CHRIST CHURCH, PHILADELPHIA

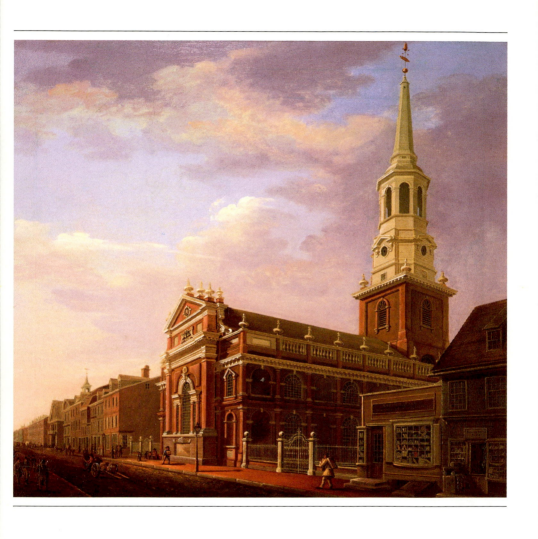

CHRIST CHURCH, PHILADELPHIA

THE NATION'S CHURCH IN A CHANGING CITY

DEBORAH MATHIAS GOUGH

A BARRA FOUNDATION BOOK
UNIVERSITY OF PENNSYLVANIA PRESS
Philadelphia

Copyright © 1995 by The Barra Foundation.
All rights reserved.
Printed in the United States of America.
Library of Congress Cataloging-in-Publication Data

Gough, Deborah Mathias.
Christ Church, Philadelphia : the nation's church in a changing
city / Deborah Mathias Gough.
     p.   cm.
Includes bibliographical references and index.
ISBN 0-8122-3272-0
    1. Christ Church (Philadelphia, Pa).—History.   2. Philadelphia
(Pa.)—Christ history.   I. Title.
BX5980.P5C65   1995
283'.74811—dc20   *94-48373*
                                           CIP

Cover and Frontispiece: Christ Church *by William Strickland (1788–1854),*
oil on canvas, 1811. Courtesy of the Historical Society of Pennsylvania.
Design: Adrianne Onderdonk Dudden

To my Mother and the memory of my Father

CONTENTS

LIST OF MAPS   ix
LIST OF ILLUSTRATIONS   xi
LIST OF TABLES   xv
ACKNOWLEDGMENTS   xvii
FOREWORD BY JAMES TRIMBLE   xxi
LIST OF ABBREVIATIONS   xxiii

Introduction   1

CHAPTER ONE
Founding an Anglican Church in a Quaker Colony   5

CHAPTER TWO
Establishing a Governing Structure Without a Bishop   23

CHAPTER THREE
Conflict Within a Framework of Stability: The Rectorship of Archibald Cummings   43

CHAPTER FOUR
Politics and the Clergy: The Rectorship of Robert Jenney   67

CHAPTER FIVE
The Maturation of the Philadelphia Church: The Rectorship of Richard Peters   87

CHAPTER SIX
Interdenominational Relations   111

CHAPTER SEVEN
Christ Church in the Revolutionary Years   127

CHAPTER EIGHT
Establishing the Protestant Episcopal Church   151

CHAPTER NINE
Christ Church Enters the Nineteenth Century   163

CHAPTER TEN
A Church of Firsts: Christ Church Activities Under White   187

CHAPTER ELEVEN
The Separation of the United Churches   209

CHAPTER TWELVE
Christ Church After Bishop White: The Rectorship of Benjamin Dorr   223

CHAPTER THIRTEEN
Christ Church Struggles to Survive in the Late Nineteenth Century   251

CHAPTER FOURTEEN
Reviving an Urban Church: The Rectorship of Louis Washburn   287

CHAPTER FIFTEEN
From Depression to Postwar Boom: Christ Church Adjusts to Changing Times   321

CHAPTER SIXTEEN
Continuity in Changing Times: The Rectorship of Ernest Harding   349

CHAPTER SEVENTEEN
Christ Church Enters Its Fourth Century   383

BIBLIOGRAPHY   395
INDEX   417

MAPS

Map 1 *Philadelphia 1770–1780*   *94*

Map 2 *The consolidated city, 1854*   *231*

Map 3 *Philadelphia, 1860, with Center City Episcopal churches*   *245*

Map 4 *Philadelphia, 1914, with Center City Episcopal churches*   *303*

Map 5 *Christ Church membership distribution within Philadelphia, 1964*   *356*

Map 6 *Christ Church membership distribution outside Philadelphia, 1964*   *357*

Map 7 *Independence Historical Park, 1970s*   *370*

Map 8 *Area surrounding Christ Church, 1980s*   *391*

ILLUSTRATIONS

Frontispiece   *Christ Church* by William Strickland, 1811
Figure 1   Carved wooden coat of arms of King William III   *8*
Figure 2   Baptismal font brought from England in 1697   *26*
Figure 3   Flagon, paten, and chalice made by John East   *27*
Figure 4   Tombstone, Christ Church burial ground   *28*
Figure 5   Franklin's Old Bookshop, next to Christ Church   *46*
Figure 6   Christ Church, 1788   *50*
Figure 7   Brass chandelier brought from London in 1744   *52*
Figure 8   The Reverend Richard Peters   *56*
Figure 9   The Reverend William Smith   *71*
Figure 10   St. Peter's Church, Philadelphia   *76*
Figure 11   East prospect of the city of Philadelphia   *92–93*
Figure 12   Memorial Plaque for Mary Andrews   *97*
Figure 13   Interior of Christ Church, wineglass pulpit   *99*
Figure 14   The Reverend Jacob Duché and his wife, Elizabeth Hopkinson
                 Duché   *132*
Figure 15   The first bishop's chair   *158*
Figure 16   St. James Episcopal Church, 7th Street above Market   *168*
Figure 17   Bishop William White   *169*
Figure 18   The second bishop's chair, c. 1809   *172*
Figure 19   The Reverend James Abercrombie   *175*
Figure 20   Communion table crafted by Jonathan Gostelowe   *191*
Figure 21   Baptismal font crafted by Jonathan Gostelowe   *192*

Figure 22 Christ Church Hospital *194*

Figure 23 Smyth hatchment *215*

Figure 24 The Reverend Benjamin Dorr *224*

Figure 25 Benjamin Dorr at the communion table *236*

Figure 26 Christ Church Hospital *239*

Figure 27 Christ Church and the celebrated Carpet Hall *252*

Figure 28 The Reverend Edward Foggo *254*

Figure 29 Christ Church, showing attached schoolhouse *256*

Figure 30 Second Street, north of Market, c. 1876 *258*

Figure 31 Interior of Christ Church, looking east *262*

Figure 32 Interior of Christ Church, looking west *263*

Figure 33 Christ Church Chapel, Pine Street above Nineteenth Street *265*

Figure 34 Market Street at Delaware Avenue *272*

Figure 35 The Reverend C. Ellis Stevens *274*

Figure 36 The Buchanan altar *277*

Figure 37 The Reverend Louis Cope Washburn *289*

Figure 38 226 South Second Street *292*

Figure 39 Neighborhood House *295*

Figure 40 High school Sunday school class *298*

Figure 41 Bread line during the Great Depression *300*

Figure 42 Christ Church prior to the construction of Morris Park *310*

Figure 43 Christ Church with Morris Park *311*

Figure 44 Henry Compton tablet *312*

Figure 45 Diocesan exhibit at the Sesquicentennial *313*

Figure 46 The Reverend Felix Kloman *322*

Figure 47 United Nations Chapel *328*

Figure 48 People gather to sign the "Christ Church Declaration" *337*

Figure 49 Photograph of the ladder that snapped, stranding a man at the top *339*

Figure 50 E. A. deBordenave and verger Harvey Mertz lead procession *340*

Figure 51 The Reverend Ernest Harding in pulpit *350*

Figure 52 Wharton house, 336 Spruce Street *354*

Figure 53 Congregation with Ernest Harding at the lectern *355*

Figure 54 Christ Church burial ground *359*

Figure 55   Francis Murphy leads a boys' choir in the loft   *361*
Figure 56   Christ Church decked out for the Magna Carta service   *371*
Figure 57   Christ Church seal   *372*
Figure 58   Christ Church chancel after the removal of the colored glass
window and the restoration of the Gostelowe altar   *374*
Figure 59   The Reverend James Trimble   *384*

COLOR SECTION

Second Street north from Market Street with Christ Church
Watercolor by William Mason, interior before 1830s alterations
Stained glass windows
The Risen Christ Commissioning His Apostles
The Age of Martyrdom
The Conversion of Constantine
The Conciliar Window
The Liberty Window
The American Window

TABLES

Table 1 Tax assessment in Philadelphia, 1709   *24*

Table 2 Tax assessment in Philadelphia, 1756   *69*

Table 3 Tax assessment for Philadelphia Anglicans, 1756   *81*

ACKNOWLEDGMENTS

This book began twenty years ago as a doctoral dissertation at the University of Pennsylvania—a dissertation that covered the first one hundred years of Christ Church. It was shaped by Richard Dunn, who taught me the advantages of doing thorough, painstaking research, and by Michael Zuckerman, who taught me to look at every issue from a variety of viewpoints and who could almost always see something in my research that eluded me. Mike has suffered with me, off and on, for twenty years, giving support and encouragment along with his insights.

The dissertation would have stayed on microfilm if it had not been for the interest of Julia Leisenring and Robert McNeil. The impetus for a book length history of Christ Church came from Julia Leisenring, who spearheaded the 1981 Antiques Show of Christ Church antiques for the benefit of the Hospital of the University of Pennsylvania. The articles that were included in the *Catalog* for that show were the first step in the production of this book. Mrs. Leisenring interested McNeil in underwriting both those articles and in commissioning a full length history of Christ Church.

As a result, a call from Mr. McNeil in 1982, followed by an interview in 1983, led me once again to delve into the history of Christ Church. After all, at that point I only had two hundred years to research and the inquisitive side of me wondered what had happened since 1800. In addition to generous monetary support, Mr. McNeil has offered kind words and encouragement; while he may have wondered whether I would ever finish, he never let on.

Along the way I have been helped by a variety of people and institutions. A post doctoral travel grant from the American Council of Learned Societies let me research the 1790s. I was aided greatly in my research by the archivists at the Historical Society of Pennsylvania in Philadelphia; the Library Company of Philadelphia; the Urban Archives at Temple University, Philadelphia; the Archives of the Protestant Episcopal Church in Austin, Texas; and the Presbyterian Historical Society in Philadelphia aided me greatly in my research. Through the cooperation of the Special Collections staff of the McIntyre Library of the University of Wisconsin-Eau Claire, I obtained manuscripts from the State Historical Society of Wisconsin. Glen Colliver at the Archives of the Episcopal Diocese of Pennsylvania in Philadelphia located information I could not have otherwise found.

Two research assistants, Alison Games and Sharon Holt, provided invaluable assistance, doing a whole range of often tedious research that was impossible to complete in Wisconsin.

The staff of Christ Church, particularly Bruce Gill, the curator, and the Reverend James Trimble, have provided invaluable information and encouragement. Arlene Cusuman, the long-time church secretary, willingly assisted me whenever I asked. I am also grateful to the many parishioners, former parishioners, and former staff of Christ Church who agreed to be interviewed.

Once the manuscript was completed, I benefited from the advice of a variety of people. Mike Zuckerman and Joan Rezner Gundersen read it in its early stages. I am particularly indebted to Jon Butler, who, when asked to evaluate the manuscript for publication, chose to do a detailed, page-by-page critique, including the rewriting of sentences, and then read it once again when the revisions were complete. The final manuscript has been vastly improved as a result of his wise counsel.

All the maps have been expertly done by Alice Thiede of Carto-Graphics of Eau Claire, Wisconsin; working with a patient and knowledgeable person with whom I could speak face-to-face has been a tremendous help.

The book would have far fewer pictures if it were not for the tenacity of Elizabeth Jarvis. When hired to help locate pictures for the book, she took the project to heart, becoming as determined as was I that the book provide a comprehensive visual representation of the history of Christ Church.

On a personal level, I want to thank my colleagues in Academic Advising at the University of Wisconsin-Eau Claire for supporting me in my research and writing; it has been difficult to complete a monograph while employed in a non-history-related profession, but my colleagues and my supervisors at the University of Wisconsin-Eau Claire have always done what they could to encourage my efforts.

Without the aid of my family, however, the book would never have been completed. My parents, who encouraged my scholarly activities from a young age, continued to encourage me and to give me confidence as I took on this task.

Academic marriages have many rewards. My husband, Bob, has read and critiqued this book, providing valuable insights and innumerable citations. I have benefited from his knowledge of urban history in particular and social history in general. He has always been there to help with the kids or the house when I "had to work on my book." And, most importantly, he has been a tremendous emotional support, suffering through my "anti-book" moods and quietly encouraging me to keep working at it.

My children, Andrew and Ellen, do not remember when their mother was not writing a book. I appreciate their patience and hope when they see the book in print they will see the benefits of perseverance.

FOREWORD

The conception and growth of this history of Christ Church, Philadelphia, like that of the church itself, is a tribute to belief, cooperation, acceptance, and intensely devoted labor. As the parish celebrates its tercentenary in 1995, it gratefully acknowledges the many hands, hearts, and minds that have wrought the church's history so powerfully. *Christ Church, Philadelphia: The Nation's Church in a Changing City* provides an opportunity to share that experience with the wider community.

The project began fifteen years ago when Julia B. Leisenring and her associate Patricia Carson proposed to me that Christ Church be featured at the 1981 Antique Show. For more than a year they collected, analyzed, and photographed material objects related to the church's history. Their hard work produced an extraordinary exhibit entitled "Art, Architecture, and Archives." They also approached four scholars to write articles on particular aspects of the church's history. Thanks to the gracious support of Robert L. McNeil, Jr. and the The Barra Foundation, which underwrote publishing costs, the articles appeared in the exhibit catalog. Leisenring and Carson later adapted some of their photographs to create *A Guide to Christ Church, Philadelphia*, an invaluable resource to anyone who visits the historic site.

The idea of a complete history of Christ Church followed naturally. The Barra Foundation agreed to support such a book, and Deborah Gough was asked to undertake the work. Her 1978 University of Pennsylvania doctoral dissertation on Christ Church during the Colonial years provided the basis for an expanded narrative of the church's three-hundred-year presence in Philadelphia. As the final, fitting gesture, the University of Pennsylvania

Press was approached to publish the book. For in the earliest years of the Academy, as the University of Pennsylvania was called in 1749, its founder Benjamin Franklin chose members of Christ Church to lead the institution.

Founded in 1695 by thirty-nine Anglican colonists in an atmosphere hostile to any formal ties with the Church of England, Christ Church was established in 1779, and was soon seen as the "mother church" of what was to become the Protestant Episcopal Church in the United States. The evolution of Christ Church through three centuries of adversity and adaptation, continuity and change, diversity and tradition reminds us of the religious values that have shaped our history. Though these values are often under siege, we must continue in courage and the faith that God cares for every human being. We preach this "comfortable gospel" in this old place and so maintain a living testament to the religious faith that has made this nation great.

JAMES A. TRIMBLE
Rector, Christ Church, Philadelphia
June 1994

ABBREVIATIONS

CSP	Calendar of State Papers
DAB	*Dictionary of American Biography*
HMPEC	*Historical Magazine of the Protestant Episcopal Church*
HSP	Historical Society of Pennsylvania
LC	U.S. Library of Congress
PEC	Archives of the Protestant Episcopal Church, Austin, Texas
POC	William Penn Papers, Official Correspondence
PMHB	*Pennsylvania Magazine of History and Biography*
SPG	Society for the Propagation of the Gospel in Foreign Parts
WMQ	*William and Mary Quarterly*, 3d series

INTRODUCTION

In 1695 thirty-nine Anglican colonists living in Quaker-dominated Philadelphia banded together to found Christ Church. Taking advantage of the religious freedom guaranteed in the charter for the colony of Pennsylvania, they were determined to recreate the religious life they had known in England, and in the process challenge the hegemony of the Quakers. Despite their courage, the future could not have looked bright. With no minister, no financial support from England or the colonial government, no church hierarchy to guide them, the task of successfully estsablishing an Anglican church in a city whose political, social, and economic leadership was entirely Quaker must have seemed daunting. Yet, succeed they did. Three hundred years later Christ Episcopal Church is a thriving congregation serving the needs of an ever-changing city, as well as a national shrine visited by thousands of tourists each year.

The history of Christ Church, the national shrine, is in itself fascinating. The spiritual home to numerous revolutionary leaders, as well as President George Washington, the final resting place of seven signers of the Declaration of Independence, Christ Church deserves the title of "the nation's church." Similarly, the pivotal role played by both lay and clerical leaders in the formation of the Protestant Episcopal Church and the outstanding leadership provided by Bishop William White to the national church make Christ Church truly the "mother church" to Episcopalians.

But Christ Church has always been more than a shrine. Its history is one of a congregation struggling to adjust to new and often adverse conditions at the same time that it focuses on serving the needs of its members. During the early colonial period the challenges were twofold. First, the members had to adjust to an environment in which the Church of England—the established state church in the mother country—was a despised minority religion. Forced to deal with religious freedom and a religiously heterogeneous environment, Christ Church members had to develop a new philosophy toward other religions and new strategies for promoting their own doctrines long before the disestablishment of the 1780s and 1790s forced most American denominations to do so. At the same time they had to adjust to the lack of state support, a loss that left the church in an almost continual financial crisis. Just as important, the church had to create a governing structure that worked in the absence of both a resident bishop and the traditional social and political hierarchy that provided stability in England. While this structural void led to almost continual power struggles and intensified every controversy, Christ Church eventually developed authority structures uniquely suited to the American environment, authority structures that served as the model for the Protestant Episcopal Church.

Following the crises caused by the American Revolution—the loss of members, the departure of two clergymen, the destruction of property—Christ Church had to deal with a new reality. No longer a part of the Church of England, Christ Church members took the lead in establishing a new denomination. At the same time they had to adjust to the decreasing role played by their leadership in the political arena. Turning their attention to religious and philanthropic societies instead, Christ Church leaders in the early nineteenth century broke new ground in religious education and actively encouraged missionary efforts. Their efforts to deal with the new reality—the increasing domination of evangelical religions and the new style of religion they encouraged—were initially unsuccessful, but Christ Church eventually found its niche as a "low church" alternative.

The most daunting challenge faced by Christ Church as early as the 1830s was dealing with the everchanging character of the city around it. Located in what quickly became the commercial district of Philadelphia, it had to compete with new churches built near the fashionable neighborhoods to the west. Thus Christ Church was one of the first churches to face the difficult questions that would become commonplace among urban churches in the late nineteenth and twentieth centuries. And while most churches in the neighborhood chose to move and others closed, Christ Church never considered abandoning its "old city" location or its magnificent building. Instead, as early as the 1850s, long before it became fashionable, Christ Church leaders chose to use its history to ensure its future.

From the 1850s until the present the challenge for Christ Church has been twofold: to maintain and serve a congregation large enough to remain viable and to preserve and promote the church building as an historic treasure. Only by balancing these two missions could the financial security of the church be assured at the same time that it retained a reason to remain open. In the late nineteenth century, as the neighborhood bacame primarily immigrant and as internal controversy plagued the church, it became uncertain whether Christ Church had a future as more than a museum. But the twentieth century brought new leadership and a new vision—a vision that saw the neighborhood and the city in general as an opportunity to serve rather as a problem to overcome. As the church's social service activities increased, Philadelphians once again came to see Christ Church as an important part of the city's present and future, as well as its past.

The post-World War II period brought new problems for the church. With no real residential neighborhoods remaining in the area, social services could no longer define the church's programming. Instead, the church chose to take the lead in another area: it launched a national campaign to use Christianity to fight communism. The expansion of its focus from the city to the nation saved the church from becoming a museum and meant that when a residential neighborhood redeveloped in Society Hill in the 1950s and 1960s, and in "Old City Philadelphia" in the 1970s, the church was still there to serve. In fact, by the late 1980s the church had come full circle, defining itself as a "neighborhood church" for the first time since before the Civil War.

The history of Christ Church is multifaceted. It is the history of an institution that was central to the political and religious life of colonial and revolutionary Philadelphia and crucial to the development of the Protestant Episcopal Church. It is the history of a congregation and its leaders struggling against great odds to keep the church alive after its glory years were over, finding new and creative missions for the church to fulfill. But it is also the history of ordinary people worshiping in a magnificent building, finding a religious community that fulfilled their needs, and using the strength and inspiration gained at Christ Church to serve God and their neighbors in both common and uncommon ways.

CHAPTER ONE

FOUNDING AN ANGLICAN CHURCH IN A QUAKER COLONY

While the founding of a new congregation was a common and normally routine event in colonial America, there was nothing common or routine about the founding of Christ Church. To Anglicans in Pennsylvania and England it represented the establishment of true Christianity and "English civilization" in a colony that, from an Anglican viewpoint, was ruled by "heathens." To the Quakers it represented a potential threat to their "holy experiment" and an end to religious peace in their colony. The first twenty years of Christ Church history were largely defined by conflicts between these two groups. Yet, remarkably, despite their strikingly different worldviews and longstanding antipathy, by 1720 the two religions had learned to coexist peacefully in Pennsylvania, long before such religious tolerance had been established in other colonies.

It would have been difficult to find a more striking contrast within Christianity at the time than that between members of the Church of England and the Society of Friends, or Quakers. In order to understand the early history of Christ Church, we must understand the basic principles of these two religions.

The Church of England was, first and foremost, the established, state-supported church in the mother country. In the seventeenth and eighteenth centuries this meant far more than merely receiving support from tax dollars, although that in itself was important. Most English at the time considered an established church absolutely essential to the orderly functioning of society. To assure correct outward behavior, the state had to promote inward virtue, or religion. Any form of religious freedom would inevitably allow "freedom *from* religion," something an ordered society could not allow.[1]

In seventeenth-century England, church and state were intimately connected. The King or Queen headed the church, appointing the bishops, who were then allowed to serve in the House of Lords. Ecclesiastical laws, including doctrine, had to be approved by Parliament. In return for accepting secular control over certain matters, the church received considerable power and privileges. Ecclesiastical courts, which handled divorces and tried cases involving morals, had coercive power, including the ability to give out jail sentences. Parish churches were supported by taxes. Those not belonging to the Church of England, called dissenters, were banned from holding office, and, while given freedom of worship in 1689, still had to pay taxes to support the state church.[2]

Two characteristics set the Church of England apart from dissenting groups—its episcopal form of government and its adherence to the Book of Common Prayer. Even Anglicans who did not believe that apostolic succession was crucial for a true church did insist that the episcopate was necessary to keep order in the church and to maintain the proper relationship between church and state. Anglicans also firmly believed in the need for a set liturgy; to an Anglican, the Book of Common Prayer was both the symbol and the reality of the national church. No matter what personal or theological controversies might rock the church, the prayers would remain the same, providing continuity with the past and a sense of oneness with Anglicans throughout the realm. While not all Anglicans understood the theoretical justifications for a set liturgy, they did share a devotion to the Book of Common Prayer as a beautiful, awe-inspiring form of worship.[3]

The unity provided by the Book of Common Prayer was intended to include all English men and women, for membership in the Church of England went with citizenship, unless one renounced it. This inclusiveness meant that the characteristics of a congregation mirrored those of society, with people of various socioeconomic groups meeting in church each Sunday. Inclusiveness also meant that members of the Church of England varied greatly in their devotion to the church, their acceptance of its teachings, and their moral behavior. While ecclesiastical courts disciplined certain immoral behavior, excommunications were rare and "moral purity" was not expected.

Despite the efforts of the state to include all citizens in the Church of England, many English citizens renounced their membership, becoming dissenters. Of these dissenting groups, perhaps the most vexing for Anglicans were members of the Society of Friends, because of both their beliefs and their persistence. Founded in 1652 by George Fox, the Society of Friends, or Quakers as they later came to be called, belonged to the left wing of the English Reformation. Accurately called a form of "group mysticism," the Quaker beliefs revolved around the concept of the "Inward Light." Fox preached that all people—not just Christians, and not just those living in the time of the early church—had God or Christ within themselves. God continued to speak *directly* to everyone, and salvation came when a person acknowledged the light within and agreed to live according to its dictates.[4]

Although a simple concept, the doctrine of the "light within" had profound consequences. If God dwelt within each person, then priests were not needed as intermediaries and even churches were superfluous. So, Quakers abolished the ordained ministry, relying instead on lay ministers. They denounced not only liturgical worship but all preplanned worship. Instead, Friends held a "silent meeting," where each individual could join in mystic union with God, and where anyone could speak when he or she felt moved by God to do so.

Quakers were perhaps best known for the actions that resulted from their beliefs. Believing that "the honor which belongs to God he would give to no man, and the honor which belonged to any man he gave to every man," Friends refused to participate in the many contemporary practices that showed more respect for some people than others.[5] They refused to use any titles, did not take their hats off as a sign of respect, and always used "thee and thou" instead of "you," since the latter was used to give distinction. Quakers also refused to take an oath, even in court, believing that such oaths blasphemed God. And, in what would become their most well known belief, Quakers adamantly supported pacifism, arguing that war was against all that was taught by "the Prince of Peace." Moreover, like Puritans, Quakers insisted that their members give up all "vain and empty customs" that "divert the mind from the witness of God," including most kinds of recreation.[6]

Since God spoke to everyone, it followed, according to Fox and his followers, that it was wrong, if not blasphemous, for a government to tell

7

FIGURE 1
Carved wooden coat of arms of William III, King of England at the time of the founding of Christ Church (1689–1702). It is believed this crest marked the pew reserved for the royal governor and later for President Washington. The crest originally had three crowns and the letters "W" over the lion and "R" over the unicorn. Courtesy of Christ Church. Photograph by Louis W. Meehan.

anyone what to believe. When they founded Pennsylvania, an important aspect of their "experiment" was the institution of religious freedom. Among the laws agreed on before the Quakers left England was one assuring all people who believed in God that they would not be "molested or prejudiced for their Religious Persuasion or Practice" or forced to "frequent or maintain any Religious Worship, Place or Ministry whatever."[7]

In 1695 Quakers, not Anglicans, dominated Pennsylvania. In fact, to Anglicans, the entire structure of the new colony seemed a world turned upside down. In government, King William, Queen Mary, and the Anglican parliament had been replaced by the proprietary rule of the Quaker Penn and a colonial Assembly dominated by Quakers, who seemed often to forget

CHAPTER ONE

that they were, in actuality, still under royal rule.[8] (See Figure 1 for royal coat of arms from Christ Church.) Pacifism had passed from being the absurd belief of an impotent minority to being the dangerous policy of an entire government. Quaker judges refused to administer oaths. The Quaker government also outlawed cards, dice, masques, revels, and the theater, all of which Anglicans enjoyed. Worse still, the Anglicans, who were used to holding all government jobs, were virtually shut out of these by the Quakers. Economically the Anglicans were also at a disadvantage, since the best land in the city belonged to Quakers, and a few wealthy Quakers dominated the commercial life of the city.

While religious freedom ensured Anglicans the right to start a church, the lack of an established church and the total absence of the church hierarchy that so efficiently governed in England made the success of such a church seem doubtful. Christ Church could not depend on revenue from taxes, nor did it have a house and land for its minister; thus its financial situation did not look good. Without a bishop anywhere in the colonies, let alone in Philadelphia, the establishment of a normal church life was also impossible; ministers could not be ordained without going to England, nor could the laity be confirmed.

In 1695 the future of Christ Church may not have seemed promising, but that of Philadelphia did. The city was already established as the Delaware River's chief port, serving Pennsylvania, West Jersey, and what is today Delaware. It was an impressive city, even in these very early days. A visitor in the early 1700s commented that Philadelphia was "most commodiously situated between two navigable Rivers. The Houses are very stately; the Wharfs and Warehouses numerous and convenient."[9] While there were only around 1,500 people living in Philadelphia in 1695, when Christ Church was founded, it was already a thriving business center. We know that five years earlier the city had 22 shopkeepers and 119 craftsmen, including 34 in the building industry, 26 in the clothing trade, and 14 in food processing.[10]

But Philadelphia in 1695 was still a country town and would remain so for many years to come. Pigs and goats roamed the streets at will. Each morning cows were taken out through the streets to pasture. It was not until the 1710s that householders began paving walks in front of their houses and much later before any streets were paved.[11]

*   *   *

It was in this environment that a small group of lay Anglicans—without the aid of a minister or other churches—decided to found Christ Church. The founders of Christ Church represented a cross section of the city's population. On both the 1693 and 1696/97 tax list Christ Church members appeared in equal numbers above and below the mean. Included in the twenty-six members for whom we have information were six merchants, one lawyer, one physician, two bakers, three carpenters, two surgeons, and one dyer. Perhaps most interestingly, two men who appeared on the Surveyor General of the Customs 1692 list of pirates were among the founders of Christ Church![12]

The founders did include several wealthy and prominent men. Joshua Carpenter, who listed his occupation as "brewer," was the second wealthiest man in the city in 1693.[13] Robert Quary, another well-to-do Anglican, represented the New Pennsylvania Company, a group of London merchants who were attempting to compete with the established Quaker merchants in Pennsylvania. Quary was perhaps the most politically prominent of the founders; he had served as secretary of council and deputy governor in South Carolina and in 1697 was appointed a vice-admiralty judge for Maryland, Pennsylvania, and West Jersey. Jasper Yeates, another founder, was a wealthy merchant from Wilmington; politically active, he was a leading spokesman for the interests of the three lower counties of Pennsylvania which would eventually form Delaware.[14]

In 1695, while holding services under the leadership of the schoolmaster John Arrowsmith, these Anglicans purchased a lot on Second Street. They completed the building some time in 1696. There is little information about the original church's appearance, but cash books and travelers' accounts indicate that the church apparently was a small brick structure; a belfry was added in 1709. Two travelers' accounts refer to it as a "very fine church" and a "great church," but it could not have been very large; after it was enlarged in 1711 it still had only forty-two pews.[15]

The site chosen for the church was in the heart of Philadelphia. It was the retail center of the young city; two years earlier, in 1693, the public market had been moved to Second and High Street (now Market), one short block from the church. On Wednesdays and Saturdays farmers would bring their varied produce to be sold. Here butchers slaughtered their animals in front of their stalls, bakers and tradesmen of all kinds hawked their wares, and all Philadelphians came to buy the necessities of life. The old prison was also located on High Street, east of Second Street. On its balcony, in full view of throngs of people, wrongdoers were whipped or executed by hanging. Escapes from this prison were common. The area around Second and High also soon became the governmental center; the city government, the county courts and the Pennsylvania Assembly all met in the County Court House, built down the center of High Street at Second in 1710.[16]

Despite its commercial activity, the area around Christ Church in 1695 retained a certain degree of country atmosphere. It is reported that a large duck pond lay to its rear, where, tradition has it, a great Indian feast took place. To amuse their guest of honor, William Penn, the Indians purportedly held a foot race around the entire pond. To the southeast of Christ Church, between Second and Front Streets, stood a "grassy sward, close cropt by nibbling sheep" that were pastured there until slain and sold. Not too far away on south Second would stand Edward Shippen's house with his "great and famous garden" and a "herd of tranquil deer" on his front lawn.[17]

While they built the church themselves, Philadelphia Anglicans no doubt hoped for help from England in supporting it. After all, the bishop of London, Henry Compton, who had jurisdiction over the Church of England in the colonies, had insisted that the rights of Anglicans be guaranteed in the charter given to William Penn. As a result of his letter to the privy council, the grant of Pennsylvania to Penn stated that whenever twenty inhabitants of Pennsylvania requested a preacher be sent by the bishop of London, "such Preacher or Preachers *shall and may be* [sent] and reside within the said Province without any denial or molestation whatsoever."[18] Moreover, the English church, which had only recently taken an active interest in its colonial branches, was particularly concerned that the Quakers (or "heathens" as they were referred to by some Anglicans of the period) not completely control religious life in Pennsylvania.

The primary champion of Christ Church's cause in England turned out to be the governor of Maryland, Francis Nicholson. In fact, it was probably Nicholson who fulfilled the provision in the charter by asking the bishop to send a minister to Philadelphia. We know that Nicholson, at the urging of Philadelphia Anglicans he met during a visit to the city in 1694, repeatedly asked English authorities to provide an annual subsidy for Christ Church. His efforts paid off in 1697 when the privy council agreed to provide fifty pounds a year for a minister and thirty pounds for a schoolmaster in Philadelphia.[19]

The congregation must have anxiously awaited the arrival of an ordained clergyman. In the interim, the schoolmaster, John Arrowsmith, officiated in the new church, reading the service, but unable to preside at communion. He was reported to be "very well beloved, not only by our own people, but by all in general."[20]

The first ordained minister of Christ Church, Thomas Clayton, about whom we know little, arrived in 1698. He probably graduated from Cambridge University in 1690, and it appears that he was on his way to a parish in Maryland when he stopped in Philadelphia and agreed to remain. His stay in the Quaker city was short; he died in September 1699. Edward Portlock, a former chaplain in the British army on his way to a post in Perth Amboy, New Jersey, served Christ Church for a few months after Clayton's death.

Finally, in November 1700, Evan Evans, an energetic Welshman, took over the Philadelphia church at the direction of the bishop of London. Evans graduated from Oxford University in 1695 and then held positions as a curate and rector of two churches in Wales. Evans served Christ Church with distinction from 1700 to 1717, receiving an honorary doctorate from his alma mater in 1714.[21]

* * *

Once the small band of Philadelphia Anglicans had acquired a permanent minister, they responded to the hostile situation in which they found themselves with the zeal of martyrs and the enthusiasm of crusaders. Compromise and accommodation, attitudes that were becoming increasingly common among Anglicans in England when dealing with dissenters, were not in the vocabulary of Philadelphia Anglicans. As Robert Quary put it, they felt they were "stigmatized with the grim and horrid titles of treacherous and perfidious fellows, dissenters and schismaticks from the Establish't Religions, which is Quakerism."[22] If the members of Christ Church were to establish an environment remotely resembling that which they had known in England, they had to curb the power of the Quakers.

Anglicans addressed the problem of Quaker domination on two fronts— political and religious. From 1700 to at least 1704 the vestry of Christ Church, as well as individual Anglicans, engaged in an almost continual battle with Penn and the Quaker political leaders. The Anglicans' ultimate aim was to make Pennsylvania a royal colony. Once it was, as Portlock put it, "Christianity will flourish in this Province, Quakerism will be rooted out, and the Church will be more than conqueror."[23] While involvement of the Church of England in such politics was not new—after all, bishops in England served in the House of Lords—it was unusual for individual congregations to be so active. The actions of the early Christ Church vestry set the stage for the involvement of that church in the political life of Pennsylvania throughout the colonial period.

Anglicans worked hard to convince the English authorities that the Quaker-dominated government in Pennsylvania was irresponsible, unreasonable, and an actual danger to its citizens. They complained about the refusal of the government to appropriate money to provide a defense for the colony, despite the fact that pirates menaced the coastline as a result of England's war with France and Spain. The vestry wrote to the Board of Trade, the committee that handled all colonial business for the crown, arguing that Anglicans were "expos'd to all the miseries imaginable, not only from a publick enemy, but from pyrates and Indians, the wofull experience of which we have lately felt . . . for want of a Militia."[24]

Anglicans made other accusations which are impossible to prove or disprove, but which were designed to raise suspicions in England. They accused the Quakers of purposely harboring pirates and illegal traders. Moreover, they characterized the Quaker judicial system as inept; they maintained that Quakers protected their own, allowing a woman who admitted killing her baby and a man who raped a servant to go free.[25]

The Anglicans' primary complaint involved a Pennsylvania law that made affirmations as binding as oaths in all court proceedings, contrary to English law. Although judges were allowed to administer oaths, since all judges were Quakers, Anglicans could rarely find a judge willing to do so. The vestry, individual Anglicans, and Anglican ministers in rural parishes surrounding Philadelphia waged a constant battle against each new oath law, even hiring an agent to argue their case in England. Anglicans who were appointed to offices used the issue to disrupt government. Some refused to serve. Others refused to administer oaths to those who wanted to take them or refused to accept affirmations from Quakers, thus halting judicial proceedings. This issue was not completely resolved until 1722 when England changed its law, allowing affirmations without God's name to be used in court.[26]

The Anglicans' efforts in the political arena were ultimately unsuccessful. Each time England disallowed an oath law, the Quaker-controlled legislature passed a new one. English authorities became less and less sympathetic to Anglican complaints as time went on. Moreover, the main goal of making Pennsylvania a royal colony was never achieved, since Parliament refused to rescind any colonial charters. In 1711 it appeared that Penn, who was tired of fighting both the legislature in Pennsylvania and the English government, would give the Anglicans their wish and sell the colony to the crown, but he suffered a debilitating stroke before he could do so. In the end Anglicans had to learn to live with a Quaker proprietor and a government dominated by Quakers.

At the same time that the Anglicans fought the Quakers in the governmental arena, they battled in the religious arena as well. Anglican ministers sought to convert all dissenters, including Quakers. Their first approach, initiated by Thomas Clayton, was to try to convince entire religious groups to rejoin the church. In 1698 Clayton wrote letters to Quakers, Keithian Quakers, a group that had broken away from the Society of Friends, and Baptists, asking each group to end its "schism" and return to the one true church.[27] While this action may appear arrogant, he was following the approach taken by the Church of England in the mother country. As a comprehensive church, the Church of England had never been oriented toward individual conversions. Instead, it had tried to negotiate with whole denominations to bring them back into the fold.[28]

This approach was as unsuccessful in Philadelphia as it had been in England. The Baptists sent a letter that cataloged all the practices of the Church of England that they considered contrary to scriptures, suggested that it was not a "rightly constituted church of Christ," and asked not to be blamed for their "peaceful separation."[29] The Keithian Quakers, whose founder would eventually join the Church of England, were a bit more sympathetic. The author of their reply refused to say anything that would "lessen that love and esteem that we have for each other," but at the same time rejected the suggestion that the Keithians join the Church of England.[30]

Evan Evans, who took over as minister in 1700, took a different, more aggressive approach in dealing with dissenters. Evidencing seemingly boundless energy, Evans dedicated himself to converting individual Quakers and to bringing Anglicans, many of whom he considered on the brink of heathenism, back into the fold. He regularly traveled to the surrounding areas up to forty miles away to preach, and in seven years he baptized eight hundred people. He took particular joy in preaching to the Welsh settlements at Merion and Radnor, which he visited every two weeks for four years. In Philadelphia he used evening lectures to try to reach both Anglicans and Quakers. He felt that the "Society of young men" that met together every Sunday after evening prayer "to read ye Scriptures and Sing Psalms" was a particularly effective conversion tool. "Those Quakers, that Durst not appear in the day at the Publiq Service of the Church, for fear of disobligeing their Parents or Masters would stand under the Church windows att night, till many of them pluck't up so much Courage, as to come to ye Church it selfe."[31]

Evans's labors were greatly aided by the establishment in 1701 of the Society for the Propagation of the Gospel in Foreign Parts, or SPG, a private missionary society in England supported by prominent men and women within the Church of England. Having heard that many colonists lacked "the Administration of God's Word and Sacraments, and seem to be Abandoned to Atheism and Infidelity," they joined together to ensure that "a sufficient Maintenance be provided for an Orthodox Clergy to live amongst" these colonists.[32] This marked the first time that officials of the Anglican church in England involved themselves with missionary work.

From the start, the leaders of the SPG made it clear that they intended to do more than provide ministers to Anglicans—they intended to build Anglican congregations by converting dissenters, particularly Quakers. To accomplish this, they went on the offensive, attacking Quakers and their beliefs, rather than merely preaching the doctrines of the Anglican church. They chose as their first two missionaries men whose intemperate views, love of controversy, and hatred of Quakers were well known. George Keith, who by this time had become an Anglican priest, was despised by orthodox Quakers as a traitor to their cause; John Talbot referred to Quakers as "worse than Infidels . . . [serving] no God but Mammon & their own Bellys." In addition, the SPG equipped these men with one thousand copies of the most extreme anti-Quaker tracts available.[33]

The arrival of Keith and Talbot in Philadelphia in November of 1702 ushered in several years of virulent confrontation between Quakers and Anglicans, an approach supported by Christ Church members. The vestry thanked the SPG for sending Keith, "whose unparalleled zeal . . . whose frequent preaching . . . whose strenuous and elaborate writing made him highly and signally instrumental in promoting the Church."[34]

Keith and Talbot spent more than six months in Philadelphia and the surrounding area between November 1702 and April 1704, preaching to crowds that overflowed the church, engaging the Quakers in public debate whenever possible, and even attempting to speak at Quaker meetings. To their apparent surprise, they found the Quakers "generally very uncivil and rude . . . declining all discourse with us, and returning nothing to our kindly offers to inform them but reproaches and railings and gross reflections." Despite his persistence, by Keith's own admission, his efforts at conversion were largely unsuccessful.[35]

Keith's arrival led to an extended and often nasty debate in the press. The most interesting occurred in the competing Quaker and Anglican almanacs of the time. A former Keithian turned Anglican, Daniel Leeds treated readers of his Almanac to anti-Quaker tirades interspersed with information on the movement of the planets and other scientific topics. In 1705 he also included a carefully reasoned explanation of Anglican doctrine and practices clearly designed to convert Quakers. The Quaker Jacob Taylor countered in his Almanac by defending Quaker practices, arguing that to Anglicans "forms and Distinctions are a Deity," and accusing Leeds of plagiarism. The rancorous exchange continued until 1711 when Taylor decided to "Let spleen depart and this Contention die."[36]

Despite the longstanding hostility between Anglicans and Quakers that led to these exchanges, within fifteen years of the founding of Christ Church, the Anglicans united and aggressive front against the Quakers had disappeared and within twenty-five years the days of confrontation in both politics and religion had come to an end.

Political confrontation between Anglicans and Quakers had declined dramatically by 1710. Once it became clear that Pennsylvania would not become a royal colony, ambitious individuals within the Anglican church realized that they had to cooperate with the Quakers to gain power. Penn and his supporters, in turn, welcomed help in battling a group of Quakers who had turned against the proprietor. Thus, when Evan Evans went to England to attend to some personal business in 1708, he met with Penn and returned with a letter directing Penn's deputy, James Logan, to consult with Evans regarding the new governor, Charles Gookin. In 1713, when Evans once again returned to England, Logan reported that they had "always had a good understanding with each other." Such a statement certainly could not have been made ten years earlier.[37]

At about the same time that individual Anglicans began cooperating with Quakers, Christ Church as an institution withdrew from the political fray. After 1707 the vestry wrote only one letter opposing Quaker policies, and it was written to the Pennsylvania Assembly, not to English authorities, thus recognizing the legitimacy of the Pennsylvania government. Anglican missionaries in the area outside Philadelphia who had often written on political topics wrote their last political letters dealing with the oath issue in 1712.[38]

The decline in Anglican hostility toward Quakers in the strictly religious sphere is harder to trace than the change in the political sphere, but it is clear that open antagonism and vigorous efforts to convert Friends began to lessen just about the same time that tension in the political arena was easing. Evan Evans had initially welcomed the strident methods of Keith and Talbot and in 1704 had written to Keith recounting his own methods and successes in converting the Quakers.[39] But after that year his letters never again emphasized his dealings with Quakers; instead he concentrated on internal problems within Christ Church. Moreover, Evans was the last rector of Christ Church to focus on the conversion of Quakers.

The end of Anglican-Quaker confrontation can also be seen in the Philadelphia press. Not one anti-Quaker pamphlet or article was published in Philadelphia after 1710. The decision of Jacob Taylor and Daniel Leeds to end their battle merely reflected the overall change in Anglican-Quaker relations.

The importance of this change can best be seen in a comparative framework, for Anglicans in other colonies took far longer to accept the legitimacy of other religions, and religious conflict continued in most colonies until the time of the American Revolution. In the 1720s Massachusetts and Connecticut experienced an intense and at times vicious battle between members of the established Congregational church and Anglicans that climaxed with the conversion to the Church of England of Timothy Cutler, the rector of Yale College, and three of his students in 1722. At the same time, the governor of South Carolina, Francis Nicholson, the deeply committed Anglican who had helped Christ Church, tried to strengthen the largely symbolic establishment of the Church of England in that colony; this resulted in battles between Anglicans and the large number of dissenters. New York, where the Church of England had a much disputed establishment in the lower counties, also witnessed religious tensions in the 1720s, with dissenters in Hempstead trying to take over the Anglican parsonage, arguing that their minister should get the support provided by taxes. Then in the 1750s the successful attempt by New York Anglicans to control the newly created King's College created anti-Anglican feeling in that colony. The drive to establish an Anglican episcopate in the colonies in the 1760s, which we will discuss in Chapter 6, led to fierce exchanges between Anglicans and non-Anglicans in New England and New York. Virginia also saw an increase in Anglican-dissenter battles in the 1760s, primarily involving the Baptists.[40]

Pennsylvania experienced less religious conflict than other colonies primarily because it had no state church. While the early leaders of Christ Church believed that having no state church at all was worse than having a dissenting church as the established church, as was the case in New England, in reality the absence of a state church eliminated the main source of tension and conflict among religious groups. "Dissenters" could not attack the church for its domination or persecution of others, and once the Quakers became a minority in their own colony, which they were by the 1730s, Anglicans could no longer complain that they were being discriminated against.

Moreover, once Anglicans came to terms with the reality of all denominations being equal under the law, they began thinking of other denominations as equal, something that was not possible in a colony where one branch of Christianity was officially sanctioned. When it became clear that Pennsylvania was not going to become a royal colony, Christ Church leaders began to deal with the environment that really existed, not that which they hoped for or that which they feared. They found that their church could and did prosper without being established and without having a royal government. Peaceful coexistence, combined with legitimate, vigorous competition proved to be conducive to the health and prosperity of the Church in Philadelphia. This knowledge contributed to a sense of confidence that Anglicans in other colonies did not have.

NOTES

1. In the first part of the seventeenth century the argument for an established church had been based on theological grounds, the belief that the Church of England offered the only way to salvation. By the 1690s more practical considerations had taken over. See particularly William Warburton, *The Alliance between Church and State: or the Necessity and Equity of an Established Religion and a Test Law, demonstrated from the essence of Nature and Nations* (London: F. Giles, 1736).

2. The Act of Toleration did allow dissenters to hold office if they could demonstrate "occasional conformity" (taking communion in a Church of England congregation at least once a year), but this loophole was closed in 1710. For a good discussion of the Anglican view on church-state relations see David Little, *Religion, Order and Law; A Study in Pre-Revolutionary England* (New York: Harper and Row, 1969), 132ff.

3. See Horton Davies, *Worship and Theology in England from Watts and Wesley to Maurice, 1690–1850* (Princeton, N.J.: Princeton University Press, 1961), especially p. 29. Arthur Warne, *Church and Society in Eighteenth Century Devon* (Newton Abott: David and Charles, 1969), 11–21.

4. The term "group mysticism" is used by Howard H. Brinton, *Friends for Three Hundred Years* (Philadelphia: Pendle Hill Publications, 1964), xiii. A good brief summary of Quaker beliefs is found in the introduction by Rufus Jones to *The Journal of George Fox* (New York: Capricorn Books, 1963). The primary contemporary work on Quaker theology was Robert Barclay's *Apology*. I have used *Barclay's Apology in Modern English*, ed. Dean Freiday (privately printed, 1967).

5. Rufus Jones, introduction to *The Journal of George Fox*, 39.

6. *Barclay's Apology*, 389.

7. "Laws agreed upon in England by the Governour and Divers of the Free-Men of Pennsylvania," attached to William Penn's "Frame of Government," *The Papers of William Penn, Volume 2, 1680–1684*, ed. Richard Dunn and Mary Maples Dunn (Philadelphia: University of Pennsylvania Press, 1982), 225.

8. See *Lawmaking and Legislators in Pennsylvania: A Biographical Dictionary*, ed. Craig W. Horle and Marianne S. Wokeck (Philadelphia: University of Pennsylvania Press, 1991–), vol. 1.

9. John Oldmixon, *The British Empire in America Containing the History of the Discovery, Settlement, Progress and Present State of All the British Colonies, on the Continent and Islands of America* (London, 1708) in Nancy Sirkis, *Reflections of 1776: The Colonies Revisited* (New York: Viking Press, 1974), 88.

10. Mary Maples Dunn and Richard Dunn, "The Founding, 1681–1701" in Russell Weigley, ed., *Philadelphia, A Three Hundred Year History* (New York: W.W. Norton and Company, 1982), 11, 20–21. The Dunns are here summarizing material from Hannah Benner Roach, "Philadelphia Business Directory, 1690," *Pennsylvania Genealogical Magazine* 23 (1964): 95–129.

11. Edwin Bronner, "Village into Town: 1701–1746" in Weigley, ed., *Philadelphia*, 57; Joseph Kelley, *Life and Times in Colonial Philadelphia* (Harrisburg, Pa., 1973), 51.

12. The only source we have for the early supporters of Christ Church is a letter they sent to Governor Francis Nicholson of Maryland, who had contributed to the new church. Thirty-six men signed the letter; they probably represented most if not all of the literate Anglican men in Philadelphia; Robert Quary and others to Governor Nicholson, Jan. 18, 1696/97 in William Perry, ed., *Historical Collections Relating to the American Colonial Church*, 5 vols. (Hartford, Conn., 1871; reprint ed., New York: AMS Press, 1969), 2: 5–7. (While I will use new style dates in the text, I will use both old and new style dates in the notes.) The 1693 tax list is in *PMHB* 8 (1884): 85–105; the manuscript of the 1696/97 list is in Philadelphia County, Miscellaneous Papers, HSP. Information about the signers of the letter is found in Charles Keith, "The Founders," in Louis Washburn, ed., *Christ Church, Philadelphia: A Symposium* (Philadelphia: Macrae Smith Co., 1925), 94–100.

13. See Roach, "Philadelphia Business Directory, 1690," 103.

14. For information on Robert Quary, see Gary Nash, *Quakers and Politics: Pennsylvania 1681–1726* (Princeton, N.J.: Princeton University Press, 1968), 195.

15. Keith, "The Founders," 96–97. The earliest reference to the church being completed is Quary et al. to Governor Nicholson, Jan. 18, 1696/97. John Watson in the earliest edition of his *Annals* asserted that the first church was made of wood. But Benjamin Dorr, a rector of Christ Church in the nineteenth century, challenged that version, arguing convincingly that the first church must have been brick. When Willis Hazard revised the *Annals* he accepted Dorr's arguments. *Annals of Philadelphia and Pennsylvania in the Olden Times*, enlarged and revised by Willis Hazard, 3 vols. (Philadelphia: J.M. Stoddard, 1884), 1: 378. Dorr bases his argument on several factors: there are references in the cash books to buying 37,000 Flemish bond bricks, the type used for the outside of buildings, when the church was enlarged in 1711; the travelers certainly would not have referred to a wooden structure as great, since Philadelphia already had many brick homes; and the present church building was begun as an addition to the first. Benjamin Dorr, *A Historical Account of Christ Church, Philadelphia* (Philadelphia: R.S.H. George, 1841), 7–14; Accounting Warden's Journal, April 1709, May 1711; John Oldmixon, *The British Empire*, 88; Gabriel Thomas, *An Historical and Geographical Account of the Province and Country of Pennsylvania* (London: A. Baldwin, 1698), 52.

16. Ellis P. Oberholtzer, *Philadelphia: A History of the City and Its People*, 4 vols. (Philadelphia: J. Clarke Publishing Company, [1912]), 1: 73, 103.

17. Watson, *Annals of Philadelphia*, 1: 38. Oberholzer, *Philadelphia*, 1: 39.

18. Grant of Pennsylvania to William Penn, March 4, 1680, Perry, *Historical Collections*, 2: 5.

19. Francis Nicholson to Archbishop Thomas Tenison, March 18, 1695/96, February 28, 1696/97, and June 30, 1697, Fulham Papers, American Colonial Section, in Lambeth Palace, microfilm, Van Pelt library, University of Pennsylvania (hereafter referred to as Fulham Papers), 2: 51–52, 87, and 92–93.

20. Ibid., Feb. 28, 1696/97, Fulham Papers, 2: 87; Richard Sewell to Francis Nicholson, Oct. 9, 1697, Fulham Papers, 7: 11.

21. William B. Sprague, *Annals of the American Pulpit*, 5 vols. (New York, Arno Press, 1969, reprint of 1857–1869), 5: 22–25.

22. Robert Quary, "A Brief Narrative of the Proceedings of William Penn," Perry, *Historical Collections*, 2: 4.

23. Edward Portlock to Archbishop of Canterbury, July 12, 1700, Perry, *Historical Collections*, 2: 16.

24. Vestry to Board of Trade, Jan. 28, 1700/1701, Board of Trade Papers, Proprietary, VI, pt1 G13 (printed in *Calendar of State Papers, Colonial Series, America and West Indies 1574–1737* (London: 1860–   ), 19 (1701), no. 101.

25. Vestry to Board of Trade, October 27, 170l, Board of Trade Papers, Proprietary, VI, pt1 G13, *Calendar of State Papers*, 20, no. 271; Robert Snead to John Houblon, April 25, 1698, ibid., 16, no. 403.

26. See Winfred T. Root, *The Relations of Pennsylvania with the British Government, 1695–1765* (New York: D. Appleton and Company, 1912), 234–55 for a good discussion of the oath question. For Anglican efforts to have laws disallowed in England see Board of Trade Papers, Proprietary, VII, pt2,082, transcripts, HSP. For discussions of Anglican efforts to disrupt the government see, for example, James Logan to William Penn, June 24 and Sept. 29, 1703, *Correspondence Between William Penn and James Logan*, 2 vols., ed. Edward Armstrong, in Historical Society of Pennsylvania, *Memoirs*, 9 and 10 (1870, 1872), 2: 193, 243–44.

27. The Keithian schism, which tore apart the Society of Friends from 1690 to 1693, started as an attempt by George Keith, a Scottish Quaker, to introduce more doctrinal rigidity into the Society by requiring adherence to a formal Confession of Faith. At least eighty-seven Philadelphia Quaker men were among Keith's followers. Keith himself returned to England and in 1699 converted to the Church of England. While it is unclear how many of his followers followed his example, we do know they had demonstrated sympathy for the Anglicans, allowing them to use their meeting house and housing the Anglican schoolteacher, John Arrowsmith, when he first arrived. For the details of the Keithian controversy see Gary Nash, *Quakers and Politics: Pennsylvania 1681–1726* (Princeton, N.J.: Princeton University Press, 1968), 144–60.

28. See George Every, *The High Church Party, 1688–1718* (London: Church Historical Society, 1956), chaps. 1 and 2.

29. We do not have any of the letters Clayton wrote, but he discusses his efforts in a letter to Governor Nicholson, Nov. 29, 1698, Perry, *Historical Collections*, 2: 14–15. The Baptist reply, John Watts et al. to Thomas Clayton, March 11, 1699, is in David Spencer, *The Early Baptists of Philadelphia* (Philadelphia: W. Syckelmoore, 1877), 35–38.

30. For the Keithian reply see Thomas Martin to Thomas Clayton, Sept.16, 1698, Fulham

2 0

Papers, 7: 18. Perry reprinted the letter (*Historical Collections*, 2: 12–13, 500), but incorrectly identifies the author as Thomas Makin, an orthodox Quaker.

31. Evan Evans, "The State of the Church in Pennsylvania, most humbly offered to ye Venerable Society for the Propagation of the Gospel in Foreign Parts," Perry, *Historical Collections*, 2:33–34.

32. The quote is from the charter of the SPG, which is found in David Humphreys, *An Historical Account of the Incorporated Society for the Propagation of the Gospel in Foreign Parts. . .* (London, 1730; reprint ed., New York: J. Downing, 1969), xvi.

33. See John Nelson, "Anglican Missions in America, 1701–25: A Study of the Society for the Propagation of the Gospel in Foreign Parts" (Ph.D. diss., Northwestern University, 1962), 96. For Talbot's quote see John Talbot to Secretary of the SPG, Sept. 7, 1724, in Edgar Pennington, *Apostle of New Jersey: John Talbot, 1645–1725* (Philadelphia: Church Historical Society, 1935), 184. Talbot's earlier letters are filled with similar quotes.

34. Vestry of Christ Church to Secretary of the SPG, [1704], quoted in Ethyn Kirby, *George Keith, 1638–1716* (New York: D. Appleton and Century Co., 1942), 144.

35. George Keith, "A Journal of Travels from New Hampshire to Caratuck, on the Continent of North America," *HMPEC* 20 (1951): 424, 431.

36. See, for example, Jacob Taylor, *An Almanack for the Year of Christian Account 1709* (Philadelphia, 1708); Daniel Leeds, *An Almanack for the Year of Christian Account 1708* (Philadelphia, 1707). For the end of the dispute see Leeds, *Almanack, 1711* and Taylor, *Almanack, 1711*.

37. For the political situation during these years see Nash, *Quakers and Politics*, 241–273. For a sample of the Penn-Logan correspondence about Quary and Logan see Armstrong, *Correspondence*, 2: 169, 195, 277–78, 289, 291, 313, 317. The quote is from James Logan to William Penn, Sept. 7, 1713, William Penn Papers, HSP.

38. The letter from the vestry concerned the oath law of 1723. See Christ Church Vestry Minutes, Nov. 1723. The letters from the missionaries are not extant. They are referred to in James Logan to William Penn, June 29, 1712, Logan Letter Book, 1712–1715, James Logan Papers, HSP, p. 15.

39. Evan Evans to George Keith, Oct. 25, 1704, Perry, *Historical Collections*, 2: 20–21.

40. See Gerald Goodwin, "The Anglican Middle Way in Early Eighteenth Century America" (Ph.D. diss., University of Wisconsin, 1967), chap. 2; Joseph Ellis, *The New England Mind in Transition: Samuel Johnson of Connecticut, 1696–1772* (New Haven, Conn.: Yale University Press, 1973), 88–98; Sidney G. Bolton, "The Anglican Church of Colonial South Carolina 1704–1754: A Study in Americanization" (Ph.D. diss., University of Wisconsin, 1973), chaps. 5 and 6; Jean Paul Jordan, "The Anglican Establishment in Colonial New York, 1693–1783" (Ph.D. diss,, Columbia University, 1971), chap. 4; Carl Bridenbaugh, *Mitre and Sceptre* (London: Oxford University Press, 1962), 144–340; Frederick V. Mills, Sr., *Bishops by Ballot: An Eighteenth Century Ecclesiastical Revolution* (New York: Oxford University Press, 1978), 35–71; Rhys Isaac, *The Transformation of Virginia 1740–1790* (Chapel Hill: University of North Carolina Press, 1982).

CHAPTER TWO

ESTABLISHING A GOVERNING STRUCTURE WITHOUT A BISHOP

The earliest Christ Church members had to do more than combat Quakers. They also had to build up a congregation, establish a worship life, raise money, and, perhaps most important, create a governing structure that would work without the presence of a bishop. A look at the church from 1705, ten years after its founding, until 1726, after a generation of churchmen had grown up in Philadelphia, can tell us how successful they were at accomplishing these goals.

The easiest task turned out to be attracting members. Between 1709 and 1717, 190 couples had their children baptized. To accommodate its growing numbers, the congregation enlarged the church in 1711, but by 1720 the vestry once again complained that the church was too small.[1] We do not know whether these members were Anglican immigrants or Quaker converts.

Strikingly, the early congregation remained relatively representative of the city as a whole. As can be seen from Table 1, the mean tax assessment of Christ Church members appearing on the 1709 tax list was almost identical to that for the entire city. While Christ Church members were slightly

TABLE 1. Tax Assessment in Philadelphia in 1709

Tax assessment (in pounds)	Total population and percents	Christ Church members and percents
To 36	81 (19.0)	9 (23.1)
37–42	77 (18.1)	6 (15.4)
43–60	74 (17.4)	4 (10.3)
61–75	74 (17.4)	9 (23.1)
76–100	5 (1.2)	0 (0.0)
101–150	73 (17.1)	4 (10.3)
151–239	23 (5.3)	5 (12.8)
240+	18 (4.2)	2 (4.9)
Total number	**425**	**35**
Mean	**£97.4**	**£97.3**

SOURCE: Peter J. Parker, "Rich and Poor in Philadelphia, 1709," *PMHB* 99 (1975): 3–19.

overrepresented in the higher brackets, the overall distribution was very similar to the city as a whole.[2]

Christ Church included members prominent in government and society. Robert Quary remained an active member until his death in 1714, serving on the vestry for many years. Robert Assheton, a relative of William Penn, was a lawyer who served as provincial attorney general and prothonotary or clerk of the Pennsylvania Supreme Court; it has been said that he had more influence on the legal forms of his day than anyone else. His two sons were also prominent. William, who was a vestryman of Christ Church from 1718 to 1723, served as judge of the vice admiralty court, and as a member of the Provincial Council, the governor's prestigious advisory board, before dying at the age of thirty-three. Ralph, who was appointed clerk of the Provincial Court when he was eighteen, went on to serve on the Provincial Council, and as Master of the Court of Chancery. William Trent, the founder of Trenton, New Jersey, also played a prominent role in Christ Church. One of the wealthiest merchants in Philadelphia, he was elected to the Pennsylvania General Assembly from Philadelphia five times and served twice as Speaker; he also served on the Provincial Council and as a justice of the Pennsylvania Supreme Court. Charles Read served as alderman and mayor of Philadelphia.[3] Christ Church members were probably relieved to have among them the editor of the first newspaper in Philadelphia, since it meant Quakers could not use it to promote their beliefs. Andrew Bradford, whose father William had been run out of town by the Quakers, returned in 1712 and in

1719 established the first newspaper south of Boston, the *American Weekly Mercury*. He also served as postmaster until 1737.[4]

* * *

Once Evan Evans arrived in 1700, members of Christ Church had a full complement of worship services and religious lectures available to them. In addition to morning and evening prayer on Sunday, Evans held services on all holy days and on Wednesdays and Fridays. He also gave a lecture in the evening of the last Sunday of each month in preparation for the Communion service, which was celebrated the first Sunday of each month.[5] Since all of these worship services were taken from the Book of Common Prayer, worshiping at Christ Church provided Anglicans with a sense of continuity with their religious and cultural life in England and an immediate bond with Anglicans who had emigrated from different parts of England.

The typical Sunday morning service in colonial churches during the colonial period consisted of three parts: the morning prayer, the litany, and, on Sundays when Communion was not observed, Antecommunion (the part of the Communion service up to the Exhortation and Invitation to the Table), with a thirty- to forty-five-minute sermon. On Communion Sundays those not taking communion, which probably consisted of most of the congregation, left after the offering that followed the sermon.[6] As was common among English clergymen, but not universal in the colonies, Evans wore a surplice, which in the eighteenth century was ankle length and full cut. He probably did not wear a cassock; these had gradually fallen out of use in England in the eighteenth century and there is no mention of one in the Christ Church records.[7]

Evening prayer was actually said in the afternoon, sometimes as early as 2:30, giving those who had attended morning services time for lunch but little more. Unfortunately we have no record of exactly when Christ Church held its services, or how many people attended both morning and afternoon.

Anglicans who attended these services not only experienced the beauty and dignity of the services, they also received a thorough grounding in the Bible. Throughout the course of a year, the entire Old and New Testaments were read. In addition, the services in the Book of Common Prayer contained all the essential elements of the church's theology.

Music would not have been the highlight of the service at this time. Because Christ Church had no organ, the clerk would have recited any responses or psalms before the congregation sang them. The years Evan Evans

served at Christ Church were transitional ones in the music of the Anglican church. The so-called "Old Version" of the metrical psalms by Sternhold and Hopkins, which first appeared in 1562, had dominated the musical life of the Anglican church for more than a century. In 1696 the "New Version" by Tate and Brady appeared, consisting of paraphrases rather than translations of the psalms. In 1698 the bishop of London accepted the "New Version" for use in his diocese, which included the colonies. We do not know when Christ Church adopted it, but it was probably around 1707 when Trinity Church in New York did. Whichever version of the psalms they used, the congregation probably only sang them to five or six tunes. In fact, because the clerk's recitation of each line broke the psalm up into "disconnected fragments," it was not uncommon for the congregation to start out with one tune and end up with another.[8]

FIGURE 3
Flagon, paten, and chalice made by John East, given by Queen Anne, 1709. Courtesy of the Philadelphia Art Museum.

Little is known about the actual interior of the first church in which these services were held, although it probably followed the standard arrangements of Anglican churches of the time. The altar table would have been a simple wooden table, covered with an expensive red or green carpet. Both the altar and pulpit were at the east end. The massive walnut baptismal font, which is still in use today, probably stood at the back of the church. Purportedly the font used when William Penn was baptized, it came from All Hallows Church, Barking-by-the-Tower, London in 1697 (see Figure 2). In 1708 Queen Anne sent the church a three-piece silver communion set including a chalice, flagon, and footed paten (see Figure 3). Seven years later Robert Quary's will provided for a matching flagon to be made.[9]

At the same time Christ Church provided for the worship needs of its adult members, it also provided for the educational needs of its children. For most of Evans's rectorship the congregation at Christ Church had a schoolmaster, and as early as 1709 there are references to a schoolhouse owned by the church. While we have no school records, the instructions given to SPG

Tombstone in the Christ Church burial ground. Photograph by Louis W. Meehan.

schoolmasters can give us an idea about what was taught. As would be expected in a church-supported school, the main goal of an SPG schoolmaster was "instructing and disposing Children to believe and live as Christians." The schoolmaster was to teach the children to read, so "they may be capable of reading the Holy Scriptures and other pious and useful Books." The children had to memorize and understand the meaning of the catechism and attend church morning and afternoon on Sunday and on other days of worship. The schoolmaster taught the children prayers and graces, as well as manners and morals, "especially respect for the minister of the parish." Education was also of a practical nature: the schoolmaster taught writing and arithmetic "in order to [fit the children] for useful Employment." Perhaps surprisingly, given the stereotype of harshness in colonial education, the schoolmaster was instructed to "rule by love rather than by fear."[10]

The schoolmaster at Christ Church could draw on an extensive church library to help in his teaching. In fact, Christ Church housed the first library in the colony outside a private home. Sometime between 1698 and 1701 Thomas Bray, an English clergyman with a strong interest in the colonial church, sent approximately 290 volumes to Philadelphia. Most of the books were of a theological nature, but Bray also sent a few volumes of classical and modern literature, one law book, and sixteen relatively esoteric medical texts. Today only 176 of the original volumes remain, housed in the Library Company of Philadelphia.[11]

The leadership of Christ Church also provided a final resting place for its members. In August 1719 the church bought a lot on Mulberry (Arch) Street at the corner of Fifth to serve as a burial ground. (See Figure 4 for an early tombstone.) At the time this lot was on the outskirts of town.[12]

*   *   *

In several respects church life in Pennsylvania was very different from that in England. The absence of a state church combined with the lack of a resident bishop caused serious problems for Christ Church.

Without tax support, the financial situation of Christ Church was always far more precarious than that of English churches. In fact, financial problems were a constant concern for the church throughout the eighteenth and much of the nineteenth century. In the early years the vestry used collections, voluntary subscriptions and burial fees to support the church. Pew rents for people who did not buy their pews were first introduced in 1717, but because most people bought their pews, these did little to improve the financial situation of the church. The minister's salary was provided by voluntary subscription undertaken each year. Thus, while the rector could live in a church owned house, his salary could fluctuate greatly from year to year. Even after Evans left to take a parish in Maryland because of a lack of financial security in Philadelphia, the vestry refused to provide his successor with a more secure income.[13]

The absence of an established ecclesiastical structure also set the Pennsylvania church apart from the church in England. The lack of a resident bishop to ordain and monitor the behavior of ministers and confirm the laity has been widely chronicled, but bishops were only one piece of a complex ecclesiastical structure that had grown up over the years in England and was not present in Pennsylvania. The exact powers of different groups varied from one parish to another in England, but who had the right to exercise power was rarely in doubt. For example, the right to choose the rector of a local church in England sometimes rested with the king, sometimes with wealthy laymen, and sometimes with the bishop. Similarly, the power of the vestry, which was usually a self-perpetuating body in both England and America, and the churchwardens, one of whom was chosen by the vestry and one by the rector, was also clearly defined by a combination of canon law and local tradition in England. English churches also had an informal authority structure based on a well-defined social hierarchy. Ministers knew that the local gentry could make their lives miserable and end their chances of advancement if offended.[14]

In Philadelphia it took years to determine the roles the congregation, the vestry, and the bishop should play in the life of the church. Moreover, because no established social hierarchy existed in the city it was never clear which lay members should have a prominent role in the church. The way in which pews were assigned in Christ Church is symbolic of the lack of clear leadership. In England and in colonies such as Virginia, pews were assigned based on a person's status in the community.[15] With the exception of the governor's pew, Christ Church never did this. Whether one bought or rented a pew, a person inherited the right to that pew. Thus the seating pattern reflected the length of time a family had been in the parish more than it did their socioeconomic status.

It is within this framework of developing governing structures—of a congregation struggling to adapt the varying power structures that they had known in England to a new environment—that we should look at the various conflicts that engulfed Christ Church in the early eighteenth century.

For, while the church got off to a good start under Evan Evans, it fell on hard times from 1715 to 1726, as a series of disputes preoccupied the leadership. Some of the incidents that occurred are fascinating in themselves, but their long-term importance lies in helping us understand how Christ Church members learned to live with their new situation, gradually developing governing structures suitable to that environment.

Internal problems at Christ Church began as early as 1705, when Evans and Robert Quary came into conflict. While the exact issues involved are unknown, they were no doubt rooted in Quary's desire to dominate the church and Evans's resistance to such domination. While a fellow clergyman reported in 1712 that Evans had "owned [his] precipitancy, and Expressed [his] sorrow for differing with Colonel Quary" and had "repented his imprudent . . . and rash representations of men of Note and distinction," there is no indication that Evans ever really accepted domination by local laymen. It was probably in part this lack of deference that led to the decrease in subscriptions that, in turn, eventually forced Evans to find a more secure parish in Maryland.[16]

Far more serious problems developed while Evans traveled to England in 1714 to settle some personal matters. The center of the controversy was the Reverend Francis Phillips, the man chosen by the vestry to substitute for Evans. Phillips was extremely popular during his first few months in the city. Robert Jenney, the priest the bishop of London had chosen to substitute for Evans, would, upon his arrival in late 1714, report his finding that Phillips had such a "good character" and "was so well beloved by the People that it was impossible to dispossess him."[17] Yet, despite Phillips's popularity, less than two years after his arrival he sailed for England in disgrace, leaving behind him a badly divided congregation.

Phillips's problems began in February 1715, when he was accused of slandering three prominent Philadelphia women and of propositioning a fourth. According to the allegations of two men, John Smith and William Jones, about whom we know nothing, Phillips had boasted that he had slept with three women: the wife of William Trent, the Anglican provincial councillor; the daughter of John Moore, the collector of the customs and a founder of Christ Church; and a Mrs. Newman. At the same time, Smith and Jones accused Phillips of propositioning Elizabeth Starkey, a servant of the Reverend John Humphreys, the Anglican minister at Chester, Pennsylvania, with whom Phillips was staying.[18]

While it is impossible to prove or disprove these charges, there are certainly grounds to doubt their validity. Elizabeth Starkey later testified that she made the accusations against Phillips only because her master promised her her freedom and twenty pounds. Moreover, Phillips had a good point when he argued that the words he allegedly spoke were "so ridiculous and groundless that no man in his wits could ever be guilty of such scandalous folly."[19] It is curious that the main charge against him was only *saying* that he had slept with three women, a charge that was almost impossible for him to disprove. But if the charges were untrue, the motives for the attack on Phillips is unknown. Moore was an opponent of Phillips, but it seems strange that he would have encouraged slander against his own daughter.

These accusations, whether true or false, caused a sensation in the Quaker city. Two of the aggrieved men, Trent and Moore, had Phillips arrested at eleven or twelve o'clock on a Saturday night and "dragged . . . barelegged for near one half mile to the prison." Bail was set at two thousand pounds for one charge against him and one thousand pounds for the other, even though no bail was required in this type of case. To add to Phillips's humiliation, Anglican Peter Evans, the sheriff who happened to be courting the slandered Miss Moore, refused to allow Phillips to send for the bail and forced him to stay in the regular jail cell rather than in the undersheriff's house, as was customary for persons of rank. Thus the members of Christ Church awoke on Sunday morning to find their church doors shut because their minister was in jail. Infuriated by this treatment of their beloved minister, two or three hundred men and boys marched to the jail on Sunday, demanding Phillips's release. Once they obtained his release, they went on to attack the house of John Smith, one of the accusers. During the following two nights the crowds became more and more disorderly, breaking windows in the homes of Moore and Trent. According to the prominent Quaker Isaac Norris, several Friends "of best repute . . . were obliged to accompany the [Night] Watch for some Nights, to prevent mischief." Meanwhile, Peter Evans, the jailer, decided to champion his fiancée and challenged the minister to a duel. Phillips wisely ignored the challenge and Evans was later indicted for his gallant efforts.[20]

Phillips was brought to trial despite the crowd's support, found guilty of slander, and fined twenty pounds. However, he refused to acknowledge the authority of the court, maintaining that he could only be tried in an ecclesiastical court. Governor Charles Gookin, who had backed Phillips from the beginning of the controversy, forgave his fine and forced the court to clear him of all charges. Unfortunately for Phillips, the bishop of London was not so magnanimous; in October of 1715, eight months after the controversy began, Phillips and Gookin received letters from the bishop ordering Phillips to vacate Christ Church. He obeyed this directive and left immediately for England, where he intended to plead his case before the bishop. We do not know the outcome of that appeal.[21]

By the time Phillips left he had alienated part of his congregation, demonstrating that, as he put it, while the Anglicans "live in the midst of our enemies . . . our greatest foes prove to be those of our own house." With the aid of Governor Gookin, Phillips had been able to retain possession of the church building throughout the controversy. His opponents held services first at the Swedish church and then, when that became too small, at the courthouse, with Robert Jenney or ministers from the countryside officiating. When Phillips left Christ Church for England, many of his supporters also left the church. Gookin reportedly went to the Swedish service, which, an SPG missionary reported, "he understands as much as I do Arabick." Others went to the Presbyterian or Baptist churches, or just stayed home.[22]

In England, charges like these would have been handled relatively quickly and easily: an ecclesiastical court would have either acquitted or convicted Phillips, and the bishop would have then taken appropriate action. In the absence of such authority, various individuals and groups entered the fray.

Phillips's rectorship provided the vestry with its first real opportunity to assert its rights in the selection of a minister. Perhaps because Phillips was the first minister chosen by the vestrymen themselves, they strongly supported him, writing the bishop of London protesting the "unchristian and barbarous treatment the Reverend Mr. Phillips our worthy minister has met with." They even went a step further, asking the bishop to license or officially install Phillips as rector of Christ Church. This move is particularly remarkable because Evans planned to return from England to his rectorship in Philadelphia. Obviously the vestry had little regard for church law or for the feelings of Evans.[23]

But the vestry did not act alone in the Phillips controversy; as we have seen, prominent laymen were among the most important participants in the dispute. Some charged that they actually caused the controversy, making false accusations because they objected to Phillips's condemnation of their own "vicious" behavior.[24] However, these lay leaders were far from a united force. While the aggrieved Moore and Trent worked hard to get Phillips expelled from the pulpit of Christ Church, Governor Gookin did everything in his power to support Phillips.

The role of the governor in the Pennsylvania church was complex. While Gookin had no legal power in religion, English authorities expected him to play a prominent role in protecting the rights and overseeing the interests of the church because he was the highest official of the Anglican faith in the colony. Gookin took his role as protector of the church very seriously. He also saw the Phillips controversy as a means toward two positive ends. He could get revenge on Trent and Moore, who were his political enemies. And, by defending an embattled clergyman he believed he could ingratiate himself with the English authorities and assure his appointment as royal governor if Pennsylvania were sold to the crown. His strategy ultimately backfired, however, since the bishop ruled against Phillips.[25]

Less prominent members of the congregation also became involved in the controversy. One hundred and four members of the congregation wrote to the bishop defending their minister against "malicious insinuations."[26] This tendency on the part of members of the congregation to express their own opinions, rather than leaving it up to the vestry, would be an important theme in Christ Church history, complicating the power structures still further.

In this case, part of the cause of the controversy seems to have been a power struggle between prominent laymen and less well-to-do Anglicans. One of Phillips's enemies argued that the whole problem was caused by "the meaner people Acting in Opposition, and purely in opposition to the Better sort," while one of Phillips's supporters argued that the wealthy men, whom he called "Church papists," objected because Phillips directed his sermons at all the members, rather than catering to the whims of the important ones.[27] The limited economic data we have support this picture. Comparing the tax assessment of Phillips's supporters whose names appear on the 1709 tax list with a sample of Christ Church members as a whole, we find that the mean value of the estates of Phillips's supporters was £59.9 while the mean for Christ Church members overall was £97.3. The numbers involved are not large enough to draw firm conclusions, but they do indicate that less wealthy members of the church felt they had a right to influence the choice of a rector.[28]

Area clergymen also believed they had an important role to play in solving this dispute. In the absence of a bishop, they considered themselves responsible for the welfare of the church and the policing of clergy in the area. Shortly after Phillips's arrest they began an inquiry into his behavior, including a formal meeting to which they invited Phillips and his accusers. Phillips did not attend, and no doubt as a result of this, the clergy found

CHAPTER TWO

against him. When he refused to "quietly . . . withdraw himself," they decided to "entirely disown him as unfit for the station which he holds." Reporting this to the bishop, they requested that he "purge the Church of so bad a member and rid us of so scandalous a Brother." This interference was not appreciated by the Christ Church vestry; twelve vestrymen wrote the bishop of London arguing that the clergymen's "attendance upon their own cures would have been much more commendable, then [sic] to Suffer themselves to be Sowers and Spreaders of Strife and Sedition."[29]

All participants in this dispute apparently realized that the bishop of London had ultimate authority, so the best they could do was to attempt to influence his decision. Indeed, the disunity among the laity on this issue only increased the bishop's power and retarded the growth of lay authority in the Philadelphia church. When the bishop ordered Phillips to come back to England, no one challenged the order.

The departure of Francis Phillips and the return of Evan Evans in late 1716 did not end conflict and controversy within the congregation. When Evans returned to Philadelphia in late 1716, he found himself almost totally without a stipend, no doubt the consequence of years of conflict in the church. As a result, in February of 1718 he left to take a parish in Maryland.[30]

Evans's departure ushered in the low point in the prerevolutionary history of Christ Church, an eight-year period of instability and conflict. Unable to find a minister who would stay for more than a few years, the vestry tried to keep the church open and healthy but seemed to spend most of its time fighting with the governor, with the ministers it did attract, and with the authorities in England.

The nineteen months after Evans left, during which time the large congregation had no regular minister, provided the laymen of Christ Church with an opportunity to decide who should have the most power. At first it appeared that the governor would be allowed to assume that role, but within a year the vestry had clearly indicated that it wanted to be in charge. In 1717, when Sir William Keith, a Scottish baronet, arrived in Philadelphia to replace Gookin as governor, the vestrymen immediately asked him to become a member of the vestry, and in 1718 he was elected chair of that body. Despite his reputation as a freethinker in matters of religion, the vestrymen called on him again and again to play the role that the local gentry did in England. They asked Keith to write to the bishop requesting a minister and schoolmaster, gave him authority to recruit area missionaries to supply the church, and asked him to negotiate with a possible minister. But an abrupt change took place in 1719. Although the details are unknown, it appears that Keith took his leadership role a bit too far, usurping what the vestry felt was its power. As one vestryman put it, because Keith had taken it "upon him to overrule [the vestrymen] and entirely [deprive] them of the freedom justly due," he was not reelected to the vestry.[31] More important, no governor was ever again elected to the vestry. In effect, the leaders of Christ Church rejected the role of government in religion that was so commonplace in England and began, probably unwittingly, to accept the separation of church and state that the founders of the church in Philadelphia so abhorred.

When the new rector, John Vicary, arrived in September of 1719, he found a vestry just beginning to discover its "rightful authority" and a proud baronet whose power had just been repudiated. Thus, despite his being an "ingenious preacher" who at first "gave general satisfaction to the people in the Exercise of every part of his sacred office," Vicary soon came into conflict with both the governor and the vestry. While Vicary's power struggles with Keith were primarily personal and therefore not very revealing, his conflicts with the vestry were symptomatic of the problems caused when anyone attempted to enforce canon law rigidly in the chaotic colonial environment. The problems began in 1721 when Vicary became ill. The rector clearly believed that he should continue to control things from his bed, whereas the vestry assumed that in the absence of a functioning rector it should take control. Vicary maintained that the vestry could not even meet officially without a rector, which, while technically correct, was not realistic in a colony without any other ecclesiastical government. And when the vestry hired a lay reader to continue services, something that was quite common in the colonies but was considered "an irregularity founded upon necessity" by the bishop, Vicary insisted that it was against church canons.[32] Vicary never adjusted to church life in Philadelphia; he refused to accept that, as another minister put it, "no people that have common sense will be huff'd into compliance when the power of acting is in themselves."[33] He returned to England in 1723, an ill and embittered man.

For the next three years, the vestry of Christ Church continued its increasingly desperate search for a minister. Its primary concern was to keep the church open and functioning. In the environment of Pennsylvania, where many denominations flourished and denominational loyalty among laypeople seemed slight, the vestrymen knew that if regular services were not held members could go elsewhere and might not come back when a new minister arrived. With the shortage of ministers, the church was forced to accept some less-than-reputable men.

The vestry first turned to John Urmston, a former missionary in North Carolina, who was visiting Philadelphia and was desperate for a job. It soon found, however, that the "misfortune" of drunkenness "that drove him from Carolina and other places Still attended him and his behavior became Such at Philadelphia as is not proper to be mentioned or allowed in any Sober Society." The vestry attempted to starve Urmstrom out by withholding his salary, but eventually had to resort to bribery, giving him his back pay in exchange for his departure. Urmston moved to a parish in Maryland, from which he was soon removed by the bishop's commissary. He wandered to North Carolina where he burned to death, supposedly having fallen into the fireplace while drunk.[34]

In July 1724 the vestry asked Richard Welton to accept the rectorship of Christ Church. In an important try for independence, it did not bother to ask the bishop of London to license Welton as was required by church law. Perhaps the vestrymen knew that such a license would be denied. Welton was a nonjuring priest, a member of a diminishing group of English priests who refused to accept the Glorious Revolution in 1688 that replaced the Catholic king, James II, with his Protestant daughter Mary and her Dutch husband William. Nonjuring priests remained loyal to the Stuart line of succession, refusing to take the oath of loyalty to the king of England, who at this time was King George I, as was required of all priests. Welton's situation was even more irregular because he had been consecrated a bishop by Ralph Taylor, a nonjuring bishop. Since three bishops were required to consecrate a new bishop, even the nonjurors did not accept Welton's consecration.[35]

Welton's political and ecclesiastical views seemed to have been of no concern to the vestry. While vestryman Peter Evans maintained that they had been "well-assured" that Welton had taken the oath to the king before they hired him, the vestry continued to support him after his views were known. Even after hearing his farewell sermon in which he warned that "after my Departure Grievous Wolves shall Enter in, among you, not sparing the Flock," it endorsed a certificate of good behavior.[36] There is certainly no evidence that there were any nonjurors among the leaders of the church. Rather, it appears that keeping the church open was more important to the leaders than dealing with English political disputes.

Governor Keith was not so willing to ignore Welton's past. A former nonjuror himself, he promptly informed the bishop that the clergyman at Christ Church was reading prayers and preaching "without mentioning the King, Prince and Royal Family according to the rubric." As a result, in the fall of 1725 Welton was served with the king's "Writ of Privy Seal," commanding that he return to England. Once again the congregation had to give in to English authorities—this time George III—and give up their choice for a minister.[37]

*　*　*

During the ten-year period from 1714 to 1724, the vestry of Christ Church tried to keep the church open, while trying at the same time to establish vestry authority to choose a minister and run the affairs of the church. However, the vestrymen ultimately found that their authority was really quite limited and the "power of acting" ultimately was not in "themselves." They had to stand by while the bishop summoned Phillips home and the king ordered Welton to return to England. Their attempts to fill the rectorship themselves had been a failure.

When Welton left in 1725, the vestry finally admitted defeat and asked the bishop of London to send them a minister. However, the new bishop, Edmund Gibson, who had taken office in 1723 determined to take an active role in the affairs of the colonial church, was not pleased with the past conduct of the lay leaders of Christ Church. While eager to settle a strong minister in this important area, he was concerned about the treatment the minister would receive. Thus, in order to obtain a new minister, the congregation had to convince the bishop of both its subservience to English authorities and its willingness to treat a minister fairly. The vestry had to put aside its search for power and even had to cooperate with Keith, whose damning reports had no doubt greatly influenced Gibson.

Governor Keith and Peter Evans, two men who agreed on few other things, wrote to Bishop Gibson to dispel his bad impression of Christ Church. Keith assured the bishop that he "never knew any place where a minister has had more honor and respect paid to him than the people are generally fond to express here," and Evans guaranteed that whoever the bishop sent would have "just ground to convince [him] that the Vestry and congregation of that church, are not only true and loyal Subjects to his majesty, but are sincere well-wishers and hearty members of the Church of England as by Law Established."[38] As a result of this show of respect and loyalty, the bishop agreed to send a new rector for Christ Church.

1. No membership or pew lists exist for this time period. The baptismal records are located in the Christ Church Archives. Reference to the need for a larger church can be found in the Vestry Minutes, Aug. 11, 1720.

2. Of the 190 people who had their children baptized from 1709 to 1717, only 39 appear on the 1709 tax list, the only one remaining from this period. For the tax list see Peter J. Parker, "Rich and Poor in Philadelphia, 1709," *PMHB* 99 (1975): 3–19.

3. Information on the Asshetons can be found in Nash, *Quakers and Politics*, 212, and in J. Thomas Scharf and Thompson Wescott, *History of Philadelphia*, 3 vols. (Philadelphia: L.H. Everts Corp., 1883), 2: 1506–7. For William Trent see Nash, *Quakers and Politics*, 55. For Charles Read, see Oberholtzer, *Philadelphia*, 1: 138.

4. See Scharf and Westcott, *History of Philadelphia*, 1: 200, 206, 220.

5. Keith, "A Journal of Travels," 432. The Accounting Warden's Journal, Christ Church Archives, that lists communion offerings, confirms that Communion was celebrated monthly.

6. For a detailed description of an eighteenth-century Anglican service see Marion J. Hatchett, "A Sunday Service in 1776 or Thereabouts," *HMPEC* 45 (1976): 369–85. The earliest sermons we have from Christ Church were preached by Archibald Cummings in the 1730s. While varying in length, I have estimated that they would have been at least thirty-five minutes long. See Archibald Cummings, *The Danger of Breaking Christian Unity in Two Sermons Preached At Christ Church in Philadelphia* (Philadelphia: Andrew Bradford, 1737); Cummings, *Faith Absolutely Necessary but Not Sufficient to Salvation* (Philadelphia: Andrew Bradford, 1740). We have no records for Communion at Christ Church, but the missionaries in the countryside consistently reported small numbers of communicants, ranging from seventeen to fifty, while the number of parishioners were often reported at two or three hundred. See, for example, William Becket to SPG, Sept. 1, 1722, Thomas Crawford to SPG, Aug. 31, 1708, Perry, *Historical Collections*, 2: 35–36, 5: 16–18.

7. For references to cleaning the surplice, see Accounting Warden's Journals, 1712.

8. See Herbert Boyce Satcher, "Music of the Episcopal Church in Pennsylvania in the Eighteenth Century," *HMPEC* 18 (1949): 373–74. The first version of the Book of Common Prayer published in the colonies in 1710 by William Bradford contained the "New Version"; Peter Lutkin, *Christian Music in the Church*, 69, quoted by Satcher, "Music of the Episcopal Church," 374.

9. For an in-depth discussion of the furnishings of Anglican churches in Virginia, see Dell Upton, *Holy Things and Profane: Anglican Parish Churches in Colonial Virginia* (Cambridge, Mass.: MIT Press, 1986), chap. 6. The only indication of the location of the pulpit is found when the new church was being built. On March 16, 1732 the vestry ordered the pulpit to be moved to the west end when it was completed and then on July 31, 1740 it ordered it returned to the east end. See Bruce Cooper Gill, "Christ Church in Philadelphia: Furnishings, the Early Years," in *The Catalog of the 1981 Antique Show: A Benefit for the Hospital of the University of Pennsylvania* (Philadelphia: Revere Press, 1981), 130, for information on the baptismal font and silver.

10. Clifton Brewer, *A History of Religious Education in the Episcopal Church to 1835* (New Haven, Conn.: Yale University Press, 1924; reprint, New York: Arno Press, 1969), 28–29.

11. Bray sent more than £2400 worth of books to churches throughout the colonies to help reform both the clergy and the laity. For the most recent discussion of Thomas Bray, see John

Van Horne, ed., *Religious Philanthropy and Colonial Slavery: The American Correspondence of the Associates of Dr. Bray 1717–1777* (Urbana: University of Illinois Press, 1985). For two discussions of the Christ Church library, see Louis C. Washburn, "The Library" in Washburn, *Christ Church, Philadelphia: A Symposium*, 157–72 and Edwin Wolfe, "The First Library of Christ Church," in *The Catalog of the 1981 Antique Show*, 148–51. Washburn includes a complete list of the books.

12. Vestry Minutes, May 15, 1719, Aug. [illeg.], 1719.

13. The Accounting Warden's Journals list the collections for each Sunday. For the introduction of pew rents, see Vestry Minutes, February 3, 1717/18. The parsonage is mentioned in the Journals in 1709. When Evans announced his departure in 1718 the vestry reported that "little or nothing" had been raised for his support in the previous year. See Vestry Minutes, Feb. 1717/18. The discussions with the prospective rector can be followed in the Vestry Minutes, May 15, June 17, June 25, 1719. It is not clear when pew rents began to be used to pay the minister's salary, although we know it was the practice by the 1740s.

14. Warne, *Church and Society in Eighteenth Century Devon*, chaps. 1 and 2; A. Tindal Hart, *The Eighteenth Century Country Parson* (Shrewsbury, England: Wilding 1955), 87–93; Borden W. Painter, "The Anglican Vestry in Colonial America" (Ph.D. diss., Yale University, 1965), chap. 1; Anthony Armstrong, *The Church of England, the Methodists and Society 1700–1850* (London: H.S. Romman and Littlefield, 1973), chap. 1.

15. For an extensive discussion of seatings in Virginia churches, see Upton, *Holy Things and Profane*, 177–88.

16. Bishop Compton to Secretary of the SPG, Dec. 17, 1705, SPG Letters, A2 no. 101; George Ross to Secretary of the SPG, June 30, 1712, SPG Letters, A7, pp. 508–9. For a detailed discussion of Quary's efforts to dominate the church, see Deborah Gough, "Pluralism, Politics and Power Structures: The Church of England in Colonial Philadelphia" (Ph.D. diss., University of Pennsylvania, 1978), 78–85.

17. For Phillips's career in Connecticut see E. Edwards Beardsley, *History of the Episcopal Church in Connecticut*, 2 vols. (New York: Hurd and Stoughton, 1866), 1: 26; Robert Jenney to Secretary of SPG, Jan. 4, 1714/15, Perry, *Collections*, 2: 81. Jenney stayed in Philadelphia during Evans's absence but was never recognized by the vestry as the minister of Christ Church.

18. For accounts of these bizarre events see John Newberry to the Reverend William Vesey, Nov. 30, 1715, Perry, *Collections*, 2: 94–97; Francis Phillips to Secretary of SPG, March 23, 1714/15, ibid., 2: 90–93.

19. See Phillips to Reverend Dr. [identity unknown], May 16, 1715, Fulham Papers, 7: 59–60; Phillips to Reverend Sir, Aug. 15, 1715, Fulham Papers, 7: 73–74; Phillips to Secretary, March 23, 1715, Perry, *Historical Collections*, 2: 90–91. For the affidavit of Elizabeth Starkey and others backing her up see Fulham Papers, 7: 61–64.

20. Isaac Norris to Benjamin Coole, July 18, 1715, Norris Letter Book, Isaac Norris Papers, HSP, 1: 267–68. Evans's challenge and the court proceedings can be found in Perry, *Historical Collections*, 2: 512.

21. Newberry to Vesey, Nov. 30, 1715, Perry, *Historical Collections*, 2: 94–97. For a good narrative account of this controversy see Charles Keith, *Chronicles of Pennsylvania from the English Revolution to the Peace of Aix-la-Chapelle 1688–1748* (Philadelphia: Patterson and White, 1917), 564–67.

22. Francis Phillips to Reverend Sir [probably the bishop], May 22, 1715, Fulham Papers, 7:

65–66; "Extracts from the Journal of Reverend Andreas Sandel, 1702–19," *PMHB* 30 (1906): 448–49; John Talbot to Bishop Robinson, [October 1715], Fulham Papers, 7: 74 (printed in Pennington, *Apostle of New Jersey*, 160–61); Newberry to Vesey, Nov. 30, 1715, Perry, *Historical Collections*, 2: 94–97.

23. Charles Gookin, Vestry, and Wardens of Christ Church to Bishop John Robinson, April 20, 1715, Fulham Papers, 7: 51–52. See also Vestry of Christ Church to Bishop John Robinson, Aug. 12, 1715, Fulham Papers, 7: 69–70.

24. Newberry to Vesey, Nov. 30, 1715, Perry, *Historical Collections*, 2: 95.

25. For the best account of Gookin's political career see Nash, *Quakers and Politics*, 312–19. For examples of Gookin's efforts to ingratiate himself and explain his actions see Charles Gookin to Secretary of SPG, Dec. 1, 1711, SPG Letters, A7, p. 497; Charles Gookin to Bishop John Robinson, May 2, 1711; Gookin to Secretary of SPG, Aug. 12, 1716, SPG Letters, A11, p. 231.

26. Members of Christ Church to Bishop John Robinson, March 7, 1714/15, Fulham Papers, 7: 43–44.

27. John Humphreys to Secretary of SPG, n.d., SPG Letters, A10, p. 139; Newberry to Vesey, Nov. 30, 1715, Perry, *Historical Collections*, 2: 96. See also Jenney to Secretary of SPG, Jan. 4, 1714/15, ibid., 2: 81.

28. See Table 1 for the distribution of the city as a whole. Only twenty-nine of the ninety-one men who signed the letter appear on the tax list.

29. Clergy to Bishop John Robinson, March 17, 1714, Perry, *Historical Collections*, 2: 84–87; Vestry of Christ Church to Bishop, Aug. 12, 1715, Fulham Papers, 7: 69–70.

30. Vestry minutes, February 1718.

31. See Vestry Minutes, March 11, April and May 1718, May and June 1719; Peter Evans to Bishop Edmund Gibson, n.d. (c.1725), Smith Manuscripts, PEC, 3: 2–3, Perry, *Historical Collections*, 2: 516–57.

32. To follow the dispute see the Vestry Minutes, January and February 1721/22. Canon law allowed lay readers, but it was normally approved by the bishop. Vicary and the vestry had different definitions of "necessity." Vicary also had a series of disputes with Governor Keith; see Gough, "Pluralism, Politics and Power Struggles," 108–12.

33. William Harrison to Secretary, May 31, 1722, SPG Letters, A16, p. 159, Perry, *Historical Collections*, 2: 127–28. Harrison was a missionary who supplied Christ Church.

34. Evans to Bishop Gibson (c.1725), Smith manuscripts, PEC; John Talbot to Secretary of SPG, Dec. 9, 1723, SPG Letters, A17, p. 250; Perry, *Historical Collections*, 5: 133; Vestry Minutes, May, August and October 1723; Jacob Henderson to Bishop Edmund Gibson, March 13, 1731/32. Aug. 7, 1731, Perry, *Historical Collections*, 4: 302–3, 308–9.

35. For an account of Welton's life see John Fulton, "The Nonjuring Bishops in America," in *The History of the American Episcopal Church*, 2 vols., ed. William S. Perry (Boston: J.R. Osgood, 1885), 1: 542–44.

36. Evans to Bishop Gibson (c.1725), Smith Manuscripts, PEC; Richard Welton, *The Certain Comforts of God the Holy Ghost & Preached at the Episcopal Church in Philadelphia, Feb. 4, 1725/26* (n.p., n.d); Vestry Minutes, Jan.13, 1726.

37. William Keith to Bishop Edmund Gibson, July 20, 1724, Fulham Papers, 7: 114–15 and April 8, 1726, Perry, *Historical Collections*, 2: 137–38 and 146–48.

38. Keith to Bishop Gibson, April 8, 1726, Perry, *Historical Collections*, 2: 147; Evans to Bishop Gibson (c.1725), Smith Manuscripts, PEC.

CONFLICT WITHIN A FRAMEWORK OF STABILITY: THE RECTORSHIP OF ARCHIBALD CUMMINGS

The arrival in 1726 of Archibald Cummings, the bishop's choice for rector, ushered in a new phase in the history of Christ Church. During his rectorship it became clear that in many ways the Anglican community had entered a period of relative stability. The consequences of religious freedom and the lack of an established ecclesiastical governing structure still led to conflicts and controversies, and the increasingly factional nature of political life in Pennsylvania also would cause problems for the church. But after 1726 the conflicts occurred against a background of stability, not chaos.

One indication of this new era was the increasing length of time rectors served at Christ Church. Between 1695 and 1726 ten men had ministered at the church, four sent by the bishop and six others who had officiated on a regular basis. The longest continuous stay had been seven years. In contrast, between 1726 and 1776 only three ministers served as rector, Cummings for fifteen years, Robert Jenney for twenty, and Richard Peters for twelve.

The Philadelphia that Archibald Cummings came to know was also more stable and developed than the city that Evan Evans had entered twenty-five years before. Its physical layout, its economy, and its social and cultural life had all matured. It was, of course, much larger. The population had increased from approximately 2,200 in 1700 to around 8,000 in 1734. More important was the change in the composition of the population; between 1726 and 1755 approximately 40,000 Germans and 30,000 Scots-Irish settled in the Quaker colony, with enough remaining in the city to change its character permanently. The number of black slaves also increased; by the 1740s approximately 10 percent of Philadelphia's population was black.[1]

New ethnic groups brought new religions to the city. Quakers were increasingly in the minority in their colony, constituting perhaps only one-quarter of the population of Philadelphia in 1742. By the 1740s the Presbyterians, who had built a church in 1704, almost equaled the Quakers in numbers, though not in wealth or power. The Germans took longer to establish their religious life than did the English or Scots-Irish, but in 1732 the German-Reformed and Lutherans formed a joint congregation. In 1732 St. Joseph's Chapel, the first Catholic church, was erected. Penn's policy of religious freedom had resulted in religious heterogeneity of unprecedented proportions.

The economy of Philadelphia had also greatly matured in the quarter of a century since Evans's arrival. The city thrived by importing and making things needed in the rural areas and by exporting what was grown there. The number of ships leaving Philadelphia quadrupled during the 1730s.[2] Artisans took advantage of the needs of the countryside to rise to what would be considered today to be middle-class, or, even in some cases, upper-class status. Benjamin Franklin, who arrived in 1723 to work as a printer and would become one of Christ Church's most famous pewholders, is merely the best known of many success stories.

The increasingly diverse population combined with economic prosperity led to a boom in places providing entertainment and in organizations providing social opportunities for the inhabitants. Coffeehouses and taverns remained the center of both business and pleasure; in 1744 it was estimated that one out of every ten buildings in the city served alcohol. But increasingly, as voluntary associations developed, Philadelphians had other places to meet. Some of these groups were limited to people of one faith or ethnic group, but many were places where people of different religions could mix. In 1729 the first of many ethnic societies, the Society of Ancient Britons (Welsh) was established, to be followed soon by the Society of the Sons of St. George's for the English. The 1730s saw the establishment of the first Freemasons' lodge, St. John's, the elite fishing club "Colony in Schuylkill," and the prestigious Dancing Assembly. Benjamin Franklin founded the first volunteer fire company in 1736 and others soon followed. Members of Christ Church joined all of these organizations.[3]

The cultural life of the city had also improved. In 1727 Franklin founded his Junto or "Leather Apron Club," a group of artisans who met to discuss books, and in 1731 the Library Company, the first of several subscription libraries, was founded. For those who were interested in buying books, there were two well stocked bookstores, Benjamin Franklin's (see Figure 5), which sold mostly secular volumes, and Andrew Bradford's, which contained books geared "almost wholly to religious interests," particularly Anglicanism. That Bradford could make a living selling Bibles, The Book of Common Prayer, and Tate's and Brady's *A New Version of the Psalms of David* indicated both that the number of Anglicans had increased and that some of them took their religion seriously.[4]

The political life of the colony had also changed considerably by the second quarter of the eighteenth century. In 1727 John Penn, eldest son of William and Hannah, took over as proprietor from Penn's widow, Hannah, who had been largely inactive. He found a political situation that was far more stable than the often chaotic and shifting political factions that had existed when his father was proprietor. An economic recession had reinvigorated political debate from 1722 to 1726, but for the most part people were willing to leave politics in the hands of a stable elite. Antiproprietary sentiment still existed—centered, as we will discuss, largely in Christ Church—but the fifteen years that Cummings would serve Christ Church were relatively calm ones in Pennsylvania politics.[5]

* * *

Archibald Cummings seems to have been the right man to lead an Anglican congregation in this cosmopolitan city, for the congregation grew and prospered during the early years of his rectorship. We know little about his background, but his published sermons give an idea of his theology. Undogmatic and middle-of-the road, he strove to inculcate Christian virtues in his members and to keep them away from the more extreme religions of the day: deism, a popular philosophy that stressed reason over revelation and believed God created the world but then assumed no authority over it, and "enthusi-

FIGURE 5
*Franklin's Old Bookshop,
next to Christ Church.
Courtesy of the Historical
Society of Pennsylvania.*

asm," or "evangelical religion," which stressed the need for an immediate conversion experience and deemphasized the liturgical service that characterized the Anglican church.

In 1729 Cummings urged his fellow clergy to use a "solemn and devout Manner of reading Divine Service," making certain that they did not appear "cold or lifeless." Sermons should also be delivered in a serious manner. While he believed that "the less Controversial and more Practical they [sermons] are, the more Usefull and Edifying they will prove," he reminded the clergymen that they must also "insist on the mysterious Points of our Religion . . . for Christianity proposes to its Votarie Things to be believed, as well as to be done." He went on to argue that moral duties could never be inculcated with as much power from reason as by "the wholesome Words of our Lord Jesus Christ."[6]

Cummings preached to an increasingly large congregation. In 1734 he baptized 149 children, compared to the 57 that were baptized in 1720. These members included a number of Quakers who, as their wealth increased, became tired of the strict Quaker lifestyle and turned to the Church of England. Joseph Shippen, William Plumstead, Joseph Redman, and Phineas and Thomas Bond were among those who abandoned Quakerism and joined Christ Church.[7]

While we cannot reconstruct the entire congregation, we do know that Christ Church continued to attract some of the most distinguished citizens of Philadelphia. Many were active in politics. Prominent merchants Thomas Tresse and Charles Read and physician John Kearsley served in the Pennsylvania Assembly. Other members served on the Provincial Council; the lawyer, Ralph Assheton, physician Thomas Graeme, who would also serve on the Pennsylvania Supreme Court, Thomas Lawrence, the merchant son of the Maryland official who had worked with Francis Nicholson to help the founders of Christ Church, and Thomas Hopkinson, a lawyer who devoted much of his time to scientific experiments, all served on this advisory body. Many more members of the church served in the Corporation, the government of Philadelphia, including merchants Jacob Duche, Sr., William Till, and Samuel Hassell. Many members of Christ Church were also prominent in the legal system in Pennsylvania: Joshua Maddox, a merchant by trade, served on the orphan court, the court established to deal with matters of probate, for eighteen years and by his death "had almost become personified in [Pennsylvania] with the administration of its local justice"; and lawyer Tench Francis became widely known as the most distinguished lawyer in the city.[8] Other Christ Church members were prominent in areas outside government. Wealthy merchants and tradesmen included Charles Willing, who accumulated twenty thousand pounds; James Bingham, a saddler and large landowner; and Phillip Syng, Sr. and Jr., silversmiths. Gustavus Hesselius, a distinguished portrait painter who designed the interior of the State House, was probably the only Philadelphian to make his living as an artist at this time.

Despite all these wealthy and prominent members, Christ Church's congregation remained inclusive and diverse, influenced by its position as the state church in England. Christ Church continued to attract people of all classes throughout the colonial period.

* * *

Christ Church's ministerial stability allowed the vestry in 1727 to decide to build a larger church building, something that had been discussed for ten years.[9] However, because of difficulty raising the needed funds, construction proceeded in three phases. Between 1727 and 1735, the western half of the church was built as an addition to the old building. Then, in 1735 the vestry acknowledged that since the old building had fallen into a ruinous state it was necessary to complete the outside of the building as soon as possible, a task that took four years. It was not until 1743 that the inside of the building was finally begun. The building, but not the steeple, was finally completed in August 1744, seventeen years after its start. The final cost was £3010.10.0.[10]

For most of this time Dr. John Kearsley had supervised the construction of the building, often on a daily basis, and advanced a sizable amount of money. In fact, the project may never have been completed without his relentless efforts. By 1743 Kearsley was impatient and frustrated; he complained of not having received any acknowledgment for his work, but rather having been "frequently loaded with Calumny, and ill treated by Members of the Congregation." But when the building was finally completed, the vestry acknowledged that "the Uniformity and Beauty of the Structure" was "greatly owing to the Assiduity, Care, panes and Labour of . . . Doctor John Kearsley."[11]

Construction of the steeple began in 1751. John Harrison, a founder of the Carpenter's Company, designed the brick tower. The soon-to-be celebrated architect and carpenter, Robert Smith built and probably aided in the design of the wooden spire. Finally completed in 1754, the steeple cost £3219.9.8.[12] Much of this amount was raised by a method popular in colonial

America—a lottery. Tickets cost four Spanish dollars each, or approximately one pound, with 15 percent going toward the steeple. It took two sales attempts, but the vestry did eventually raise the £2,000 it needed to complete the project.

In April 1755 eight bells, cast by Thomas Lester and Thomas Pack of the Whitechapel foundry in London, arrived. The first time they were rung it was reported that one of the ringers died "by his ignorance and ill-judged management of the bell rope." Fortunately, that was the last such incident to occur. "The chimes were the wonder of the town and their fame spread over the province. They were rung on the evenings preceding market days for the enjoyment of the country people . . . and often the gaping yeomanry invaded the church to beg the ringers to show them the source of the fine sounds." For almost a century they were the only bells in the city capable of playing a tune.[13]

When the new church building was completed, it was one of which all Philadelphia could be proud (see Figure 6). The newspaper, the *Pennsylvania Packet*, declared that Christ Church "in point of elegance and taste, surpasses everything of the kind in America." A contemporary Philadelphian, Joseph Sanson exclaimed: "It is the handsomest structure of the kind that I ever saw in any part of the world; uniting in the peculiar features of that species of architecture, the most elegant variety of forms, with the most chaste simplicity of combination."[14]

Recognized today as one of the handsomest and most elaborate Palladian churches in America, it stood in great contrast to the plain style that characterized so many of the buildings in the Quaker City. Both the interior and the exterior of Christ Church were greatly influenced by the architecture of post-fire London, particularly the churches of Christopher Wren, but Christ Church is not a copy of any church in England. Yet no "drawings" have been found and there is no reference to any architect in the records. While some have given credit for the design to Kearsley, it is unlikely that he had the necessary knowledge or skill to design such an elaborate edifice. It is more likely that the designs were imported from England and have since disappeared.[15]

The ornate Georgian exterior of the church today is very similar to its original appearance, laid in Flemish bond brick, with extensive wood and stone trim. The two-storied facade is divided into eight bays by brick pilasters. The east end is dominated by a large Palladian window, believed to be the first such window in America. The balustrade, or railing, as well as the east pediment are adorned with flaming urns, once wooden, now cast iron.

FIGURE 6
Christ Church, Philadelphia, 1788. Engraving by James Peller Malcolm, from Universal
Magazine. *Courtesy of the Historical Society of Pennsylvania.*

The square brick tower is topped by an octagonal wooden spire. Christ Church members were clearly making a cultural as well as an architectural statement when they agreed upon its design; they were rejecting the Quaker insistence on simplicity at the same time that they were making certain that it was the Church of England that dominated the skyline of Philadelphia. The Palladian east window made a theological statement as well; the rising sun which streamed in symbolized the Resurrection.[16]

The original interior (see the 1780s print in Figure 13, pp. 99 below) had elaborate painting and plush furnishings, rather than the plain white interior that exists today. The walls around the window and the ceiling of the chancel were covered with trompe l'oeil decoration, a style of painting used to give the impression of three-dimensional work, probably done by Gustavus Hesselius. The organ gallery was decorated with crimson velvet drapery and tassels, and elaborate curtains were hung from the gallery windows. Some of the box pews, which were probably unpainted wood, were upholstered "with cushions, silk lace, crimson velvet, carpets, silver fringe, brass tack and hooks, green binding and tassels." The magnificent chandelier, with twenty-four "branches" (Figure 7), which still hangs in the center of the church, was imported from England in 1744. The candles in the chandelier along with an unknown number of oil lamps and brass wall sconces, three of which remain, lighted the church. The pulpit of the 1740s, about which we know nothing, stood on the north side of the center aisle, with the communion table in the center of the chancel. An organ, purchased for £200 in 1728, was installed near where the organ is today.[17]

*   *   *

At the same time that a new church was begun, attempts were made to formalize the governing structure. In 1728 the vestry adopted formal rules for selecting vestrymen and running its meetings. The size of the vestry was increased from fifteen to twenty, to be chosen by the congregation on Easter Monday, as it still is. The congregation was then to choose one church-warden, with the rector selecting the other. The vestry was to meet once a month and anyone not attending these meetings was fined one shilling. Parliamentary procedures were also outlined, including the rule that no person could speak more than twice on the same matter without receiving permission.[18]

The bishop of London attempted to establish some order in the overall ecclesiastical affairs in Pennsylvania as well. Bishop Gibson appointed Cum-

FIGURE 7
Brass chandelier brought from London in 1744. Photograph by Bruce Cooper Gill.

mings, who remained as rector of Christ Church, as his first commissary for Pennsylvania. The bishop outlined in detail the duties he expected a commissary to fulfill: the commissary was to hold an annual visitation at which he would communicate the bishop's directives to the clergy; he was to examine the licenses of all priests officiating in the colony, make certain that the churches and parsonages were in good repair, report to the bishop on efforts of the courts to suppress vice, and, most important, keep an eye on the morals of the clergy. Overall, he was to provide leadership for the Anglican church in the colonies and report to the Bishop when action against a clergyman was required.[19]

While the bishop took the power of the commissary seriously, neither clergy nor laity in Pennsylvania did. Cummings regularly reported to the bishop and the SPG on the state of the country parishes and recommended candidates for orders, and the bishop often solicited his advice. But Cummings's fellow clergymen and the laity rejected his leadership as commissary. Robert Jenney, who succeeded Cummings as rector of Christ Church and as commissary, wrote that "the Laity laughed at [his commission], and the Clergy seemed to despise it."[20] As a result, both Cummings and Jenney kept a low profile in their role as bishop's representative.

*　*　*

While Christ Church prospered and grew under Cummings's leadership, it also had to deal with two major controversies. Evangelical religion, which burst forth during the Great Awakening, would change the face of religion in America forever and would cause Christ Church problems for the next century. However, controversies caused by political divisions were actually more damaging for Cummings.

In 1739 members of the Anglican community, along with other churches in Philadelphia, were forced to deal with the colonial wide revival known as the Great Awakening. The earliest manifestation in Philadelphia of this new style of religion—a style that played to the emotions of people at mass meetings and called people to repent and be saved—had been felt among Presbyterian and Dutch Reformed groups. The arrival in Philadelphia of the renowned English evangelist George Whitefield in November 1739 brought the full force of the revival to the colony. Whitefield, an Anglican priest who was part of the evangelical branch of the Church of England that had already produced revivals throughout the mother country, combined the promise of a warm, personal relationship with God with the threat of eternal damnation. He was also one of the greatest orators "since the days of the apostles." The famous English actor, David Garrick, commented that Whitefield could reduce "throngs to tears by simply pronouncing 'Mesopotamia.'" The combination of a tremendous voice, a charismatic personality, and an appealing message enabled Whitefield to draw followers from all denominations.[21]

Whitefield also encountered a large number of opponents, including his fellow Anglican ministers in Pennsylvania. While these clergy began as cautiously friendly toward the newly arrived cleric, often allowing him to use their churches, they turned against him once they observed his style, heard his doctrine and experienced his attacks on the clergy for "hypocrisy and false Doctrine." They soon closed their churches to him and preached openly against him and his doctrines.[22]

Archibald Cummings exemplified this pattern. At the urging of his congregation, Cummings allowed Whitefield to preach at Christ Church during his two visits to Philadelphia in 1739. Cummings later reported that he believed Whitefield to be a "well-meaning tho' rash Young Man" who had "imbibed some mistaken Notions of Religion"; the rector thus urged the evangelist to go study the principles of the church. However, when Whitefield returned to Philadelphia in April 1740 he found the doors of Christ Church closed to him and Cummings on the attack. Cummings was particularly disturbed by Whitefield's charge that Anglican clergymen, including Bishop Gibson and John Tillotson, Archbishop of Canterbury and head of the English Church, preached justification by works. Cummings, therefore, began preaching against Whitefield, and then published two of these critical sermons. He accused Whitefield of advocating antinomianism, the position that faith alone is necessary to salvation and that good works are neither necessary for salvation nor do they necessarily follow santification. By totally stressing "justification by faith" and ignoring good works, Cummings argued that Whitefield abandoned the theological basis for moral behavior.[23]

Cummings's refusal to allow Whitefield to preach in Christ Church did not stop Anglicans from hearing him, and Cummings reported that initially large numbers of his congregation followed Whitefield. While the rector believed that his own sermons had exposed what he considered to be the irrationality of Whitefield's doctrine to the "sensible part of mankind among us," greater numbers were led by their passions. Some, he reported, "have . . . forsaken the church and joined themselves to Dissenting Congregations; others threaten to follow them and several have refused to contribute to my Subsistence which was bare and precarious before."[24]

The long-term consequences of the Great Awakening for the church in Philadelphia, as well as throughout Pennsylvania, were far less ominous than Cummings's comments suggested. The divisions caused by Whitefield were momentarily increased with the death of Cummings and the fight over his successor, but by 1743 the new rector reported that "the part set up by Whitefield here has affected the Presbyterians much more than the Church, not above two or three of Character having left us."[25]

The relatively short-term effect of Whitefield on Anglicans is not surprising since part of Whitefield's appeal was his novelty and his commanding presence; even the deist Franklin went to hear him. One Anglican minister was amazed "to see how fond the common people here are of novelties in religion and how easily they become prey to seducers."[26] But while Whitefield's style may have been alluring, his Calvinist theology was far from the mainstream beliefs of the church. Not having been raised on predestination—the Calvinist theology that maintains that God has preordained who will be saved and further argues that those who have not had a conversion experience are clearly not among them—Anglicans did not respond to Whitefield's message as instinctively as Presbyterians who were Calvinists. More important, once Whitefield left Philadelphia, his Anglican followers had to go to a Presbyterian, Moravian, or Baptist church to find a similar theology and style of worship. While religious tensions in Pennsylvania had cooled, denominational loyalties were still too strong for many to take this route.

*   *   *

A second controversy that occurred in the 1730s—one that would involve both the politics of the province and issues related to who controlled the ecclesiastical power structure in Philadelphia—had more effect on the short-term history of Christ Church than did the Great Awakening. The central character was a young cleric named Richard Peters, a man who would eventually have an illustrious career in both politics and religion in Pennsylvania. Peters came to Philadelphia in 1735 hoping to start a new life (see Figure 8). He had unwittingly committed bigamy, finding out only after he married a woman while a student in Holland that the servant girl he had married as a young man was not dead, as he had thought. He and his second wife (if one believes Peters's version of the story) had agreed to separate amicably. He chose Philadelphia as his new residence because he was related through marriage (not his) to Andrew Hamilton, the prominent politician and lawyer who is principally remembered for his defense of John Peter Zenger.[27] Shortly after Peters arrived it appeared that he had indeed embarked on a successful and fulfilling life. Lodging with Clement Plumstead, a provincial councillor, Peters associated with some of the most important people in Pennsylvania, including Thomas Penn, one of William Penn's sons. Peters's fervent desire to remain in the ministry also seemed to be gratified; in August 1736 the vestry of Christ Church asked him to become the assistant rector.[28]

Cummings did not support Peters's candidacy, however, and his opposition led to divisions within the church that would last for decades. Cummings, who seemed to assume that the bishop would not license Peters, did not make his opposition public until the bishop actually agreed to license the young cleric. At that time Cummings informed Peters and the congregation that he could not accept him as his assistant. Cummings gave two reasons for

FIGURE 8
The Reverend Richard Peters. Portrait by "Miss Crawford" after John Wollaston. Courtesy of the Historical Society of Pennsylvania.

opposing Peters. First, he feared that Peters's bigamist past would hurt the reputation of the church among dissenters; he told the bishop that he was confronted with religious groups who "upbraid us for having entertained one as our Teacher who (as they Say) was forced to fly from Justice." Second, he and several other area clergymen opposed Peters's theology, arguing that he "pleaded for the sufficiency of Reason" and "seemed to extoll and establish natural religions, so far as to destroy the necessity of Divine inspiration." While this accusation was partly based on Peters's sermons, it was in good part guilt by association. Cummings charged that Peters was "much caressed by our Modern Infidels and concealed Deists, a mere Tool to Andrew Hamilton, " who was a self-styled "freethinker" or deist, although no evidence demonstrates that Peters shared his views.[29]

Peters knew that no matter what Cummings's reasons were for opposing him, he could not remain as an assistant rector without the rector's approval. Certain vestrymen attempted to achieve a reconciliation between the two men, but in June Cummings preached a sermon Peters felt was aimed at him. He, in turn, preached two farewell sermons and retired to a lucrative and powerful secular life as secretary to the proprietors.[30]

The dispute did not end with Peters's resignation. His supporters bombarded the Bishop with letters throughout the summer and voted Cummings's supporters off the vestry the following Easter. At the same time, those who sided with Cummings also pleaded their case before the Bishop. The bishop sided with Cummings, but this did not quiet Peters's friends. As late as August 1738, Cummings's supporters still complained of divisions within the congregation, and when Cummings died some six years later the entire controversy would begin again.[31]

The controversy over Richard Peters illustrates the relationship between religion and politics, for politics determined much of the opposition to Peters. In the early 1720s the political peace of the province was broken by a fierce battle over paper money and related economic measures, with the proprietor and his supporters opposing paper money and Governor William Keith and a group of Philadelphia merchants supporting it. Keith's supporters included many if not most of the Anglicans in Philadelphia; even after he returned to England and calm returned to the colony, many Philadelphia Anglicans continued to oppose the proprietary faction vigorously.[32]

Peters's alliance with the proprietary group understandably upset anti-proprietary Anglicans. In fact, while Cummings objected to Peters's friends, it was really their political rather than their religious principles that offended him. For what Peters's friends—Quakers Jeremiah Langhorne, James Logan, and Clement Plumstead; Presbyterian William Allen; and freethinker Andrew Hamilton—all had in common was not their religious views but their attachment to the proprietor.[33] In a heated letter to a friend in England, Peter Evans, the Christ Church layman, asserted that Hamilton had "always a spight against Mr. Cummings" and wanted to divide the congregation. But Cummings, by gaining the "love and esteem of mankind in general here" had allowed the congregation to keep "two Members of our Church representatives for this County in Legislation, a great Mortification to that Monster." He argued that the only thing that stood in the way of Hamilton gaining total domination was "the united Body of the Church." Evans, along with antiproprietary legislators John Kearsley, Thomas Leech and Thomas Tresse, led the fight against Peters.[34]

At the same time that antiproprietary supporters inside Christ Church opposed Peters, proprietary supporters *outside* Christ Church actively supported his candidacy. Jeremiah Langhorne, a prominent Bucks County *Quaker*, wrote to his relative Bishop Gibson in favor of Peters. Ferdinando John Paris, a man who would become the colonial agent in London for the proprietor in 1740, also lobbied the bishop on Peters's behalf, reporting his failure to the Presbyterian William Allen.[35] It is understandable that Cummings and his supporters resented this interference by people of other religions.

While politics may have been the root cause of opposition to Peters, the controversy soon came to center on conflicting claims of authority within Christ Church. Specifically, the vestry, which had been quiet since Cummings's arrival, once again tried to exert its authority. Refusing to consider the matter closed once Peters resigned, the vestrymen held an official meeting without Cummings's presence, a violation of canon law. They wrote to the bishop testifying that Peters had given "great satisfaction to our Congregation in General" and thanking Gibson for granting Peters a license. In a second letter, eighteen vestrymen went still further, arguing that because they built their own church and maintained their minister without any outside assistance, both the laws of England and the canons of the Church gave them "the right of Patronage, that is, the right of presenting any Minister or Ministers, against whom there lies no legal objection to your Lordship for your Lycense." Ignoring the canon that required assistants to be approved by the rector, the vestry was, for the first time, declaring its independence from both its rector and the bishop of London.[36]

In response to the vestry, Bishop Gibson assured its members that he never claimed any power other than that of licensing. In theory, this assurance legitimized the vestry's growing assertions of authority. In reality, the vestry's right to select its ministers would not be firmly established until the 1760s. As long as there were disagreements within the congregation about who the minister should be, the bishop would continue to be influential in the choice. While those members who disagreed with any decision of the bishop protested his power, others, particularly those in the minority, openly solicited his interference.

The second phase of the Peters controversy, which began in April of 1741 with the death of Archibald Cummings, illustrates how divisions within the congregation increased the power of the bishop of London. At first the vestry seemed properly submissive, informing the bishop that it would accept anyone he sent, but it soon became apparent that the wounds of the 1737 dispute were being reopened and intensified. At the same time that the vestry was writing in such a docile fashion to Bishop Gibson, eighty-one members of the congregation were petitioning him to license Richard Peters, arguing that it was time that Peters's "talents may be no longer buried in a Lay tho' Honorable Employment." They were opposed by thirty-seven members of the congregation who wrote to the bishop arguing that if Peters were selected "it will Effectually disperse and drive out the Greater Number of the Devout and Religious part of the Congregation."[37]

The reasons people opposed Peters had in fact increased, with his opponents falling into three categories: (1) those who charged that his morals since taking lay employment were not up to the standards of a clergyman; (2) the still lingering group of Whitefield's followers who objected to Peters's stand against the revivalist; and (3) those who continued to be influenced by "old Differences," who now added the charge that Peters had "voluntarily" accepted a lay position without the approval of the proper authorities, a technical violation of church canons. These three groups, according to Peters's supporters, made up one-third of the congregation.[38]

Peters could once again count on the support of people outside Christ Church. Ferdinando Paris took the lead in presenting Peters's case before the bishop, meeting with him on several occasions.[39] John and Thomas Penn and Governor George Thomas also lobbied the bishop on his behalf. Peters himself wrote to the Penns, seeking their aid with a particularly blunt statement: "as the State of this Province is at present circumstanced it may not be unserviceable to your Family to have a good Friend over the Church of Philadelphia." He assured them that "in any station you may depend on my Services your Interest being as dear to me as my own."[40]

While the dispute was shaped by political forces, like the first phase of the

Peters controversy, it came to center on the basic question of authority in the colonial church. As the controversy progressed, the positions of both the members of Christ Church and the bishop of London became more extreme.

Peters's opponents, led by John Kearsley and Peter Evans, could not count on the vestry to represent their views, so they turned to area clergymen. Six clergymen, all of whom were serving as SPG missionaries, wrote to the bishop arguing that Peters's appointment would "prove the overthrow of the peace and unity of the Church at Philadelphia." This action infuriated Peters's supporters on the vestry, who considered it to be unwarranted interference in the life of their church. Peters reported to Paris that he had trouble preventing the vestry from "going into a vote against the Missionarys & from proceeding to an immediate appointment of me without leaving his Lordship any Choice." Instead, the vestrymen settled for writing to the clergy asking them to retract their statement, arguing that the clergy, by "putting a negative" on Peters, had essentially taken away their right to select a rector. Two missionaries did retract their endorsement, but the first letter had already negatively influenced the bishop.[41]

While the vestry, at the urging of Peters, largely kept quiet, trying not to alienate the bishop, fifteen members of the congregation were bolder. In a letter written to unidentified "gentlemen," who from the context of the letter must have been in England, they suggested that "no Minister be received into our Church till the Right of Nomination be settled between the Bishop and the Congregation," since the "Bishop of London's sending ministers here" without the consent of the people "may be made Ill use of." They asked these "gentlemen" to see if Pennsylvania were really annexed to the diocese of London or any other diocese in England or "whether there is any manner of Occasion to do more than appoint and Induct without application to any Bishop whatsoever."[42]

Richard Peters and Ferdinando Paris made a more startling proposal— suggesting that secular authorities assume greater power over Christ Church. They, too, questioned the validity of the bishop of London's jurisdiction, but they argued that "the right of Licensing" should be in the proprietor or governor. Peters added, in a letter to one of the proprietors, John Penn, that the fees required for licensing could "add considerable to your Royalties." That any clergyman would suggest that the right of licensing should rest with a secular official is surprising. Even in Virginia, where the governor had considerable power in church affairs, ministers were licensed by the bishop. Peters's suggestion is even more unorthodox because John Penn was at least a

CHAPTER THREE

nominal Quaker. Such an idea would have been considered heresy by the Anglican founders of Christ Church. This proposal shows how great an impact the absence of any clear authority structures and the presence of factional politics in Pennsylvania had on the church in Philadelphia.[43]

So far this dispute fits neatly into historians' arguments for the rise of the vestry and democracy in the colonial church. However, the end result does not support this argument. The bishop did not capitulate and Peters did not become the rector of Christ Church. At one point Gibson became so angry that he allegedly threatened to approve no one for Christ Church until the vestry gave up its right of selection. He backed off from this position, but had an equally effective one with which to replace it. He argued that he had a right to choose his commissary, that his commissary had to be the rector of Christ Church, and that Peters was not suitable for the job. He based his opposition to Peters on the negative letters written by the clergy, the fact that he had taken lay employment without the bishop's permission, and that his moral standards had not been those of a clergyman since entering his lay position.[44]

By May 1742 the Christ Church vestry capitulated. The members wrote an extremely obedient letter to the bishop asking him to send the church a rector and assuring him that the vestry and members of the congregation would consider it their duty to "zealously" pursue measures likely to "promote true piety and virtue, secure the peace of this church . . . supported by a strict observance of the wholesome rules and canons of the church of England . . . always bearing a due regard to the rights and jurisdiction of your lordship." Gibson, for his part, did agree not to decide unilaterally on a rector; he sent the vestry his nomination and waited for its approval before licensing the new rector and commissary.[45]

The bishop's candidate, Robert Jenney, who had been embroiled unwittingly in the Phillips controversy discussed in Chapter 2, had actually lived in Philadelphia for several years before becoming an assistant minister at Trinity Church in New York City. He later served as an SPG missionary in Rye and Hempstead, New York. No doubt because of his personal experience with the Philadelphia congregation, Jenney demanded concessions from the vestry before accepting the position; the vestry had to assure him in writing that he would be well received and that he would have all the rights and privileges that Cummings had had.[46]

The efforts of the congregation and of the vestry to exert their power seem to have only made it more difficult for the church to obtain a minister.

Tired of controversy and aware that without the bishop's cooperation they would be without a minister, the vestry agreed to accept Jenney as rector without even meeting with him personally or hearing him preach. Once again the principle of lay power had given way to the desire for a minister.[47]

* * *

The Cummings rectorship had been an important one in the history of Christ Church. A spectacular new church building was almost complete when he died. The congregation had grown and included many prominent Philadelphians. Christ Church had been chosen by the bishop as the seat of his commissary. Most important, a relatively stable church life had been established.

But Cummings's years in Philadelphia had also been turbulent ones. The three factors that would cause the church the most trouble during the colonial period—evangelical religion, the intrusion of factional politics into the life of the church, and the absence of an established governing structure—all haunted Cummings. All three would cause problems for his successor as well.

NOTES

1. Gary Nash, *The Urban Crucible* (Cambridge, Mass.: Harvard University Press, 1979), 54, 102–3, 109; Bronner, "Village into Town, 1701–1746," 47.

2. Bronner, "Village into Town," 36–39; Nash, *Urban Crucible*, 119–21.

3. Carl Bridenbaugh, *Cities in the Wilderness: The First Century of Urban Life in America, 1625–1742* (New York: Knopf, 1938), 269, 439–41. The estimate on the number of places selling liquor was made by a grand jury in 1744. Oberholzer, *Philadelphia*, 1: 150.

4. Bridenbaugh, *Cities in the Wilderness*, 456; Carl Bridenbaugh and Jessica Bridenbaugh, *Rebels and Gentlemen: Philadelphia in the Age of Franklin* (New York and London: Oxford University Press, 1942), 86–87.

5. Nash, *Quakers and Politics*, 318–35, discusses the maturing political situation.

6. Archibald Cummings, *An Exhortation to the Clergy of Pennsylvania at Philadelphia, September 24, 1729* (Annapolis, Md.: W. Parks, 1729).

7. We have no pew lists from this period. The number of baptisms stayed well over one hundred per year throughout the 1730s. See Frederick Tolles, *Meeting House and Counting House* (New York: W. W. Norton and Co., Inc., 1948), especially 139–43, for information on Quaker conversions.

8. Biographical information has been gathered from a variety of sources including George Roberts, "History of Christ Church Hospital," *PMHB* 45 (1976): 89–90; Burton Alva Konkle, *The Life of Andrew Hamilton, 1676–1741: Day Star of the Revolution* (Philadelphia: National Publishing Company, 1941), 51–53, 57; Scharf and Wescott, *History of Philadelphia*, Ober-

holtzer, *Philadelphia*; Henry Simpson, *Lives of Eminent Philadelphians Now Deceased* (Philadelphia: W. Brotherhead, 1859); *DAB*, s.v. Francis, Tench.

9. See Vestry Minutes, February 1717, July 1721, June 3, 1725, April 1, 1727.

10. Vestry Minutes, May 25, 1735, May 7, 1739, May 1, 1742; Robert Jenney to Bishop of London, June 24, 1743; Perry, *Historical Collections*, 2: 234. I am relying heavily on Charles Peterson's excellent and detailed account of the construction of Christ Church; see Charles Peterson, "The Building of Christ Church," in *The Catalog of the 1981 Antiques Show*, 123–47. The vestry spent a large part of its time for twenty-five years discussing ways to raise money. At one point it became so desperate it allowed the fundraisers to keep 10 percent of whatever they raised from people who were not members of Christ Church; see Vestry minutes, July 1, 1725.

11. Vestry Minutes, April 16, 1743, Aug. 27, 1743, Oct. 23, 1743.

12. Peterson in "The Building of Christ Church," 136–38 argues that Smith designed the steeple. However, the only reference in the Vestry Minutes is to a draft drawn up by Harrison. See L. Arnold Nicholson, "Historic Christ Church in Philadelphia Faces Problems," reprint of article in the Today Magazine, *Philadelphia Inquirer*, n.d., Christ Church Archives. See also "The Steeple Account," Christ Church Archives. The lottery is discussed in the Vestry Minutes, Oct. 27, 30, 1752 and Feb. 22, 1753.

13. Watson, *Annals of Philadelphia and Pennsylvania in Olden Times*, 1: 384. *Pennsylvania Magazine*, 4: 169, quoted in Oberholtzer, *Philadelphia*, 197; Robert W. Shoemaker, "Christ Church, St. Peters, St. Paul's in Historic Philadelphia," American Philosophical Society, *Transactions* 48 (part 1, 1953): 189.

14. Watson's *Annals*, 1: 383; Shoemaker, "Christ Church," 188.

15. Historians have suggested several churches that may have influenced the architectural design, including St. Andrew-by-the-Wardrobe, St. James in London, and St. James Piccadilly. The interior, it is said, seems to echo St. Bride's Fleet Street. See Hugh Morrison, *Early American Architecture from the First Colonial Settlements to the National Period* (New York: Oxford University Press, 1952), 537–38; Donald Friary, "The Architecture of the Anglican Churches in the Northern American Colonies: A Study of Religious, Social and Cultural Expression" (Ph.D. diss., University of Pennsylvania, 1974), 368. Charles Peterson, "The Building of Christ Church, Philadelphia," *Catalog of the 1981 Antique Show*, 135, has concluded that the plans were imported from England.

16. The quote is from George Tatum, *Penn's Great Town: 250 Years of Philadelphia Architecture Illustrated in Prints and Drawings* (Philadelphia: University of Pennsylvania Press, 1961), 28. For the description I am indebted to Tatum, Peterson, and Friary.

17. Friary, "The Architecture of the Anglican Churches," 835–36; Gill, "Christ Church," 130; Christ Church Vestry Minutes, Sept. 2, 1728. The Accounting Warden's Journal indicates that Gustavus Hesselius was paid £13.10.

18. Vestry Minutes, April 19, 1730.

19. Edmund Gibson, "Methoduc Procedenti contra clericos irregulares in Plantationibus Americanis," in Arthur Cross, *The Anglican Episcopate and the American Colonies* (New York: Harvard Historical Studies, 1902), 294–309.

20. For Cummings's notes on his first visitation see "Notes" in the Society Autograph Collection, HSP. For his concern for the missions see, for example, Archibald Cummings to the Secretary of the SPG, Oct. 3, 1729, Nov. 11, 1730, June 29, 1731, SPG Letters, A22, pp. 328–29 and A23, pp. 171–72 and A23, p. 269; Robert Jenney to Bishop Sherlock, May 23, 1751, Fulham Papers, 7: 314–15.

21. The quote is from Joseph Kelley, *Pennsylvania: The Colonial Years* (Garden City, N.Y.: Doubleday, 1980), 206. The best work on the Great Awakening in the middle colonies is Martin Lodge, "The Great Awakening in the Middle Colonies" (Ph.D. diss., University of California, Berkeley, 1964). See also Charles Maxson, *Great Awakening in the Middle Colonies* (Chicago: University of Chicago Press, 1920); Arnold A. Dallimore, *George Whitefield: The Life and Times of the Great Evangelist of the Eighteenth Century Revival* (London: Banner of Truth Trust, 1970); Harry Stout, *The Divine Dramatist: George Whitefield and the Rise of Modern Evangelism* (Grand Rapids, Mich.: W. B. Eerdmans, 1991).

22. For clergy comments on Whitefield, see Cummings, *Faith Absolutely Necessary*, iv–xv (the quote is from iv); George Ross to Secretary of the SPG, Aug. 1, 1740, Perry, *Historical Collections*, 2: 204–5; Alexander Howie to Secretary of the SPG, July 17, 1740, ibid., 207. The clergy particularly objected to Whitefield's written attacks against John Tillotson, Archbishop of Canterbury, and against the popular English devotional work, *The Whole Duty of Man*.

23. Archibald Cummings to Secretary of the SPG, Nov. 14, 1739, SPG Letters, B7, pp. 232–33, Perry, *Historical Collections*, 2: 210; George Whitefield's *Journals, 1737–1741, to Which is Prefixed His "Short Account" and "Further Account"* (Gainesville, Fla.: Scholars' Facsimiles and Reprints, 1969), 337–42. Cummings describes his growing alarm in his published sermon *Faith Absolutely Necessary* and in a letter to the SPG, July 31, 1740, SPG Letters, B7, 279–80, Perry, *Historical Collections*, 2: 210–11. For Whitefield's account of his relations with Cummings, see his *Journals*, 337–42, 404.

24. Whitefield visited Philadelphia three times, November 1739, and April and November 1740. The Pennsylvania papers reported crowds ranging from 6,000 to 15,000 people on successive visits. For an account of his visits, see Whitefield's *Journals*. The estimates are reported in Bronner, "Village into Town," 49. Cummings to Secretary of SPG, July 31, 1740, SPG Letters, B7, pp. 279–80, Perry, *Historical Collections*, 2: 210–11.

25. Robert Jenney to Bishop Gibson, June 24, 1743, Fulham Papers, 7: 305–306. Other missionaries reported things returning to normal even earlier; see, for example, William Currie to Secretary of SPG, May 2, 1741, SPG Letters, B9, no. 110; William Becket to Secretary of SPG, Sept 26, 1742, SPG Letters, B10, no. 126.

26. Alexander Howie to Bishop Gibson, Nov. 13, 1739, Fulham Papers, 7: 248.

27. See Konkle, *Life of Andrew Hamilton*.

28. For a more detailed discussion of Peters's background, see Hubertis Cummings, *Richard Peters, Provincial Secretary and Cleric 1704–1776* (Philadelphia: University of Pennsylvania Press, 1944), or Joseph Fairbanks, "Richard Peters (c. 1704–1776) Provincial Secretary of Pennsylvania" (Ph.D. diss., University of Arizona, 1972). Peters's detractors argued that he was fleeing the threat of prosecution. See Peter Evans to Thomas Moore, August 2, 1737, Smith Manuscripts, PEC, 3: 4–5, Perry, *Historical Collections*, 2: 521–23, Christ Church Vestry Minutes, Aug. 12, 1736.

29. Archibald Cummings to Bishop Gibson, June 15, 1736, July 22, 1737, Fulham Papers, 7: 174–75 and 189–90. Cummings expressed reservations to the bishop in a letter of May 11, 1736, Fulham Papers, 7: 170–71. Gibson's reply is in Bishop Gibson to Richard Peters, Sept. 12, 1736, Richard Peters Papers, HSP, 1: 25 (hereafter Peters Papers). All indications are that deism was far less widespread in Philadelphia in the 1730s than the clergy indicated. In several cases they seem to be lumping deists and Quakers together. See Gough, "Pluralism, Politics and Power Struggles," 142–47.

30. Cummings and Peters both published their sermons. See Cummings, *The Danger of*

Breaking Christian Unity; Richard Peters, *The Last Two Sermons Preached at Christ's Church in Philadelphia, July 3, 1737* (Philadelphia: Benjamin Franklin, 1737).

31. Bishop Gibson to Archibald Cummings, n.d, Fulham Papers, 7: 231; Archibald Cummings to Bishop Gibson, Aug. 12, 1738, Fulham Papers, 7: 238–41; Vestry of Christ Church to Bishop Gibson, n.d. (c.1738), Fulham Papers, 7: 242–3.

32. For information on the politics of the era see Gary Nash, *Quakers and Politics*, 331–35. When Keith left Philadelphia, to die in a debtor's prison in England, his wife stayed behind, living in seclusion and poverty. She is buried in the Christ Church courtyard. For information on Mrs. Keith, see Watson, *Annals*, 3: 192.

33. Alexander Howie to Bishop Gibson, Aug. 19, 1737, Fulham Papers, 7: 218. See also Archibald Cummings to Bishop Gibson, July 22, 1737, Fulham Papers, 7: 189–90.

34. Peter Evans to Thomas Moore, Aug. 2, 1737, Smith Manuscripts, PEC, Perry, *Historical Collections* 2: 523. For the names of some of Peters's opponents see Members of Christ Church to Bishop Gibson, June 21, 1738, Smith Manuscripts, PEC, 3: 12, Perry, *Historical Collections*, 2: 529–30; Some Vestrymen (of Christ Church) to Bishop Gibson, n.d., Smith Manuscripts, PEC, 3: 8, Perry, *Historical Collections*, 2: 525–26.

35. Jeremiah Langhorne to Bishop Gibson, May 28, 1736 and Aug. 3, 1737, Fulham Papers, 7: 172–73 and 208–9; Langhorne to Bishop Gibson, Aug. 3, 1737, ibid., 208–9; Ferdinando Paris to William Allen, Dec. 18, 1737, Perry, *Historical Collections*, 2: 527.

36. Some Vestrymen of Christ Church to Bishop Gibson, n.d., Fulham Papers, 7: 204–5; Vestry of Christ Church to Bishop Gibson, n.d., Fulham Papers, 7: 242–43. Bishop Gibson had never actually granted Peters a license, but the vestry seemed to think that his letter allowing Peters to officiate at the pleasure of Cummings was the same thing.

37. Members of Christ Church to Bishop Gibson, May 18, 1741, Fulham Papers, 7: 271–72.

38. Churchwardens and Members of Christ Church to Bishop Gibson, 1741, Perry, *Historical Collections*, 2: 225–27; Part of the Vestry to George Ross and Missionaries, May 7, 1741, Penn Manuscripts, Penn Papers, HSP, 7: 97; John Kearsley to Secretary of SPG, June 18, 1741, SPG Letters, B9, no. 89; Kearsley to Secretary, Aug. 3, 1741, ibid., no. 91; Peter Evans to Thomas Moore, April 20, 1741, May 14, 1741, Smith Manuscripts, PEC, 3: 16 and 21.

39. Paris's efforts can be followed in a series of letters. See Richard Peters to Ferdinando Paris, April 25, 1741, POC 3: 149; Paris to Peters, June 27, 1741, POC 3: 179; Paris to Peters, July 16, 1741, POC, 3: 187; Peters to Paris, Oct. 25, 1741, Peters's Letter Book, 1739–43, Peters Papers, HSP, 52; Paris to Peters, Jan. 20, 1742, Samuel Hazard et al., eds., *Pennsylvania Archives*, 8 series (Philadelphia and Harrisburg: J. Severns, 1852–1935), series 1, 1: 628.

40. George Thomas to Bishop, May 14, 1741, Fulham Papers, 7: 265–66; Peters to John Penn, Oct. 24, 1741, Peters Letter Book, 1739–43, HSP, 36–37; Thomas Penn to Ferdinando Paris, April 25, 1741, POC, 2: 151; Peters to John and Richard Penn, April 27, 1741, POC 3: 157. It appears that John Penn, who was in England, spoke to the bishop in person.

41. Clergy to Bishop, April 23, 1741, Smith Manuscripts, PEC, 3: 17, Perry, *Historical Collections*, 2: 534; Peters to Paris, May 7, 1741, POC, 3: 161; Part of the Vestry to George Ross and Missionaries, May 7, 1741, POC 7: 97.

42. Members of Christ Church to "Gentlemen," n.d., Peters Papers, HSP, 1: 26.

43. Richard Peters to John Penn, Oct. 24, 1741; and Richard Peters to Thomas Penn, Oct. 24, 1741, Peters Letter Book, 1739–43, Peters Papers, HSP, 36–37 and 50.

44. Ferdinando Paris to Richard Peters, July 7, 1741, POC, 3: 181 discusses the bishop's objections to Peters.

45. Vestry Minutes, March 29, May 1, 1742; Vestry of Christ Church to Bishop of London, May 27, 1742, Fulham Transcripts, LOC, Pennsylvania, no. 10.

46. Robert Jenney to Vestry, April 12, 1742 and Oct. 12, 1742 in Vestry Minutes, July 6, 1742 and Oct. 20, 1742.

47. The negotiations involved in bringing Jenney to Philadelphia can be followed in the Vestry Minutes and in the following letters: Thomas Penn to Robert Jenney, Dec. 23, 1741, Fulham Papers, 7: 291–92; Jenney to Bishop, Jan. 14, 1741/42, Fulham Papers, 7: 293; Jenney to Thomas Penn, Jan. 14, 1741/42, Fulham Papers, 7: 291–92; Vestry to Bishop Gibson, Nov. 17, 1742, Fulham Papers, 7: 298–99; Jenney to Bishop Gibson, Dec. 8, 1742, Fulham Papers, 7: 300.

POLITICS AND THE CLERGY: THE RECTORSHIP OF ROBERT JENNEY

The arrival of Robert Jenney to assume the rectorship of Christ Church in November 1742 ended another crisis. A submissive vestry wrote thanking the bishop for sending Jenney and assuring his lordship that the congregation was behaving itself, "becomeing true Members of a Christian Church."[1] Jenney would serve for twenty years, and these years saw great progress. As we have seen, the congregation finished building the new church shortly after he arrived and built the steeple ten years later. Jenney also presided over the building and opening of St. Peter's Church, a church that would be united with Christ Church for more than seventy-five years. During his rectorship Christ Church obtained a permanent assistant minister for the first time and, under this assistant's leadership, started a ministry to the blacks of Philadelphia. Jenney's years, as we will see in a later chapter, also saw the Anglicans of Philadelphia take the lead in the founding of the Academy (later College) of Philadelphia.

But while Jenney should have been able to point with pride to the accomplishments achieved under his rectorship, he and his assistant William Sturgeon both became overwhelmed and eventually embittered by the continuing intrusion of factional politics into the life of the church and the divisive influence of evangelical Anglicans.

* * *

Jenney's congregation continued to contain a reasonable cross section of the white population of Philadelphia. While an analysis of the 1756 tax lists, summarized in Table 2, indicates that Christ Church was overrepresented at the highest levels and underrepresented at the lower levels, it was still far from "being the church of the elite" as it has sometimes been portrayed. In fact, the number of Anglicans at the lower end of the economic spectrum is surprisingly high; because less affluent Philadelphians were also likely to be the most transient, locating them in church records is difficult without membership records for the specific tax year. The diversity of the congregation can also be seen in the occupations of the members; during the 1750s the congregation contained eighty-two merchants, twenty-five sea captains, ten lawyers, and ten doctors, all occupations whose members were generally of above average wealth and stature. There were also seventeen seamen, eight barbers, four bakers, twelve shoemakers, five innkeepers, and a variety of skilled artisans.

Christ Church tried to serve the needs of its poorer members. Despite the city's establishment of an almshouse in 1732, churches and other private agencies still handled most poor relief. Christ Church continued the traditional role of the church in England; it maintained a Charity School for most of the colonial period, and distributed the money donated monthly at Communion services to the poor within its parish. The recipients, who were almost entirely women, ranged in number from ten to twenty-four a month.[2]

Under Jenney's leadership Christ Church also extended its ministry to Philadelphia blacks. By the 1740s, approximately 10 percent of the population of 11,000 were black, most of them in slavery. While importation of slaves had increased greatly in the 1730s, Cummings had baptized only four blacks during his fifteen-year rectorship. In sharp contrast, Jenney baptized twenty-five blacks (out of a total of 136 baptisms) in his first year in Philadelphia, and after five years in Philadelphia he had baptized more than fifty blacks or more than 5 percent of the city's black population. In 1746, after much urging from Jenney, the Society for the Propagation of the Gospel agreed to provide an annual stipend of £30 for an assistant minister of Christ Church to serve as "Catechist for the Negroes."[3]

The selection of the assistant minister to catechize the blacks marked the

TABLE 2.   Tax Assessment in Philadelphia in 1756

Tax assessment (in pounds)	Philadelphia population (with cumulative %)	Christ Church members (with cumulative %)
8–10	415, or 17.8%(17.8)	18, or 8.3% (8.3)
11–12	456, or 19.5% (37.3)	27, or 12.5% (20.8)
13–16	427, or 18.3% (55.6)	19, or 8.8% (29.6)
17–25	402, or 17.2% (72.8)	33, or 15.3% (44.9)
26–40	328, or 14.1% (86.9)	52, or 24.1% (69.0)
41–46	144, or 6.2% (93.1)	33, or 15.3% (84.3)
61–100	98, or 4.2% (97.9)	17, or 7.9% (92.2)
101–150	30, or 1.3% (98.6)	9, or 4.2% (96.4)
151–250	23, or 1.0% (99.6)	7, or 3.2% (99.6)
251+	11, or 0.5 % (100.0)	1, or 0.5% (100.0)
Total number	**2,334**	**216**
Mean	**£27.4**	**42.1**

SOURCES: Karin Peterson, "Christ Church, Its Congregation Between 1750 and 1760" (Seminar paper, University of Pennsylvania, 1975); Hannah Benner Roach, "Taxables in the City of Philadelphia, 1756," Genealogical Society of Pennsylvania *Publications* 22 (1961–62): 3–44. The taxed did not include the entire population, only those with houses, lands, tenements, rent charges, bound servants, and slaves assessed at eight pounds or more.[4]

first time that the vestry was allowed to choose a minister, albeit with the rector's approval. Because the vestry and Jenney agreed on the selection, the bishop willingly licensed their choice without comment. Unfortunately, this did not mean the end of conflict over ministerial selection.

The man chosen, William Sturgeon, came from a background quite different from that of previous ministers of Christ Church. The first Christ Church minister born in America, Sturgeon was raised in the Congregational church in New England and educated at Yale.[5] Perhaps it was this background that allowed him to get along so well with Jenney, who had lived for many years among Congregationalists. While the two ministers had problems with other ministers and with the vestry, they seemed to have remained close to each other until Jenney's death.

Sturgeon's ministry among the black population, which was limited in the early years to teaching them the catechism, expanded in 1757 when the Bray Associates expressed interest in educating blacks in Pennsylvania. Sturgeon convinced them to allow him to open a school for blacks, most of them slaves. The mistress in charge of the thirty or more blacks, who worked under Sturgeon's supervision, was instructed to "teach the boys to read, the girls to read, sew, knit and mark," to take them to church every Wednesday and Friday, and to make certain that "all her Endeavours [were] directed towards making them Christians." Sturgeon examined them on the catechism after the Wednesday service.[6] Sturgeon continued his supervision of the school until he retired to the country in 1766, when Francis Hopkinson and Edward Duffield, two Anglican laymen, took over. Based on the success of the Philadelphia school, the Bray Associates opened schools in other colonies. Given the widespread fear that educating blacks would make them less subservient and might lead to rebellions, this school should be considered a major accomplishment for the church in Philadelphia.

* * *

In the 1740s and 1750s Philadelphia Anglicans—and Christ Church—made a visible impact on Pennsylvania politics. In just three decades Christ Church members went from being a few dissident voices in a Quaker-dominated government to holding many important political positions in an increasingly heterogeneous colony. Because of the fractious nature of politics in the 1740s and because the Anglicans involved in politics included two clergymen who believed in using the church for political ends, the advances Christ Church members made in government had complex effects on the life of the church.

In stark contrast to the case in earlier years, most Anglicans prominent in politics supported the proprietor, Thomas Penn, who took over sole control of the proprietorship in 1746. That support was made easier by Thomas Penn's conversion to Anglicanism. The Provincial Council, the body appointed by the proprietor to look out for his interests and to advise the governor, changed from having ten out of twelve Quaker members in the 1730s to having at least ten out of seventeen Anglican members from 1754 to 1764. Councillors Thomas Hopkinson, Lynford Lardner, Thomas Lawrence, William Till, James Hamilton, Edward Shippen, and Benjamin Chew were all members of Christ Church at one time or another. These proprietary supporters, who were primarily merchants, also controlled the Corporation of Philadelphia (the body that governed the city) and held a host of other appointed political positions.[7]

The two Anglican clerics active in politics also supported the proprietor. Richard Peters continued to serve as secretary to the Penns and as a provincial councillor. While not on the staff of Christ Church, he did serve on the vestry from 1745 to 1752. In 1754 he welcomed another Anglican cleric, William

FIGURE 9
The Reverend William Smith, D.D. (1727–1803). Portrait by Gilbert Stuart. Courtesy of the University of Pennsylvania Art Collection.

Smith, to the Quaker City. A twenty-seven-year-old Scotsman, Smith came to Philadelphia in 1754 to teach at the newly established Academy of Philadelphia and became provost of the newly established College of Philadelphia in the following year. Described by John Adams as "soft, polite, insinuating, adulating, sensible, learned, industrious, indefatigable," Smith played an active role in religion, education and politics in Pennsylvania for the next forty years. While never holding office, he immediately became an ardent supporter of and articulate spokesman for the proprietor[8] (see Figure 9).

Not surprisingly, given the diversity of the Christ Church congregation, there also continued to be members who supported the Quaker-controlled, anti-proprietary assembly. Benjamin Franklin, who rented a pew at Christ Church although he was never an active member, was a leader of the anti-proprietary group in the 1750s. In addition, three Christ Church members— Thomas Leech, Daniel Roberdeau, and John Hughes—continued to serve as antiproprietary assemblymen. Unfortunately, it is impossible to know how many of their fellow parishioners voted for them and how many supported the proprietor.

The importance of these political affiliations increased in the 1740s as political controversies once again enveloped the colony. This time the issue was, at least on the surface, the defense of the colony. In 1739 England declared war on Spain and in 1744 France joined the side of Spain, thus increasing the number of privateers attacking colonial shipping and raising the possibility that Pennsylvania would be attacked by the French coming down from Canada or by their Indian allies. A peace treaty was signed in 1748, but the French and Indian War broke out in 1754, once again putting Pennsylvania at risk. Indian attacks on settlers in western Pennsylvania plunged the colony into an intense struggle over how to defend itself. Proprietary supporters tried to disfranchise the Quakers because of their pacifist principles and urged the resignation of Quaker assemblymen who could not in good conscience vote for defensive measures.

The debate over the defense of the colony soon became intertwined with issues of proprietary rights and economic policy. Believing that the Assembly's power came from its control over money, Penn refused to allow it to issue paper money, a decision that affected most Pennsylvanians adversely. Penn further alienated people of all religions by refusing to allow his lands to be taxed. This in turn contributed to the Assembly's refusal to defend the colony; if Penn were not going to allow his lands to be taxed to defend the colony, then many in the Assembly decided that they would not do it for him. While proprietary officials tried to put all the blame on the Quakers' pacifist beliefs, the situation was not that simple.[9]

These controversies would not have caused problems for Christ Church if everyone had supported Robert Jenney's belief that politics should be kept out of the life of the church. Jenney argued that a priest "should be under no obligation to any man which might cause him to help further that man's political designs." Similarly, he believed politically prominent men should not try to influence the church. He particularly feared the interference of the proprietor. He even objected to Thomas Penn's endorsement of his own candidacy, arguing that Penn "being of another Religion or rather none at all, ought not to interfere in this matter."[10]

Peters and Smith had a far different view of the role of the clergy. Peters believed that a minister, in or out of a rectorship, could, when necessary, try to persuade Anglicans to support a particular party.[11] While Peters generally worked behind the scenes and avoided controversy, Jenney still resented his political involvement. Like Peters, Smith believed that every minister should instruct the people on both temporal and spiritual "law and duty." Ministers should be particularly vocal when liberty was at stake for "where would protestant religion be without protestant liberty."[12] Both he and Peters apparently believed that "liberty was at stake" whenever the power of the proprietor was threatened, for they believed that the Anglican church was the natural ally of the proprietary faction in its fight against the Quaker assembly and that all clergymen should encourage this alliance.

While Peters stayed in the background, using his conciliatory style to influence people, Smith became embroiled in a series of political disputes almost immediately on his arrival in Philadelphia. These disputes led to anti-Anglican articles in the paper, Anglican clergymen attacking each other, and even the involvement of the vestry of Christ Church in the political controversies.

Smith's first political battle revolved around the defense of the colony. Smith led the fight both against the Quaker-supported militia bill and for the disfranchisement of Quakers. He wrote a series of pamphlets and newspaper articles that elicited strong responses, many of them focusing on his role as an Anglican cleric. An article in the *Pennsylvania Journal* concluded sarcastically that such essays as those written by Smith could not be the work of a clergyman of the Church of England, but rather of a "frantick Incendiary," a "Minister of the infernal Prince of Darkness, the *Father* of *Lies*." Another charged that Smith was attempting to impress his superiors so that he would be appointed Bishop of America.[13]

Smith soon found himself opposed by the antiproprietary vestryman Daniel Roberdeau and, when asked to choose, the vestry sided with Roberdeau. The controversy centered on issues of integrity. Roberdeau publicly accused Smith of saying that he did not actually support the proprietor but only wrote on his behalf because Penn had no one else. Infuriated by this slight on his integrity, Smith published an affidavit made before Mayor William Plumstead in which he adamantly denied saying anything of the sort. In response, Roberdeau published an affidavit from the Christ Church vestry stating that he had been a member since his infancy and had "always supported the Character of an Honest Vertuous, religious upright sober man." Smith was upset by the failure of the vestry to back him publicly. He argued that a majority of the vestry supported him, but when he finally solicited signatures attesting to his good character, only three current vestrymen were among the forty-five members of Christ Church who signed.[14] This extraordinary action—a vestry indirectly questioning the integrity of an Anglican cleric—showed how great an impact politics and Smith's behavior had on Christ Church.

Smith's antiproprietary stance brought him more serious trouble in 1758. In that year he and his father-in-law, William Moore, were jailed for publishing an article in the local newspapers that purportedly libeled the Quaker-controlled Assembly. Despite Smith's minimal role in its publication, he was tried by the Assembly, found guilty, and sentenced to be jailed during the Assembly's sessions until he submitted to the authority of the Assembly. Refusing to do so, Smith was arrested each time the Assembly met in 1758 and 1759. Realizing that this could go on forever, Smith decided to sail for England to appeal his case to English authorities. This proved to be a wise step, for the privy council decided in his favor and Smith returned to Pennsylvania to resume his antiproprietary activities.[15]

Clergymen outside of Philadelphia reacted with alarm at this attempt "to brand with Disgrace and Ignominy, the Character of a Clergyman of the Church of England, who is placed at the Head of a Seminary of Learning," as Smith put it. The archbishop of Canterbury, the bishop of London, and the secretary of the SPG all expressed support and sympathy for Smith's plight, believing, no doubt, as did Robert McKean, an Anglican minister in New Brunswick, New Jersey, that the case was "a severe stroke levelled at the interests of the Church of England thro' the person of Mr. Smith."[16]

Yet the clergy associated with Christ Church saw the situation differently. Jenney and Sturgeon, who were jealous of Smith's influence and disapproved of his conduct, both wrote to England *attacking* Smith. At the same time they tried to protect themselves against any attacks Smith might make against them. Writing to Archbishop Thomas Secker, Jenney expressed his concern for "the practice of some Clergymen here to intermix what is their true and real business with Politics in civil affairs and being so zealous therein as to blame and even revile those of their Brethren who cannot approve of their conduct in this particular." He asserted that Smith had "declared his prepossession against me with a design to trip up my heels as he expressed it." Similarly, Sturgeon argued that Smith's attempts to insinuate that he was "better qualified . . . to execute the Office of a Pastor than the present ministers" had led some of the "Chief People" to lose their esteem and affection for Sturgeon. He, too, expressed apprehension that Smith would "attempt something to [Sturgeon's] disadvantage" while he was in

England. While Jenney had remained politically neutral, Sturgeon openly sided with the Assembly. He asserted that the Assembly had been "so much offended by his [Smith's] conduct that he was taken into custody by their order, and he is now going home to obtain some redress for his imagined grievances."[17]

We do not know what affect these events had on the congregation, but we do know that Jenney quickly became an embittered man. He thought Smith had attempted to turn his parishioners against him and accused Peters of orchestrating every controversy he had with the vestry. In 1750 he complained that "we have some men in this Congregation who, having a great Opinion of their own extraordinary parts & Qualities, think they shew them best by creating Trouble and Vexation to their minister." These men he later identified as Peters and his supporters.[18] Clearly Jenney felt besieged and unhappy. Such resentment must have affected his performance as rector and his relations with his parishioners.

The political controversies and ministerial conflicts also affected the decision to build a new Anglican church in Philadelphia, since Jenney feared that any new church would be dominated by Peters. Despite the fact that by 1740 Christ Church was "too little by one half to hold the members," in 1753 Jenney opposed the proposal made by a group of Christ Church members to build a new church at the south end of the city. Two years earlier he had reported to the SPG that Peters's supporters were planning to build a new church for him, and while Jenney admitted there was a need for one, he feared the effects of raising "altar against altar." The group did not give up; after convincing Penn to donate the land, in 1758 they appeared before the vestry with a specific proposal for the construction of a new building.[19] This time the vestry agreed to the plan.

While there is evidence that politics led some people to want to build a new church, men from both political camps supported the proposal. Peters reported to Penn that "those who live in the South part of the town and applied for a new Church . . . always will be friends of good Government, and of the Proprietaries and their Governors." Yet of the men who signed the letter to Penn asking for the land, seven of the nineteen whose political affiliation could be determined were antiproprietary. Moreover, Peters, while wanting to return to the ministry, had made it clear to Penn that he did not want to "meddle" with the church in Philadelphia.[20]

It is much more likely that the men involved in requesting the new church were motivated by their place of residence. By 1760 settlement in

Philadelphia extended as far south as Christian Street, which was fourteen long and often muddy blocks from Christ Church. Of the eighty-one petitioners, none lived in the ward in which Christ Church was located or in the large ward to the north; at least twenty-eight lived in three of the four most southern wards, those farthest away from Christ Church.[21]

No matter what the real motivations of the new church's supporters, the perceived threat of Peters becoming its rector greatly influenced the actions of the vestry. Jenney convinced the vestry that unless it wanted "to ruin the peace, unity and concord of our Church and gratify the worst motives of our enemies" it should make the new church a "chapel of ease" to the old. Under this concept, which was common in England, both churches would make up one congregation under one rector and as many assistants as were needed, and would be governed by one set of churchwardens and vestrymen, so that "nothing done by one, separate from the other, shall be good and valid."[22]

The plan advocated by Jenney and adopted by the vestry differed from the arrangement for other chapels in one important respect: rather than there

FIGURE 10
St. Peter's Church, Philadelphia. Print by André Breton, 1829. Private collection.

being a curate or assistant minister in charge of the new church, the two churches were to be served by the same ministers, who would supply them "in such order and manner, that neither of the said churches shall claim or enjoy the service of any particular minister oftener than the other."[23] This unique arrangement, which resulted in the establishment of the "United Churches of Christ Church and St. Peter's," grew out of Jenney's determination that the churches not become competitors and that the wrong forces not gain control of St. Peter's. He knew that a popular assistant minister, if left alone in control of St. Peter's, could as easily become the center for the wrong kind of religion or for a political party as could the rector of a separate church.

Once the organizational structure of the new church was determined, the congregation proceeded fairly quickly to build St. Peter's. Begun in 1758, it was completed in 1761 at a cost of £2,310. John Kearsley once again supervised the construction and Robert Smith contracted to build the church. Located at Third and Pine Streets, St. Peter's was a simple two-story rectangular brick building without either tower or steeple (the present steeple was added in the nineteenth century). While it was larger than Christ Church, seating more than nine hundred people, it did not dominate the landscape as did its parent church; in fact, only its cupola distinguished it from a Quaker meetinghouse (see Figure 10). The interior was also far simpler than that of Christ Church. With its high back pews and pulpit at the west end, it remains today largely as it was originally.[24]

With the addition of another church, the United Churches needed more ministerial support. In February 1759, at the request of his father, a long-time vestryman, the vestry asked the bishop of London to ordain Jacob Duché, Jr. as a deacon and license him as an assistant minister for Christ Church. Duché, who was in England studying at Cambridge University, had grown up in Christ Church and had, according to the vestrymen, "from very early years of his life been strongly inclined to the ministry." As we will see, Duché would serve Christ Church well for almost twenty years, eventually becoming rector. Peters reported that Duché was "the best Preacher I ever heard," adding that "all Strangers even of the best Education, join with us in this Opinion."[25]

* * *

While Jenney spent most of his rectorship concerned with Peters, Smith, and the influence of politics, in the end it was an evangelical minister and his supporters who caused him the most serious trouble. Jenney's problems with those of evangelical leanings began with the arrival in Philadelphia of William Macclenachan in 1759. Born and raised in Ireland as a Scotch-Irish Presbyterian, Macclenachan migrated to New England in 1734 and served as a Congregational minister in Maine for twenty years. In 1755 he converted to the Church of England and accepted a post at a frontier mission in Maine for the SPG. Unhappy in that position, he next secured a parish in Virginia. In May 1759, on his way back from visiting that parish, he stopped in Philadelphia. As was common practice with visiting clergymen, Macclenachan was invited to preach at Christ Church one Sunday; because Sturgeon was ill, he was asked to officiate the following Sabbath as well. According to Macclenachan's report, the Monday after his second appearance a group of parishioners asked him to remain in Philadelphia to perform his clerical functions "on Probation," with the long-term hope of making him an assistant minister.[26] Because Jenney had been partially paralyzed since 1757 and Duché had not yet returned from England, leaving all the parochial duties to Sturgeon, Macclenachan's arrival must have seemed fortuitous to many.

Information about Macclenachan is second hand, but he clearly belonged to the evangelical wing of the Church of England. Like Whitefield, he adhered to a Calvinist theology, stressing the parts of the Thirty-Nine Articles and the Book of Common Prayer that dealt with the fallen state of man and man's dependence on God's grace, themes that had been de-emphasized or ignored by most eighteenth century Anglicans. He also often preached and prayed extemporaneously, much to the dismay of Jenney.[27] William Smith reported that

With a huge Stature, and voice more than Stentorian up he started before his Sermon, and instead of modestly using any of the excellent forms provided in our Liturgy . . . he addressed the Majesty of heaven with a long Catalogue of epithets, such as "Sin-pardoning, all-seeing, heart-searching, . . . God—We thank thee that we are all here today and not in hell." Such an unusual manner in our Church sufficiently fixed my attention, which was exercised by a strange extempore rhapsody of more than twenty minutes, and afterwards a Sermon of about sixty minutes more; which I think could hardly be religion, for I am sure it was not Common Sense.[28]

Despite Macclenachan's popularity, the vestry did not immediately agree to accept him as an assistant minister. It was pointed out that the church already had one assistant and had asked the Bishop to license Jacob Duché and that the church had neither the need for nor the resources to support a third assistant. However, after receiving a petition from seventy-four people asking that Macclenachan be made an assistant, the vestry, in consultation with Jenney, agreed on May 10, 1759 that Macclenachan could "have the liberty and use of the pulpit to preach in as a lecturer only, during the pleasure of . . . Dr. Jenney, church wardens and vestry." This privilege would be allowed him only if he produced the proper references and if his supporters raised his salary by subscription.[29]

By the time Macclenachan had obtained the proper letters of recommendation, Jenney and the vestry had come to firm but opposing opinions about the cleric. The vestry agreed to appoint him as assistant minister, writing the bishop in October 1759 for a license. Jenney, on the other hand, refused to sign the letter to the bishop. Instead he joined with Sturgeon, Duché, who had by now returned from England, and four area clergymen in requesting that the Bishop not license Macclenachan. Jenney complained bitterly that Macclenachan had been "forced upon him notwithstanding his known 'dislike' of the Man, and that such action was "directly contrary to all the Rules and Discipline of the Church of England." However, he did not dismiss him. Rather, Jenney hoped the bishop would deny Macclenachan a license. While waiting to hear, Jenney allowed Macclenachan to officiate, but refused to allow him to administer the sacraments or to perform parochial duties.[30]

Macclenachan's supporters argued, however, that the bishop's opinion was irrelevant since the *congregation* had the right to choose its ministers without the interference of the rector or the bishop. One hundred thirty members informed Jenney that "rest assured as we pay our Clergy we have right, and shall insist on the services of such who we conceive can serve us." In response to rumors that Duché had told Macclenachan that the evangelist could not officiate anymore because he did not have the Bishop's license, they were even more direct. They told Jenney that Macclenachan already was invested with "all the powers necessary for the discharge of any duties pertaining to his office," for "his Lordship's License means nothing here . . . without a previous Presentation from the *People*." Just in case Duché had not gotten the message, they added that he would do well to "consider before he meddles with other men's affairs, whether he ever had such a Presentation from the Congregation." Thus, even as the vestry was trying to fully establish its authority in Christ Church, members of the congregation were already questioning that authority and asserting their own.[31]

While this argument was a logical extension of the argument made by some of Peters' supporters that the bishop's authority was not valid in Pennsylvania, it undermined the entire system of government of the Church of England; all Anglican ministers had to be licensed by a bishop. Yet it had the support of about half the Christ Church congregation. One hundred seventy-seven members of Christ Church signed one of several documents supporting congregational rights, about 31 percent of those who held pews in 1750. Considering known mobility and death rates during this period, this must represent at least half of the 1750 pewholders who remained in Christ Church in 1759.[32]

In May 1760 the Bishop fulfilled Jenney's wish, denying Macclenachan a license. Surprisingly, it was neither Macclenachan's theology nor Jenney's disapproval that led to the Bishop's decision, but rather his behavior before coming to Philadelphia. He had, according to the SPG, seriously neglected his churches while a missionary and, moreover, had already contracted with a parish in Virginia. Jenney, having received the support he needed, informed the vestry and Macclenachan on June 18, 1760 that the evangelist could no longer use the pulpit of Christ Church.[33]

When the vestry accepted Jenney's decision, a large group of Macclenachan's supporters seceded from Christ Church. On June 24 they signed the "Articles of Agreement" for a new church they called St. Paul's. They reported two weeks later that they had already raised eighteen hundred pounds toward the erection of a new church building. This new building, when completed in late 1761 or early 1762, was the largest Anglican church in Philadelphia, seating more than one thousand people. Located on Third Street between Walnut and Spruce, its architecture was greatly influenced by St. Peter's: it was a simple, two-story rectangular structure with a Palladian east window and did not even have a cupola.[34]

The seceders still considered themselves "loyal members of the Church of England" but wanted nothing to do with the church hierarchy. The Articles of Agreement stated that the building could only be used for performing the "liturgy, rites, ceremonies, doctrines and true principles of the established church of England" and that only ordained Anglican priests could officiate. However, the articles made no mention of the bishop's license, requiring only that all ministers and assistants be chosen by a majority of the congregation. As William Smith put it, they wanted "an Independent Church of England-a strange sort of Church indeed."[35]

Despite William Smith's charges that the founders of St. Paul's were "Presbyterians and Baptists," that they were primarily from the "lower sort,"

TABLE 3.   Tax Assessment for Philadelphia Anglicans in 1756

Tax assessment (in pounds)	Christ Church members (with cumulative percent)	St. Paul's Church members (with cumulative percent)
8–10	18, or 8.3% (8.3)	4, or 7.5% (7.5%)
11–12	27, or 12.5% (20.8)	2, or 3.8% (11.3%)
13–16	19, or 8.8% (29.6)	7, or 13.1% (24.5)
17–25	33, or 15.3% (44.9)	12, or 22.6% (47.2)
26–40	52, or 24.1% (69.0)	19, or 35.8% (83.0)
41–60	33, or 15.3% (84.3)	2, or 3.8% (86.8)
61–100	17, or 7.9% (92.2)	4, or 7.5% (94.3)
101–150	9, or 4.2% (96.4)	0, or 0.0% (94.3)
151–250	7, or 3.2% (99.6)	3, or 5.7% (100)
251+	1, or 0.5% (100.0)	0, or 0.0% (100)
Total	**216**	**53**
Mean	**£42.1**	**£41.2**

SOURCE: Hannah Benner Roach, "Taxables in the City of Philadelphia, 1756," *Genealogical Society of Pennsylvania Publications* 22 (1961–62): 3–44.

and that they were "supported by the Quaker Party," in reality members seem to have been a cross section of Anglicans. Of the 114 people known to have been involved in the founding of the new church, 73, or 64 percent, are known to have been previously associated with Christ Church. Moreover, the socio-economic make-up of the founders of St. Paul's was almost identical to the overall economic profile of Christ Church (see Table 3); the means of the tax assessments differed by less than one pound.[36]

William Smith's charge that St. Paul's was "supported by the Quaker Party" is harder to assess. Four leaders of the antiproprietary and anti-Smith segment of Christ Church did join St. Peter's.[37] However, since Jenney and Sturgeon were also on the antiproprietary side, people did not have to leave Christ Church to find compatible political views.

In fact the founders of St. Paul's probably left Christ Church to follow Macclenachan for the obvious reason: they wanted to belong to an evangelical Anglican church. Like many of their fellow churchmen in England, they had become tired of the overly reasoned, scholarly style of preaching they had been receiving, and longed for a more emotional religion that required a strong personal commitment. Macclenachan represented the best of both worlds: an evangelical minister willing to use the liturgy of the Church of England. For while Pennsylvania Anglicans were willing to modify the governing structure of the Church of England, downplaying or even abandoning the power of the bishops, they remained loyal to the Book of Common Prayer. This mutual attachment would eventually bring about a reconciliation between St. Paul's and the United Churches, but only after the death of both Macclenachan and Jenney.

* * *

Jenney's rectorship, which ended with his death in 1762, had not, from his point of view, been an overwhelming success. The presence of Smith and Peters and the political squabbles associated with them concerned and frustrated Jenney for most of his rectorship. Moreover, in the last years of his life he had to watch a large number of members secede from his church to found an Anglican church based on views he abhorred. Yet, the Anglican church in Philadelphia did continue to grow during his twenty year rectorship, as evidenced by the building of St. Peter's as well as St. Paul's. If a rector with a conciliatory approach could be found, the future of Christ Church still looked bright.

NOTES

1. Vestry of Christ Church to Bishop Gibson, Nov. 17, 1742, Fulham Papers, 7: 298–99.
2. Christ Church Journals, 1743, 1744 and 1745. For information on poverty in Philadelphia at this time see Nash, *The Urban Crucible*, 127.
3. Because the blacks were all referred to in the baptismal records by only their first names, we can assume that they were slaves. For the number of baptisms, see Christ Church Baptism Records, 1726–1761. For Jenney's interest in a catechist see, for example, Robert Jenney to Secretary of SPG, Jan. 26, 1744, SPG Letters, B12, no. 37, Perry, *Historical Collections*, 2: 235–36. For a discussion of blacks in Philadelphia during this period see Nash, *The Urban Crucible*, 109–10.
4. Peterson used a broad definition of membership, including those married at Christ Church. Therefore these numbers provide only a rough idea of the congregation.
5. Richard Shelling, "The Reverend William Sturgeon, Catechist to the Negroes of Philadelphia and Assistant Rector of Christ Church 1747–66," *HMPEC* 8 (1939): 388–401.
6. For an excellent discussion of the founding and development of the school, as well as all known letters discussing it, see Van Horne, ed., *Religious Philanthropy and Colonial Slavery*. The quote is from William Sturgeon to the Rev. John Waring, Nov. 9, 1758, Van Horne, ed., *Religious Philanthropy and Colonial Slavery*, 135–36.
7. See G. B. Warden, "The Proprietary Group in Pennsylvania 1754–1764, *WMQ* 21 (1964): 367–89; Judith Diamondstone, "The Philadelphia Corporation 1701–1776" (Ph.D. diss., University of Pennsylvania, 1969); and Stephen Brobeck, "Revolutionary Change in Colonial Philadelphia: The Brief Life of the Proprietary Group," *WMQ* 33 (1976): 410–34.
8. For biographical information on Smith see Thomas Firth Jones, *A Pair of Lawn Sleeves: A Biography of William Smith* (Philadelphia: Chilton Book Company, 1972). The quote is from

p. 2. For information on the founding of the Academy and College, see Edward R. Cheyney, *History of the University of Pennsylvania 1740–1940* (Philadelphia: University of Pennsylvania Press, 1940), 17–52. We will discuss the founding of the College in Chapter 6.

9. For a discussion of Pennsylvania politics during this period see James Hutson, *Pennsylvania Politics, 1746–70: The Movement for Royal Government and Its Consequences* (Princeton, N.J.: Princeton University Press, 1972), chap. 1.

10. Robert Jenney to Thomas Penn, Jan. 14, 1742, and Robert Jenney to Secretary of SPG, Jan. 14, 1742, in Edward Pennington, "The Reverend Robert Jenney," American Antiquarian Society, *Proceedings* 61 (1941): 168.

11. Thomas Penn to Richard Peters, Nov. 17, 1760, Thomas Penn Letter Book, Penn Papers, HSP, 6: 328–34.

12. William Smith to Thomas Barton, published as the preface to Barton's *Unanimity and Public Spirit* (Philadelphia: Franklin and Hall, 1755).

13. *Pennsylvania Journal and Weekly Advertiser*, April 22, 1756. "Humphrey Scourge," "Mild Advice to a Certain Parson," *Pennsylvania Journal*, March 25, 1756.

14. *Pennsylvania Journal*, May 20, 1756; June 10, 17, 1756; Christ Church Vestry Minutes, June 15, 1756; *Pennsylvania Journal*, June 17, 1756. The list of names supporting Smith is in Smith Papers, HSP, vol. 1, no. 14. It does not appear to have ever been published. For a general discussion of the Roberdeau affair, see Ralph Ketcham, "Benjamin Franklin and William Smith, New Light on an Old Quarrel," *PMHB* 88 (1965): 142–63.

15. For a detailed discussion of the episode, see Don Roy Byrnes, "The Pre-Revolutionary Career of William Smith, 1751–1780" (Ph.D. diss., Tulane University, 1969), chap. 7, or William Ridell, "Libel on the Assembly, a Pre-Revolutionary Episode," *PMHB* 52 (1928): 176–92, 249–79, 342–60. For Smith's side of the story see "A Brief Narrative of the Case of Reverend Mr. Smith," Perry, *Historical Collections* 2: 267.

16. Smith's Petition to the Privy Council, quoted in *The Papers of Benjamin Franklin*, vol. 8, ed. Leonard Labaree et al. (New Haven, Conn.: Yale University Press, 1965), 31; McKean to Secretary of SPG, Feb. 5, 1758, Perry, *Historical Collections*, 2: 270–73. See also Phillip Bearcroft to William Smith, May 30, 1758, Smith Manuscripts, PEC, 1: 24; Archbishop Secker to Robert Jenney, July 18, 1759, Lambeth Palace Papers, transcripts, Library of Congress, 1123, II, no. 143; Thomas Penn to William Smith, May 26, 1758, Penn Letter Book, 15: 322–24.

17. Robert Jenney to Archbishop Secker, Nov. 27, 1758, Perry, *Historical Collections*, 2: 273–74; William Sturgeon to Archbishop Secker, Nov. 29, 1758, Perry, *Historical Collections*, 2: 269.

18. Robert Jenney to SPG, Oct. 13, 1750, SPG Letters, B18, no. 151. Jenney had a series of conflicts with the vestry about who should choose the churchwardens and the clerk. He was particularly upset in 1750 when the vestry took control of the pew rents, which had previously all gone to him, and cut his salary in order to pay Sturgeon. Peters maintained that he had not done anything to hurt Jenney and withdrew from the vestry when the controversy came out in the open. See Richard Peters to Thomas Penn, March 20, 1752, POC, 5: 235.

19. C. P. B. Jeffreys, *The Provincial and Revolutionary History of St. Peter's Church, 1753–1783* (Philadelphia, n.d.), 15; Robert Jenney to Secretary of SPG, June 20, 1751, SPG Letters, B19, nos. 103–104; Subscribers to Thomas Penn, Aug. 1, 1754, Penn Papers, 7: 109 (printed in Jeffreys, *St. Peter's*, 19); Christ Church Vestry Minutes, June 20, 1758.

20. Richard Peters to Thomas Penn, June 1, 1756, quoted in Dietmar Rothermund, *The Layman's Progress: Religious and Political Experience in Colonial Pennsylvania 1740–1770* (Philadelphia: University of Pennsylvania Press, 1961), 179; Peters to Penn, June 2, 1753, POC, 1: 63.

21. Karin Peterson, "Christ Church, Its Congregation Between 1750 and 1760," identifies the wards of residence of these men. For the settlement of the city in 1762 see the Clarkson-Biddle map in Martin P. Snyder, *City of Independence: Views of Philadelphia Before 1800* (New York: Praeger Publishers, 1975), 63.

22. Robert Jenney to Vestry, June 20, 1758, quoted in Jeffreys, *St. Peter's*, 19.

23. Vestry Minutes, Aug. 19, 1761.

24. Articles of Agreement for Building a Church, John Kearsley et al. and Robert Smith, Christ Church Archives; Tatum, *Penn's Great Town*, 156; Harold Rose, *The Colonial Houses of Worship in America Built in the English Colonies Before the Republic 1607–1789 and Still Standing* (New York: Hastings House, 1963), 206. The cost is discussed in Vestry Minutes, March 5, 1763. Friary, "The Architecture of the Anglican Churches," 355–57. Tatum attributes the building to William Smith, while Harold Rose believes Samuel Rhodes designed it.

25. Vestry Minutes, Nov. 10, 1758, Feb. 27, 1759; Richard Peters to his sister, Dec. 2, 1762, Smith Papers, HSP, vol. 2, no. 107.

26. William Macclenachan to Archbishop Secker, n.d., received Aug. 23, 1760, Lambeth Palace Papers, 1123, II, no. 195. For information on his background see Frederick L. Weis, *The Colonial Churches and the Colonial Clergy of the Middle and Southern Colonies 1607–1776* (Lancaster, Mass.: Society of the Descendents of the Colonial Clergy, 1938).

27. For information on Macclenachan's evangelical leanings, see "An Address of some Presbyterian Ministers to his Grace the Archbishop of Canterbury in behalf of Reverend Mr. Macclenaghan," May 23, 1760, Smith Manuscripts, PEC, 3: 38, Perry, *Historical Collections*, 2: 307–8; William Macclenachan to Archbishop Secker, received Aug. 23, 1760. For a good discussion of the theology of the early evangelicals in England, see L. E. Elliott-Binns, *The Early Evangelicals: A Religious and Social History* (Greenwich, Conn.: Lutterworth Press, 1953), chap. 21.

28. William Smith to Archbishop Secker, Nov. 27, 1759, quoted in Horace Smith, *Life and Correspondence of the Reverend William Smith*, 2 vols. (Philadelphia: S.A. George, 1879), 2: 225.

29. The first round of conversations seem to have been informal. See William Smith to Archbishop, November 27, 1759, Horace Smith, *William Smith*, 1: 223 and Vestry Minutes, May 10, 1759. For other accounts of these events see Missionaries and Other Clergy of the Church of England to Bishop Sherlock, Oct. 21, 1759, Lambeth Palace papers, 1123, II, no. 153.

30. Vestry Minutes, Sept. 27, 1759. For a copy of the letter to the bishop, see "The Address of the Church Wardens and Vestry of Christ Church . . . to the Bishop of London," Oct. 3, 1759, Lambeth Palace Papers, 1123, II, no. 147; Missionaries and Other Clergy of the Church of England to Bishop Sherlock, Oct. 21, 1759, Lambeth Palace Papers, 1123, II, no. 153; Robert Jenney, "Order for Regulating the Duty of his Congregation," Nov. 1, 1759, included in William Smith's letter to the Archbishop, Nov. 27, 1759, Horace Smith, *William Smith*, 2: 223.

31. Members of Christ Church to Robert Jenney, Nov. 1, 1759, Smith Manuscripts, PEC, 3: 44.

32. Ibid.; Members of Christ Church to Archbishop, n.d., received August 23, 1760, Lambeth Palace Papers, 1123, II, no. 194; Articles of Agreement of St. Paul's Church, in Norris S. Barratt, *Outline of the History of Old St. Paul's Church* (Philadelphia: Colonial Society of Pennsylvania, 1917), 194–97. These all expressed the same sentiment.

33. Philip Bearcroft to William Macclenachan, Feb. 20, 1760, SPG Letters, B6, no. 280, explains the reasons. The letter to Jenney was reported in the minutes of the Convention of Clergy in Philadelphia, 1760, Perry, *Historical Collections*, 2: 298; Robert Jenney to Vestry, June

18, 1760, Vestry Minutes, June 18, 1760; see also Robert Jenney to Macclenachan, June 17, 1760, Smith Manuscripts, PEC, 3: 43, Perry, *Historical Collections*, 2: 310.

34. Members of Christ Church to Archbishop, n.d., received August 23, 1760, Lambeth Palace Papers, 1123, II, no. 194. See Barratt, *Old St. Paul's Church*, 194–97; Friary, "The Architecture of the Anglican Churches," 355–57, 868–72.

35. Members of Christ Church to Archbishop Secker, n.d., received Aug. 23, 1760, Lambeth Palace Papers, 1123, II, no. 194; "Articles of Agreement," Barratt, *Old St. Paul's Church*, 194–97. William Smith to Bishop of London, Nov. 13, 1766, Perry, *Historical Collections*, 2: 414.

36. Smith made his charges in a letter to the Secretary of the SPG, Aug. 26, 1760, SPG Letters, B21, no. 276, Perry *Historical Collections*, 2: 325 and in William Smith to Archbishop, July 1, 1760, Perry, *Historical Collections*, 2: 321. The baptism, marriage, and vestry records as well as one pew rent list of Christ Church were used to determine the background of these men. Because of the incomplete nature of the records we can conclude that the number of former Christ Church members was probably considerably higher. Fifty-eight founders of St. Paul's could be found on the list; they were compared to 204 members of Christ Church. See Roach, "Taxables in the City of Philadelphia, 1756."

37. Smith to Archbishop Secker, July 1, 1760, Perry, *Historical Collections*, 2: 323; Smith to Secretary of the SPG, August 26, 1760, SPG Letters, B21, no. 248, Perry, *Historical Collections*, 2: 325. The antiproprietary members included Daniel Roberdeau, who had had the public disagreement with Smith; John Ross, who was a close ally of Franklin; Thomas Leech, who had served as Speaker of the Assembly when Smith was declared in contempt; and John Baynton, whom Peters described as "bitter on the side of the Party." Richard Peters to Thomas Penn, Oct. 2, 1756, *PMHB* 31 (1907): 246–47. Ross's friendship with Franklin is clear from a series of letters he wrote.

THE MATURATION OF THE PHILADELPHIA CHURCH: THE RECTORSHIP OF RICHARD PETERS

Jenney's death in January 1762 offered the vestry and congregations of the United Churches their first opportunity to choose their own minister, a choice that would profoundly shape the congregations' future. In 1762 tensions about the relationship between the church and politics, about the role of evangelicals within the church, and about who had power within the church had yet to be resolved. Unless the vestry acted wisely in their choice of a new rector, the 1760s could be even more contentious than the 1750s had been.

Yet, surprisingly, after a year of indecision, in December 1762 the vestry made a decision that ushered in the most peaceful period in the colonial history of Christ Church. While few changes occurred in the authority structures, the men who led the churches during these prerevolutionary years were able to adapt to the informal structures that had developed over the years. The ministers of the United Churches put differences aside and showed no inclination to compete for power among themselves, with the vestry, or with William Smith. And as they struggled to define the Anglican church in America, they came to accept theological diversity to a degree not yet reached in England.

Such peace would not have been predicted at the time of Jenney's death. The candidates for the rectorship differed greatly in personality, theology, and in political opinions, and the vestrymen seem to have had extreme difficulty choosing among them. William Sturgeon, the loyal assistant to Jenney, if chosen, could have been counted on to continue Jenney's anti-Smith, anti-Peters attitude. William Smith brought controversy wherever he went and firmly believed in using the church to further his political beliefs. A popular preacher, Smith's rational beliefs led him to oppose virulently any form of evangelicalism or mysticism.[1] Peters, at sixty, was the oldest and most widely respected Anglican cleric in Pennsylvania. By 1762 Peters had rejected the deistic tendencies of his youth and embraced a personal, pietistic, and deeply committed style of religion that gained him favor with evangelical Presbyterians and Lutherans.[2] His political involvement had also decreased as he got older, but he still served on the Proprietary Council and aligned himself with the proprietor. Jacob Duché could have been seen as a compromise candidate. He had never taken an active role in politics, and thus might have satisfied Jenney's supporters, but he was quietly aligned with the proprietary camp and thus acceptable to Smith and Peters. But Duché's age was against him; at age twenty-four, he was not even old enough to be ordained a priest!

Jenney had made his choice for his successor clear. In a letter to the vestry outlining the qualities needed in a rector, he warned that the rector should "not be under any . . . Attachment . . . to any great Man," nor should he have any "slur upon his reputation" such as polygamy or "conceit of himself as overbears others," obvious references to Smith and Peters. He then went on to openly endorse Sturgeon for the job because of "his Attachment to the Church and Knowledge of its Constitution," and "his Piety, moral Behavior and prudent Conduct toward all men." He must have known that at least some vestrymen disagreed with him, for he concluded by saying that he had given his true sentiments, "however they may be resented by you."[3]

Immediately after Jenney's death in January 1762 the vestry adopted a compromise arrangement that was, unfortunately, doomed to failure: it promoted both Duché and Sturgeon to ministers and placed them on an equal footing (despite Duché's status as a deacon).[4] Even before Duché left for England to be ordained, the two ministers had had a falling out. Sturgeon resented and feared working with a young, talented minister with good connections, yet who remained without priestly orders. Duché commented to Smith: "as to Sturgeon, know he is below my Notice, nor shall I ever have anything to do with him." By the end of the year the vestry had concluded that "Mr. Duché and Mr. Sturgeon not being upon the best terms together, the Congregation would be perpetually kept in hot water by their differences" if a new rector were not selected.[5]

Thus in December 1762 the vestry had to reconsider their earlier choices. In a profoundly significant decision, the vestry *unanimously* chose Richard Peters as rector of the United Churches. Sturgeon and Duché remained as ministers, but in reality served as assistants. In May 1763, twenty-two years after Bishop Gibson rejected his candidacy, Peters received a license from the bishop of London.[6]

While this decision surprised many people, only Sturgeon expressed opposition. Duché seemed genuinely pleased. The young cleric wrote to the archbishop of Canterbury that Peters had been "a Father to me almost from my Infancy" and that he was so pleased that now he had "a Friend, a Counsellor & Guide whose Age and Superior Abilities will always stand me in much stead and facilitate my Duty in almost every Instance." Since he was still young, he could look forward to being rector of the United Churches one day.[7]

The unanimous choice of Peters by a vestry that had previously been divided and indecisive is difficult to explain. While some objections to Peters had diminished over the years—particularly the moral ones—other potential problems remained. As mentioned earlier, Peters's religious views had changed, but by 1762 he had so completely rejected his earlier rationalistic beliefs that he had raised new objections. Sometime in the early 1760s Peters came under the influence of the German mystic Jakob Boehme and his English disciple William Law. Boehme and Law completely rejected the applicability of human reason in matters of religion and stressed a personal mystical piety that led their adherents to such heights of mystical union with God that they sometimes had trouble communicating with their fellow humans. William White, who served as Peters's assistant from 1772 to 1775, later remembered that while Peters could be "exceedingly entertaining on any ordinary and on any literary Subject . . . from the moment of turning the Conversation to Religion, he was in the Clouds." When Peters supplied the churches from June until December 1762 while Duché was in England. Peters's close friend, the Presbyterian William Allen, reported that "most people in the place . . . have been much dissatisfied with Mr. Peters' adoption of Mr. Law's Mystical Divinity." Yet the vestry did not seem to hold this against him.[8]

Peters's political connections were less important than they had been in 1741, since he had resigned as secretary to the proprietor in 1760, but they still could have caused objections. Peters still served on the Provincial Council and his selection meant that Smith would have greater influence in the United Churches. Yet a vestry that still contained fourteen of the vestrymen who supported Roberdeau against Smith chose Peters as rector. In fact, Peters even suggested that his connection with the proprietor was one of the reasons he was chosen. He explained that the vestry "considered my good circumstances and connections with Persons of Influence, and thought they could turn these to their Benefit."[9]

While some may have seen advantages in hiring a person with political influence, it appears that the main reason Peters was hired was because of another personal quality—his "charity." Independently wealthy, Peters agreed to serve the churches without pay until the debt incurred in building St. Peter's was paid. While the vestry never actually mentioned the financial factor, Duché explained that Peters's "extraordinary Benevolence" meant that he would not need support. This meant, of course, that Duché's own salary did not have to be diminished.[10]

With Peters's selection as rector the vestry had rejected Jenney's advice regarding a politically neutral church. In 1766 the leadership further repudiated Jenney's vision by forcing Sturgeon to resign. As early as 1764 his jealousy and resentment had so affected his performance that the vestry asked him when he planned to make good on his promise to leave soon. Sturgeon responded that he "resolved to continue his duties," but by 1766 the situation had so deteriorated that he "voluntarily resigned" and moved to the countryside.[11]

Sturgeon's story is one of the saddest episodes in the history of Christ Church. In 1763 the SPG had cut off his stipend as "Catechist to the Negroes," ostensibly because he had not been conducting his duties, despite the vestry's assertions to the contrary.[12] After his resignation Smith, who reported that Sturgeon had "at Times a very bad State of Body, which has to all Appearances often affected his Mind, & led him to do many weak things," effectively blocked Sturgeon's application for an SPG missionary assignment at Trenton or Oxford. Heavily in debt and with several small children, Sturgeon moved to the country. There his luck only worsened. Within a space of fifteen months, in 1768 and 1769, Sturgeon's wife and four children died and his house burned to the ground, leaving him only a few beds and the clothes on his back. With no income and no house, he was left with three sons, nine years old and younger, to support. In a letter to the SPG reminiscent of Job, he maintained, "I will not despond, since it is the Will of Heaven, the Lord gave and the same divine Arm hath taken a Way, Oh! that I may ever be enabled to praise his holy Name." While he still had hopes of returning to the ministry, he was never able to obtain a cure.[13]

*   *   *

Peters had lived in Philadelphia for a quarter of a century before he became rector. He had seen the city grow from a large town, which was in many ways as much rural as it was urban, into a true city. The Christ Church steeple still dominated the sky-line, but the view from the river, as seen in Figure 11, was far different in 1762 from what it had been in 1737. During his rectorship he would witness the emergence of Philadelphia as the premier city in America in terms of population, economic growth, scientific achievement, and artistic endeavor. Between 1765 and 1775 the population of Philadelphia grew from 18,000 to 25,000, making the city the largest in the colonies. (See Map 1 for physical size of city.) The population growth of the city was both a cause and an effect of economic growth. When the Seven Years' War ended in 1763, immigrants from Germany and Ireland once again flooded the city and pushed back the frontiers of Pennsylvania. The merchants of Philadelphia provided these newcomers with much-needed goods and services. At the same time, the increased agricultural production of the Pennsylvania hinterland, combined with droughts in Europe and increasing importation of food in New England, greatly increased the exporting business of Philadelphia merchants. All this activity enabled Philadelphia to recover quickly from the inevitable depression that followed the end of war-related economic activity. By 1775 ships entered and left the city ports at record rates.[14]

Christ Church members played an important role in this mercantile activity. Thomas Willing, son of the prosperous merchant Charles Willing, joined with Robert Morris, a former clerk in his father's firm, to form one of the leading mercantile firms in Philadelphia. Like other wealthy merchants, Willing dabbled in politics, serving as mayor, assemblyman, and eventually as a justice on the supreme court. He served on the vestry of Christ Church where he was joined by fellow merchants Thomas Lawrence, Jr., John Baynton, Redmond Conyngham, William Plumstead, and Alexander and Charles Stedman, to mention a few.

FIGURE 11

East prospect of the city of Philadelphia, taken by George Heap (c. 1715–1752) from the Jersey shore, under the direction of Nicholas Scull (1687–1761), Surveyor General of the Province of Pennsylvania. Engraving by Gerard Vandergucht, 1754. Shows the steeple of Christ Church. Courtesy of the Historical Society of Pennsylvania.

creased substantially in the 1760s and while most recipients of aid continued to be women and children, the ranks were swelled by displaced soldiers, poor immigrants, and people fleeing the fighting on the frontiers. Christ Church members attempted to meet the needs of these people. In 1772, for example, Richard Peters, John Kearsley and Robert Morris joined with the Catholic priest Robert Harding in founding "the Society of the Sons of St. George, Established at Philadelphia, for the Advice and Assistance of Englishmen in Distress."[15]

While some Philadelphians knew only poverty, the city was prosperous enough to have a greatly expanded cultural life. Anglicans played a particularly important role in the blossoming musical life of Philadelphia. James Bremner, the organist of Christ Church from 1767 to 1770 and then again in 1774, was one of the foremost musicians in prerevolutionary Philadelphia. A

successful composer, he set up a school teaching harpsichord, guitar, and violin. Bremner's most enduring contribution to Philadelphia was to the education of Francis Hopkinson. Hopkinson, who had grown up in Christ Church, could be considered a "Renaissance man." A poet, literary essayist, artist, and accomplished musician, Hopkinson would become famous as an outspoken patriot and pamphleteer during the American Revolution. In the 1770s he became organist of Christ Church and considerably improved the musical program there. On Bremner's departure, Hopkinson assumed the musical leadership of the Philadelphia community.[16]

Philadelphia Anglicans were also enthusiastic supporters of science. In the 1740s Christ Church vestryman Jacob Duché, Sr., the father of the assistant minister of Christ Church, sponsored a series of scientific lectures in his home which were later transferred to the College of Philadelphia. In the 1760s Philadelphians founded two scientific societies: Dr. John Morgan and Samuel Powel provided leadership for the American Society for Promoting and Propagating Useful Knowledge, Held at Philadelphia, while Dr. Thomas Bond, Richard Peters, William Smith, John Penn and James Hamilton revived the American Philosophical Society. Two other Anglicans, Francis

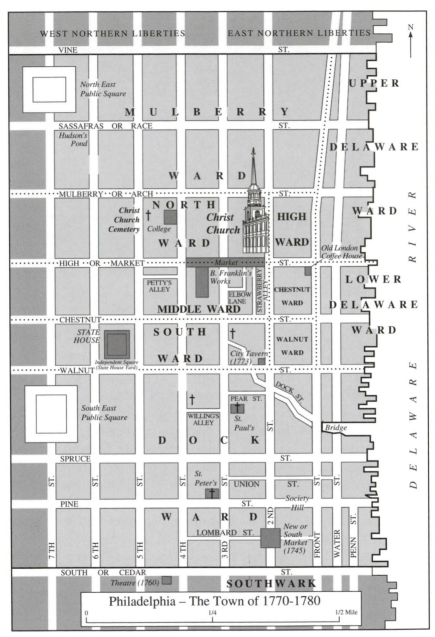

MAP 1
Philadelphia, 1770–1780.

Hopkinson and the Reverend Jacob Duché, were among those who joined both societies and formed the bridge that helped unite the two in 1769. Anglicans also were in the forefront of medicine. In 1765, under the leadership of John Morgan, the trustees of the College established the first medical school in the colonies, an idea originally conceived by Presbyterian William Shippen. Morgan and two other Christ Church members, Thomas Bond and Benjamin Rush, served as faculty of the new school.[17]

Both the economic and cultural elite who increasingly joined Christ Church and the rank and file from all socioeconomic segments of the city's population must have found Peters to be a far different type of rector from Jenney. Using a conciliatory style that he had developed throughout his years in politics, Peters worked hard to avoid controversy. He tolerated diversity and, in general, set an example that brought peace to the United Churches.

However, Peters also tolerated—even encouraged—Smith to take an active role in the life of the church and, as a result, shortly after Peters's selection, Smith plunged the United Churches into the heat of the political battles that engulfed Pennsylvania in the 1760s. The issue this time involved the attempt of the "Quaker faction," led by Benjamin Franklin, to change the province from a proprietary colony to a royal colony. In stark contrast to the first attempt by early Anglicans to obtain royal rule, this time it was an Anglican minister, William Smith, who led the fight *against* a royal governor.[18] In October 1764 Smith, who was supplying the churches while Peters was in England, held a meeting *in Christ Church* to protest the royal government effort and to sign petitions. The response the meeting elicited in the press was exactly what Jenney had been trying to avoid. A satirical piece by an unknown author strongly criticized both Smith and Duché. The author argued that "Some stiff-necked People of your Communion may imagine that your Church was prostituted to vile worldly Purposes upon this Occasion; and that your Communion Table was defiled by Petitions and Writings about Politics" but since "matters of more Consequence were transacted than that of Religion," those who protest should keep silent.[19]

Smith's use of the church for political purposes could have caused serious problems for Peters if it had not been for the relative calm that fell on Pennsylvania politics. The Royal Government movement, which ended in failure in 1768, was the last political controversy to divide Pennsylvania until the Revolution. As a result, Jenney's worst fears of constant political turmoil within Christ Church did not come true.

At the same time that political tensions within Christ Church eased, so too did tensions caused by power struggles. With Peters's conciliatory style leading the way and with all the ministers of the United Churches comfortable with the power of the laity, the informal governmental structures were allowed to work effectively.

For the first time since Peters arrived in 1737 the leadership of the Anglican clerical community was clear. Peters and Smith willingly shared the leadership role, with Peters serving as the elder statesman, while Smith was the energetic leader. Peters explained to the SPG that he left the bulk of the larger church matters to Smith since he was "young and can do much better than I can was my health better."[20] In fact, when the bishop of London decided not to appoint a commissary, Smith's way became clear to act as the surrogate bishop many had earlier accused him of being. Smith had always been active in advising the bishop and the SPG, but prior to 1764 he had been only one of many voices. From that year until the Revolution he served as the English authorities' main source of information and advice about Pennsylvania. While SPG missionaries might resent his power, they had little choice but to court his favor. He wrote to England regularly, reporting on vacant churches, suggesting which minister should be sent where, endorsing the requests of individual churches, and recommending people for orders. Such activity had previously caused conflict with the rector of Christ Church, but now Peters welcomed it.[21]

At the congregational level, authority structures also worked smoothly. In 1767, after forty-five years of trying, the United Churches finally obtained a charter and adopted bylaws. In most respects the bylaws repeated the rules established in 1730, but there was an important change in the procedures for choosing a rector. At the insistence of the congregation, the vestry could not recommend anyone to the bishop for the position of rector until at least one month after the vestry had voted, so that members might have time to express any "reasonable objection to the Person." Members of the United Churches still could not vote on their rector, as could their fellow Anglicans at St. Paul's, but the bylaws did at least acknowledge the demand for congregational authority that had surfaced several times during the history of Christ Church.[22]

Perhaps the new era that Peters's rectorship ushered in was best symbolized by the motto chosen for the United Churches: "Unity in Peace and Love." Given the previous history of the churches, such a motto had to be considered as a "hope" rather than a reality. It was, in some ways, prescient; with the exception of the Revolution, which divided all of society, the United

FIGURE 12
*Memorial plaque for
Mary Andrews, c. 1769,
located on the wall of
Christ Church. This very
early example of Ameri-
can memorial art may
have been the work of
John Folwell working
from Batty Langley's de-
signs. Photograph by
Louis W. Meehan.*

Churches would experience more than a half century of comparative "peace" if not total "unity" until their separation in 1832.

*   *   *

The Peters rectorship also saw two major improvements in the sanctuary of Christ Church. In 1769 the vestry used a bequest of Mary Andrews to purchase the now famous "wineglass pulpit." (See Figure 12 for a Memorial Plaque honoring Andrews.) Designed and constructed by Philadelphia cabinetmaker John Folwell, the new pulpit must have been a striking addition to the sanctuary. Its "grand curving staircase, gilded decoration and decorated canopy supported by a large square ionic column and topped with a carved gilded dove" was made even more spectacular by the addition of nearly £800 worth of upholstery and tassels draped over it. In reaction to the Great Awakening and the renewed emphasis on preaching, the vestry placed the pulpit in the center of the chancel, directly in front of the Palladian window, rather than on the north side of the center aisle as its predecessor had been (see Figure 13). The communion table, which had occupied the place of prominence, now stood behind the pulpit, and was carried out in front on Communion Sundays.[23]

The purchase in 1766 of a new organ for James Bremner to play vastly improved the musical portion of the service. Built by Philip Feyring, it had three manuals, 27 stops, and a total of 1,607 pipes. Francis Hopkinson attempted to improve the singing in the churches. In 1763, anticipating the installation of organs in both churches, Hopkinson had published *A Collection of Psalm Tunes with a Few Anthems and Hymns, Some of Them Entirely New, for the Use of the United Churches of Christ Church and St. Peter's Church, in Philadelphia, 1763*. He indicated in the preface that organs would be a "needless expense" unless the congregations could "join their Voices with them in the singing of Psalms." Therefore, besides printing the psalms, he "prefixed a few Rules for Singing, in as clear and easy a Manner as possible; so that Children, with very little Attention, may understand them." When Bremner returned to England, Hopkinson took over as organist. His efforts obviously had some effect: in 1772 the congregation participated in singing "The Hallelujah Chorus," and when John Adams visited the church during the meeting of the First Continental Congress in 1774 he reported that "the organ and a new choir of singers were very musical."[24]

Peters and the vestry also had the unpleasant task of supervising a large number of repairs to Christ Church, or the "old church" as it was already being called. In 1767 Peters made the kind of report that would become all too familiar to vestries of Christ Church. He stated that the church needed

white washing and new Painting, that a great Deal of the Glass in the Windows was broken and the Leads for the most part wanted repair and to be soldered again: that the Roof leaked in several Places, and the Tenants and Mortars [tenons and mortises] of the Balustrades as well as the Coping Boards were all rotten and that the work at the east end of the Church was so bad as to be in Danger of falling.

FIGURE 13
Interior of Christ Church, showing the wineglass pulpit. Eighteenth-century engraving attributed to James Peller Malcolm (1767–1815). Courtesy of the Historical Society of Pennsylvania.

Acknowledging the need, the vestry also had to recognize that it had no way of paying for these repairs, since it still owed £900 for St. Peter's. Once again Peters came to the rescue, agreeing to lend the vestry the money, which eventually totaled £464.17.4, a debt which was still unpaid when he resigned in 1775.[25]

An even greater blow came in 1772 when members discovered that the steeple, which was less than twenty years old, was in a ruinous state: "the Ends of the great Timbers [were] so rotten as to be mere Powder, and the other parts likewise very much decayed." A subscription drive, including a door-to-door canvassing of members, raised the necessary £644.2.10.[26] By the end of Peters's tenure Christ Church was in excellent physical condition.

* * *

Theological diversity, with its potential for disunity, was much more difficult to deal with than crumbling steeples, but Peters showed himself equally good at handling spiritual matters. Despite the building of St. Paul's, the demands of evangelicals continued to cause problems within Christ Church. Fortunately Peters's patience and acceptance of diversity allowed him to handle the situation effectively.

The potential for conflict once again centered on the choice of an assistant minister. With the resignation of Sturgeon and the increasing age and ill health of Peters, it became obvious that the congregation needed another assistant. But the diversity of candidates made the choice a potentially divisive one. One group within the congregation strongly supported the candidacy of John Porter, an evangelical priest who, like Duché and Peters, followed William Law. Porter had stopped in Philadelphia in 1768 on his way to Maryland, and, as a result of his preaching had won the support of "some of the most respectable members" of the congregation, including the churchwardens and eight other vestrymen. Not surprisingly, Smith opposed Porter and threatened to end his association with the church if Porter were even given a trial.[27]

In fact, Smith supported another candidate for the assistant minister's position, Thomas Coombe. Coombe, who was in England for ordination at the time, came from a wealthy merchant family, had grown up in Christ Church, and had studied under Smith. No doubt as a result of this background, his theology was much closer to Smith's than to Peters's. He complained to the provost that "the plain Doctrines of Christ & his Apostles are less valued among you, than the mysterious Rhapsodies of Law & Behmen."

While Coombe sided with Smith against mysticism, he seems to have gone beyond him in rejecting systematic theology and the importance of following the doctrines of the Church of England. He asserted that "orthodoxy seems to be a word without any determinate meaning; since that which is *orthodoxy* at Rome, is heterodoxy in England." He summarized his beliefs this way: "He is the *best* Christian who conforms his life the nearest to the moral *precepts* of the gospel." Despite his rationalistic views, Coombe was a popular preacher. In 1771 Joseph Hutchins, a parishioner visiting in England, reported that Lord Chief Justice DeGrey had "shed Tears in Approbation of [Coombe's] Eloquence whilst he was preaching a Charity Sermon."[28]

While Smith was ready to fight over the choice of an assistant minister, Duché and Peters both chose a conciliatory course. Peters refused to appoint any assistant minister until unity could be achieved. Porter, it seems, followed the lead of his friends; in 1769 when he expected to pass through Philadelphia, he reported that he was reluctant even to stay with Peters because of "the present unfavorable Light in which flying Fame reports me to stand among the Clergy of Philadelphia."[29] Porter's untimely death ended this stage of the controversy.

However, the choice of an assistant minister was still not easy, for another candidate, William White, threatened Coombe's chances for appointment.[30] White, the son of a vestryman, was no closer theologically to Peters and Duché, but was far less outspoken and critical than was Coombe. White's theology, which will be discussed in more detail in later chapters, has been accurately described as one of a group of men who "were disposed to emphasize, perhaps too much, the rational and intellectual side of Christianity," but who "never yielded its supernatural claims altogether in favor of mere rationalism." "If they were, as a rule, somewhat lacking in fire, they were strong in judiciousness and moderation." Emphasizing "common understanding," White sought to "set theology's feet solidly on the ground of the empirical."[31] While his views were in many ways similar to Coombe's, he had much more respect for "orthodoxy" and the teachings of the Church of England. His preaching style was certainly not as popular as that of Coombe, Duché, or even Smith, but in his earlier years it was still impressive. A friend described him as "an ingenious, rational preacher, whose discourses were stored with excellent matter; & altho' delivered in a simple & unpretending manner, were well calculated to inform the minds, & amend the hearts of his hearers."[32]

Rather than support White for the assistant's job, Peters chose a compromise course. In June 1771 he urged the vestry to appoint *both* Coombe and White as assistant ministers. The vestrymen would have willingly agreed but knew that the church could not afford it. Once again Peters came to their aid; he offered to pay each man £100 a year during his incumbency, thus giving up most of the small salary he had just recently begun to receive. White helped as well: also independently wealthy, he agreed to serve for whatever the vestry could afford. The vestry finally agreed to hire both Coombe and White and reported in February 1774 that the congregation was satisfied with the appointment of the assistants.[33]

Unfortunately, even Peters's generosity did not solve the financial problems of the churches. In 1774 the salaries of the staff plus a mere fifty pounds for repairs resulted in a deficit of more than £190. As a result the vestry was forced to ask the congregation for permission to raise the pew rents 50 percent for three years. While the rent increase narrowly passed, the parishioners showed their displeasure by voting out of office fourteen of the twenty vestrymen at the next election.[34] This reluctance of members of the United Churches to pay for the normal support of the churches and their ministers would continue to be a problem into the nineteenth century.

* * *

The United Churches now had in place a team of ministers that would have lasted them into the nineteenth century had the Revolution not intervened. The vestry, with Peters's encouragement, had knowingly chosen an extremely disparate group in terms of age, theology and personality.

Fortunately for the congregation, despite occasional disagreements, all the ministers consciously chose to put differences aside and work together. Of all the ministers, White was the most tolerant of divergent beliefs. Well known in his later years for his ability to "perceive and acknowledge the existence of good qualities, without regard to the opinions of the party professing them," he remained close friends with Peters, Duché, and Coombe until their deaths. His relations with Smith in later years were a bit more complex, as we will see, but, having studied with him at the college, he respected him as his mentor and forgave his excessive concern for politics and land speculation.[35] Smith and Peters remained friends until the rector's death; their long political and ecclesiastical association seemed to compensate for their differences over theology.[36] Thomas Coombe privately expressed negative opinions about Peters, Duché, and Smith, but he did not publicly disagree with them. When preparing to return home from England, Coombe wrote that he was coming home "in the Spirit of Peace and Silence" and believed that he and Duché "may yet live quietly together, not to do so, & be in the same Church, would justly fix Odium on us both."[37]

The ability to maintain ecclesiastical harmony at Christ Church contrasted sharply with the Anglican situation in England where minor differences over theology caused major controversies within the church throughout the eighteenth century.[38] There were many reasons for this. The Philadelphia clergymen downplayed systematic theology and emphasized what religion should mean to the common man. They aimed at producing pious and moral parishioners rather than theologians. Moreover, Philadelphia's heterogeneous environment had led Anglican leaders to accept other denominations as legitimate and thereby expanded the bounds of orthodoxy. The clergy also may have realized that the presence of ministers with varying beliefs and styles of religion within one church could be a competitive advantage, especially for a denomination with a tradition of universalism.

The laity within the United Churches appeared even more willing than the clergy to accept divergent beliefs. Except for the complaints about Peters's sermons, there were no known objections to any of the ministers. This was no doubt in part because all the clergymen were well liked. More important, average laypeople were far more concerned with style and manner of delivery than with theology. When Sturgeon visited Philadelphia in 1746 the vestry asked him to preach a *published* sermon rather than preaching his own because it wanted to judge his "voice and delivery," rather than to determine his theology.[39] Similarly, contemporary accounts of Duché and Coombe all emphasize their style and delivery rather than their theology.[40] So long as the ministers' sermons were comprehensible and delivered well, the members of Christ Church did not seem to care about their theology.

Perhaps unknowingly, by the time of the Revolution the members and clergy of the United Churches had redefined what it meant to belong to the Church of England. Rather than stress belief in the Thirty-Nine Articles, the theological statement of the Church of England, or strict adherence to the church canons that were held so dear in England, Philadelphia Anglicans merely asked that a minister be properly ordained, use the Book of Common Prayer, and not cause divisions within the church. As we will see, this extremely tolerant attitude, which in some ways captured the essence of the Church of England as a "universal church," would make it much easier for Philadelphia Anglicans to unite with their brethren in the northern and southern colonies after the Revolution.

Reactions to three evangelical groups in Philadelphia in the 1760s and 1770s revealed how the clergy of the United Churches defined acceptable religious practices. St. Paul's Church presented the most enduring challenge. In 1768 the St. Paul's congregation chose as their minister William Stringer, a former cheesemonger from London, who had been irregularly ordained by "Erasmus," a self-styled "bishop" from Greece. At this point, even Peters, who had tried to be patient with the church, insisted that he would not "hereafter have any Connection with the Minister or Congregation." Clearly, lack of a proper ordination made Stringer unacceptable. But four years later, when the St. Paul's vestry asked the bishop of London to ordain Stringer, the Philadelphia clergy endorsed the request and willingly accepted the church back into the fold. Stringer had turned out to be, according to Peters, a "quiet, inoffensive and good man" who gave "constant attendance to his Duty which he punctually performs according to the Rites and Ceremonies of our Church."[41] This adherence to the Book of Common Prayer, combined with a proper ordination, made Stringer acceptable, despite his evangelical beliefs and the unorthodox charter of St. Paul's.

George Whitefield and his followers provided a more difficult situation for the Anglican clergy. His itinerant preaching and abandonment of the Prayerbook stretched the bounds of acceptable practices, but he did expect people to go back to established churches when he left. Moreover, he had established a following among Philadelphia Anglican laity that was hard to ignore.

Thus the attitudes of the Philadelphia clergy toward Whitefield varied. Smith, not surprisingly, was strongly opposed to the evangelist, whose tenets, he argued "tend to hurt order and a regular ministration of the Gospel." White agreed: years later he explained that he strongly disapproved of Whitefield's disregard for his ordination vows and believed that the exciting of "animal feelings" led to insincere conversions and turned more people away from religion than it saved. Duché, on the other hand, was more favorably disposed. An area minister reported that Duché "appeared more openly than the others [ministers] in preaching up his Doctrines and espousing his cause."[42]

Peters, who as rector ultimately decided whether Whitefield could preach in the United Churches, was personally more ambivalent, but, as was his style, he based his final decision on pragmatic considerations. Because he had strongly opposed Whitefield during his earlier visits, and remembered the discord he had caused, he was surprised and upset when in 1763 "the Congregations . . . by the Church wardens, signified . . . that they were one and all desirous that Mr. Whitefield should be invited . . . to preach in the Churches." However, after consulting with Duché, Sturgeon, and other friends of the church, he agreed to allow Whitefield to preach so as to "prevent dissatisfaction and further disunion among the members, who might when displeased go over to Mr. McClenachan." He hoped that Whitefield's excesses might "really confirm those that belong to us and perhaps get us an increase." After hearing Whitefield, who he found refrained from "his usual censure of the clergy" and spoke with "greater moderation of sentiments" than he had previously, Peters's opinions moderated. Yet, in 1764, despite his more favorable opinion of the evangelist, he complied with the archbishop's order that Whitefield not preach in the churches again. Members of the United Churches who wanted to hear him had to go to St. Paul's or to the college. In 1770, presumably because Archbishop Secker had died in 1768, Peters once again allowed Whitefield to preach in St. Peter's.[43]

The third evangelical group that Philadelphia clergy dealt with—the Methodists—clearly did not fall within the bounds of acceptable behavior. The Methodist movement in England, founded by John Wesley in 1738, had much in common with the evangelicals; Methodists also stressed a deeply spiritual religion, the need for a conversion experience, and the importance of Christ's sacrificial death on the cross. But they differed from this group in several important respects; most important, from the Philadelphia clergy's point of view, Methodists, while technically still within the fold of the Church of England, were far less dedicated Anglicans. They extolled the idea of lay preachers and lay societies outside of the control of clergy. Their preachers preferred to remain itinerant, preaching throughout the country rather than leading one congregation. Holding revival meetings in the open air or in any church or hall open to them, they often completely abandoned the liturgy of the Book of Common Prayer. In the late 1760s Thomas Webb, a British soldier, founded the first Methodist society in Philadelphia, and in 1769 Richard Boardman and Joseph Pilmore, two of John Wesley's deputies in America, arrived in Philadelphia. With their assistance, the Methodists founded St. George's Chapel (later St. George's Methodist Episcopal Church).[44]

While certain aspects of the Methodist evangelical style no doubt appealed to Duché and Peters, who seem to have had some social contact with them, their total disrespect for church authority structures made cooperation impossible.[45] Methodist ministers were never allowed to preach in the United

Churches. Methodists did not fall within the bounds of orthodoxy as defined by the clergy of Christ Church and St. Peter's, and St. George's was never considered to be a sister church.

* * *

Peters's rectorship was the most peaceful of any in the colonial period. While financial problems continued to plague the church, other problems—jealousy among clergy, competing elements in the authority structure, and the presence of evangelical ministers—were all kept under control. This peace, of course, was ended by the Revolution. However, the ability of the United Churches to rebound after the Revolution and to take a leadership role in the formation of the Episcopal church was a direct result of the resolution of problems that had occurred under Peters's leadership.

NOTES

1. For a brief discussion of Smith's theology see Sydney A. Temple, Jr., *The Common Sense Theology of Bishop White* (New York: King's Crown Press, 1946), 9–11.
2. Peters discusses his new beliefs in a letter to Conrad Weiser, Feb. 24, 1746, Peters Papers 2: 72. For an evangelical minister's endorsement of him see Gilbert Tennent to Peters, Jan. 26, 1757, Society Collection, HSP.
3. Robert Jenney to Vestry, n.d. (1757?), Perry, *Historical Collections*, 2: 246–50.
4. The decision was originally made as a temporary one, but in June it was reaffirmed. See Vestry Minutes, Jan. 16 and June 8, 1762. Peters reported that the vestrymen had "altered their minds two or three times this Week." See Richard Peters to William Smith, June 10, 1762, Smith Papers, HSP, vol. 2, no. 88.
5. Duché to Smith, April 9, 1759, Hawks Papers, Smith Manuscripts, PEC, no. 33; Richard Peters to William Smith, Jan. 15, 1763, Smith Papers, HSP, vol. 2, no. 113-14.
6. Vestry Minutes, Dec. 6, 1762. Wardens and Vestry of the United Congregation to Bishop Osbaldeston, Jan. 21, 1763, Fulham Papers, 8: 3–4; Bishop Osbaldeston to Vestry, May 24, 1763, Fulham Papers, 8: 9. It was no doubt fortunate for Peters that Bishop Gibson, who had been involved in the earlier controversy, had died in 1748.
7. Jacob Duché to Archbishop Secker, Feb. 2, 1763, Smith Manuscripts, PEC, 3: 32.
8. "The Autobiography of William White, " ed. Walter Herbert Stowe, *HMPEC* 22 (1953): 389. William Allen to Thomas Penn, Feb. 25, 1768, POC, 10: 136; Diary of Richard Peters, Aug. 7, 1762, Peters Papers, HSP.
9. Richard Peters to William Smith, Jan. 15, 1763, Smith Papers, HSP, vol. 2, no. 113-14.
10. Jacob Duché to Archbishop Secker, Feb. 2, 1763, Smith Manuscripts, PEC, 3: 32. Peters also mentioned the financial aspect in his explanation to Smith; see Richard Peters to William Smith, Jan. 15, 1763, Smith Papers, HSP, vol. 2, no. 113-14. Christ Church's debt stood at £1,265.5 against an annual income of only £809.10.0.
11. Vestry Minutes, Oct. 30 and Nov. 19, 1764. For comments on Sturgeon's jealousy and

lack of effectiveness see William Plumstead to Richard Peters, Nov. 19, 1764, Penn Papers, Saunders-Coates, 177; William Smith to SPG, Sept. 21, 1766, SPG Letters, B21, no. 254.

12. John Ross, a founder of St. Paul's, had written a letter against Sturgeon. At about the same time Smith reported that he felt the churches could and should support Sturgeon themselves. See John Ross to SPG, July 2, 1762 and William Sturgeon to SPG, Nov. 20, 1763, SPG Letters, B21, no. 219 and no. 281 and Vestry Minutes, March 30 and April 27, 1763.

13. William Sturgeon to John Waring, Aug. 3, 1769, in Van Horne, *Religious Philanthropy and Colonial Slavery*, 287. For Smith's role see William Smith to SPG, Sept. 21, 1766 and May 6, 1768, SPG Letters, B21, no. 254 and no. 259.

14. Nash, *Urban Crucible*, 313, 326, 246–52, 254–55. For an excellent discussion of Philadelphia merchants see Thomas M. Doerflinger, *A Vigorous Spirit of Enterprise* (Chapel Hill: University of North Carolina Press, 1986).

15. For a discussion of poverty in Philadelphia see Nash, *The Urban Crucible*, 325–30. For the Society of the Sons of St. George see Bridenbaugh and Bridenbaugh, *Rebels and Gentlemen*, 239.

16. Oscar G. T. Sonneck, *Francis Hopkinson . . . and James Lyon* (New York: DaCapa Press, 1967), 27–29.

17. Sonneck, *Francis Hopkinson*, 331–39; see also Brooke Hindle, *The Pursuit of Science in Revolutionary America, 1735–1789* (Chapel Hill: University of North Carolina Press, 1956); Whitfield J. Bell, Jr., *John Morgan: Continental Doctor* (Philadelphia: University of Pennsylvania Press, 1965); Bridenbaugh and Bridenbaugh, *Rebels and Gentlemen*, 281–91. Benjamin Rush did not join Christ Church until 1787.

18. For a thorough discussion of the drive for royal government see James Hutson, *Pennsylvania Politics*.

19. *An Address of Thanks to the Wardens of Christ Church and St. Peter's and the Rev. W—S—h, D.D. . . . Provost of the College and Tool to the P—r and Jacob Duché AM & MVD from F—A—n DD and Jn E—g in their own Name and in the Name of all the Presbyterian Ministers in Pennsylvania* (Philadelphia: Anthony Armbrustor, October 26, 1764).

20. Richard Peters to Secretary of SPG, Dec. 12, 1766, SPG Letters, B21, no. 129.

21. See, for example, William Smith to Secretary of SPG, Sept. 21, 1766, no. 254; Oct. 22, 1768, Feb. 22, 1769, Aug. 10, 1769, and Jan. 14, 1771, SPG Letters, B21, nos. 254, 261, 262, 264, and 268.

22. Christ Church had tried to obtain a charter in 1721 and in 1749, but John and Thomas Penn did not want to favor one church by granting it a charter. See Vestry Minutes, July 31, 1721 and April 21, 1749. For information on the charter see Minutes, April 20 and 27, 1767.

23. This discussion is taken from Bruce Gill, "Christ Church," 130–31.

24. For Adams's quote see Bridenbaugh and Bridenbaugh, *Rebels and Gentlemen*, 148. For a discussion of the organ and Hopkinson's book see Satcher, "Music of the Episcopal Church," 382–88. A copy of Hopkinson's Psalmbook is in the Christ Church Archives.

25. Vestry Minutes, June 15, 1767.

26. Vestry Minutes, May 20, June 4, Aug. 24, Nov. 22 and Dec. 14, 1771; Jan. 8 and 10 and Nov. 16, 1772.

27. Jacob Duché to Richard Peters, Oct. 18, 1768, Peters Papers, 6: 65; William Smith to Richard Peters, Oct. 14, 1768, Peters Papers, 6: 64.

28. Thomas Coombe to William Smith, Aug. 1, 1770, Hawks Papers, Smith Manscripts, PEC, no. 27, Thomas Coombe, Jr. to Thomas Coombe Sr., Oct 1, 1771, Coombe Family Papers,

folder 21. Coombe referred to his admiration for Samuel Clarke, who was the father of modern Arianism. Joseph Hutchins to William Smith, June 19, 1771, Hawks Papers, Smith Manuscripts, PEC, no. 52. For other positive comments on Coombe's sermons, see "Diary of Josiah Quincy, Jr.," April 24, 1774, quoted in *Inscription in St. Peter's Church Yard*, comp. William W. Bronson (Camden, N.J., 1879).

29. Jacob Duché to Richard Peters, Oct. 18, 1768, Peters papers, 6: 65; John Porter to Richard Peters, Dec. 30, 1769, Peters Papers, 6: 99.

30. Coombe believed that neither Peters nor Duché wanted him for the position. See Thomas Coombe, Jr. to Thomas Coombe Sr., Aug. 7, 1771 and Jan. 5, 1770, Coombe Family Papers, folders 21 and 19.

31. William Manross, *A History of the American Episcopal Church* (New York: Morehouse Press, 1935), 118; Temple, *Common Sense Theology of Bishop White*, 9.

32. James Taylor, "Memoir of Bishop White," ed. John D. Kilbourne, *PMHB* 92 (1968): 50.

33. Vestry Minutes, June 19, July 3, and Nov. 16, 23, and 30, 1772.

34. Vestry Minutes, Feb. 28 and April 4, 1774.

35. Taylor, "Memoir of Bishop White," 58–59. For evidence of White's fondness for Peters, see, for example, William White to Richard Peters, Nov. 30, 1770, Walter Herbert Stowe, ed., *Life and Letters of Bishop William White* (New York: Morehouse Press, 1937), 250–51. For White's relationship with Duché see "Autobiography of William White," 406–7. For his friendship with Coombe see, for example, Thomas Coombe to William White, Nov. 29, 1777, in William S. Perry, "Life of William White," typescript, Rare Book Room, University of Pennsylvania, chap. 3, part 2, pp. 14–15. For his comment on Smith see White, "Autobiography of William White," 387.

36. Smith did report Peters's "irregular" sermons to the bishop and Peters chastised Smith for caring too much for worldly matters, but they remained friends. See Richard Peters to William Smith, Jan. 17, 1765, Smith Manuscripts, HSP, vol. 2, no. 165.

37. Thomas Coombe, Jr. to Coombe, Sr., May 1, 1771, Coombe Family Papers, folder 20. For his negative opinions see Thomas Coombe, Jr. to Thomas Coombe, Sr., Dec. 6, 1769, Coombe Family Papers, folder 17.

38. While there were certainly fewer and less intense controversies in the eighteenth-century English church than in the seventeenth, the high church/low church battles still surfaced regularly, and evangelicals and Methodists caused serious divisions within the church. See Charles J. Abbey and John H. Overton, *The English Church in the Eighteenth Century*. 2 vols. (London: Longman and Green, 1878), esp. vol. 2, chap. 1–4; Elliott-Binns, *The Early Evangelicals*, chap. 19.

39. Vestry Minutes, Dec. 6, 1746.

40. See, for example, Joseph Hutchins to William Smith, June 19, 1771, Hawks Papers, Smith Manuscripts, PEC, no. 42; "Diary of Josiah Quincy, Jr.," April 24, 1774, quoted in *Inscriptions in St. Peter's Church-Yard*; "Social Life in Philadelphia in 1782, Extracts from the Journal of James Alexander, June, 1762," *PMHB* 10 (1886): 335–36. Despite their differing theologies, John Adams indicated that Coombe was a "copy of Duché"; see John Adams, *Diary and Autobiography of John Adams*, ed. L. H. Butterfield, 2 vols. (Cambridge, Mass: Harvard University Press, 1962), 2: 149.

41. Stringer's background is found in Bishop of London to Richard Peters, Nov. 25, 1768, Smith Manuscripts, PEC, 3: 71–72; Richard Peters to Bishop of London, Dec. 6, 1769, Smith Manuscripts, PEC, 3: 73, Perry, *Historical Collections*, 2: 443–45. For their change of attitude

see Richard Peters, William Smith, Jacob Duché and Thomas Coombe to Bishop, Dec. 5, 1772, Fulham Papers, 8: 50–51.

42. "Autobiography of William White," 388–89. For Coombe's comments see Thomas Coombe to William Smith, Aug. 1, 1770, Hawks Papers, Smith Manuscripts, PEC; Hugh Neill to Secretary of SPG, Oct. 17, 1763, B21, no. 119, Perry, *Historical Collections*, 2: 354–55. For Smith's attitudes see William Smith to Secretary of SPG, May 8, 1765, B21, no. 251, Perry, *Historical Collections*, 2: 381. The meetings were also discussed in *The Journals of Henry Muhlenberg*, 3 vols., trans. Theodore Tappert and John W. Doberstein (Philadelphia: Lutheran History Society, 1947–1948), 1: 652, 654, 702, 709, 718; 2: 2–4, 15, 37, 50.

43. Richard Peters to Archbishop, n.d., Perry, *Historical Collections*, 2: 392–93. The Archbishop's letter is referred to in Hugh Neill to Secretary, Oct. 18, 1764, B21, no. 121, Perry, *Historical Collections*, 2: 381. References to his preaching in St. Peter's can be found in an anonymous record of revivals in the Christ Church Archives. Coombe refers to his preaching in the United Churches; Thomas Coombe to William Smith, Aug. 1, 1770, Hawks Papers, Smith Manuscripts, PEC, no. 27.

44. For a discussion of the differences between Methodists and evangelicals see Elliot-Binns, *The Early Evangelicals*, chap. 12. For a discussion of the early Methodist movement in Philadelphia see Doris Elizabeth Andrews, "Popular Religion and the Revolution in the Mid Atlantic Ports: The Rise of the Methodists 1770–1800" (Ph.D. diss., University of Pennsylvania, 1986); J. Manning Potts and Arthur Bruce Moss, "Methodism in Colonial America" in *The History of American Methodism*, ed. Emory S. Bucke (New York and Nashville: Abington Press, 1964), 1: 79–80, 82–86.

45. The evidence here is ambiguous. Pilmore speaks highly of Duché, referring to him as "a precious Child of God, and a Spiritual Minister of Jesus." See *The Journal of Joseph Pilmore*, ed. Frederick E. Maser and Howard T. Maag (Philadelphia: Message Publishing Company for the Historical Society of the Philadelphia Annual Conference of the United Methodist Church, 1969), March 17, 1771. And while Pilmore never mentions Peters, in 1770 the bishop of London chastised him for "paying too much attention to new and irregular Preachers." See Daniel Burton (Secretary of the SPG) to William Smith, Aug. 17, 1770, Hawks Papers, Smith Manuscripts, PEC no. 10.

CHAPTER SIX

INTERDENOMINATIONAL RELATIONS

While the leaders of the United Churches focused most of their attention on the internal needs of the congregation during the colonial period, they could not ignore the other religious groups that existed in Philadelphia. By the 1740s the "Quaker city" had become the most religiously heterogeneous city in the British empire. Quakers and Anglicans were joined by large numbers of German Lutherans and German Reformed, Scots-Irish Presbyterians, as well as Catholics, Baptists, and a variety of German sects. As a result, Anglicans in the later colonial period had to adjust to the kind of religious climate that would become commonplace in nineteenth-century America, a climate in which no group could claim dominance. Precisely because the situation in Philadelphia was a harbinger of things to come throughout America, it is important to understand how Anglicans dealt with the existence of so many other denominations.[1]

The religious composition of the city in 1770 differed greatly from what it had been in the first half of the eighteenth century. Quakers now represented only around 13 percent of the population, while German Lutherans, Reformed, and Moravians constituted almost 25 percent, Presbyterian congregations accounted for around 12 percent and Anglican churches served 18 percent of the population.[2]

Although it is impossible to examine how the Anglican laity felt about their fellow citizens of other denominations, it is clear that the Anglican clergy sought to avoid confrontation and conflict whenever possible. Anglican leaders accepted the right of other denominations to exist in the city and neither expected nor worked for the Church of England to be established in Pennsylvania. However, because they still hoped that their denomination would become the largest and most powerful religious group in the city, they never exemplified a modern ecumenical spirit.

Relations between Anglicans and Quakers continued to improve throughout the colonial period. Quakers ceased to be a religious threat when they lost their missionary zeal and turned inward, actually disowning more members than they accepted. Indeed, many of these disaffected Quakers joined the United Churches; at least six of the men who served on the vestry in the 1750s and 1760s came from Quaker families.[3] Yet the end of confrontation between Anglicans and Quakers did not lead to any real cooperation between the two groups. While individual Anglicans and Quakers might cooperate in politics or in charitable ventures, the two groups went their own separate ways most of the time.

Christ Church leaders in the 1740s and 1750s had several precedents to guide them in their dealings with the Lutherans. Relations with the Swedish Lutheran congregations that had been founded in Pennsylvania before the first Anglican congregation was organized had been cordial from the beginning. Swedish ministers regularly attended meetings of Anglican clergy, and Swedish bishops were made members of the SPG. One of the original Swedish missionaries, Erick Bjork, summarized the relationship well: "We have always been counseled and instructed from Sweden to maintain friendship and unity with the English, so that we and the English Church shall not reckon each other as dissenters like the Presbyterians, Anabaptists, Quakers, &c., but as Sister Churches."[4]

Pennsylvania Anglicans had had far less contact with German Lutherans prior to the 1750s, but there was a tradition of cooperation between the state churches in England and Germany. Efforts to unite the two churches had begun under Queen Anne, whose husband was a Danish Lutheran, and were renewed, unsuccessfully, with the succession of a German, George III, to the throne of England.[5]

William Smith and Richard Peters hoped that they could succeed in

Pennsylvania where English leaders had failed by uniting Anglicans and Lutherans. In the 1750s they attempted to use the German Society, an organization originally designed as a nonsectarian effort to provide educational and religious services for Pennsylvania Germans, to further the cause of the Church of England. Smith, in a letter to the archbishop of Canterbury, asserted that the German Society was "but one part of the same noble scheme in which the venerable Society [the SPG] are engaged." He went on to make the surprising claim that he could offer a scheme for uniting the Anglicans and the Germans "which I am sure would easily take effect," but that this was not the time for such a move.[6] While the German Society failed to achieve any of Smith's goals, in 1766 Smith once again appeared optimistic about a union. He informed the bishop of London that there was an "extremely good disposition among the Lutheran clergy to be united to our Church." By 1768 Peters also believed that union was near. He reported that Charles Wrangel, the Swedish Lutheran commissary in Pennsylvania, was "zealously desirous to promote a stable Union between the Church and the Swedish and Lutheran Congregations here." Having given up on the German Society, Smith and Peters now suggested that this union could be accomplished by establishing a professorship of divinity at the College of Philadelphia "wherein German and English youths might be educated" in both languages so they could serve in places where "there is a mixture of both Nations." This, they felt, "would conciliate us all and make us live and love as one Nation." This proposal was endorsed by the bishop but never implemented.[7]

German Lutherans ignored the Anglican overtures. While Lutheran ministers maintained friendly relations with the Anglicans, even inviting them to Lutheran ministerial meetings, they never considered union. Henry Muhlenberg, the unofficial head of the German Lutheran church, found the Anglican church to be dead to the spirit of Christ, with the ministers too concerned about "the empty shell or cicatrix of ordination in apostolic succession."[8]

Relations between the Anglican and Presbyterian clergy were considerably more ambivalent than those between Anglican and Lutheran ministers. Christ Church leaders never considered the Presbyterian Church to be a "sister church" and never had any hopes of uniting with that denomination; the most they could hope for was individual converts. Their relationship with Presbyterians was further complicated by the schism in the Presbyterian church in 1741 between the New Side—the group that supported the personal religion and revivalism of the Great Awakening—and the Old Side—the group that stressed doctrinal orthodoxy and rejected the techniques of the revivalists. Yet, despite their less-than-positive opinion of Presbyterians, Anglican ministers agreed that conflict should be avoided if possible.

Anglicans generally avoided conflict with New Side Presbyterians merely by lack of contact. While the New Side Presbyterians had such energy and attracted so many converts that they were indeed a potential threat to the Anglicans, Christ Church leaders never openly attacked them. Anglicans instead concentrated their energies on providing refuge for those disillusioned with the revivalists.

Anglicans had far more contact with Old Side Presbyterians and consequently had far more potential for conflict. Many of the Old Side Presbyterian ministers felt they had more in common with Anglicans than they did with their revivalist brethren. This common bond, combined with the generally weak state of the Old Side Presbyterians, led them to cooperate with the Anglicans during the 1740s and 1750s. However, this cooperation was always one of convenience, based on mutual advantage rather than genuine regard. When either side sensed that it had less to gain from the cooperation than the other side did, conflict occurred.

The history of the College of Philadelphia exemplifies the relations between Anglicans and Old Side Presbyterians during the 1750s and 1760s, as it also reveals Anglican attitudes toward interdenominational cooperation in general. The Academy of Philadelphia, founded in 1749 and expanded to a college in 1755, was the brainchild of Benjamin Franklin. Often cited for its educational innovation, its approach to religion was just as novel. Unlike all the other colleges and universities in England and in the colonies that were controlled by one denomination, the College of Philadelphia was to be nondenominational. The trustees and teachers were to be drawn from all religions and no creed was taught to the students. Religion was not entirely ignored, but only those tenets on which all could agree were taught. Students were required to attend worship on Sundays, but could go to any church they desired.[9]

Despite this nondenominational approach, Philadelphia Anglicans strongly supported the Academy. Eighteen of the first twenty-four trustees were Anglicans, nine of them serving on the vestry of Christ Church.[10] This situation contrasted sharply with that in New York City. There, Anglicans and Presbyterians battled bitterly over control of King's College. Believing their church to be rightfully established in the city, and conceiving of education only in sectarian terms, New York Anglican leaders fought for and won control of the only college in the province. Such sectarian sentiment was not unknown in Philadelphia. Robert Jenney objected to the Academy both because, as Smith put it, "it was not made a Church Establishment & all the Masters to be of that Persuasion," and because Peters had such an important part in it.[11] But the number of Anglicans on the board of trustees indicated that Jenney was in the minority. Most of the leadership of Christ Church had come to accept interdenominational cooperation as a good thing.

Perhaps it was this acceptance of cooperation that led Franklin to choose Anglicans to take a leading role in the Academy. As one of his biographers has indicated, Franklin "identified liberal, sophisticated and intellectual Christianity" with Anglicanism, and thus felt that the goals of his College could best be achieved by Anglicans. Franklin considered only Anglicans to head the school. When Richard Peters, his first choice, refused to serve, Franklin temporarily gave up his scheme since he knew of no one else "suitable for such a trust." When the Academy eventually opened, it was headed by David Martin, a less well known Anglican, and had Peters as the president of the board of trustees. When Martin died in 1753, the trustees chose the young Anglican cleric, William Smith, to head the school.[12]

William Smith shared Franklin's belief that only Anglicans could be counted on to provide a liberal, nonsectarian education. In 1763, writing to Peters, he reaffirmed his desire that the foundation of the College "should be wide and Catholic." But he reminded his friend that the Presbyterians, if they gained a majority, "would not wish the same in return."[13] To someone who believed that the Church of England was the most liberal and the most nearly perfect religion in the colonies, a "catholic plan" for a college meant that while all religious persuasions could be represented among the trustees, the faculty and the students, and no sectarian doctrine would be taught in the classroom, the Church of England would have a controlling voice.

These two conflicting themes—that the College should be nonsectarian but that the Church of England should have the greatest influence—were apparent throughout the history of the College in the colonial period. In 1763 Smith wrote to Peters: "Our Catholic Plan let us ever adhere to. It is our Glory, let Bigots think as they will." Yet in the previous year he had asserted in a letter to the archbishop that, because the charter chose an Anglican clergyman as provost, it led the way "by a sort of Prescription to all future appointments of a chief Master." He concluded that "on the whole, the Church is on as good a Footing in this Seminary even as at New York."[14]

The trustees also attempted to keep the school nonsectarian while maintaining a strong Anglican influence. In 1765 the board adopted a "fundamental resolve" to do its "utmost to ensure that the excellent plan" of the institution would not be narrowed, and that neither the Church of England nor dissenter, they stated it this way: "At the same time that we shew all due this sounds liberal, one should note that at the time twenty-one of the twenty-four trustees and the provost were Anglicans! Moreover, at the same time that the trustees made this pledge, they assured the archbishop that they would hold themselves "inexcusable" if they allowed the "interest of the Church" to deteriorate. In a letter to Samuel Chandler, a leading English *dissenter*, they stated it this way: "At the same time that we shew all due Regard to our national Church, we shall never violate our Faith pledged to other religious Denominations."[15]

The Presbyterians had their own designs for the College. When Francis Alison, an Old Side minister, agreed to head the Latin School in 1752, the synod decided that his taking the position had "a very probable tendency, not only to promote the good of the public, but also of the church," since it was the only institution available for educating Old Side ministers.[16]

The College of Philadelphia was not nonsectarian in the modern sense of the word and the potential for problems was present from the beginning. Yet relations between Anglicans and Presbyterians were amazingly peaceful for the first decade of the College's history. As long as the Old Side Presbyterians needed the College, they accepted Anglican domination.

The unification of the Old and New Side Presbyterians in 1758 changed the situation. Old Side Presbyterians no longer needed the alliance with the Anglicans and began to see it as detrimental; New Side Presbyterians, who were numerically superior within Philadelphia, actually rejected candidates for the ministry because they had been educated at the College. While this infuriated Alison and his Old Side colleagues, it also contributed to a growing realization that the College was not a suitable training ground for Presbyterian ministers. Moreover, their struggles to avoid domination by New Side ministers made the Old Side people associated with the Academy far less willing to accept domination by Anglicans.[17]

Thus, beginning in 1761 a series of conflicts occurred at the College that eventually ended the alliance between Anglicans and Presbyterians. These conflicts began innocuously enough. In 1761, Alison convinced the trustees to change the tradition of using the Book of Common Prayer for the morning and evening prayers at the College. The new rules stated that the prayer was to be "either agreeable to a form, or otherwise as the Person officiating may choose." A year later the Presbyterians moved on to a new grievance. When Peters rather routinely informed Alison that he intended to read the prayers at Commencement, as had been custom, Alison responded "in a great passion that he would not go unto the Commencement" if that were to be the case and William Allen, a Presbyterian trustee and friend of Peters, accused Peters of attempting to "introduce the Liturgy into the Commencement." We do not know the immediate outcome of this dispute, but by 1765 a compromise had been reached; some Anglican prayers were used, but the service ended with prayers by Alison.[18]

This Presbyterian assertiveness led some Anglicans to believe that *they* were being dominated. In 1763 Hugh Neill, the missionary at Trinity Church, Oxford, complained that the College was "dwindling away . . . into a mere Presbyterian Faction." He asserted that "members of our Church are ill treated in the College and not chosen into offices tho' better qualified than others" and that Presbyterians were intent on destroying Smith's influence, since he was the only Anglican teacher. While Smith refuted most of Neill's accusations, he did comment to Peters that "we may have Reason to suspect a Design to draw us from our Plan the other way," that is, in favor of the Presbyterians, something that "must not be suffered."[19]

In 1766 an event occurred that effectively ended Presbyterian cooperation at the College: three Presbyterian graduates of the College sailed for England to take Anglican orders and become S P G missionaries. Alison bitterly complained that the College had "artfully got into the hands of Episcopal Trustees" and as a result "Young men educated here get a taste for high life & many of them do not like to bear the poverty & dependence of our ministers." Rather than attempting to gain more influence in the college, Alison and William Allen took a more extreme step; they applied for and received a charter turning the Presbyterian Academy, a school in NewArk, Delaware that Alison ran, into a College. From this time on Alison spent more and more time at NewArk. John Ewing, the other Presbyterian professor at the College, actually went to England to raise money for the Delaware school.[20] Both Ewing and Alison continued their positions at the College of Philadelphia, but their hearts were with the school at NewArk.

Thus the most successful interdenominational cooperation of the colonial period came to an end. While the alienation of the Presbyterians eventually caused the college and the Anglicans problems during the Revolution, that should not overshadow the originality and foresight that went into the planning and operating of the college during its first fifteen years. It was an accomplishment of which Philadelphia Anglicans deserved to be proud.

* * *

At about the same time that Presbyterians and Anglicans were becoming disenchanted with their cooperative effort at the College, the renewed efforts of some northern colonial Anglicans to obtain a resident bishop further strained relations between the two denominations in Pennsylvania. Anglicans had lobbied for an American bishop throughout the colonial period, but in the 1760s Anglican clergymen in New York, New Jersey, Connecticut, and Massachusetts decided to intensify their efforts. Having converted to the Church of England primarily because of a deep-seated belief in the necessity of apostolic succession, they believed the episcopal form of government to be divinely ordained, not just the best form available. In the 1760s they began a campaign to force the English government to put politics aside and grant them the necessary bishop.[21]

These demands for a bishop proved to be extremely ill timed, arriving in England at the height of the Stamp Act controversy. But the bishop of London's response that their address "was unseasonable and from peculiar Circumstances of the Times, tended to *throw difficulties in the way of Government*," only further convinced these clergymen that *their* efforts *alone* would bring a bishop to America. In their response they apologized for their bad timing, but suggested that since the crisis had now ended they saw no reason not to renew their request.[22]

At the same time the northern clergy wrote to the archbishop, the Convention of Clergymen in New York, New Jersey, and Connecticut decided to launch a public crusade to quiet the fears of dissenters. The result, Thomas Bradbury Chandler's tract, *An Appeal to the Public in Behalf of the Church of England in America*, published in 1767, had exactly the opposite effect. Chandler offered a traditional and reasoned defense of the episcopal form of government and explained how essential the exclusive powers of the bishop— ordination, confirmation, and church government—were to the welfare of the church and what hardships were caused by the absence of a bishop in America. But he ran into trouble when he tried to answer the objections of dissenters. Unable to treat these objections as anything more than bigotry, he argued that "every Opposition to such a Plan, has the Nature of Persecution, and deserves the Name," and that anyone who would oppose such a plan "if armed with power . . . would bring us, if they could, to the Stake, or the

Gibbet." Not surprisingly, the *Appeal* actually galvanized opposition more than it enlisted support.[23]

Although historians often have argued that the Pennsylvania clergy opposed the introduction of a bishop into the colonies, such was not the case.[24] Instead, all evidence indicates the clergy openly supported an American bishop, but opposed the specific campaign of Chandler and his colleagues. The Philadelphia clergy communicated to their English superiors their desire for a bishop often during the late colonial period. In 1762 Smith wrote to Archbishop Drummond urging that bishops be sent. He argued, as had others, that if the burden of having to cross the ocean for ordination were not soon removed, the "comparative number of Church People" would gradually diminish, leaving them "in a manner to be at length wholly swallowed up among the numerous surrounding Sects who severally flourish in the full enjoyment of their Religious Rights." Smith also argued that allowing "the Church to continue in her present languishing condition," could lead the colonists to think about independence, since "it is well known that . . . the Church is one of the firmest Props of Monarchy, and the English Constitution, while the various Denominations of Independents, Quakers and other Sectaries, are more Republican in their principles."[25]

Under the leadership of Smith, the Anglican clergy of Pennsylvania as a group petitioned their superiors to send bishops to America on several occasions. In a letter sent to Archbishop Secker in 1760, congratulating him on his ascension to the see of Canterbury, the clergy, including Smith, Jenney, Sturgeon, and Duché, bemoaned the terrible condition of the church in America and suggested that his "Grace's Primacy in the Church Militant may be rendered eminently glorious by introducing the Episcopal Character into America." Clergymen also expressed their support individually. Sturgeon had argued for a bishop as early as 1758, and while Peters expressed his views to the archbishop in person and thus left no record, one of the leaders of the bishopric crusade indicated that Peters was "well affected to the cause of episcopacy."[26]

While the clergymen associated with Christ Church supported the idea of a resident bishop, they lacked the fanatical zeal of their northern brethren, and, as a result, they opposed the methods, intensity, and timing of the episcopate campaign of the 1760s. Basic to the differing approaches of the Philadelphia clergy and the northern group were their differing views of the episcopate and the church in general. While Peters and Smith felt that a bishop was necessary for the smooth functioning of the church, neither believed that the episcopal form of government was divinely ordained. More-over, Philadelphia Anglican clergymen had come to view the Church of England as the best but not the only legitimate religion. As Peters put it, he considered the "doctrines and disciplines" of the church neither "perfect, nor established on the despotick Principle of crushing all other Churches & maltreating their Members. 'Tis indeed a good natured Church & were it not so it would not retain the Ardency of my Affections."[27]

Because the Philadelphia clergy did not believe a bishop was required for a true church, they were able to see the problems in the approach taken by Chandler and his colleagues. Since both Smith and Peters kept in close contact with English officials and were politically savvy, they knew that further petitions were useless, if not detrimental to the cause.[28] And having spent years trying to avoid confrontations with dissenters, they wanted to avoid a public debate that would further alienate the Presbyterians.

The condition of the governing structures in the church in Philadelphia and in Pennsylvania in general also influenced the views of Smith and Peters. The peaceful situation of the United Churches after 1760 reduced the need for a bishop. Moreover, Smith's efforts to consolidate his power over the clergy in the area could only be hurt by the appointment of a bishop. While the provost coveted the prelacy for himself, he knew that his chances of appointment were slim.[29] As an alternative to a bishop, in 1762 Smith had proposed that three people be appointed to serve as both Commissary to the bishop of London and agent for the SPG. Smith openly suggested that he be appointed to this position for Pennsylvania and New Jersey. The rejection of this plan by the New Jersey clergy and their subsequent affiliation with the New York convention did not incline Smith to champion their cause.[30]

While the Philadelphia clergy did not approve of Chandler's approach, once the controversy associated with the publication of the *Appeal* began, they had no choice but to enter the fray. The Presbyterians, already feeling dominated by the Anglicans at the College of Philadelphia, reacted strongly to news of the clergy's crusade for a bishop. The issues of Anglican influence at the College and the call for an episcopate reinforced and fed on each other, increasing the intensity of each dispute and effectively ending the spirit of cooperation that had existed, at least on the surface, between Anglicans and Presbyterians.

Presbyterian leaders quickly answered Chandler's arguments. In March 1768 the *Pennsylvania Journal* published articles written primarily by Francis Alison with the aid of John Dickinson, a political ally of the Presbyterians. These articles were a passionate, vituperative attack on the entire Church of

England and a calculated effort to link the episcopate scheme and thus the Anglicans to the general attack on American liberties that the authors felt was in progress. It was as if the Presbyterian leaders felt relieved of a tremendous burden imposed on them by their cooperation with the Anglicans and were attempting to make up for, even perhaps atone for, those years of peace.[31]

The articles contained the usual arguments against bishops, stressing that there was no guarantee that they would be given only limited powers, and the standard assertions that the early church did not have bishops and that apostolic succession was not necessary for a valid ordination.[32] The Presbyterians also engaged in a wholesale attack on the idea of an established religion and on the Church of England in particular. They accused the church of persecution, of corrupting and obscuring the "pure word of God" by "human inventions" (the episcopate among them), and of allowing sinners to buy pardons. Moreover, Dickinson argued, Anglicans were "attached to slavery and despotism," and thus only dissenters could guard American liberty.[33]

No matter what their personal feelings about Chandler, the Anglican clergy had to answer these attacks as a matter of pride. Smith reported to the bishop in May of 1768 that although he "could have wished our side had not given any cause yet they must not be left unsupported, and I am determined now to contribute my mite for great openings are given to detect their shameful misrepresentations." Smith's mite appeared in the newspapers in September and he and other unknown Anglicans continued their defense through January 1769. These writers defended the church against the full range of Presbyterian attacks. Denying a link between the bishopric issue and the Stamp Act, Smith assured his readers that Anglicans would join with men of all denominations in defending colonial liberties whenever they were in danger. He argued more effectively than Chandler that the Presbyterians raised false fears about the episcopate since tithes, simony and ecclesiastical courts with powers over non-Anglicans were impossible in America without a total abrogation of the colonial charters. And he spent four articles refuting the most serious charge, that the church had "corrupted and obscured the pure word of God with human inventions."[34]

Smith did more than defend the church; he went on the attack, arguing that Presbyterians wanted to take over the country and that they were, in fact, the persecutors. Dredging up well-known episodes from New England history, he and his colleagues argued that in order to have America to themselves, the dissenters went to great lengths to keep all Anglican influence out, to keep the people ignorant of the true character of the Church of

England, and to convince them that it was the Anglican church that was evil and persecuting.[35] They therefore opposed an American episcopate because it would allow the church to grow faster.

Although the newspaper exchanges between Philadelphia Anglicans and Presbyterians were fierce and destroyed earlier attempts at cooperation, there were important differences between the conflict in Pennsylvania and a similar newspaper battle in New York. Participants in the Pennsylvania dispute seemed to regret the controversy.[36] The Presbyterian "Centinel" made a clear distinction between Pennsylvania Anglicans and their northern brethren, asserting that only one or two clergy of that province had been consulted by Chandler and arguing that they were "Men of too much Understanding to complain without Reason, and too well acquainted with the Charter and Laws of the Province not to know that they enjoy the same Liberty as any other religious Denomination." Similarly, Smith ended his series with a challenge to Presbyterians, asking "whether union among ourselves in America, or the common cause of protestantism are likely to be promoted by vilifying and traducing a Church, which I will still say, is the main bulwark of the reformation."[37] New York Anglicans would never have considered such cooperation with a church they did not consider legitimate.

Differences between the two colonies can also be seen in the termination of the newspaper battles. Even though Presbyterians had concluded their series in July of 1768, they published only four rebuttals during the four months that Anglicans ran their essays. This lack of an antagonist caused "the Anatomist" to end his series earlier than planned. Both sides blamed the early ending on the need for unity in the face of the Townshend Acts.[38] But imperial questions did not keep the Presbyterians and Anglicans in New York from continuing their intense battles until April 1769. In that colony, where Anglicans openly aimed at total domination of the Calvinists and where the episcopate issue was close to the heart of the clergy, local religious and political considerations were far more important than imperial debates. In Pennsylvania, the Presbyterians knew that Anglicans accepted the legitimacy of other religions and therefore they felt safe concentrating their attention on attacks on their political liberties, confident that their religious liberties were secure.

* * *

The last two decades of the colonial period in Philadelphia did not witness a true ecumenical spirit in the City of Brotherly Love. However, compared with the battles Anglicans waged against Presbyterians in New York and New Jersey, against Congregationalists in New England, and against Baptists in Virginia, the clergy of the United Churches got along remarkably well with their brethren in other denominations. Without an established church to cause friction, and with a long history of heterogeneity, Philadelphia Anglicans, as well as Philadelphians of other denominations, were in an ideal position to set a model for interdenominational relations for the new nation in the nineteenth century.

NOTES

1. For a good discussion of the early diversity of religions in the Delaware Valley and how each one adapted to this new situation see Jon Butler, *Power, Authority, and the Origins of American Denominational Order: The English Churches in the Delaware Valley 1680–1730*, American Philosophical Society, *Transactions* 68 (1978).

2. Robert Gough, "Toward a Theory of Class and Social Conflict: A Social History of Wealthy Philadelphians, 1775 and 1800" (Ph.D. diss., University of Pennsylvania, 1977), 138. For information on the Germans see Theodore E. Schmauk, *A History of the Lutheran Church in Pennsylvania 1638–1800* (Lancaster, Pa.: New Era Press, 1902); J.H. Dubbs, *History of the Reformed Church in Pennsylvania* (Lancaster, Pa.: New Era Press, 1902). For information on the growth of Presbyterians, see Guy Klett, *Presbyterianism in Colonial Pennsylvania* (Philadelphia: University of Pennsylvania Press, 1937).

3. For information on disownments see Jack Marietta, *The Reformation of American Quakerism, 1748–1783* (Philadelphia: University of Pennsylvania Press, 1984), 55. Trying to determine conversion in Philadelphia is next to impossible because of the nature of the records and the problems with names. None of the converted Quakers who served on the vestry have a baptism recorded. Of the 120 Quakers disowned from the Philadelphia meeting from 1751 to 1760, the names of 23 appear as either having children baptized or holding a pew; however, there is no way of knowing if they are the same people or merely have the same name. Stephen Brobeck found that seven of the fifty-nine men in his 1750 non-Quaker elite had been raised as Quakers. Robert Gough found that seven of his forty-eight Anglican elite in 1775 had been Quakers. See Stephen Brobeck, "Changes in Composition and Structure of Philadelphia Elite Groups 1756–1790" (Ph.D. diss., University of Pennsylvania, 1972); Gough, "Toward a Theory of Class and Social Conflict," 189.

4. For a discussion of Swedish-Anglican relations see Nelson Rightmyer, "Swedish-English Relations in Northern Delaware," *Church History* 6 (1946): 101–15; or William A. Bultmann, "The Society for the Propagation of the Gospel in Foreign Parts and the Foreign Settler in the American Colonies" (Ph.D. diss., University of California at Los Angeles, 1951), chap. 1. The quote is from *The Records of Holy Trinity (Old Swedes Church), Wilmington, Delaware from 1697–1773*, trans. Horace Burr (Dover, Del.: 1890), 143.

5. Norman Sykes, "Ecumenical Movements in Great Britain in the Seventeenth and Eighteenth Centuries," in *A History of the Ecumenical Movement*, ed. Ruth Rouse and Stephen Neill (Philadelphia: Westminster Press, 1954), 152–67.

6. Archbishop Secker to William Smith, Feb. 1, 1755 and William Smith to Archbishop Secker, Nov. 1, 1756, Smith Manuscripts, PEC, 1: 10 and 20. For a brief account of the history of the German Society—officially referred to as the Society for Propagating Christian Knowledge among the Germans Settled in Pennsylvania—see *The Papers of Benjamin Franklin*, 5: 203ff. Michael Schlatter, a leading Reform minister, originally conceived the idea.

7. William Smith to Bishop of London, Dec. 18, 1766, Fulham Papers, 8: 31–33, Perry, *Historical Collections*, 2: 411–13. Richard Peters to Bishop Terrick, Aug. 30, 1768, Fulham Papers, 8: 36–39, Perry, *Historical Collections*, 2: 432–33; Bishop of London to Richard Peters, Nov. 25, 1768, Smith Manuscripts, PEC, 3: 72.

8. *The Journals of Henry Melchior Muhlenberg*, 1: 456, 480, 684; 2: 372.

9. "Proposals Relating to the Education of Youth in Pennsylvania," in *Benjamin Franklin and the University of Pennsylvania*, ed. Francis N. Thorpe (Washington, D.C.: U.S. Government Printing Office, 1893), 61. For a good account of the founding of the Academy, see Cheyney, *History of the University of Pennsylvania*, 17–54.

10. For biographical sketches of the trustees see Thomas Montgomery, *A History of the University of Pennsylvania from its Foundation to A.D. 1770* (Philadelphia: George W. Jacobs, 1900), 53–108.

11. For a discussion of the King's College controversy see Bridenbaugh, *Mitre and Sceptre*, 144ff.; Ellis, *The New England Mind in Transition*, 174–96. For Jenney's attitude see William Smith to SPG, Nov. 1, 1756, in Horace Smith, *Life of William Smith*, 1: 143; Robert Jenney to Secretary of the SPG, June 20, 1751, SPG Letters, B10, 103–4.

12. Melvin Buxbaum, *Benjamin Franklin and the Zealous Presbyterians* (University Park, Pa: Pennsylvania State University Press, 1975), 156; Benjamin Franklin, *Autobiography*, ed. Max Farrand (Berkeley and Los Angeles: University of California Press, 1949), 134. Little is known about David Martin. He had served as sheriff of Hunterdon County, New Jersey and Peters described him as "a perfect good Scholar and a man of good Temper." See William L. Turner, "The College, Academy and Charitable School of Philadelphia . . ." (Ph.D. diss., University of Pennsylvania, 1952), 257. Smith had captured Franklin's attention by a book he had written. *A General Idea of the College of Mirania* described a nonsectarian college very similar to the College of Philadelphia. See *The Works of William Smith, D.D., Late Provost of the College and Academy of Phialdelphia*, 2 vols. (Philadephia: H. Maxwell, 1803), 2: 225–26.

13. William Smith to Richard Peters, March 2, 1763, Smith Papers, HSP, vol. 2, no. 120.

14. William Smith to Richard Peters, June 17, 1763, Smith Papers, HSP, vol. 2, no. 141; William Smith to Archbishop of Canterbury, April 17, 1762, Perry, *Historical Collections*, 2: 570–71.

15. Trustees of the University of Pennsylvania, Minutes, University Archives, June 14, 1765, pp. 262–63; Trustees to Archbishop of Canterbury (written by Richard Peters), June 24, 1764, pp. 265–66; Trustees to Samuel Chandler, June 14, 1764, 266–67.

16. *Records of the Presbyterian Church in the United States of America . . . 1706–1775* (Philadelphia, 1904), 206.

17. For the problems between the Old and New Sides after the reunion see Leonard J. Trinterud, *The Forming of an American Tradition* (Philadelphia: Westminster Press, 1964), 152ff.

18. Trustees Minutes, March 10, 1761. Diary of Richard Peters, May 13, 14, 19, 1762, Peters Papers, HSP; Trustees Minutes, May 30, 1765, p. 295.

19. Neill's letter cannot be located. Its contents are summarized in Archbishop of Canterbury

to Jacob Duché, Sept. 17, 1763, Perry, *Historical Collections*, 2: 389–91. Isaac Hunt, a graduate of the College, expressed similar opinions in a pamphlet, written during the Paxton riots, *A Looking Glass . . . No. II*, in John Dunbar, *The Paxton Papers* (The Hague: Martinus Nijhoff, 1957), 310; William Smith to Richard Peters, Aug. 27, 1763, Smith Papers, HSP, vol. 2, no. 148.

20. Francis Alison to Ezra Stiles, April 15, 1764, *Extracts from the Itineraries and other Miscellanies of Ezra Stiles*, ed. Franklin Dexter (New Haven, Conn.: Yale University Press, 1915), 424–26. See Elizabeth Ingersoll, "Francis Alison, American Philosophe 1705–1799" (Ph.D. diss., University of Delaware, 1974), 493.

21. For a discussion of the New England clergy's attitude toward the episcopate see Joseph Ellis, *The New England Mind in Transition*. For good discussions of this second phase of the campaign for bishops see Bridenbaugh, *Mitre and Sceptre*, 171–340; Frederick V. Mills, Sr., *Bishops by Ballot: An Eighteenth Century Ecclesiastical Revolution* (New York: Oxford University Press, 1978), 35–71. For a useful review of the literature, see Frederick V. Mills, "The Colonial Anglican Episcopate: A Historiographical Review," *Anglican and Episcopal History* 61 (1992): 325–45.

22. The bishop's letter is quoted in Edgar Pennington, "Colonial Clergy Conventions," *HMPEC* 7 (1939): 201. The clergymen's response is summarized in Thomas Bradbury Chandler to Samuel Johnson, Jan. 19, 1767, in *Samuel Johnson, President of King's College, His Career and Writings*, 4 vols., ed. Herbert Schneider and Carol Schneider (New York: Columbia University Press, 1929), 1: 389–91.

23. "The Seabury Minutes of the New York Clergy Convention of 1766 and 1767," ed. Walter Stowe, *HMPEC* 10 (1941): 144–46; Thomas Bradbury Chandler, *An Appeal to the Public in Behalf of the Church of England in America* (New York, 1767), 39; Bridenbaugh, *Mitre and Sceptre*, esp. chap. 9; Mills, *Bishops by Ballot*, 35–53; Patricia Bonomi, *Under the Cope of Heaven, Religion, Society and Politics in Colonial America* (New York: Oxford University Press, 1986), 199–216.

24. Mills is the most recent historian to argue that Philadelphia clergy opposed a bishop; see *Bishops by Ballot*, 46–48. Mills does admit that Peters had supported a suffragan bishop, but believes that he changed his mind because of the opposition of the Penns to a resident bishop. While the Penns did oppose such a bishop, there is no evidence that this influenced either Smith or Peters unduly. In general, Mills's account of the church in Pennsylvania is incomplete.

25. William Smith, "State of the American Church presented to Archbishop Drummond, Bishop of London and others May, 1762," copy in Christ Church Archives.

26. "To the Most Reverend His Grace THOMAS, Lord Archbishop of Canterbury . . . The Humbler Address of the Missionaries and other Clergy of the Church of England residing in and near the Province of Pennsylvania, May 1760," Perry, *Historical Collections*, 2: 317–19. William Sturgeon to Bishop Sherlock, Nov. 29, 1758, Fulham Papers, Perry, *Historical Collections*, 2: 268; Samuel Auchmuty to Samuel Johnson, June 12, 1766, Schneider and Schneider, *Samuel Johnson* 1: 362–63.

27. Richard Peters to Thomas Penn, June 2, 1753, POC, 6: 63.

28. See Richard Peters to Bishop of London, Nov. 14, 1766, Perry, *Historical Collections*, 2: 409–10; William Smith to Bishop of London, n.d. (c. February, 1772), Smith Manuscripts, PEC, 1: 75; Richard Peters to Archbishop of Canterbury, Oct. 17, 1763, Perry, *Historical Collections*, 2: 391–95.

29. Smith reported to Peters in 1763 that the authorities wanted a "man or men of Years &

great Name." Moreover, several of the legacies for an American bishop specified that he had to be born in the archdiocese of Canterbury, which Smith was not. See William Smith to Richard Peters, April 24, 1763, Smith Papers, HSP, vol. 2, no. 122.

30. William Smith to Bishop of London, April, 1762, Perry, *Historical Collections*, 2: 571–72. The rejection of the plan by New Jersey clergy is discussed in Chandler's "Summary of Address of New Jersey Convention to the Bishop of London, Dec., 1766" in his letter to Samuel Johnson, Jan. 19, 1767, Schneider and Schneider, *Samuel Johnson* 1: 391ff.

31. The articles appeared under the names "The Centinel," "Remonstrat," and "The North Briton" in the *Pennsylvania Journal* from March 24, 1768 until July 28, 1768.

32. See "The Centinel," *Pennsylvania Journal*, no. 1, March 24, 1768; no. 2, May 19, 1768; no. 10, May 26, 1768; no. 12, June 19, 1768; no. 15, June 30, 1768; no. 18, July 21, 1768; no 19, July 28, 1768.

33. The quote is from "The Centinel," *Pennsylvania Journal*, no. 17, July 14, 1768; see also no. 4, April 14, 1768, no. 5, April 21, no. 6, April 28, no. 7, May 5, no. 8, May 12, no. 11, June 2, no. 16, July 7, no. 17, July 14; "The North Briton, no. 61, *Pennsylvania Journal*, Nov. 10, 1768. Richard Hooker, "John Dickinson on Church and State," *American Literature* 16 (1944): 82–98, argues that John Dickinson definitely wrote numbers 6, 7, and 8 and may have written number 16.

34. William Smith to Bishop of London, May 6, 1768, Perry, *Historical Collections*, 2: 429; *Pennsylvania Gazette*, "The Anatomist," no. 1, Sept. 8, 1768; no. 12, Nov. 24, 1768; no. 13, Dec. 1, 1768; no. 14, Dec. 8, 1768; no. 15, Dec. 15, 1768; no. 16, Dec. 22, 1768; no. 17, Dec. 29, 1768; no. 18, Jan. 5, 1769.

35. "The Anatomist," no. 3, *Pennsylvania Gazette*, Sept. 22.

36. Mills, *Bishops by Ballot*, 73–76, makes this point, but incorrectly relates it to the need for Presbyterians and Anglicans to join in supporting the proprietor. That political cooperation had already ended.

37. "The Centinel," no. 13, *Pennsylvania Journal*, June 15, 1768; "The Anatomist," no. 19, *Pennsylvania Gazette*, January 12, 1769.

38. For Alison's comments see Bridenbaugh, *Mitre and Sceptre*, 301. For Smith's comments see "The Anatomist," no. 19, *Pennsylvania Gazette*, Jan. 12, 1769.

CHAPTER SEVEN

CHRIST CHURCH
IN THE
REVOLUTIONARY YEARS

If Richard Peters and the other leaders of the United Churches had assessed the situation of their churches in 1770, they could have been rightfully pleased and proud. They had two large churches that housed two prosperous congregations. These congregations could boast of four well liked ministers, two of them young enough to lead the churches into the next century. Most important, peace reigned within the churches and within the Anglican community in Philadelphia. And while interdenominational relations had been tense at times in the 1760s, they were still the most peaceful and most "ecumenical" of any colony in America.

But the world of Philadelphia religion, politics, and culture was about to change dramatically. The Revolutionary struggle, which affected all Americans, brought particularly grave consequences to the Church of England. With its ecclesiastical government inextricably connected to the secular English government and with even its theology and Prayer Book determined by Parliament, it suddenly became unclear whether the church had a future in a Philadelphia beyond the king's control.

The story of Christ Church and the American Revolution

had a happy ending—the church survived and its leaders played an important part in the founding of the Protestant Episcopal Church. But this ending came only after years of hardship. Many members of Christ Church figured prominently in the drive toward independence and the Revolutionary War, but for the church as an institution the war had serious consequences. Two ministers of the United Churches plus Provost Smith were arrested, with the two ministers fleeing to England and Smith moving to Maryland. The church's influence in the College ended. The parishioners themselves became bitterly divided, with whigs fighting loyalists and neutrals for control of the vestry. And wartime inflation and the departure of many of its members ravaged the church's finances.

*   *   *

During the early years of the resistance movement the members and clergy of the United Churches, like the city, united in opposition to the English actions. In 1765, when word reached Philadelphia that the Stamp Act, which taxed almost all printed materials, had been passed, Anglicans joined members of all other denominations in supporting a boycott of all British goods. Six Anglicans, including Thomas Willing, John Ord, and Francis Wade from Christ Church, served on the twenty-two-member committee formed to enforce that boycott.[1]

The clergymen associated with the United Churches joined the laity in opposing new taxes imposed from England, but they continued to believe in the good intentions of the English government and to emphasize the mutual benefits drawn from the colonists' connection with England. This combination of beliefs would characterize the clergy's position throughout the pre-revolutionary struggle. Smith expressed their views well in a letter to an English cleric; the Stamp Act and any other tax measure not passed by colonial legislatures, Smith asserted, "will ever be looked upon so contrary to the . . . inherent rights of Englishmen, that among a People planted nursed and educated in the high principles of Liberty it must be considered as a Badge of Disgrace impeaching their . . . affinity and Brotherhood to Englishmen." At the same time he maintained that since "no oppression was intended nor the Consequences foreseen or duly wished," he disliked the publications that painted a picture of English officials as oppressors.[2]

This support for resistance measures sharply contrasted with the attitude of most Anglican clergy in New England and New York. In fact, the northern Anglican clergy constituted the only organized group opposing resistance in the early stages. Because of its timing, the opposition to the Stamp Act quickly became entwined with the fight for an American Bishop. As a result, the clergy's desire to please those officials from whom they were seeking a favor was combined with their natural tendency to prefer hierarchy over democracy and their distrust of the Calvinists who were leading the resistance; all these factors led them to speak out openly against the resistance movement.[3] But the situation of the Pennsylvania clergy, as we have noted, was far different. They were used to cooperating with the Presbyterians and had accepted "democratic" forms of government in both church and state. Thus petitioning England to protect liberties did not seem inconsistent with their loyalty to the crown.

Between 1769 and 1774 both the Philadelphia community as a whole and the members of Christ Church became less united in their approach to the controversy with England. In 1769 the Townshend Acts, which imposed taxes on a variety of imports, divided Philadelphia merchants. Six Anglicans—including John Gibson, George Clymer, John Cadwalader, William Masters and John Shee from the United Churches—served on committees enforcing a boycott of English goods. But three other Anglicans—Tench Francis, Joseph Swift and William West—joined the merchants who actively worked to end the boycott.

After the traditional Philadelphia leadership failed to avidly support the resistance movement, a small group of younger, more radical men challenged their power and worked to politicize the city. The reaction of Philadelphia to the Tea Act, which established a monopoly to import tea, thus assuring that the colonists paid a hated import tax, indicated they had some success. Despite the opposition of many conservative merchants, the radicals, through a carefully orchestrated publicity campaign, awakened the citizens to the dangers of this act. A committee, which included Peter Knight of Christ Church and eight other Anglicans, made certain that the tea never landed in Philadelphia.[4]

The Boston Tea Party, with its destruction of property, and the resulting passage of the Coercive or Intolerable Acts in 1774, which closed the port of Boston, transferred the Massachusetts government to a military governor, and required the quartering of troops in private homes, further polarized feelings in Philadelphia. But because the radicals purposely chose not to alienate any but the ultraconservatives, a wide variety of Philadelphians continued to be involved in the resistance movement. The radicals also consciously attempted to include all religious groups in their committee structure, ensuring that Anglicans would be involved.

The Anglicans who served on the resistance committees in 1773 and 1774 were aligned with the moderate faction. Neither the ultraconservatives, who opposed all resistance, nor the radicals, who more fully supported the actions of Boston revolutionary leaders, had more than a few representatives in Christ Church. In this respect the Anglican congregation probably mirrored opinion in the city, which had not yet been won over by the radicals.

The Anglicans' moderation evidenced itself in the reaction to Boston's request for aid and that city's suggestion that a continental congress be called. Five Anglicans served on the nineteen-member committee elected to reply to Boston's request: four moderates—John Gibson, John Nixon, Thomas Penrose and the Reverend William Smith—and one radical—George Clymer of St. Peter's. Perhaps surprisingly, the committee chose Smith to write the reply. Exhibiting a tone that was "faintly disapproving and indecisive," Smith endorsed a congress but argued that a boycott should be used only as a last resort. He even suggested that Boston pay for the tea![5]

Radical leaders strongly objected to this letter. To rally support for Boston's plight they called for a "solemn Pause" on June 1, 1774, the day the Boston Port Act was to go into effect. Once again the United Churches responded cautiously, refusing to hold special services, as some churches did. Christ Church's muffled bells were rung continuously, indicating that someone with access to the bells supported the radicals. But Richard Peters indignantly announced in the *Pennsylvania Packet* that "the Bells were not rung with his knowledge or Approbation, and that, by his express Direction, there was no particular Observance of that Day, in either of the Churches under his Care."[6] Since the vestry minutes contain no objection to this nonobservance, the lay leadership must have shared Peters's sentiments.

Despite the radicals' displeasure, Smith and his fellow moderate Anglicans continued to serve on all the important committees steering the resistance movement throughout the summer of 1774. At a mass meeting in June Smith made an eloquent and effective speech, calling for unity and dispassionate actions. He served with Willing, Hillegas, and Robert Morris, as well as with St. Peter's members Nixon, Clymer, and Adam Hubley as delegates to the Provincial Convention called to draft instructions for the delegates to the Continental Congress. Smith even served on the committee that wrote the instructions that called on England to renounce any power over internal legislation in America and to repeal all taxation, all quartering acts, the Coercive Acts, and a variety of trade regulations.[7] Up until this point the moderate position of the Anglican members represented well the opinion of Philadelphia in general.

* * *

In September 1774 the moderately conservative residents of Philadelphia welcomed the delegates to the First Continental Congress. Many of these men visited Christ Church. In fact, for most of the next sixteen years Christ Church served as a home away from home for Anglicans participating in the national congresses and governments. An already distinguished congregation became more distinguished with the addition of men such as George Washington, James Mason, and even Congregationalists such as John Adams.

Delegates who never worshiped at Christ Church still heard one of its ministers on a regular basis. In September 1774 the Continental Congress chose Jacob Duché as chaplain. Attempting to find a minister who would offend neither the Anglican nor the Calvinist members of the congress, Samuel Adams suggested Duché, "a gentleman of piety and virtue, who was at the same time a friend of his country"[8] (see Figure 14). Duché's initial appearance before the Continental Congress made quite a stir and established him as a favorite of John Adams and other resistance leaders. Part of the effect was the result of fortuitous circumstances; the psalm for the day as indicated in the Prayer Book happened to be the thirty-fifth, which begins, "Plead my cause, O Lord with them that strive with me; fight against them that fight against me." John Adams reported that it "seemed as if Heaven had ordained that Psalm to be read on that morning." Duché's style equally impressed the delegates; Silas Deane remarked that Duché had prayed "with such fervency, purity and sublimity of style and sentiment . . . that even Quakers shed tears."[9]

The Continental Congress not only placed Duché and Philadelphia in the limelight, it also greatly increased the power of the radical leaders in Philadelphia. Once the Congress endorsed a boycott, something moderate Philadelphians had opposed, the radicals no longer had to compromise. In November 1774 their entire slate of sixty-six men was elected to serve on the Committee of Inspection to enforce the boycott. The triumph of the radicals did not end the participation of Anglicans in the resistance movement; in fact, because of the radicals' continued desire to include all religious denominations, the Anglicans actually increased their representation on the Committee of Sixty-

FIGURE 14
The Reverend Jacob Duché (rector, 1775–1779) and his wife, Elizabeth Hopkinson Duché, portrait by their son, Thomas Spence Duché (1762–1790). Courtesy of the Historical Society of Pennsylvania.

Six from what it had been on the Committee of Forty-Three. The twenty Anglicans included Robert Morris, Emmanuel Eyre, Francis Wade, Richard and Thomas Willing, and James Worrell of Christ Church. However, not all Anglicans endorsed the radicals' victory. Fourteen Anglicans had run on the conservative ticket, which was badly defeated. Smith, perhaps sensing the mood of the city, had refused to run for reelection.[10]

The battles of Lexington and Concord in April 1775 further strengthened the radicals' hand. Philadelphians responded with patriotic zeal, almost immediately forming neighborhood militia units. Even the reluctant Assembly gave in, endorsing the militia units and appointing a twenty-five-person Committee of Safety in June 1775; this committee would largely run Pennsylvania for the next year and a half.

Anglicans continued to join their Presbyterian neighbors in supporting the struggle. Although many opposed the specific tactics used by the radicals, as a group they suffered none of the serious divisions that plagued the Quakers. Included on the Committee of Safety were Philadelphia Anglicans George Gray, John Cadwalader, Robert Morris, Robert White, Thomas Willing and Benjamin Franklin, who had recently returned from England. Christ Church was also well represented in the Continental Congress, with Willing and Franklin serving in 1775. Christ Church members flocked to the militia, with Richard Peters, Jr., the nephew of the rector, serving as a captain and secretary of the officers, and many others serving as officers.[11]

While non-Quakers in Philadelphia generally supported the arming of the province as a necessary precaution, the military phase of the revolutionary struggle presented painful alternatives for the Philadelphia clergymen who had taken oaths to support the king. Fighting against the king's forces was far different from petitioning Parliament or boycotting English merchants. Moreover, the clergy were no longer allowed the luxury of silence. As they explained to the bishop of London, "the time is now come . . . when even our Silence could be misconstrued, & when we are called upon to take a more public part."[12]

Finally forced to make their positions publicly known or by their silence be branded enemies to their country, the clergy seem to have been motivated by two factors: their genuine attachment to the rights of America and their concern for the welfare of the church. Even when writing to the bishop of London they admitted that "our Consciences would not permit us to injure the Rights of this Country. We are to leave our families in it, and cannot but consider its Inhabitants entitled, as well as their Brethren in England to the

Right of *granting their own money*." Moreover, they knew that if they did anything "which might have the appearance of drawing them [the people] to what they think would be a Slavish Resignation of their Rights, it would be destructive to ourselves, as well as the Church." Smith was deeply concerned with dispelling the notion that the clergy of the church were "Tools of Power, Slavish in their tenets and privately Enemies to the principles of the [Glorious] Revolution." If such notions predominated, he reminded the bishop, "it would give a deadly wound to the Church in this country."[13]

Thus, the clergy of the United Churches agreed to take their turns preaching to the militia during the summer of 1775. More important, in contrast to 1774 when even the ringing of bells was considered inappropriate, they agreed to observe the fast day proclaimed by the Continental Congress for July 20, 1775. Such an observance was a violation of the church canons which allowed only the king to proclaim fast days, but the clergy obviously felt the occasion called for unusual actions. Because of their willingness to bend the rules, the Christ Church congregation was honored by having the Continental Congress as a group worship in their church on that fast day. Chaplain Duché preached a stirring sermon endorsing the struggle for American liberties.[14]

While historians have given much attention to Duché's sermons, the sermons of Smith and Coombe were equally well received; together they demonstrate three basic themes in the clergy's approach to the revolutionary struggle. First, all the ministers endorsed the colonists' defense of their liberties in the most emphatic language. Second, they charged England with being the aggressor, picturing the colonists as merely defending their lives and property from destruction; Anglican clergy could only justify a *defensive* war against the mother country. Third, they extolled the blessings of union, disavowed any thoughts of independence, and prayed for reconciliation. This was the combination of beliefs that the clergy had espoused since 1765 and that most would continue to espouse in July 1776.

These themes can be seen clearly in Coombe's fast sermon preached on July 20, 1775. He presented an eloquent defense of the colonists' rights and a strong attack on the actions of England. He argued that the men of Britain

have at length assumed a right to *demand* the fruits of our labor, & to appropriate them to their own peculiar purposes. Bent upon effectuating their dark designs, they have sacrilegiously lifted the sword against the constitution, and have severed the most inviolable compacts. And because we dared a refusal of obedience to their sanguine edicts, they have led on their armies to the battle, & their hostile navies surround our coasts.

Asserting that the measures taken by the colonists "were purely defensive," he continued: "We ask but for peace, liberty and safety."[15]

At the same time Coombe emphasized the benefits the connection with England had brought. He asserted that the "growth and importance" of the colonies had been increased by their connection "with a wise and powerful nation, whom we were taught, from our cradles, to look up to with filial reverence." He added that the colonies could take comfort in knowing that the present struggle was not "owing to any restlessness on our part, or weariness of that ancient form of government . . . but to that lawless lust for dominion on hers."[16]

Duché's sermons expressed similar views, but his chaplaincy imbued his remarks with the rhetoric of the resistance movement. When justifying resistance, he appealed explicitly to the social compact theory of government, combining it with Christian theology. He argued that

inasmuch as all Rulers are in fact the Servants of the Public . . . whenever these Rulers abuse their sacred trust, by unrighteous attempts to injure, oppress, and enslave those very persons, from whom alone, under GOD their power is derived—does not humanity, does not reason, does not scripture call upon the Man, the Citizen, the Christian of such community to STAND FAST IN THAT LIBERTY WHERE CHRIST . . . HATH MADE THEM FREE.[17]

Duché was also, however, strongest among the clergy in his denunciation of independence. In the sermon he preached to the Continental Congress he argued that "as to any pretensions to, or even desire of independency, have we not openly disavowed them in all our petitions, representations and remonstrances? Rather than advocating independence, Duché prayed that God would "restore that brotherly union and concord, which ought to subsist inviolate in the great family to which we belong."[18]

These sermons placed the Philadelphia clergy squarely on the side of the colonists in their struggle for justice and, because the concept of independence did not yet have wide support in Philadelphia, they were well received. The Continental Congress had Duché's sermon published, while the militia units published the sermons of Coombe and Smith. Smith's sermon, which presented the same arguments as those of his fellow clergymen, went through several printings in a few weeks. Thus, until January 1776 the position held by the Anglican ministers—support of peaceful resistance and even defensive warfare aimed at reconciliation—allowed them to remain within the mainstream of the resistance movement.

The publication of *Common Sense* in January 1776 and the concurrent news from England that King George had declared the colonists in rebellion and ordered that all colonial ships be seized changed the situation dramatically. For the first time the Philadelphia press openly debated the issue of independence and its proponents began to woo supporters openly. But Philadelphia was still not a radical stronghold; independence did not yet appear inevitable and opponents of a break with Britain were not yet branded traitors by the community at large.[19]

While the laity within Christ Church were probably as divided as the city as a whole, the Anglican clergymen all still opposed independence in 1776.[20] Smith, in a series of articles written under the pseudonym "Cato" and in a tract entitled *Plain Truth,* presented the strongest attack on *Common Sense* published in Philadelphia. He argued forcefully that the English constitution was the best in the world and reminded his readers that at the beginning of the struggle "we considered our connection with *Great Britain* as our chief happiness—we flourished, and grew rich and populous, to a degree not to be paralleled in history." He argued that reconciliation with Great Britain was their "sole resource" and was within easy reach. For those who were not swayed by his faith in England, Smith expounded on the horrors of war and the extremely slight chance that the colonies could win. He argued that war would lead to Spain and France dividing up the colonies, or to a New England dictatorship, or to "all misery of anarchy and intestine war."[21]

Smith's views had not changed from when he gave his well-received sermon to the militia, but the situation in Philadelphia had changed drastically. The radicals, who now openly argued for independence, considered Smith an enemy of resistance. In January 1776 the Philadelphia Committee of Safety investigated charges that Smith had spoken disrespectfully of the Continental Congress.[22] A month later the Congress gave Smith a chance to express his views publicly and thereby show which side he was on. They asked him to preach the funeral oration for General Richard Montgomery, the heroic soldier killed in the ill-fated Canadian expedition. Speaking at the service held at Christ Church, Smith stated the same views he had stated in his sermon of 1775. Quoting from a congressional resolution of July 1775, he expressed satisfaction that the Continental Congress supported him in praying for reconciliation. Unlike 1775, this time his sermon was not well received. John Adams described the oration as an "insolent performance" and a motion in the Congress that Smith be thanked and asked for a copy of the speech to be published was opposed with such "spirit and vivacity from every part of the room" that it was withdrawn.[23]

While the clergy of the United Churches agreed with Smith's positions, if not with his outspokenness, the laity were divided. In fact, "Cato"'s main adversary, "Cassandra," was actually James Cannon, a teacher at the College of Philadelphia and a member of Christ Church. Cannon, who served as secretary of the ultraradical Committee of Privates and has been described as one of the six core members of a "conspiracy of revolution," was the most effective spokesman for independence in Philadelphia. While Smith argued for reconciliation, Cannon argued that negotiating with Britain was useless, since Parliament could not make commitments that would be binding for future legislatures. He saw independence as the only answer.[24]

Members of the United Churches who held public office were also increasingly divided. In the assembly elections of May 1776 Thomas Willing and Alexander Wilcocks of St. Peter's ran as anti-independence candidates, while George Clymer ran as a pro-independence candidate. Wilcocks and Clymer both won, while Willing was narrowly defeated, showing the still-divided nature of Philadelphia opinion. Similarly, Anglicans in Philadelphia were represented in the Continental Congress in 1775–76 by the conservative Thomas Willing, moderate Robert Morris, and radical Benjamin Franklin. And while Christ Church member William Adcock joined the radicals, serving as president of the Committee of Privates, John Kearsley, nephew of the man responsible for building Christ Church, was paraded around town as an ultra-tory.[25]

These divisions remained when the issue of independence came to a head in July 1776. Seven signers of the Declaration of Independence are buried in the Christ Church burial ground or in the churchyard itself. These include five who voted for independence: Benjamin Franklin; Francis Hopkinson; James Wilson, a representative from Carlisle who later joined St. Peter's in 1778; George Ross, a delegate from Delaware; and Joseph Hewes of North Carolina. They also include Benjamin Rush, a radical who was elected to the Continental Congress after the vote on independence and who converted to the Episcopal Church in 1787. Those interred at Christ Church also include Robert Morris, who became known as the financier of the American Revolution and who played a large part in the success of the war effort, but who absented himself from the vote because of his reservations about Independence. He was not alone in his reservations: Christ Church member Thomas Willing voted against independence and, as a result, was defeated in elections for Congress held the next week.

* * *

Members of Christ Church were accustomed to political divisions within their church. However, after July 4, 1776 political decisions could be life-threatening, both for individuals and for the church. For individuals, moderation became impossible, dissent became treason and even neutrality among public figures became difficult. And while other churches could maintain neutrality as institutions and not be suspect, Christ Church did not have that luxury. Because it owed its existence to the government of England, the Revolution threatened its very existence. Moreover, that connection made its leaders immediately suspect. To make matters worse, since prayers for the king were a part of its liturgy, the church had to take a stand immediately.

Anglican clergymen had to balance the needs of the church and their own careers with their consciences. At ordination each priest took an oath to "bear faith and true allegiance to the King's Highness . . . and to . . . assist and defend all [his] jurisdictions," as well as swearing to perform the liturgy of the Church of England verbatim, including the prayers for the king.[26] Adhering to that oath meant closing the churches and enduring persecution and even imprisonment. Yet, even for clergy willing to break their oath, the way was not clear; if the "rebellion" were quickly crushed, the careers of whig clergymen would be over. It is therefore not surprising that the clergy in Pennsylvania could not agree on a position and that some seemed to vacillate.

Jacob Duché, who had been chosen rector in October 1775 when Peters retired, asked the vestry to decide whether to omit the prayers for the royal family from the liturgy or to close the churches. On July 4 he called a special meeting to ask the vestrymen whether it was best "for the peace and welfare of the congregation, to shut up the churches or to continue the service, without using the prayers for the Royal Family." The vestry decided that it was necessary "for the peace and well being of the churches, to omit the said petitions" and requested the rector and assistant ministers to do so.[27]

Duché agreed to preside at services that omitted the prayers for the king and even agreed to continue as chaplain to the Continental Congress after independence, but he never fully accepted independence. In October 1776 he resigned his position as chaplain, a position he said he took because he thought the churches were in danger "and hoped by this means to have been instrumental in preventing those ills I had so much to apprehend." Duché's belief in the American cause gradually declined and when he was arrested by British General William Howe in September 1777, his friends won his release by assuring Howe that Duché had not only changed his opinion on the rebellion but had inserted prayers for the king in the worship service that very day.[28]

Duché completed his political pilgrimage in October 1777 when he wrote his famous letter to General Washington, requesting either that the general ask the Congress to rescind independence and cease hostilities immediately or that he negotiate with the British himself. The letter caused a sensation; while toryism among the Anglican clergy was expected, Duché had symbolized Anglican patriotism. Now he was denounced as an "apostate," "the first of villains," and a "Judas."[29] The most poignant response came from Francis Hopkinson, Duché's brother-in-law and close friend from college days. He wrote to Duché:

Words cannot express the grief & Consternation that wounded my Soul at sight of this fatal performance. . . . I would fain hope, notwithstanding your assertion to the contrary, that you wrote it, with a Bayonet held to your Breast . . . Be assured, I write this from true brotherly Love . . . I am perfectly disposed to attribute this unfortunate step to the Timidity of your Temper, the weakness of your nerves & the undue Influence of those about you. But will the world hold you so excused?[30]

Duché's vacillation had not only made him unwanted in America but also raised suspicions in England. To answer those, he sailed for England in December 1777, assuring the vestry that "as soon as he has settled his affairs, and could with safety, he would cheerfully return to the care of his churches." That day never came. He stayed in England for fifteen years, serving for most of that time as the chaplain to the Asylum for Female Orphans in Lambeth. While he enjoyed a "happy circle of literary and religious friends," he missed everything about Philadelphia, but particularly the United Churches. After the war he naively inquired about the chances of returning, even writing to General Washington, but none of his friends could give him any encouragement. Finally, in 1792, old and in ill health, Duché returned to Philadelphia, where he died in 1797. He was buried in St. Peter's churchyard.[31]

Duché's story bespoke the hard choices faced by Episcopal clergymen. Raised in a wealthy Philadelphia family, he shared his countrymen's outrage at the British measures. But, like many of his economic class, Duché disapproved of independence. Moreover, the events following independence convinced him that no good would come out of the struggle. Duché resented the younger, less wealthy men who took control of the government, some of them, as Duché put it, "so obscure, that their very names were never in my ears before, and others [who had] only been distinguished for the weakness of their understandings, and the violence of their tempers." He also reacted strongly to the destruction caused by the war. He lamented: "in America your harbours are blocked up, your cities fall one after another, fortress after fortress, battle after battle is lost . . . How fruitless the expense of blood." As White later observed, Duché was motivated by "Despair of the American Cause & to spare the Effusion of Blood."[32]

Thomas Coombe's actions after independence were far more consistent, though not necessarily any less agonizing. Coombe decided that he could not take the oath to the new government "without the saddest violation of [his] own peace of mind," but the decision "was not entered upon without some heartaches and many a sorrowful anticipation." To Coombe it came down to a choice between his "Duty" and his "interest," and he chose his duty. As a result, in September 1777, prior to the British occupation of Philadelphia, he was arrested along with forty others for evidencing "a Disposition Inimical to the Cause of America." He refused to obtain his freedom by pledging not to do anything against the colonies or give any information to the British, but he was given permission to leave the country. Prevented by illness from leaving before the British arrived, Coombe remained in the city throughout the occupation, keeping the United Churches open with the help of the British chaplains. With the departure of the British, Coombe asked the Supreme Executive Council for permission to depart for England. In July 1778 he left Philadelphia for the last time, assuring the vestry that nothing but "a conviction of my higher obligations could have induced" him to leave. He left behind his entire family, including his wife who died before she could join him.[33]

Despite his despair at leaving Philadelphia and the death of his wife, Coombe, who was at peace with himself, was able to resume a happy life in England sooner than was Duché. He served as chaplain to Lord Carlisle, who later presented him with a parish, obtained a doctor of divinity degree from Trinity College, Dublin, and eventually became a prebendary of Canterbury and one of the chaplains to the king. In 1787 he wrote to his father: "I enjoy contentment, domestic comfort and live under the habitual influence of cheerful hopes; not having one real want, and experiencing many blessings."[34]

CHAPTER SEVEN

William White took a different course from that Duché or Coombe, agreeing to take the oath to the new government. Ironically, he had been the one minister who refused to comment publicly on the resistance movement before independence. Although he firmly believed that "the late Measures of ye English Government, contradicted ye Rights which ye Colonies had brought with them to ye Wilds of America," he refused to "beat the ecclesiastical Drum" because he objected to "making . . . the Ministry instrumental to war." Therefore in some ways he was the least likely candidate to remain a patriot. He admitted that "had the Issue depended on [his] Determination, it would have been for Submission, with the determined and steady Continuance of rightful Claim." Yet, despite his original conservatism, White chose to side with the colonists immediately after independence, believing "it was the Dictate of Conscience, to take what seemed the right side." Years later he justified his position by emphasizing that it was England that had thrown the colonies "out of its Protection," and that the colonists had not been at all inclined toward independence until England's decision to seize all ships coming to America. White was rewarded for his patriotism by being appointed chaplain of the Continental Congress, a position he shared with the Reverend Edward Duffield, a Presbyterian minister.[35]

William Smith's position after the Declaration of Independence is harder to classify. Despite his strong opposition to independence, Smith never became a tory. He willingly took the oath to the new government in Pennsylvania and there is no evidence that he ever said or did anything against the American cause. However, Smith never openly supported the revolutionaries. Understandably, his failure publicly to announce a change of heart made people suspect him as a secret tory. Thus in August 1777 Smith was arrested along with Coombe. Unlike Coombe, however, Smith had already taken the oath and now agreed to promise in writing that he would do nothing to aid the British. As a result, the Supereme Executive Council allowed him to return to his property in what is now Montgomery County, Maryland.[36]

*   *   *

For the laity of Christ Church, far more than for the clergy, religion was only one of many factors to consider when deciding their position on independence. Given the heterogeneous nature of the congregation and the lack of unity in the past, it is not surprising that Christ Church members divided when it came to the Revolution. Christ Church can boast of having patriots of legendary importance among its members. Robert Morris made a heroic effort to finance the revolution, eventually being named as the "financial dictator" in 1781, and also served in the Pennsylvania Assembly. Benjamin Franklin became almost the personification of the new nation to Europeans. James Cannon wrote the new constitution for Pennsylvania before retiring from public life in 1777. Francis Hopkinson wrote propaganda pamphlets, chaired the Continental Navy Board, and served as treasurer of loans. Some say he also designed the American flag. And while Betsy Ross probably did not actually sew the first flag, she did make flags for the navy and came to symbolize the contributions of women to the American cause.[37] Similarly, St. Peter's had among its pewholders General John Cadwalader and George Clymer, who served in the Continental Congress for most of the war.

However, Christ Church also had well-known tories among its members. James Tilghman and John Lawrence were among those arrested for aiding the British; Phineas Bond, Jr. later became the British consul to the United States; and the younger John Kearsley, who had early opposed the resistance movement, was imprisoned in 1775 and died there a year later. He was attainted of treason and had his property confiscated.[38]

Overall, Christ Church members probably divided rather evenly over the Revolution. One study of Philadelphia's economic elite found that 33 percent of those who rented pews at Christ Church were patriots, 25 percent were loyalists, and the rest were neutral. Of seventy-four Christ Church members found on the 1778 or 1779 tax lists, twenty-nine were double taxed because they refused to take the oath to the new government, while the remainder must have been at least neutral toward the Revolution. At the same time twenty-seven pew renters served as officers in either the militia or the Continental army during the Revolution. In sum, statistics indicate that the Christ Church laity divided over the Revolution, with an important plurality favoring independence, but with tories comprising a substantial minority and many remaining neutral.[39]

These divisions, not surprisingly, caused serious problems for the life of the church. During the first two years of the Revolutionary War the churches were controlled by men either sympathetic to the British or, more probably, neutral. This can be seen in the way both Coombe and Duché were treated. When Coombe was arrested in September of 1777, the vestry reacted indignantly, demanding that he be given a hearing. They reminded the Supreme Executive Council that the "Connexion betwixt Ministers & People hath in every Christian State, been deem'd a Tender & Spiritual one" and suggested that his arrest was an "Infringement of Religious as well as Civil Liberty."[40] And when Coombe decided to go to England, the vestry wrote to the Bishop of London explaining his decision and approving of his conduct while serving the churches.

Similarly, when Duché announced his departure, the vestry wrote an extremely supportive letter, lamenting "the unhappy occasion that calls you from the Care of those Churches in which you have officiated with so much satisfaction. They offered their "Sincere Prayers for . . . your speedy return to your Native City and the charge of the united Churches, with the approbation of your spiritual superiors which we doubt not you will meet with upon a proper representation of your Conduct." Moreover, the vestry kept the rectorship open in the event Duché returned! Perhaps most surprising, when they received a letter from the bishop of London in September 1778 (dated March 8, 1776) granting Duché a license as rector, the vestry once again confirmed Duché as rector of the United Churches.[41]

When the British occupied Philadelphia, the leaders of Christ Church cooperated fully with the British military. Church leaders allowed prayers for the king to be reinstated and even allowed British chaplains to officiate in Christ Church. In fact, General Howe, who sat in Washington's pew at the church, made attendance at Christ Church mandatory for the officer corps. Few in Philadelphia could miss the officers marching up Second Street amid ruffles and flourishes.

The vestry election of 1778 further evidenced the neutral or tory sentiments of the Christ Church leadership. Many Philadelphia whigs—especially among the prominent and wealthy—had fled the city at the start of the occupation. Yet this flight did not cripple the United Churches. Thirteen of the men chosen for the vestry in April 1778 had been on that body in either 1776 or 1777 and most had several years of experience. A majority of vestrymen had stayed in Philadelphia despite the British presence.[42]

The end of the occupation and the increased confidence in the American cause renewed the potential for conflict. Whig members, who resented the previous loyalist domination, resolved to take control of the church. As White put it, those who remained in the city "had become in some Measure identified with the Enemy." Thus certain whig members hoped to annul the 1778 vestry elections held while many members were out of the city. Fortunately for peace, White and "some judicious Men on the same Side in Politics" convinced the more ardent whigs to wait until the next vestry election.[43]

The vestry election of 1779 finally allowed the whigs to take control. This election was not only a repudiation of the "occupation vestry," but also a vote against the past leadership of the churches in general. Only three of the twenty men who had served during the occupation were reelected in 1779.[44] The composition of those who were elected is equally revealing: twelve had never served on a vestry and only two had served on the vestry prior to 1776. In fact, only eight of the twenty vestrymen elected in 1776, the last election prior to independence, served on the vestry at all after 1778. Clearly the congregation had rejected its old leadership.[45]

The new vestry set a very different course from its predecessor. It voted the rectorship vacant—no longer keeping it open for Duché's return—and proceeded to elect William White as rector in April, 1779.[46] This momentous event was largely the result of circumstances; White was the only one of the United Church ministers left in the city. But it was also fortuitous; White led the churches for almost sixty years, and would establish Christ Church as the "mother church" of the Protestant Episcopal Church in the United States.

The new vestry also changed the bylaws to conform to the new political status of the country. At the same time it clarified issues relating to the selection and dismissal of ministers. The ministers no longer had to be licensed by the bishop of London, but simply had to have "Episcopal Orders." More important, provision was made for "dismissing" a rector or assistant minister, something that had not been possible under the colonial charter and bylaws. If the vestry received a signed statement charging a minister with "conduct disgraceful to the Pastoral Office," that body was to investigate and hold a public hearing before voting on the issue. Fourteen votes were needed to dismiss a rector and eleven to dismiss an assistant. The vestry also clarified the role of the congregation in the selection of the ministers. As in the colonial bylaws, the members were given one month to register their objection to their choice of a minister. If a majority of those members qualified to vote registered their objection in writing, the election would be void. A similar majority would also negate a vote for dismissal. The congregation confirmed these changes on June 21, 1779.[47]

The whig-controlled vestry also strengthened the ministry of the United Churches in September 1781 by electing Robert Blackwell as assistant minister. Blackwell came from a wealthy Long Island family and had served as an SPG missionary in New Jersey in the 1770s. Most important, he had unblemished patriot credentials; he had been dismissed from the SPG in 1777 for aiding the Revolution and had subsequently served as chaplain and surgeon in the Continental army.[48] Blackwell served as White's assistant until his retirement in 1811.

With the church firmly in the hands of whigs, loyalist members faced a dilemma. As White put it, the "Danger was the absenting of themselves from the Churches, in the Devotions of which, the new Allegiance was acknowledged." He reported that some did stay away for a while, but "the prejudice wore away gradually." In reality, loyalists had little choice. Unlike the situation in New York and in some areas of New England, where loyalist clergy either stayed throughout the war or returned afterward, loyalists in Philadelphia had no clergyman to rally around. White's conciliatory style and lack of crusading zeal for the revolutionary cause no doubt made their acceptance of the new situation easier. Whatever the reason, once White became rector, open conflict within the churches ended.[49]

* * *

Members of Christ Church not only had to adjust to independence, they also had to deal with a distinctly different political environment within the state government. In the internal revolution that swept Pennsylvania in 1776, Philadelphia Anglicans were, temporarily at least, the big losers. Taking advantage of the Pennsylvania constitution of 1776 that established a unicameral legislature and abolished an executive branch, Presbyterians and their allies, many of whom had never held office, took control of the government.[50]

Yet Anglicans continued to be active in state government. As we indicated, James Cannon was largely responsible for writing the new constitution and George Clymer served in the Pennsylvania Assembly throughout the 1780s. Others, including Robert Morris, Thomas Willing, John Cadwalader, Samuel Meredith, John Nixon, Richard Bache, and James Wilson, served as leaders of the anti-constitutionalist or Republican effort to gain a new constitution with a more balanced government.[51] But during the Revolution and the postwar years, Anglican influence was clearly of secondary importance in the Pennsylvania government.

Presbyterian control of the legislature directly affected causes and institutions supported by Christ Church, particularly the College of Philadelphia. The hostility Presbyterians associated with the college felt toward Anglicans in the late colonial period was increased by Smith's perceived loyalism, the outright toryism of three of the college's trustees, and the general conservative nature of that governing body. To radical Republicans, the college was a bastion of conservatism and aristocracy, a symbol of what they hoped the

Revolution would destroy. Thus in November 1779 the legislature abrogated the charter of the College, establishing instead the state controlled "University of the State of Pennsylvania." While the board of trustees included representatives from six religions, Presbyterians dominated the new college.[52]

William White, who had done his best to stop the attack on the College, at first refused to have anything to do with the new college, despite having a right to a seat on the board of trustees, a position he had held for six years under the old charter. He ultimately put the decision before the vestry, which decided that the "right accruing . . . ought not to be lost to ye Church." White then agreed to run for provost of the university, believing he could continue to serve as rector of the United Churches as well. When he lost, the trustees offered him the position of vice-provost, which he declined. White did eventually accept the legitimacy of the new institution, accepting an honorary doctorate in 1782.[53]

The private charter of the college was reinstated in 1789, but Anglicans never again dominated it. Christ Church continued to have a role in the university; White remained as a trustee until his death and other rectors have served on the board. In 1827 William DeLancey, an assistant minister of the United Churches, accepted the provost position. But the intimate connection that had existed during the colonial period would never again exist.[54]

* * *

Christ Church survived the Revolution in relatively good condition compared to many other Anglican churches and as a result, as we will see, took a leading role in the formation of the Protestant Episcopal Church. But both clergy and laity within the church realized that the Declaration of Independence ended an era in the church in more than an ecclesiastical sense. As the city expanded, as new people entered politics, Christ Church's dominant role in the public life of the city and the state ended. Both clergy and laity had to begin to adjust to a different role for the church in the new nation.

NOTES

1. Richard Ryerson, *The Revolution Is Now Begun* (Philadelphia: University of Pennsylvania Press, 1978), 264.
2. William Smith to Dean Tucker of Gloucester, Dec. 18, 1765, in Smith's "Notes on the Revolution," Smith Papers, HSP. Thomas Coombe expressed similar opinions regarding the

Townshend Acts in a letter to his father, Nov. 1, 1769, Coombe Family Papers, HSP, folder no. 17. White explained his views in his autobiography; see "The Autobiography of William White," 402–6.

3. See William H. Nelson, *The American Tory* (Boston: Oxford University Press, 1961), 12–20.

4. For a discussion of the events surrounding the Tea Act and the composition of the committee, see Ryerson, *The Revolution Is Now Begun*, 33–38, 80.

5. Ryerson, *The Revolution Is now Begun*, 43. The letter and Smith's comments about its reception are found in William Smith, "Notes on the Revolution,"pp. 6–8, Smith Papers.

6. *Pennsylvania Packet*, June 8, 1774.

7. *Pennsylvania Gazette*, June 22, 1774, contains the speech. Ryerson, *The Revolution Is Now Begun*, 59, 84–85.

8. Charles Francis Adams, ed., *Familiar Letters of John Adams and His Wife Abigail Adams during the Revolution*, 37, quoted in Clark Garrett, "The Spiritual Odyssey of Jacob Duché," American Philosophical Society, *Proceedings* 119 (no. 2, 1975): 147.

9. Garrett, "Spiritual Odyssey," 147; Edmund C. Burnett, ed., *Letters of the Members of the Continental Congress*, 8 vols. (Washington, D.C.: Carnegie Institution of Washington, 1921–1936), 1: 18.

10. Ryerson, *The Revolution Is Now Begun*, 275–81. For Smith's comments about his withdrawal see William Smith to Bishop of London, July 8, 1775, Perry, *Historical Collections*, 473–74. For a discussion of the election see Ryerson, *The Revolution Is Now Begun*, 94–96.

11. Ryerson, *The Revolution Is Now Begun*, 117–24.

12. Richard Peters, William Smith, Jacob Duché, Thomas Coombe, William White and William Stringer to Bishop of London, June 30, 1775, Perry, *Historical Collections*, 2: 470–72.

13. Ibid., 470, 472; William Smith to Bishop of London, July 8, 1775, ibid., 473–74. See also William Smith to Thomas Bradbury Chandler, Aug. 30, 1775, Smith Manuscripts, PEC, vol.6, no. 29.

14. Jacob Duché, *The American Vine, a Sermon Preached . . . Before the Honourable Continental Congress, July 20, 1775* (Philadelphia: J. Humphreys, Jr., 1775).

15. Thomas Coombe, *A Sermon Preached Before the Congregation of Christ Church and St. Peter's, July 20, 1775* (Philadelphia: John Dunlap, 1775), 4–6.

16. Coombe, *Sermon*, 25.

17. Jacob Duché, *The Duty of Standing Fast in our Spiritual and Temporal LIBERTIES* (Philadelphia: J. Humphreys, Jr., 1775), 13, ii.

18. Ibid., 18–19; Duché, *The American Vine*, v–vi.

19. See Ryerson, *The Revolution Is Now Begun*, 149–75.

20. This opposition of the ministers has to be inferred from later information. Coombe consistently opposed it. Duché argued in his famous letter to Washington that he had registered his opposition to independence prior to the event; see Jacob Duché to George Washington, Oct. 8, 1777 in C. P. B. Jeffreys, *Provincial and Revolutionary History of St. Peter's Church*, 69–70. White expressed his own hesitation in his "Autobiography," 405.

21. [William Smith], *Plain Truth, Addressed to the Inhabitants of America Containing Remarks on a late Pamphlet, Entitled Common Sense* (London: J. Almons 1776). Cato's letters appeared in the *Pennsylvania Gazette*, March 13 to April 24, 1776, and have been reprinted in Peter Force, ed. *American Archives*, 4th series (Washington, D.C., 1837–53), 5: 126–27, 188–90, 443–46, 514–17, 542–46, 839–43, 850–53, 1049–51. The quotes are from "Cato, nos. 3 and 4, Force, *American Archives,* 5: 443, 446, 515; [Smith], *Plain Truth*, 11–13, 19, 35–36.

22. See Christopher Marshall's *Remembrancer*, quoted in Albert F. Gegenheimer, *William Smith, Educator and Churchman, 1727–1803* (Philadelphia: University of Pennsylvania Press, 1943), 176.

23. Smith, "An Oration in Memory of General Montgomery and of the Officers and Soldiers who fell with him, December 31, 1775," in Smith, *The Works of William Smith*, 1: 28. John Adams to Abigail Adams, Feb. 28, 1776, in Burnett, *Letters of the Members of the Continental Congress*, 1: 434. See also Samuel Adams to Mrs. Adams, Feb. 26, 1776, ibid., 1: 365; Diary of Rich Smith, [Feb. 22, 1776], ibid., 1: 359.

24. Ryerson, *The Revolution Is Now Begun*, 167–68. For a good portrait of Cannon, see David Hawke, *In the Midst of a Revolution* (Philadelphia: University of Pennsylvania Press, 1961), 105ff.

25. Ryerson, *The Revolution Is Now Begun*, 172–73, 140, 121–32.

26. David Holmes, "The Episcopal Church and the American Revolution," *HMPEC* 47 (Fall 1978): 268–69.

27. Jacob Duché to George Washington, Oct. 8, 1777, Jeffreys, *Provincial and Revolutionary History of St. Peter's Church*, 70; Vestry Minutes, July 4, 1776.

28. "The Autobiography of William White," 407.

29. For examples of responses to Duché's letter, see Nathaniel Folson to Josiah Bartlett, Oct. 30, 1777, Burnett, *Letters of the Members of the Continental Congress*, 1: 538; Henry Laurens to Robert Howe, Oct. 20, 1777, ibid., 526; John Adams to Abigail Adams, Oct. 25, 1777, ibid., 533–34.

30. Francis Hopkinson to Jacob Duché, Nov. 14, 1777, Hopkinson Papers, HSP, vol. 2, no. 101.

31. Vestry Minutes, December 9, 1777; Jacob Duché to General Washington, April 2, 1783, quoted in Garrett, "The Spiritual Odyssey of Jacob Duché," 150; Jacob Duché to William White, Aug. 16, 1791 and Oct. 16, 1790, White Manuscripts, vol. 3, nos. 11 and 7; "The Autobiography of William White," 407. Duché was present at White's consecration ceremony at the latter's request: see William White, *Memoirs of the Protestant Episcopal Church*, ed. B. F. DeCosta (New York: S. Potter, J. Maxwell Printer, 1880), 137. My discussion of his years in England is based on Garrett's article.

32. Jacob Duché to George Washington, Oct. 8, 1777, Jeffreys, *Provincial and Revolutionary History of St. Peter's Church*, 73. For a discussion of the governmental situation in Pennsylvania, see Ryerson, *The Revolution Is Now Begun*, especially chaps. 8 and 9; and Hawke, *In the Midst of a Revolution*. See also "The Autobiography of William White," 407.

33. Thomas Coombe to Vestry of United Churches, July 7, 1778, Vestry Minutes, July 7, 1778; Vestry Minutes, Sept. 6, Sept. 10 and Dec 9, 1777; *Minutes of the Supreme Executive Council*, August 31, 1777, in *Minutes of the Provincial Council of Pennsylvania* (Harrisburg, Pa.: J. Stevens and Co., 1851–53), 11: 284, 300, 527.

34. "The Autobiography of William White," 408; Thomas Coombe, Jr. to Thomas Coombe, Sr., Dec. 5, 1787, Coombe Family Papers.

35. "Autobiography of William White," 403–6, 409. Vestry Minutes, April 15, 1779.

36. *Minutes of the Supreme Executive Council*, Aug. 31, 1777, 11: 284; June 30, 1778, 11: 525.

37. *DAB*, s.v., Hopkinson, Francis; Morris, Robert; Hawke, *In the Midst of a Revolution*, 181–200.

38. Lorenzo Sabine, *Biographical Sketches of Loyalists of the American Revolution with an Historical Essay*, 2 vols. (1864; reprint, Port Washington, N.Y.: Kennikat Press, 1966), 1: 235, 597.

39. For information on the elite, see Robert Gough, "Towards a Theory of Class and Social Conflict," 493. The tax information is found in *Pennsylvania Archives*, Series 3, vol. 14. The information on military service was provided by Pam LaJeunesse who did research for Christ Church's celebration of the nation's Bicentennial.

40. Vestry to the Supreme Executive Council of the Commonwealth of Pennsylvania, Sept. 9, 1777, Vestry Minutes, Sept. 9, 1777.

41. Vestry Minutes, Dec. 19, 1777, Sept. 7, 1778.

42. See ibid., April, 1776, 1777 and 1778.

43. "Autobiography of William White," 408–9.

44. The three who were reelected were Samuel Powel, Townsend White, and John Morris. Joseph Swift and Peter Knight ran and received four votes each. The rare tally sheet of the election is found in the Tench Coxe Papers, HSP.

45. Thomas Montgomery, "List of Vestrymen of Christ Church, Philadelphia," *PMHB* (1895): 518–26.

46. Vestry Minutes, April 15, 1779.

47. Vestry Minutes, June 21, 1779.

48. For the selection of Blackwell see Vestry Minutes, April 23 and Sept. 12, 17, 19, 1781. For Blackwell's background see Nelson Burr, *The Anglican Church in New Jersey* (Philadelphia: Church Historical Society, 1954), 585–86.

49. See Morgan Dix, *A History of the Parish of Trinity Church in the City of New York*, 4 vols. (New York: Putnam's, 1898–1906), for a discussion of the divisions in New York caused by the presence of the loyalist clergyman Charles Inglis.

50. See Owen Ireland, "The Ethnic Religious Dimension of Pennsylvania Politics, 1778–1779," *WMQ* 30 (1973): 422–48.

51. See ibid., 440–41; the legislators can be found in Robert Brunhouse, *The Counter-Revolution in Pennsylvania, 1776–1790* (Harrisburg, Pa., 1942), 337–39.

52. See Cheyney, *History of the University of Pennsylvania*, 107–8, 120–22; Brunhouse, *Counter-Revolution*, 77–79; Ireland, "The Ethnic Religious Dimension," 435–37.

53. "The Autobiography of William White," 412–13. White gives a lengthy report on the abolition of the charter, something about which he felt strongly. See also Vestry Minutes, Dec. 9, 1779.

54. From 1789 until 1791 there were actually two colleges in Philadelphia, the College of Philadelphia and the University of the State of Pennsylvania; Smith served as provost of the college. In September 1791 the Assembly united them and Smith was not chosen by the trustees to remain. See Gegenheimer, *William Smith, Educator and Churchman, 1727–1803* (Philadelphia: University of Pennsylvania Press, 1943), 87–91.

CHAPTER EIGHT

ESTABLISHING THE PROTESTANT EPISCOPAL CHURCH

While Christ Church and St. Peter's, along with many other Anglican churches throughout the United States, continued to perform their religious functions throughout the late 1770s and 1780s with few changes, in reality the denomination to which they belonged no longer officially existed in the new country. With an entire governing structure that looked to England, colonial Anglicans had lost both their traditional leaders and a part of their identity when independence became a reality. Yet thousands of Americans were still firmly attached to the doctrines, traditions, and liturgy of the Church of England and desired to remain within that communion. Some way had to be found to establish a church that maintained the essential features of the mother church at the same time that it divorced itself from all connections with all governments.

Both the overall situation of the United Churches and the type of men who led them placed the churches in an excellent position to play a major role in Anglican reorganization in the United States. In general, independence from England brought far fewer changes to the United Churches than it did to any other Anglican church in the United States. Since the churches had always been financially independent, they were not forced to look for new sources of income as were the southern churches where the Anglican Church had been established or most northern churches that had been dependent on the SPG. Because they had never had any formal relationship with the colonial government, either as an established church or as official dissenters, they did not have to adjust to disestablishment either. And the heterogeneous nature of colonial Pennsylvania meant that they were not startled by the competitive brand of interdenominational relations that emerged in the new republic. Having lived for years with the conditions the other churches were just now facing, the Pennsylvania Anglicans were natural leaders for the new church. In all these areas, William Smith, who had moved to Maryland during the Revolution and officially represented that state at the ecclesiastical conventions, had far more in common with his Pennsylvania friends than he did with his Maryland colleagues.

The attitudes of the Pennsylvania clergy toward doctrine and church government also contributed to the leadership role they assumed. Smith and White and their colleagues occupied a middle position between the "high church" beliefs of some of their northern colleagues and the "low church" attitudes of the Anglican churches in the south. This was especially true in the area of church government. Neither Smith nor White believed that the episcopate was divinely ordained as the clergy in New England did, yet they also lacked the suspicion and antagonism toward the prelacy that was common in the south.[1] Moreover, Philadelphia Anglicans had long accepted a wide variety of theological positions within the church. With great diversity among themselves, the Philadelphia Anglicans could easily accept the doctrinal positions of their northern and southern brethren, no matter how different they might seem.

The congregations of Christ Church and St. Peter's had also emerged from the war far stronger than most Anglican churches throughout the colonies. Most important, by the end of the war whig-tory divisions no longer plagued the churches; the whigs, who firmly controlled the churches, accepted loyalists and neutrals back into the fold without rancor or resentment. In Philadelphia Tench Coxe and Samuel Powel, both of whom had stayed in Philadelphia during the occupation, worked hand in hand with patriot Francis Hopkinson in the establishment of the new national church. This situation differed from that at Trinity Church in New York, for example, where supporters of the loyalist Charles Inglis fought patriot supporters of Samuel Provoost for many years.[2]

All these factors would have been of no consequence, however, had it not been for the leadership of William White. White had stood in the shadow of Peters, Smith, and Duché during his years as an assistant minister, and had been quiet for most of the revolutionary struggle. Yet in the years immediately following the war White suddenly appeared as a leader of monumental ability.

White was catapulted into national attention in 1782 with the publication of *The Case of the Episcopal Churches in the United States Considered*, a carefully wrought plan to restructure the Anglican churches in the colonies in a way that would preserve the faith, doctrine, and form of worship of the Church of England while changing the governmental structures to meet the needs of the new country.[3] This pamphlet caused great controversy at the time and continued to cause White problems thirty years later. Nevertheless, in most respects its proposals were eventually accepted as the framework for the organization of the Protestant Episcopal Church.

White's proposal for church government differed in many respects from traditional Anglicanism. Rather than authority descending from above, from the king and his bishops, the basis of authority would come from below, from the laity.[4] White argued that each individual church should retain "every power that need not be delegated for the good of the whole." Issues that could not be handled by individual churches should be decided by a pyramid of representational bodies. Lay and clerical representatives from each church would meet in district meetings. Here delegates to one of three regional conventions would be selected. At the large meetings, representatives to a triennial nationwide convention would be chosen. At all meeting levels, clergy and laity would be represented in equal numbers.[5]

White's position on the episcopate deviated even more from the traditional English position. White worked from three basic premises regarding the episcopate. First, he denied that the bishopric was divinely ordained or necessary for valid ordination. Second, he reminded his readers that "there cannot be produced an instance of lay-men in America, unless in the very infancy of the settlements, soliciting the introduction of a bishop" and that most considered it a "hazardous experiment" that could be "dangerous and destructive to their civil rights." Third, he argued that despite the hesitance of the laity to ask for a bishop, most members preferred an episcopal form of government; this, he believed, could be deduced from their adherence to this form despite the many inconveniences it caused during the colonial period.[6]

These premises may have been an accurate reflection of the views of most

American Anglicans, but they posed problems for anyone trying to organize the church. How was one to reconcile the desire for an episcopal form of government with the fears of a bishop? How could one have an episcopal church without an episcopate? White's solution was to retain the episcopate, if only because there would be "far less shock to ancient habits, and less cause of intestine divisions, than if new principles are to be sought for and established." However, in order to guard against episcopal tyranny, the prelates's power should be sharply limited. Appointed and removed by the assembly of clergy and laity, he was to serve as no more than a president of that body, "who, in conjunction with other clergymen to be also appointed by that body, may exercise such powers as are purely spiritual, particularly that of admitting to the ministry."[7]

White felt that the presence of a bishop was desirable but not absolutely necessary for the formation of the new church in the United States. Writing before the signing of the Treaty of Paris, the young cleric feared that it might be years before England recognized the independence of the United States and allowed American bishops to be consecrated. Therefore he proposed a radical and exceedingly controversial plan: the church should organize and govern itself without the aid of a bishop until one could be obtained. He argued "that the worship of God and the instruction and reformation of the people are the principle objects of ecclesiastical discipline;" therefore "to relinquish them from a scrupulous adherence to episcopacy, is sacrificing the substance to the ceremony."[8]

Historians have correctly noted the influence of John Locke on White's theory of government, but much more than political theory led White to adapt democratic principles to church government. Neither Locke nor his followers in the United States government addressed the proper relationship between laity, clergy, and bishops in an episcopal government. In answering these questions, White looked to his experience in the Philadelphia church. What White proposed in *The Case* conformed well to the basic principles of the horizontal authority structure that had gradually developed in Pennsylvania. The clergy and laity were to share (or, as the case may be, compete for) power. And the bishop, both through his unique spiritual powers and through his position as president of the convention, would have independent authority. However, the bishop's actual powers would be limited to ordaining the clergymen, just as the bishop of London's authority over the Philadelphia churches had been gradually reduced to the ordination and pro forma licensing of the clergy. In essence, White elevated the unique ecclesiastical structure that had developed in Philadelphia from an unfortunate expedient to a positive system. Having grown up under this system and having seen it work well in the 1760s and 1770s, he believed it was the best government the Protestant Episcopal Church could adopt. He no doubt also believed it was the only form of episcopal government that the laity in Pennsylvania and in the south would accept.[9]

* * *

White not only published a proposal for establishing a new denomination, he and Smith worked tirelessly for seven years to bring the plan to fruition. Had it not been for White and Smith, it is doubtful that there would have been one united Protestant Episcopal Church in the United States.

The process of organizing the church in Pennsylvania began in the United Churches. At the request of White, the vestry asked St. Paul's to send representatives to a meeting to plan a statewide convention. As a result of this meeting the Philadelphia churches sent a letter to all churches in the state asking them to send both lay and clerical representatives to a convention at Christ Church on May 24, 1784.[10]

This state convention marked the first time laity were included in an authorized ecclesiastical assembly of Anglicans. While the inclusion of laity was a logical consequence of their power in the colonial churches, White convincingly justified their presence based on the role Parliament played in the government of the Church of England.[11]

This group of clergy and laity, including representatives from seven churches outside Philadelphia, adopted resolutions that would frame the debate over the government of the new church at the national level and would eventually form the basis of the new ecclesiastical constitution. In their noncontroversial resolutions, the delegates declared that the doctrines and "uniformity of worship" of the Church of England should be maintained as "near as may be," and that three orders of clergy—bishop, priest and deacon—should also be maintained. But they went further. Following White's arguments in *The Case*, they resolved that "no powers be delegated to a general ecclesiastical government, except such as cannot conveniently be exercised by the clergy and laity, in their respective congregations" and that "to make canons, or laws, there be no other authority, than that of a representative body of the clergy and laity conjointly."[12] The convention also appointed the first standing Committee, which included White, Blackwell, and Matthew Clarkson from Christ Church, as well as John Chaloner and Dr. Gerardus Clarkson from St. Peter's.

Over the next two years, Anglicans outside New England, under the leadership of White and Smith, slowly put together the outlines of a federal church government. The climax of this organizational process came in 1785. After two informal meetings in New Brunswick, New Jersey and in New York, the "Protestant Episcopal Church" met for its first official General Convention in Christ Church on September 27, 1785. Seven states were represented, but Pennsylvania and Maryland dominated. Ten of the sixteen clergymen were from these two states and thirteen of the twenty-six laymen were from Pennsylvania, including Richard Peters, Samuel Powel, William Atlee, Edward Shippen, Joseph Swift, Dr. Gerardus Clarkson, John Wood, and Edward Duffield from the United Churches. The convention chose William White as president.[13]

This General Convention gave preliminary approval to the first constitution of the Protestant Episcopal Church and sent it to the states for ratification. Written by White and based on the proposals presented to the New York meeting by the Pennsylvania delegation the year before, the constitution established a general convention to which each state would send both clerical and lay representatives. The clergy and laity would deliberate as one body, with the bishops presiding, but they would vote separately, with a majority vote of both groups necessary to pass a measure. The General Convention rejected the more extreme suggestions of the southern delegates, which would have had the two groups vote together and would have made the bishops only ex-officio members. In deference to the southerners, they did leave it up to each state to decide whether it wanted a resident bishop. But overall, Pennsylvania's horizontal structure rather than the southerners' "democracy" had prevailed so far.[14]

The General Convention also asked the archbishops of the Church of England to consecrate any bishopric candidates recommended by the state conventions. Before any consecrations could occur, one more General Convention had to take place to deal with various objections raised by the English prelates. This meeting convened in Christ Church in June 1786 and, after an adjournment to wait for further information from England, concluded in Wilmington, Delaware in October. At both sessions Philadelphia Anglicans played a prominent role: Francis Hopkinson served as Secretary to the Convention, and he and Samuel Powel served with White and Smith on the committee of correspondence, the body set up to handle issues occurring between conventions.[15]

At the same time that the national convention worked to get bishops consecrated, the Pennsylvania convention elected its candidate for the episcopate. In September 1786 the Pennsylvania convention unanimously elected William White as its candidate for bishop and in October the vestry of the United Churches provided the necessary credentials for the bishop-elect. The vestrymen commented that, while they congratulated the Church in general,

we particularly felicitate ourselves upon the irreproachable moral character of the Person now chosen to fulfill the Duties of that Eminent Station, whose exemplary life, and soundness in the Christian Faith we have no doubt will, in future, dignify an exalted, as it has hitherto, adorned a more humble station in the Church of Christ.

White sailed for England with Samuel Provoost of New York in November. On February 4, 1787, in a ceremony performed by the archbishops of Canterbury and York and two other bishops, White and Provoost were consecrated.[16] (See Figure 15 for the first "bishop's chair" provided for Bishop White.)

This event, so momentous for the national church, was of even greater significance to Christ Church and St. Peter's. The history of those congregations would be shaped for the next fifty years by the fact that their rector was bishop of Pennsylvania. Upon his arrival back in Philadelphia in April 1787 White reported that he had been received "in my native City with all the Esteem & Affection which could be expected from the Respectability of my present Station, in Addition to the Force of old Connections & Attachments." Since the fears of an episcopate no longer applied now that the United States was independent, he found that "the Episcopalians are happy in finding their Church at last supplied with the higher Order of her Ministry & the most respectable Characters of all Denominations rejoice with her in the Event."[17]

While White's consecration was an extremely happy event for Christ Church, it did not solve the organizational problems of the Episcopal Church, since Episcopalians in New England, particularly Connecticut, rejected the "federated plan" of the middle and southern states and had begun to organize their own church. Believing that a bishop had to be obtained before any organizing of the church could be done, in March 1783 the clergy of Connecticut secretly elected Samuel Seabury, famous for his outspoken tory position, as their candidate for bishop. Unable for both political and ecclesiastical reasons to be consecrated in England, Seabury finally journeyed to Scotland and in November 1784 was consecrated by the nonjuring bishops, a group of bishops who refused to accept the legitimacy of the Glorious Revolution of 1688. While no one questioned the legitimacy of the Scottish bishops' succession, their political position was anathema to many in both England and the United States.[18]

Seabury's views on church government were even more troubling than his tory background or his unorthodox consecration. Believing that God had

FIGURE 15
The first bishop's chair of Christ Church, crafted for Bishop White in the 1780s. An oversized windsor chair made of tulip poplar and red maple, it has bamboo-turned spindles and a cage on the crest. Photograph by Louis W. Meehan.

placed ecclesiastical power squarely in the hands of bishops, he allowed the clergy only an advisory role and refused to allow any role for the laity in church government. His colleague Thomas Bradbury Chandler expressed their position plainly: "If the Bishops are not allowed to govern the Church, the Church is not under Episcopal government, and cannot be Episcopal."[19]

As a result of these diverging opinions, the chances that the northern and southern churches would unite seemed remote in 1786. Virginia and South Carolina would not accept a church in which the laity were not represented and the New England clergy appeared equally determined to resist giving any power to the laity. Moreover, many Anglicans, including Bishop Provoost, refused to accept the validity of Seabury's consecration.[20]

White and Smith were in a particularly good position to act as conciliators in this dispute because they possessed neither the intense suspicion of bishops that the southern delegates had nor the hatred of nonjuring beliefs and resentment of tories that dominated Bishop Provoost's thoughts. While Chandler found Smith's positions "commodiously flexible, yielding not only to every blast, but to the gentlest breeze that whispers," it was Smith's ability to compromise that allowed the warring sides to come together.[21] Smith and White did not work alone, of course. Samuel Parker of Massachusetts and Jeremiah Leaming of Connecticut both worked earnestly for reconciliation. But it was White and Smith who achieved the concessions and compromises from the General Convention that allowed the New England churches to join their southern brethren.

As the date for the 1789 triennial convention approached, Smith and White struggled to convince Seabury that his two main objections—the requirement that state conventions send lay delegates and the questioning of the validity of his consecration—could be solved. When it became clear that their personal assurances would not convince Seabury, White and Smith turned their attention to the General Convention which met in the State House in Philadelphia in July 1789. With Provoost absent due to illness and the delegates in a mood to compromise, the General Convention passed a resolution recognizing Seabury's consecration and amended the form of government to remove many of Seabury's objections. Under the new measures a state delegation without lay members would be considered valid. Moreover, the convention strengthened the power of the bishop by establishing a House of Bishops and allowing it veto power over legislation.[22]

In September 1789, after receiving information from the Committee of Correspondence made up almost entirely of Pennsylvania delegates, Seabury, joined by delegates from Connecticut, Massachusetts, and New Hampshire, arrived at the reconvened convention. Once the two sides met, they quickly worked out the remaining issues. They further strengthened the House of Bishops by giving it the right to initiate measures and by increasing the percentage needed to override the bishops' veto to four-fifths.[23] With these changes the constitution of the Episcopal Church was complete and a nationwide government was firmly established.

The constitution of 1789 differed in certain respects from the one proposed in 1785. Most important, the power of the bishops had been increased to the same level as that of the laity and lower clergy; the assent of a majority of each group was now necessary for any measure to pass. But despite the changes the new constitution followed quite closely from the original proposals made by White; it also closely resembled the situation of the church in Pennsylvania. The 1789 constitution essentially established a horizontal authority structure within an episcopal form of government. While earlier drafts had established somewhat of a hierarchy, with the bishops at the bottom, the final form gave equality to each group, thus establishing a true horizontal relationship among bishops, lower clergy, and laity.

* * *

One more important task faced the convention of 1789: the production and approval of a prayer book for the new church. Rather than merely removing references to the king and Parliament, the delegates chose to conduct a line-by-line revision of the Book of Common Prayer. As one of only two bishops, White had a major role in these revisions. The two assistant ministers of the United Churches, Joseph Bend, who had joined the Christ Church staff in 1787, and Robert Blackwell, and lay delegate Hopkinson also served on one of the four committees appointed to produce the new prayer book. The Convention approved it in 1789.

While many of the revisions were minor, certain changes are worth noting. The new book omitted the Athanasian Creed and made the phrase "descend into hell" optional in the Apostles' Creed, replacing it with "he went into the place of departed spirits." In place of the English custom of reading all the psalms each month, the House of Deputies chose a selection of psalms which could be used instead. At Seabury's insistence, the service of Holy Communion included the much longer and more beautiful Scottish Prayer of Consecration. Besides changing the liturgy, the Convention also made other changes. It omitted sixty-nine saints' days from the church calendar. It also added three important offices: A Form of Prayer for the Visitation of Prisoners, A Form of Thanksgiving to Almighty God for the Fruits of the Earth, and Forms of Prayer to Be Used in Families.[24]

The convention, at the insistence of William Smith, also decided to include an official hymnbook with the Book of Common Prayer, something that had never been done in England. In addition to the metric psalms, which had been used for hundreds of years, the book included twenty-seven hymns. White, who opposed hymn singing all his life, objected to their inclusion, but eventually agreed, as long as the number was lowered from the fifty-one originally selected by Smith. The inclusion of these hymns marked a revolutionary change in the music of the church.[25]

With the approval of the Prayer Book, the formation of the Protestant Episcopal Church was complete and members of Christ Church could look with pride to the role they had played in that formation. Both the initial federation of the churches in the middle and southern states and the subsequent unification with the New England states had been largely orchestrated by the clergy and laity of the United Churches. And the new Prayer Book was greatly influenced by the work of White, Smith and Hopkinson. William White certainly deserves the title "father of the Episcopal Church." Similarly, Christ Church richly deserves the title "mother of the Episcopal Church." Not only did the church serve as the site of the first national conventions, but the authority structures developed within that church during the colonial period influenced the national church government to an extent not generally recognized.

NOTES

1. Mills, *Bishops by Ballot*, 193–94, 201–2, 258–63 discusses the antagonism of the southerners toward a bishop.
2. See Clara Loveland, *The Critical Years: The Reconstruction of the Anglican Church in the United States of America 1780–1789* (Greenwich, Conn.: Seabury Press, 1956), 66–67.
3. William White, *The Case of the Episcopal Churches in the United States Considered* (Philadelphia, 1782), reprinted in *HMPEC* 22 (1953): 445–75.
4. This point was made well by Temple, *The Common Sense Theology of Bishop White*, 21–29. Temple presents an excellent overall discussion of this pamphlet.
5. White, *The Case*, 453–54.
6. White, *The Case*, 456–57.
7. White, *The Case*, 458, 454.
8. White, *The Case*, 460; see pp. 458–75 for his overall justification of the plan.
9. See Loveland, *The Critical Years*, 34–35; Temple, *Common Sense Theology*, 21–23. Mills particularly emphasizes the influence of the Revolution on the entire organization of the Episcopal church. In his discussion of the church in colonial Pennsylvania, Mills does indicate

that the relationship between laity and clergy "in an unforeseen way . . . was an omen of what was to come after the Revolution." But when he discusses the actual reorganization, he ignores this influence, preferring to discuss the political influences at work. See Mills, *Bishops by Ballot*, 77–78.

10. White, *Memoirs of the Protestant Episcopal Church*, 84–85; *Journal of the Meetings Which Led to the Institution of a Convention of the Protestant Episcopal Church in the State of Pennsylvania Together with the Journals of the First Six Conventions of the Said Church* (Philadelphia, 1790), 3–5. (Hereafter *Pennsylvania Journals*.)

11. See White, *Memoirs*, 87–92. Mills supports White's claim that it was the first official assembly to include laity. See Mills, *Bishops by Ballot*, 197.

12. *Pennsylvania Journals*, 6.

13. John Bioren, ed., *Journals of the General Conventions of the Protestant Episcopal Church in the United States of America; from the year 1784, to the year 1814 inclusive* (Philadelphia, 1817), 1–16.

14. See Loveland, *The Critical Years*, 152–55; White, *Memoirs*, 22–24, 96–99; Mills, *Bishops by Ballot*, 237–40.

15. The complicated negotiations to obtain the consecration of American bishops can be followed in Loveland, *The Critical Years*, esp. 156–60, 174–79, 192–96; and White, *Memoirs*, 111–40. Most of the relevant documents are found in Perry, *Historical Documents*; Bioren, *Journals of the General Conventions*, 35, 43.

16. Vestry Minutes, Oct. 17 and 23, 1786; White, *Memoirs*, 27–28.

17. William White to Archbishop of Canterbury, April 28, 1787, White Manuscripts, vol. 2, nos. 143.

18. For Seabury's efforts to obtain consecration see Loveland, *The Critical Years*, 93–117, or Bruce Steiner, *Samuel Seabury, 1729–1796: A Study in the High Church Tradition* (Athens: Ohio University Press, 1972), 181–224.

19. Thomas Bradbury Chandler to William White, Sept. 26, 1785, quoted in Loveland, *The Critical Years*, 144. Seabury's journey is discussed in Loveland, 93–117; Mills, *Bishops by Ballot*, 213–28.

20. Mills, *Bishops by Ballot*, 241–42, 259–60.

21. See Loveland, *The Critical Years*, 212. While Smith technically represented Maryland, by 1789 he was once again living in Philadelphia.

22. See Loveland, *The Critical Years*, 247–51; Mills, *Bishops by Ballot*, 273–77.

23. The members of the Committee of Correspondence are listed in Bioren, *Journals of the General Conventions*, 86. For the proceedings of the Convention see Loveland, *The Critical Years*, 262–63; White, *Memoirs*, 169, 232–33; Mills, *Bishops by Ballot*, 277–80.

24. For a summary of the changes see Loveland, *The Critical Years*, 263–72; James Thayer Addison, *The Episcopal Church in the United States 1789–1931* (New York, 1951; reprinted, Hamden Conn: Archon Books, 1969), 70–72. For a more complete discussion, see Marion Hatchett, *The Making of the First American Book of Common Prayer* (New York: Seabury Press, 1982), 116–36. The Proposed Prayer Book, which was largely the work of Smith, had actually been used in Christ Church briefly.

25. See Martin Dewey Gable, Jr., "The Hymnody of the Church 1789–1832," *HMPEC* 36 (1967): 254–56. For the voluminous correspondence between White and Smith on the subject of hymns see Perry, *Historical Documents*, 1: 145–83.

CHAPTER NINE

CHRIST CHURCH ENTERS THE NINETEENTH CENTURY

After a decade of struggle, by 1790 the future looked brighter for Anglican churches in America and especially for the United Churches. Led by outstanding ministers, with a congregation that included many wealthy and influential members, and having finally outgrown the controversies that so plagued the churches during the colonial period, the United Churches were in an excellent position to face the new century. While Bishop White's last years—beginning in the 1820s—would see decline and controversy, his rectorship can still be seen as the golden years of Christ Church.

The city of Philadelphia as a whole had also overcome its massive postwar problems by 1790 and entered a period of unparalleled growth and prestige. The city still stretched only nine blocks north and south and not far beyond Fifth Street to the west, but its structures had been rebuilt and repaired, and its population had increased by 9 percent since 1780, to 42,520. The economy had been revived, in part because ingenious and aggressive Philadelphia merchants had overcome the loss of trading routes within the British empire by opening up trade with countries in Europe and the Orient. By 1787 the value of exports had reached a level about

50 percent higher than before the war. The Bank of North America, formed in 1781 and headed after the war by Episcopalians Thomas Willing, Robert Morris, Tench Francis, and William Bingham, aided in this economic development.[1]

The city's political atmosphere also improved. Philadelphia hosted the Constitutional Convention and celebrated the ratification of the document it produced with perhaps the most spectacular parade in its history. Directed by Christ Church member Francis Hopkinson, it began by a cannon salute echoed by the bells of Christ Church. In 1790 Pennsylvania adopted a new constitution of its own, modeled after the federal one and much more to the liking of most members of Christ Church. A year earlier the Assembly had restored self government to the city, a right that had been taken away under the 1776 constitution. Episcopalians Francis Hopkinson, John Nixon, and Benjamin Chew were popularly elected to a new Common Council, which chose Samuel Powel as mayor.[2]

The 1790s saw their share of sorrow as well. In 1793 Philadelphia experienced the worst of four yellow fever epidemics. Of the 4,000 people who died, 398 were buried in the Christ Church burial ground, 373 more than the year before. Most Philadelphians who could fled the city, but ministers of the United Churches (along with Joseph Pilmore of St. Paul's and Absalom Jones of what would be the African Episcopal Church of St. Thomas) stayed to help their parishioners. Blackwell fell victim to the disease, but recovered.[3]

The city bounced back from the epidemic as it had from the trauma of the Revolution and faced the new century with optimism. The federal census of 1800 confirmed that Philadelphia was still the largest city in the new nation and visitors declared it a beautiful city as well. The French botanist André Michaux described it as "the most extensive, the handsomest and most populous city in the United States," while to the Duc de la Rochefoucauld-Liancourt it was not only the "finest" in the United States, but "one of the most beautiful cities in the world." Its mercantile trade continued to be second to none, with Philadelphia merchants, including Christ Church members Tench Coxe and Thomas Willing, taking a leadership role in the lucrative China trade. Philadelphia was also rapidly becoming the cultural capital of the country, "the Athens of America"; United Church members George Clymer, Joseph Hopkinson, the sculptor William Rush, William Poyntell, and John Dorsey were among those who founded the Philadelphia Academy of Fine Arts.[4]

With these developments, Philadelphia reached its apex as a preindustrial city. Yet, with the exception of governmental forms, the changes in Philadelphia between 1775 and 1800 were not fundamental. Many artisans and merchants still lived over their shops. Residential neighborhoods were still interspersed with commercial ones. While many new faces had been added to the economic and political leadership, merchants and lawyers still dominated almost every aspect of the city's life. Similarly, while Presbyterians had gained and Quakers had lost political power in the revolutionary struggle, the makeup of the city's religious life had changed little; three Presbyterian, four Episcopal, one Baptist, one Methodist, two Catholic, and two Lutheran churches and two Quaker meetings vied for the loyalty of Philadelphians as they had before the Revolution.[5]

However, by 1836, when Bishop White died, the physical appearance as well as the economic and religious life of Philadelphia had been transformed. Many of the dramatic changes in the city in the first third of the nineteenth century would directly affect the future of Christ Church. Economically, Philadelphia adjusted to a declining share of the overseas commerce by dominating the coastal trade and by leading the nation in the industrial revolution. Helped by coal transported from western Pennsylvania mines, by 1828 Philadelphia was recognized as the foremost manufacturing city in the country. Manufacturers accumulated amounts of money only dreamed of by eighteenth-century merchants and caused the gap between the rich and poor to widen and become more noticeable. Manufacturing giants also diversified the economic elite in Philadelphia. Old-style leaders like Sidney George Fischer complained that these men were concerned only with making money, rather than with the good of the community, as eighteenth-century leaders had been. Immigrants, predominantly Irish Catholics, drawn in part by jobs in the factories, diversified both the ethnic and religious makeup of the city.[6]

Industrialization also brought the beginnings of spatial differentiation. A "downtown" commercial district began to develop in the area surrounding Christ Church. By 1830 the fashionable residential area of the old city now stood in the area of Third and Spruce, near St. Peter's, while the center of the city had moved to Seventh Street. By 1840 there were 56,000 residents living west of that street and only 37,500 east of it. At the same time the northern and southern suburbs were actually growing faster than the city itself.[7]

During the first third of the nineteenth century the face of Philadelphia religion changed dramatically. One important religious change had actually begun in the 1790s. In 1794, after three years of fund-raising, the city's free blacks, with the active encouragement of Benjamin Rush and other white leaders, founded the African Episcopal Church of St. Thomas. While many of the founding members had previously been associated with St. George's Methodist Church, they voted to affiliate their new church with the newly formed Episcopal denomination, in part because of the degree of local autonomy it allowed. In 1795 White, with the support of the Pennsylvania convention, ordained Absalom Jones, one of the heros of the yellow fever epidemic, as the first black deacon in the Episcopal Church; in 1804 Jones was ordained a priest. This ordination had a price: in part because Jones did not have the required training in Greek and Latin, St. Thomas's Church had to agree not to send representatives to the Episcopal Convention. This less-than-equal status would cause problems later in the century, but at the time it no doubt seemed to blacks a small price to pay for their own church.[8]

White Philadelphians were increasingly going to churches with a more evangelical orientation. By 1828 there were twelve Presbyterian, six Methodist, and five Baptist churches, compared to six Episcopal churches and five Quaker meetinghouses.[9]

In the 1820s and 1830s all Philadelphia, but particularly the evangelical churches, felt the effects of the Second Great Awakening that swept the country. Revivalist Charles Finney brought his emotional, personal, committed style of religion to Philadelphia in 1827, holding revival meetings that called on people both to repent and to put their new beliefs into action. As a result, reform movements flourished, aiming to convert and perfect people so as to usher in the millennium.[10]

Even Episcopalians were affected by the evangelical style of the Awakening. Increasingly they divided into two camps: evangelical and high church. As we have discussed, the evangelical movement within the Church of England had been introduced into Philadelphia by William Macclenachan and continued to be represented by St. Paul's Church. But with the revival movement of the nineteenth century, evangelicals within the Episcopal Church became much more numerous and more aggressive. At approximately the same time, another group of Episcopalians were developing the "high church" position that would increase in importance as the nineteenth century progressed.

Evangelical Episcopalians stressed the sinful nature of man and his utter helplessness before God, centering their theology and their worship around the Bible rather than the classical and early Christian writers that had become popular in the eighteenth century. They encouraged the emotional aspects of religion, what White referred to as "animal instincts," and were extremely strict in their morals, condemning such entertainment as the theater, and encouraging temperance. Their attachment to the Episcopal Church was sincere, but not fanatical. While they used the Prayer Book, they did not limit themselves to it, regularly engaging in extemporaneous prayers and prayer meetings that often turned into revivals. Similarly, while they believed that the episcopacy was the best form of government, they did not think it necessary for the existence of a true church. In part because of their more flexible attitude toward the episcopate, they encouraged cooperation with other Protestant churches and were active in social reform movements.[11]

By the second decade of the nineteenth century evangelical Episcopalians, who had been opposed by low church adherents in the eighteenth century, had new opponents, a group of high churchmen centered in New York and led by the energetic and dogmatic Bishop John Hobart. Hobart had grown up in Christ Church and studied under White, with whom he remained close friends, but his views were far more rigid than those of White. High church adherents believed that for three or four centuries after the death of Christ the church was in a "pure" state, accurately reflecting the teachings of Christ. Thus, rather than focusing on the scriptures as interpreted by regenerate Christians as the evangelicals did, they tried to recreate that early church. Out of this framework came the belief that the episcopate was absolutely necessary for a true church. Similarly, the emphasis on the perpetuation of the pure church led the high church faction to advocate a church divorced from most societal issues. Rather than asking whether a movement was good for society, those with high church leanings asked whether it was good for the church, and in cases such as temperance or abolition, they always answered "no." Moving against the general religious forces within society, they therefore refused to recognize non-episcopal ordination or cooperate with other Protestants in reform organizations. Within the life of the church, high church Episcopalians stressed the sacrament of the Eucharist and the objective aspects of religion, and insisted on absolute adherence to the Prayer Book. They believed that salvation occurred through the use of the sacraments rather than by a "conversion experience" that occurred at a specific time. While they emphasized the devotional life of the Christian, they came to be identified with "order" and the "proper forms" of worship.[12]

*   *   *

While the changes in the size and structure of the city and in religious life would eventually have negative effects on the United Churches, for most of

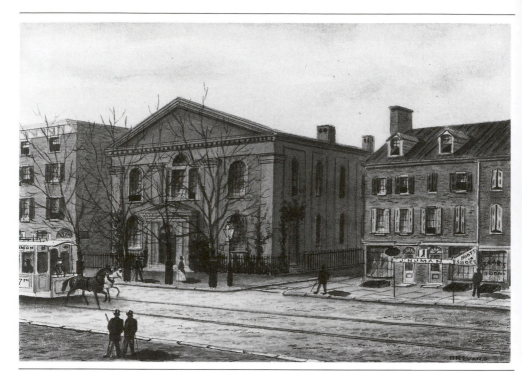

FIGURE 16

St. James Episcopal Church, 7th Street above Market. Courtesy of the Historical Society of Pennsylvania.

Bishop White's tenure the churches were in an exceptionally good position to take advantage of the growth and prosperity of Philadelphia and to compete for the allegiance of Philadelphians. In fact, by 1806 the congregations of the United Churches had become so large that they needed another church. Responding to the westward movement of the city's population, in 1809 the vestry built St. James Episcopal Church on Seventh Street above Market (Figure 16); its more favorable location made it immediately popular among Episcopalians.[13]

Bishop White served as rector for all three churches until his death in 1836 and had a profound impact on Philadelphia, the Episcopal Church, and the men who served as his assistants, as well as on the three congregations under his care (see Figure 17). Although he wrote extensive theological works in which twentieth century scholars have found some originality, and

FIGURE 17
Bishop William White (rector, 1779–1836), portrait by Thomas Sully. Courtesy of the Historical Society of Pennsylvania

served as president of a host of organizations, it was neither his theological positions nor his administrative skills that impressed his contemporaries; it was his character. Mildness, moderation, modesty, prudence, charity are the words most often used to describe him. Even when one makes allowances for the sentimentalism of the day and the biased nature of many of the sources, one is still impressed with the unanimous praise given to White. In his later years he seems to have been considered to be the Protestant version of a saint. A story about his childhood illustrates this well. One of his playmates years later recounted, "Billy White was born a bishop. I never could persuade him to play anything but church. He would tie his own or my apron around his neck, for a gown, and stand behind a low chair, which he called his pulpit: I seated before him on a little bench was the congregation; and he always preached to me about being good."[14] In his eulogy to White, Henry Onderdonk, who had served as assistant bishop under him, put the same sentiments in theological terms. White, he said, belonged to that "very small class of Christians, who bear from infancy the image of Christ, and never deface it by vice, or worldliness or by flagrant neglect. With a character so pure, it has been said of him, and not unaptly, that he was sanctified from the womb."[15]

White never let this constant stream of praise affect him. Alonzo Potter, who would later serve as bishop of Pennsylvania, commented that White "betrayed no sense of his own consequence. He invited no salutations. . . . He never claimed anything for himself." When asked by his grandson why he always took off his hat to people of the lower classes, White simply responded: "My child, would you have them polite to me and I not to them?"[16]

Despite his "saintly" character and his own high standards of conduct, White did not impose his views on others. For example, White suggested that people should show their "disapprobation of the licentious tendency of the theater, by abstaining from going there," but he added "I would not make this an essential of church communion" and would not "endeavor to enforce my opinion, otherwise than by argument."[17] He also refused to take the temperance pledge, believing that when a Christian man "had promised his body in soberness, temperance and chastity," as he had in his ordination vows, he had gone as far as language permitted him to go. His biographer and student, Bird Wilson, records that White's definition of temperance included two glasses of wine with dinner and a glass of sherry before bed![18]

White's mildness, moderation, and prudence were also central to his theological positions. His reasoned, dispassionate approach to Christianity grew naturally out of his personality. As Bishop Onderdonk argued in his obituary, his flawless character meant that although White knew and felt he was a sinner, he did not "so feel it as to exhibit the clear train of converting experience which other Christians undergo, whose piety was not so early, or has not proved so uniform and consistent." Thus "his religious feelings appeared calm and moderate and destitute of that ardor and strength which many thought the necessary . . . indications of . . . the transforming influence of religious truth. But though calm and moderate, they were deep-seated, sincere, steady and serene."[19]

White's theological positions were "low church" in the eighteenth-century sense of the term. Like most eighteenth-century Anglican clergy, White stressed reason rather than emotion in religion, looking to Scripture and history for "empirical" evidence to support his beliefs. He did not, however, reject revelation, believing that man needed divine grace to use his reasoning faculties correctly. However, both his nature and his theology led him to be repelled by the evangelicals. He opposed introducing anything into a service that would appeal to "animal sensibilities" and warned young clergymen to "carefully distinguish evangelical persuasion from that sort of preaching which is called addressing the passions."[20]

White followed his own advice, using his sermons to instruct the congregation in both doctrine and morality. Perhaps because he "felt little cause for self-reproof," he never felt called upon to use his sermons to rebuke or censure others. According to Bird Wilson, they were "calm, serious and argumentative discourses," delivered in a dignified fashion, "without much animation and entirely without action." Joseph Ingersoll, a prominent and long-time parishioner, felt that White's delivery, "so foreign from the arts of elocution, as they are generally practiced, did not deprive the sermons of their attractiveness." But Alonzo Potter reported that when, at the age of eighteen, he first met White, he found "his delivery was monotonous . . . His style was deficient in point and force, and the models on which he had unconsciously formed himself, were not favorable to a bold and commanding eloquence."[21]

White was devoted to the liturgical forms of the Episcopal Church. Both his orderly mind and his stress on the vows taken at the time of ordination led him to frown on any deviation from the prescribed order of service. He strongly believed people "should not be dependent on the occasional feelings, or the discretion, or the degree of cultivation of an officiating minister."[22] (See Figure 18 for the second bishop's chair provided for White.)

Despite his attachment to the Episcopal Church, his devotion to the episcopate was not as extreme as that of his high church brethren. In fact, he never repudiated his belief, as expressed in *The Case of the Episcopal Churches*, that under certain circumstances a church could exist without bish-

FIGURE 18
The second bishop's chair, c. 1809, made by Ephraim Haines. This Sheraton style chair is made of mahogany with turned reeded legs, carved arm supports ending in an angel face, and an elaborately curved crest rail of grapes and leaves surmounted by the bishop's miter. Photograph by Louis W. Meehan.

ops. While he believed in the "divine institution" of the episcopate and refused to allow non-episcopally ordained ministers to officiate in his churches, he thought it wise to "abstain from faulting Ordination of any other Protestant Church." Partially as a result of these views, he refused to rebaptize converts from other denominations.[23] These views would cause him problems with high church Anglicans, but they followed logically from his experience with the bishopless colonial church.

White's position on the episcopate fit well with his overall tolerance of other denominations. Having been raised in the Philadelphia Church where interdenominational feuding was avoided when possible, it is not surprising that he believed it "an indispensable duty to cultivate courtesy with those respectable ministers of other denominations with whom I have been acquainted." He cautioned the first Episcopal missionaries to China to remember that:

In the tie which binds you to the Episcopal Church, there is nothing which places you in the attitude of hostility to men of any other Christian Denomination, and much which should unite you in affection to those occupied in the same cause with yourselves. You should rejoice in their successes, and avoid as much as possible all controversy.[24]

White exhibited a similar moderation and willingness to compromise in his dealings with the newly created Methodist church in the 1780s and 1790s. Philadelphia clergy had long considered Methodists to be outside the bounds of orthodoxy, a feeling which was confirmed when the Methodists in the United States, unlike their brethren in England, formed a separate denomination in 1784. Yet, when Thomas Coke, the Methodist "superintendent" in America, approached White offering a method to unite the two denominations, White encouraged the discussions. White asserted that it is "to be expected that distinct Churches, agreeing in fundamentals, should make mutual sacrifices for a union," and argued the measures Coke proposed "cannot fail of success, unless there be on one side or on both, a most lamentable deficiency of Christian temper."[25] At the General Convention of 1792 White joined the other bishops in proposing a declaration encouraging state conventions to pursue unions with other denominations, particularly the Methodists. Declaring it the "sacred obligation" of Christians to promote union if at all possible, they expressed a willingness to "alter or modify those points [of church order] which, in the opinion of the Protestant Episcopal Church, are subject to human conventions." Perhaps not surprisingly, nothing came of these efforts.[26]

While White was comfortable dealing with other denominations as equals, he did not accept the total separation of church and state. He argued that it was "a right inherent to legislative power, to make provision for the public teaching of religion, with a view to the morals of the people," although he believed that such establishment should "be so far general as to embrace the opinions of the great majority of the people, with toleration of all others."[27] He endorsed the effort of the United Churches and others in Philadelphia to get the city council to put chains across the streets during the worship services to stop the noise. His most vigorous campaign occurred when Stephen Girard willed the city money to establish a boys' school but insisted that no clergymen be allowed on the premises. White unsuccessfully lobbied the city to reject the bequest, arguing that it was "irreligious and unchristian to accept of the public responsibility of an institution, to the pupils of which there shall be denied all instruction in religion."[28] Thus, while White took a moderate position on most theological and moral issues of the day, his belief in the importance of religion in the lives of individuals and the nation was as vehement as that of any of his contemporaries.

*　　*　　*

White successfully fulfilled his dual roles of rector and bishop because of the support of a series of exceptionally talented assistant ministers. What we know about Robert Blackwell, who was an assistant from 1781 to 1811, indicates that he resembled White in many respects. He was described as "a man of large fortune, fine appearance and singularly pleasant temper and manner" who was "a scholarly and sensible preacher of the English university cast." Horace Binney, his long-time friend and parishioner, declared that Blackwell's sermons were "to him never uninteresting," although lacking in "elocutionary display." Like White, Blackwell participated in a number of organizations; he played an active role in the Corporation for the Relief of the Widows and Children of Clergymen for more than fifty years, and served as treasurer of the diocesan and general conventions.[29]

After White became a bishop, the vestry further strengthened the position of the churches in 1787 by hiring Joseph Bend as an assistant minister. Bend, a young cleric from New York, spent only four years in Philadelphia. He subsequently accepted the rectorship of St. Paul's Church in Baltimore, a rather prestigious appointment, and became a leader of the high church party.[30]

In 1794 the vestry hired James Abercrombie, a man who had grown up in Christ Church, to replace Bend (see Figure 19). This began an association that would last for thirty-six years, the longest tenure of any assistant in the

FIGURE 19
The Reverend James Abercrombie (assistant minister, 1794–1832), portrait by Thomas Sully, original in Christ Church, Philadelphia. Courtesy of the Historical Society of Pennsylvania.

history of Christ Church. Abercrombie's youthful goal of the priesthood had been disrupted by the Revolution and then by a severe disease of the "eye lids." Instead, he pursued a mercantile and banking career and in 1792 was chosen a member of the new Philadelphia Common Council.[31] Unsatisfied by these pursuits, at the age of thirty-five Abercrombie once again turned his attention to the ministry, accepting the position of assistant minister of the United Churches in 1794.

Of the many ministers who served under Bishop White, Abercrombie is the most difficult to capsulize. He was in some ways very much like White, but in other ways it is hard to see them working together. Abercrombie's theological positions closely resembled White's. His fellow assistant minister William DeLancey described him as "a well-trained conservative clergyman contented with the existing system, disinclined to change, and confiding in authority."[32] However, their personalities were so different that only White's tolerance could have allowed him to work harmoniously with Abercrombie for so many years.

Like White, Abercrombie was devoted to the Book of Common Prayer of the Protestant Episcopal Church. In a sermon on the liturgy preached to the diocesan convention, he commented: "contemplating the amazing whole, the blaze of spiritual light dazzles the mental eye . . . excellencies are thus the distinguishing character of every part." He was considered one of the best readers of the liturgy in America. Having tamed a naturally harsh voice, his "manner of reading the Service was not only impressive but well nigh irresistible." It was said that "he read as one who fully understood what he was reading, and whose mind was earnestly occupied with the matter of it."[33] His sermons were learned, eloquent, and exceptionally well delivered. But, one observer commented that, like White's, they lacked "that deep feeling commonly called *unction*, which is always so sure to open a passage to the hearts of the hearers." His lack of emotion was attributed to another characteristic he shared with White, a devotion to scholarly activities. Abercrombie edited the short-lived *Quarterly Theological Magazine*, a religious magazine aimed at the laity which contained a potpourri of religious writings, including sermons, biblical criticism and poetry.[34]

The *Quarterly Theological Magazine* illustrated another trait White and Abercrombie shared: a tolerance for other denominations and a desire to emphasize what Christians had in common. The frontispiece of the *Quarterly* carried the following quotation: "The differences among Christians, about lesser matters, proves the truth of those great fundamental points in which they agree." Similarly, the prospectus promised that the editors would "discard the sectarian spirit so long at variance with that *spirit of unity and that bond of peace*, which ought to constitute the distinguishing marks of all Christian societies."[35]

Abercrombie's attempts at educating young men in school were more successful than his efforts to educate the general laity through the *Quarterly Theological Magazine*. From 1800 to 1817 he ran the Philadelphia Academy, a private boys' school where "he enjoyed the highest reputation as a classical teacher." His published "Charges" to his students indicate that he took the responsibility of shaping young lives very seriously. He included advice on almost every aspect of their lives, from dress ("avoid the extremes of foppery and slovenliness") to choice of friends (associate as much as possible with your superiors "in age, talents and virtuous qualifications") to "external deportment" ("let ease, gracefulness, politeness and affability, be carefully studied").[36]

His "Address to Parents, Sponsors and Guardians" illustrates his concern with his students' spiritual development. Mincing no words, he charged that many of his fifteen-year-old students were "as ignorant of the principles of the Christian religion, as the savage that roams the wilderness." After urging parents to give their children proper instruction and to set a good example by going to church themselves, he warned that "voluntary disregard of their immortal souls" would lead to the parents' own damnation, as well as that of their children.[37]

Abercrombie's personality was as different from White's as his theological views were similar. The two words used most often to describe him were "guileless" and "frank." Delancey commented that from the first he was struck by Abercrombie's "frank and open hearted manners and conversation. There was nothing assuming, dictatorial or patronizing in his demeanour." Abercrombie's mischievous sense of humor and love of life were bound to get him in trouble. Both his letters and those of his friends indicate an ability to poke fun at himself and others in authority. In 1811, for example, a clerical friend wrote about a dinner with Abercrombie and Bishop Hobart, a *very* serious primate. He reported: "Dr. Abercrombie amused himself a little at table by warmly recommending a wig to Bishop Hobart reprobating his wearing pantaloons, etc., etc." Henry Onderdonk, bishop of Pennsylvania, summarized well Abercrombie's personality at his funeral: "He was often misunderstood—frank men always are. He was often misrepresented—the unresisting and the innocent must expect to be."[38]

Abercrombie's personal life also deviated from what some considered the clerical ideal. His wife, the former Ann Baynton, died in 1805, leaving him with nine children. Unlike White, whose wife died when he was fifty, Abercrombie did not live out his life as a quiet widower. Only months after his wife's death, Abercrombie, who was referred to by a female as "your frolicsome friend," was reported to have "fallen deeply in love with Charlotte Seaton." Reporting on this relationship, a friend told her brother that she would "reserve all *scandal* until I have a personal interview with you."[39] How much scandal was caused by his relationship with Charlotte Seaton is unknown, but twelve years later, his marriage at the age of fifty-nine to Mary Jane Mason, age thirty, did provoke considerable consternation. William Meredith, a vestryman of Christ Church and a loyal friend of Abercrombie's, wrote to Mason's father warning him against "the proposed connection between your family and Dr. A." He explained that in "the world it has been received with the strongest feelings of disgust; and the most violent expressions of Hatred and Contempt for all who are suspected of promoting it." The vestry members were so upset they appointed a committee to express their "dissatisfaction . . . at his conduct" and to suggest that he offer his resignation. While Abercrombie did not lose his position at the United Churches because of the marriage, it did, no doubt, at least temporarily affect his reputation in the community.[40]

Abercrombie's family life indirectly led to another source of controversy: his financial problems. Unlike other Christ Church ministers, Abercrombie neither came from a wealthy family nor married into one. The salaries at the United Churches were not high and were actually reduced in the nineteenth century, and Abercrombie compounded his problems by having thirteen children. As a result, starting in 1800 he regularly asked the vestry for money. In fact, his motivation for founding the academy was purely financial; he reported to the vestry that the "disagreeable necessity of increasing his income led him to the severe and slavish undertaking of opening a school."[41] At times he seems to have been kept afloat by loans from William Meredith. His situation became so bad in 1818 that he began to put his hopes not on the vestry's benevolence but on the lottery! But luck not being with him, in 1827 he reported to the vestry that he was "pressed for Rent and am pennyless at home." Such continual begging must have been unpleasant for both the minister and the vestry.[42]

Despite Abercrombie's problems, he continued to have many friends and supporters throughout the years. While some were alienated by his frankness, his mischievous sense of humor and his lifestyle, others must have found these characteristics endearing. In many ways he probably provided a needed contrast to the serious, "saintly" character of Bishop White.

*   *   *

Between 1811, when Blackwell retired, and 1831 Abercrombie and White had as ministerial colleagues four of the finest ministers in the Episcopal Church. All four went on to become influential in the national church, two serving as bishops. One contemporary described three of them well:

The few clergy in the city were in some respects rather remarkable men. . . . Jackson Kemper, a young deacon, . . . very handsome, very energetic and full of zeal, . . . for some years carried all before him . . . After some years he was no longer the only young clergyman. First, came James Milnor, a lawyer of distinction. Then [William] Muhlenberg likewise, by all his family high connected. . . . [A] peculiarity about all of them was that had they not been Clergymen, they would, from their family, manners, etc. have been leaders in society.[43]

Jackson Kemper, who succeeded Blackwell, grew up in New York City and graduated as valedictorian from Columbia University. He studied theology under Bishop Benjamin Moore of New York and John Henry Hobart, then assistant minister of Trinity Church. After being ordained a deacon by Bishop White in March of 1811, he preached at St. James and as a result the vestry of the United Churches offered him the position of assistant minister on May 14, 1811.[44] Kemper remained as an assistant to White for twenty years.

Kemper's youthful exuberance and undeniable devotion to Christ made a big impression on the United Churches. As his friend and biographer put it:

Familiarity with Scripture, glowing love of his Savior, imparting to his expressions affecting power, unquestioning and loyal obedience to the divine will—these are what impressed his hearers;. . . As he preached, the delight of beneficence beamed from his features until he seemed an embodiment of his theme.[45]

But Kemper's strength was not as a scholar or a preacher, but as a "pastor"; he preferred personal ministry to all other aspects of his job. After Kemper had left Philadelphia, a parishioner who had grown up under his tutelage wrote to him that "in all cases of doubt or difficulty I was sure of a friend and counsellor who never wearied of my application, but was ever ready to afford the advice and assistance which was requisite."[46]

While Kemper greatly impressed the Philadelphia church, he was not similarly impressed with the religious life of his parishioners. Two years after his ordination he wrote that "during the short term of my ministry I have not infrequently been perplexed in mind, wondering at the mysterious Providence of God in permitting a church whose doctrines are apparently in exact transcript of the [scriptures?] to continue in so lifeless a state." This sentiment was no doubt in part occasioned by the failure of members to take communion; a friend reported to him in 1811 that while there had been a "pretty good congregation" at St. James, only sixteen had received the sacrament.[47]

Fortunately, Kemper was able to invigorate the congregations. He reported that "there are many, particularly of St. James who are becoming sensible of the vast importance of their immortal souls & who if they continue working, will soon glory in the cross of Christ." In the three years after Kemper's arrival, the confirmation classes of the United Churches, under Kemper's supervision, averaged 170 people, a considerable increase over the average of forty-four confirmands from 1807 to 1810. Considering that the three churches had fewer than 2,500 pews, the 509 people confirmed in those three years is exceptional.[48]

Kemper's success in increasing confirmations was indicative of both his theology and his missionary zeal. While he has often been identified with the high church movement in the Episcopal Church and would eventually side with it, during his years at Christ Church he was a moderate churchman who saw good in men of both camps. He shared with Hobart a deep devotion to the government and Prayer Book of the Episcopal Church and did not approve of the liberties taken by some evangelicals. But his devotion seems to have been grounded in a personal love of the church rather than on any rigid theology or historical study. Indeed, Kemper's primary concern was never with theology, nor with maintaining the "pure church," but with saving souls. It was this that made him sympathetic to the evangelicals within the church. He shared with them a deep concern with the piety of his parishioners and stressed the need for everyone to acknowledge their sinfulness and put their fate in God's hands. He felt that "a sincere acknowledgement of the depravity of human nature, of human inability and consequently of the necessity of a divine atonement will lead to the joy . . . in heaven over the repentant sinner." This concern with the souls of his parishioners led him to support prayer meetings, something his high church friends found appalling. In fact, it appears that for a while he held a "Prayer Society" at St. James. However, at the same time he believed that the primary means of attaining salvation was through the use of the "appointed means of grace," that is, baptism and communion, a position that his high church friends would have endorsed.[49]

Kemper's concern for people's souls combined with his love for the Episcopal Church led him to support expanded missionary activity within the church. As we will see, he persuaded Bishop White to take a much more active role in the western parts of the diocese, and he was the prime mover in the involvement of the United Churches in missionary activity. He himself served as a missionary agent for much of his time at Christ Church.

In 1835, shortly after Kemper left Christ Church, the General Convention elected him as the first missionary bishop for the Episcopal Church. Kemper spent the next twenty-four years traveling thousands of miles a year through the Mississippi valley, helping to organize six new diocese. Later appointed the first bishop of Wisconsin, he finished out his life at Nashotah Seminary, a training ground he had helped to found for high church clergymen.[50]

* * *

In 1814, after considerable discussion, the United Churches finally hired a fourth minister.[51] The minister chosen, James Milnor, came from a distinguished and varied background. While he stayed at Christ Church for only two years, he went on to have an extremely successful ministry in New York and became a leader in the national church. Milnor was born into a Philadelphia Quaker family, but was disowned when he married an Episcopalian. He practiced law for twenty years and became a prominent Federalist politician, serving on the Philadelphia City Council from 1800 to 1810 and as a congressman from 1811 to 1813. He flirted with Presbyterianism, but by 1809 had rented a pew at St. James.[52]

Between 1800 and 1812 Milnor gradually became disillusioned with the gaiety of political life and underwent a religious conversion. By 1812 he had become convinced that saving "one soul out of hell . . . would be more to [him] than the wealth of the Indies."[53] Refusing to run for reelection, he began his studies for the ministry and was ordained in August of 1814.

That White and Kemper would embrace Milnor, who clearly belonged to the evangelical wing of the church, indicates the open-minded, moderate character of both men, as well as the lack of clear camps within the church at this early date. Even after Milnor became the rector of St. George's in New York, from whose pulpit he became a leader of the evangelical movement, he continued to avoid controversy and to attempt conciliation. In 1815 he argued that "parties in the Church . . . should not be countenanced" as they had "disastrous consequences to the Interests of our Zion."[54] As a result, while Hobart condemned Milnor, Kemper continued to befriend him, even considering him for the assistant bishop position in Pennsylvania.

William Augustus Muhlenberg succeeded Milnor at Christ Church in 1817. The great grandson of Henry Melchior Muhlenberg, the foremost colonial Lutheran leader, William Muhlenberg had been raised as a Lutheran. His connections with Christ Church began early, however; he attended Abercrombie's Academy and, when St. James was built on land sold by his mother his family was given a pew there. They attended that church from then on.[55]

Muhlenberg was in many ways a true product of the United Churches, influenced by all its ministers. As his most recent biographer suggests, Muhlenberg was influenced by Abercrombie's attitude toward other denominations, his dislike of the position of clerk of the church, and his advocacy of singing a variety of hymns. Muhlenberg was also influenced by Kemper, having attended Kemper's Prayer Society while at the University of Pennsylvania, and being among the 180 confirmed in 1813. To Kemper he owed, at least in part, his concern for parish visitation; part of his training included accompanying Kemper when he visited the sick. After studying theology with White and Kemper, Muhlenberg was ordained a deacon in 1817, immediately assuming the duties of assistant minister of the United Churches.[56]

Muhlenberg stayed only three years. Shortly after his ordination to the priesthood he received an offer to become rector of the church in Lancaster, Pennsylvania. When the vestry refused to appoint him as permanent assistant minister, despite White's request, Muhlenberg accepted the appointment. Muhlenberg went on to become one of the most innovative leaders in the Episcopal Church. He founded one of the first Episcopal boarding schools for boys and St. Paul's College near Flushing, New York. Later, with the aid of his sister's money, he founded the Church of the Holy Communion, an innovative parish in New York City; while not a mission church, it had no pew rents and was extremely active in helping the poor, foreshadowing many of the activities that would become common during the social gospel movement at the end of the century. He also founded a hospital which was best known for having the first order of deaconesses in the American Episcopal Church. Still later he attempted a planned community for working class families.[57]

Muhlenberg is best known, however, for the memorial he and seven other people presented to the House of Bishops in 1853 and which bears his name. In an effort to further Christian unity, a goal that had always been important to Muhlenberg, the Memorial suggested that the Episcopal Church ordain priests who subscribed to its basic theology but could not ascribe to all the canons. Secondarily it called for improvements in religious education and a greater freedom within public worship. While the Memorial did not lead to any action, it was taken seriously and it did lead to an open discussion of the issues of church unity and liturgical reform for years to come.[58]

Two years after Muhlenberg's departure he was replaced by another minister who would have an outstanding ecclesiastical career. William Heathcote DeLancey came from the wealthy New York family that had been prominent before the Revolution. After graduation from Yale, he studied for the priesthood under Bishop Hobart. He served as assistant until 1827 when he resigned to become provost of the University of Pennsylvania. He returned to become rector of St. Peter's after Christ Church and St. Peter's separated in 1832 and later was appointed bishop of western New York.[59]

Like White and Kemper, DeLancey was considered by his contemporaries to be an exceptional man. At the time of his appointment to the United Churches, a fellow New York clergyman described DeLancey as "modest, liberal and charitable, firm in his own sentiments, and very kind and candid in judging those of others." He went on to ascribe to him an "amiableness of disposition, and a frankness, kindness, purity of heart, which peculiarly qualifies him for the interesting but difficult station of a collegiate pastor."[60] At his death a minister from his diocese in New York described him this way:

His Rare personal beauty contributed not a little to win men at the outset . . . the treasures of his mind, the sympathies of his heart, the urbane decisiveness of his manner and the under-stratum of piety discernible in all, left the impression upon every one he met which once framed itself in words, "He was *born to be an Apostle.*"[61]

His theological positions were probably best outlined in his consecration address in which he described the two most important ecclesiastical influences on his life—bishops Hobart and White. He indicated that he learned from Hobart "the view of evangelical doctrine and Church order with which you are all familiar and which seems to me . . . to be fundamentally connected, not with the outward prosperity of the Church alone, but with . . . the glory of the living God, and the salvation of the souls of men." He went on to say that his years in White's diocese allowed him to learn "from his example of Christian gentleness, patient energy, quiet diligence," that the most "effectual mode of retaining peace and harmony among ourselves" was "steady adherence, in all practical points, to . . . the great principles of Gospel truth and order and holiness through which the Church is blessed and man is saved." As can no doubt be inferred from these statements, DeLancey, like Kemper, became a moderate high churchman, who tried to avoid controversy.[62]

Located in a growing, vibrant city and served by such outstanding ministers, the United Churches were in an excellent position to move forward, to take new initiatives, and to attract new members. It is to these members and to their activities that we will turn in the next chapter.

NOTES

1. Richard G. Miller, "The Federalist City," in Russell F. Weigley, ed., *Philadelphia, a Three Hundred Year History* (New York: W.W. Norton and Company, 1982), 172–76, 198–99.
2. Miller, "Federalist City," 161–67.
3. Broadside Bill of Mortality, 1793, in Weigley, *Philadelphia*, 183. See John Powell, *Bring Out Your Dead: The Great Plague of Yellow Fever in Philadelphia in 1793* (Philadelphia: University of Pennsylvania Press, 1949; reprinted with a new Introduction, 1993), 236; Bird Wilson, *Memoir of the Life of the Right Reverend William White, D.D., Bishop of the Protestant Episcopal Church in the State of Pennsylvania* (Philadelphia: J. Kay, 1839), 160.
4. Wilson, *Memoir*, 161–66, 172–76.
5. Edgar P. Richardson, "The Athens of America, 1800–1825," in Weigley, *Philadelphia*, 218; Scharf and Wescott, *History of Philadelphia*, 2: 1129–1446 discusses the history of the churches in the city.
6. Nicholas Biddle Wainwright, "The Age of Nicholas Biddle, 1825–1841," in Weigley, *Philadelphia*, 259, 266–77.
7. Sam Bass Warner, Jr., *The Private City: Philadelphia in Three Periods of Its Growth* (Philadelphia: University of Pennsylvania Press, 1968, rev. ed. 1987), 58; Wainwright, "The Age of Nicholas Biddle," 281.
8. Differing accounts of this event can be found in Ann Lammers, "The Reverend Absalom Jones and the Episcopal Church: Christian Theology and Black Consciousness in a New Alliance," *HMPEC* 51 (1982): 159–84; Gary Nash, *Forging Freedom: The Formation of Philadelphia's Black Community, 1720–1840* (Cambridge, Mass: Harvard University Press, 1988), 113–30.
9. Marion L. Bell, *Crusade in the City: Revivalism in Nineteenth Century Philadelphia* (Lewisburg, Pa.: Bucknell University Press, 1977), 43–48.
10. Bell, *Crusade in the City*, describes Charles Finney's visits and the resulting problems in great detail.
11. See E. C. Chorley, *Men and Movements in the American Episcopal Church* (New York: Charles Scribner's Sons, 1946), 59–110 for an excellent discussion of the evangelical movement.
12. See Robert Bruce Mullin, *Episcopal Vision/American Reality, High Church Theology and Social Thought in Evangelical America* (New Haven, Conn.: Yale University Press, 1986), chap. 3; Chorley, *Men and Movements*, chap. 5.
13. See Vestry Minutes, May 30, Oct. 8, Oct. 10, Dec. 9, and Dec. 29, 1806; Jan. 30, March 23 and April 28, 1809; Jan. 1810. Bishop White wrote an eloquent argument in favor of building a modest church; see William White, "On Building a New Church," in Wilson, *Memoir*, 353–56. Although the vestry seems to have followed his advice, the building of St. James still left the United Churches with a $4,000 debt in 1814.
14. Wilson, *Memoir*, 21.
15. Wilson, *Memoir*, 283.
16. Alonzo Potter, in Sprague, *Annals of the American Pulpit*, 5: 286; Julius Ward, *Life and Times of William White* (New York: Dodd, Mead and Company 1892), 84–85.

CHAPTER NINE

17. William White to W. S., March 24, 1803, Wilson, *Memoir*, 392.

18. Wilson, *Memoir*, 21; Ward, *Life and Times of William White*, 78–79.

19. Quoted in Wilson, *Memoir*, 275, 271.

20. William White, *A Commentary on the Duties of the Public Ministry*, 10, quoted in William Manross, "Dr. White's Episcopate," in Stowe, *Life and Letters of Bishop William White*, 135. He opposed the introduction of too many hymns because of the tendency to incite "animal sensibilities"; see White, *Memoirs of the Protestant Episcopal Church*, 237. For a thorough study of White's theology see Temple, *The Common Sense Theology of Bishop White*. For a good summary see William Manross, "Bishop White's Theology," *HMPEC* 15 (1946): 285–97.

21. Joseph Ingersoll in Sprague, *Annals of the American Pulpit*, 5: 289; Wilson, *Memoir*, 290–91; Alonzo Potter in Sprague, *Annals*, 5: 286.

22. William White, "Address before the Special Convention of 1826," in Wilson, *Memoir*, 390.

23. William White, "Charge of 1834," quoted in Walter Stowe, "The Presbyter," in Stowe, *Life and Letters of Bishop William White*, 79. For his position on non-episcopal baptism, see William White to Dr. Caspar Morris, Dec. 19, 1832 in Stowe, *Life and Letters of Bishop William White*, 278–79.

24. William White to Rev. S. Marks, Feb. 1, 1826, in Stowe, *Life and Letters of Bishop William White*, 271; White, "Additional Instructions for the Missionaries to China," May 20, 1835, in Wilson, *Memoir*, 150–51.

25. White, *Memoir*, 413; for a good summary of Methodist attitudes toward the split with the Anglicans, see Mills, *Bishops by Ballot*, 254–56.

26. Addison, *The Episcopal Church in the United States*, 85–87.

27. William White to Francis Gorbin, Feb. 7, 1794, in Wilson, *Memoir*, 165.

28. Vestry Minutes, July 24, 1797; White, "An opinion respectfully offered to the members of the city council, on the question of their acceptance of the legacy of Stephen Girard, Esquire, for the founding and supporting of a literary institution for the education of orphans," printed in the *National Gazette*, quoted in Wilson, *Memoir*, 241.

29. Printed sketch of Blackwell in the Wallace Papers, HSP, no source noted.

30. Sprague, *Annals*, 5: 354.

31. Sprague, *Annals*, 5: 392–23.

32. Sprague, *Annals*, 5: 399.

33. James Abercrombie, *A Sermon on the Liturgy of the Protestant Episcopal Church* (Philadelphia: Samuel and Maxwell, 1808), 21–22. Comments by the Revs. Henry Mason and John Coleman in Sprague, *Annals*, 5: 395, 397.

34. From David Paul Brown in Sprague, *Annals*, 5: 396. See the Table of Contents of the *Quarterly Theological Magazine and Religious Repository* 1 (1813). The quote comes from the prospectus, iv.

35. *Quarterly Theological Magazine*, 1 (1813), iv–v.

36. David Paul Brown to Sprague, in *Annals*, 5: 396; James Abercrombie, *Charge delivered After a Public Examination of the Senior Class of the Philadelphia Academy* (Philadelphia: Smith and Maxwell, 1807).

37. "An Address to Parents, Sponsors, and Guardians," in James Abercrombie, *Lectures on the Catechism*, 2nd edition (Philadelphia, 1811), xiv, xx, xxii.

38. Benjamin Onderdonk to Jackson Kemper, Aug. 29, 1811, Kemper Papers, State Historical Society of Wisconsin, 1: 163. The descriptions of Abercrombie's personality are remarkably similar. See William DeLancey, Henry Mason, and John Coleman, all in Sprague, *Annals*, 5:

395–98. The excerpt from his funeral oration is quoted by John Coleman, in Sprague, *Annals*, 5: 398.

39. Gertrude Meredith to William Meredith, Aug. 16, 24, and 27, 1805, Meredith Papers, HSP.

40. William Meredith to Richard Mason, Dec. 21, 1816, Meredith Papers; Vestry Minutes, June 30, 1817. Abercrombie had been married in June.

41. Vestry Minutes, Feb. 20, 1800.

42. James Abercrombie to William Meredith, Dec. 23, 1810, Nov. 22, 1816, Feb. 16, 1818, Meredith Papers. To follow his requests to the vestry see Vestry Minutes, Feb. 20, 1800; April 26, May 27, 1802; Oct. 23, 1811; April 19, Sept. 1, and Oct. 29, 1819; Jan. 25 and Feb. 16, 1827.

43. Anonymous, Jackson Kemper Papers.

44. See Greenough White, *Apostle of the Wilderness* (New York, 1900); Howard Morris Stuckert, "Jackson Kemper, Presbyter," *HMPEC* 4 (1935), 130–31; Vestry Minutes, Mar 22, May 13, May 14, 1811.

45. White, *Apostle of the Wilderness*, 29.

46. A. B. Shaw to Jackson Kemper, March 20, 1832, Kemper Papers, 12: 41.

47. Jackson Kemper to James Milnor, Feb. 24, 1813 and Samuel Turner to Jackson Kemper, Nov. 4, 1811, Kemper Papers, 2: 46 and 22.

48. Jackson Kemper to James Milnor, Feb 24, 1813, Kemper Papers, 2: 46; Bishop White's List of Confirmations, Christ Church Archives.

49. Kemper to Milnor, Feb. 24, 1813, Kemper Papers, 2: 46; Benjamin Onderdonk to Jackson Kemper, October 19, 1811 and March 18, 1812, Kemper Papers, 2: 16, 20, 78;

50. Edward Hardy, Jr., "Kemper's Missionary Episcopate: 1835–59," *HMPEC* 4 (1935): 195–218; Frank E. Wilson, "Kemper's Diocesan Episcopate: 1854–1870," *HMPEC* 4 (1935): 219–24.

51. See Joshua Clay to Jackson Kemper, Oct. 12, 1814, Kemper Papers, 4: 44 for a description of the discussions surrounding the Milnor appointment; also Montgomery to Jackson Kemper, Nov. 14, 1814, Kemper Papers, 5: 53.

52. See J. S. Stone, *Memoir of the Life of James Milnor, Late Rector of St. George's Church, N.Y.* (New York: American Tract Society, 1848), 31.

53. His conversion is chronicled in a wonderful series of letters printed in Stone, *Memoir of the Life of James Milnor*. For the quotes, see 135, 157–58.

54. James Milnor to Levi Bull, Jan. 16, 1815, *Memoir*, 191.

55. Ann Ayres, *Life and Works of W. A. Muhlenberg* (New York: Harper and Brothers, 1894), chap. 1.

56. Alvin W. Skardon, *William Augustus Muhlenberg: Church Leader in the Cities* (Philadelphia: University of Pennsylvania Press, 1971), chap. 1; Ayres, *W. A. Muhlenberg*, chap. 1.

57. Vestry Minutes, Nov. 30, 1820. See Skardon, *William Augustus Muhlenberg* and Ayres, *W.A. Muhlenberg*.

58. See Addison, *The Episcopal Church in the United States*, 177–88.

59. Frederick Masterman, "Some Aspects of the Episcopate of William Heathcote DeLancey, First Bishop of the Diocese of Western New York," *HMPEC* 33 (1964): 261–77.

60. Benjamin Onderdonk to Jackson Kemper, March 6, 1822, Kemper papers, 6: 81.

61. George Hills, *The Wise Master Builder* (Syracuse, N.Y., 1865).

62. Masterman, "Episcopate of William Heathcote DeLancey," 264.

CHAPTER TEN

A CHURCH
OF FIRSTS: CHRIST
CHURCH ACTIVITIES
UNDER WHITE

The high caliber of clergy found in the United Churches in the late eighteenth and early nineteenth centuries allowed the congregations to attract outstanding members, even as competition among churches increased. These members joined the clergy in supporting a whole range of activities within the city of Philadelphia. Rejecting political involvement in favor of religious and philanthropic activities, Christ Church members were influential in founding many important Philadelphia institutions. It is indeed impressive how many "firsts" the congregation could claim during White's rectorship.

The United Church membership continued to be simultaneously diverse and disproportionately wealthy. One third of the men from the 1790 pew renters list whose occupations could be identified were merchants, attorneys, doctors, or "gentlemen." Similarly, a study of the Philadelphia economic elite in 1800 found that 34.6 percent were Episcopalians, most members of the United Churches, while only approximately 10 percent of the population at large joined that denomination.[1]

Included in this group of wealthy Episcopalians were

many who had been active in the Revolution. Merchants Robert Morris, John Nixon, and John Wilcocks had all amassed fortunes during the war. While Morris ended up in debtors' prison because of land speculation, most other Episcopalians were more prudent. Also remaining at Christ Church were merchants Matthew Clarkson and Philip Nicklin, shopkeeper William Adcock, Michael Hillegas, the first treasurer of the United States, Francis Hopkinson, who by this time was a district judge, and John Dunlap, the editor and printer of the *Daily Advertiser*.

Men who had grown up in Christ Church became prominent in the church and in the city in the nineteenth century. Nicholas Biddle, who would become famous as the president of the Second Bank of the United States, grew up in the church. Joseph Hopkinson, son of Francis, became prominent in his own right, serving as a representative to Congress and as judge of the federal district court, as well as authoring "Hail Columbia." General Thomas Cadwalader, who played a prominent role in the War of 1812, was the son of General John Cadwalder.[2]

New members of wealth and distinction also continued to join Christ Church. Henry Pratt, another merchant in Christ Church, was considered a "financial genius," second in wealth only to Stephen Girard. And John Perot, another prominent merchant, arrived in Philadelphia from Bermuda in 1781. Alexander Dallas, who would become United States secretary of the treasury under Madison, came to Philadelphia in 1783, joining Christ Church soon after.

In the nineteenth century lawyers took over the leadership roles in the church that had been filled by merchants in the eighteenth century. William Meredith, Sr. served on the vestry from 1816 to 1831, acting as accounting warden for the last two years, and was a regular delegate to both diocesan and national conventions. A prominent lawyer, he was president of the Schuylkill Bank and a member of the Philadelphia Common Council and the Select Council. His son William succeeded him at the bar in 1817 and would later succeed him in leadership roles at Christ Church. Horace Binney, the unquestioned leader of the Philadelphia bar for thirty years and perhaps the finest lawyer in the country, became an "institution" in Christ Church and in the city of Philadelphia. "Respected and admired but not loved," he served on the vestry for twenty-six years, acting as rector's warden from 1828 to 1835 and, like Meredith, served regularly at the diocesan and national levels of the church. William Tilghman, the rector's warden from 1813 to 1827, served as chief justice of the Pennsylvania Supreme Court from

1806 until his death in 1827. Besides his active involvement in Christ Church, he served as president of the American Philosophical Society and as a trustee of the University of Pennsylvania.[3]

However, one should not overestimate either the "elite" character of Christ Church or the importance of the church's position in the socioeconomic landscape of Philadelphia. While Christ Church in the nineteenth century was more of an elite institution than it had been in the eighteenth century, it still contained a majority of "ordinary citizens." Moreover, the profusion of voluntary associations in the city, as well as the increasing number of churches, meant that the wealthy and powerful had a variety of places to meet. The church in Philadelphia had never had the same symbolic and social importance that it had in eighteenth century Virginia, for example. While there were "status" churches in nineteenth-century Philadelphia, the city was too large and too heterogeneous for one or two churches to dominate the social or political scene.

* * *

Important changes occurred in the worship life of the church after 1790. Like other Episcopal churches, the Christ Church congregation began using the new American Prayer Book in 1789. The changes from the Proposed Prayerbook so upset Benjamin Rush that he left the church, but we know of no other negative comments.[4] While the services were probably shortened, the degree of continuity with the English Book of Common Prayer was so great that it is unlikely that the parishioners had trouble adjusting to the new one.

Musical practices changed as well, although not as much as in many other Episcopal churches. White maintained that he was the first in the country to introduce chanting into the service. Whether he was indeed first is not clear, but the practice seems to have been common in the Philadelphia churches by 1786. Christ Church also had a choir by the end of the Revolution.[5]

White's conservative views on music blocked more major changes. As indicated earlier, White strongly opposed the singing of hymns in church, allowing only psalms. This was in part because he believed that the selection of music should no more be left to the musicians or the ministers than the choice of prayers should be left to the clergymen. In the case of hymns, control was particularly important because of their tendency to excite "animal sensibilities" if not properly chosen. Moreover, he believed that there was "little of good poetry except the Scriptural, on sacred subjects."[6] White's strong beliefs about church music meant that the singing of hymns at Christ Church was a *rare* event. Once, according to William Smith, Abercrombie defied the bishop and ended his sermon by quoting the first line of a hymn, having arranged for the choir to pick up on it and finish the entire hymn. White was evidently not amused, and the incident was not repeated.[7]

White further believed that each psalm should have only one tune attached to it and the entire number of tunes used by the congregation should not exceed twenty. This would ensure that the people sang rather than merely listening to the clerk or the choir, something White felt important because "taking of the praises of God on the tongue has a tendency to interest the heart." The vestry agreed, instructing the clerks of the two churches in 1785 to "sing such tunes only as are plain and familiar" since the frequent changing of tunes is "generally disagreeable and inconvenient."[8]

By far the most important change in the religious life of Episcopalians after the war was their ability to be confirmed. It must have been particularly meaningful to be confirmed by a bishop who had grown up in their church. Bishop White performed his first confirmations in St. Peter's in 1787, when he confirmed twenty-two men and twenty-two women. In the next two years he confirmed 142 more members of the United Churches. While the absence of a bishop for almost one hundred years had, no doubt, made the rite of confirmation seem unnecessary to some, clearly many members were eager to partake of this importance religious observance. The equal sex distribution of the first year did not continue: of those confirmed in 1788 and 1789, ninety were women and fifty-two were men. In the following ten years White confirmed sixty-nine women and twenty-two men in the United Churches. This pattern, which was typical of religion in general in the United States, would continue in Christ Church until the twentieth century.[9]

Christ Church parishioners worshiped and sang in a building that was in much better condition than it was during the Revolution. In the 1780s the windows in Christ Church were declared "beyond repair" and new ones were put in the upper story, while stoves were provided for both churches; altogether the repairs totaled more than a thousand pounds. In 1789 the chancel of Christ Church was improved by Jonathan Gostelowe's gift of a mahogany communion table, the table still used in the church (see Figure 20). This table had a recess in the back that allowed it to fit snugly against the pulpit and ended the inconvenience of bringing the communion table out from behind the pulpit when needed. At the same time Gostelowe also gave the church a mahogany baptismal font that can still be seen at the church[10] (see Figure 21).

Not surprisingly, especially given the history of financial problems of the churches, the repairs left the churches heavily in debt. In 1789, when the churches' budget included only £152 above what was needed to pay salaries, the debt totaled £1860.16.10. The situation did not improve in the early 1790s, despite the renewed prosperity the city experienced.[11]

Philadelphia Episcopalians, it would seem, were still plagued by the tradition of a state church; despite the fact that Christ Church had been self-supporting from its founding, its members had not yet become accustomed to supporting it. In fact, the financial woes of the United Churches stemmed in large part from the failure of members to pay their pew rents. In 1794, for example, 49 percent of those renting pews in the United Churches were in arrears despite the fact that rents had not been raised since 1772 and were not unduly high.[12] Far fewer Christ Church pewholders paid their rent on time than did the members of the less wealthy Presbyterian churches. Only Third Presbyterian had a serious problem, with around 30 percent of its pew rents

FIGURE 20
Communion table crafted in 1788 by Jonathan Gostelowe, a vestryman of Christ Church. Photograph by Louis W. Meehan.

FIGURE 21
*Baptismal font crafted by
Jonathan Gostelowe.
Christ Church Archives*

in arrears in 1790. First and Second Presbyterian reported arrears of around 15 to 18 percent for the 1780s and 1790s.[13]

As the financial situation of the churches worsened, the vestry finally acted. In 1795, after much debate and apparent dissension, the vestry raised pew rents on lower-priced pews by 12 to 20 percent and on medium- and higher-priced pews by 40 to 50 percent. The following year the vestry raised burial rates. Moreover, in 1797 the vestry finally agreed that a person who did not pay pew rent for one year would be given six months to pay and then the pew would be let to someone else.[14] Delinquent pew renters and the resulting financial problems would be a continual problem for the churches, but these actions seem to have eased the immediate financial crisis.

While Christ Church members as a whole were not generous with their money, many gave generously of their time to support a wide range of religious and philanthropic activities. The most important and most enduring project, Christ Church Hospital, actually began on a small scale during the Revolution, but it became a major concern of the vestry in the 1780s. In his will John Kearsley, the man responsible for the building of Christ Church, had provided for the establishment of "an Infirmary or Alms House or Almshouses for ten or more poor or distressed women of the communion of the Church of England." He gave the churches a house on Mulberry Street (now 311 Arch Street) which he felt would be "suitable" for the almshouse, along with part of his estate. More important, at the death of his wife, his entire estate, with the exception of £500 given to his nephew, John Kearsley, was given to the church for the almshouse.[15]

Dr. Kearsley died in 1772, but it was not until Mrs. Kearsley died in 1778 that the hospital was actually established. Despite the British occupation, Christ Church Hospital opened on April 27, 1778, with three women living in the house on Mulberry (Arch) Street. By 1781 there were seven women living in the house and five more being supported as "out-pensioners."

The vestry could do no more than this because the younger John Kearsley, the already notorious tory who was also a member of Christ Church, protested the will. Despite general agreement that his claim of £4,000 against the estate was "without any support of Law or Equity," a jury awarded Kearsley £2500. This must have represented almost half the legacy left to the hospital.[16] Ironically, this money was of little use to the loyalist Kearsley, since his estate was attainted and he died in prison.

Despite the setback caused by Kearsley, Jr., as soon as the war ended the vestry began to look into better ways to serve the United Churches' poor women. The committee in charge reported in 1784 that eight pensioners lived "uncomfortably" in the house on Mulberry Street, which was too small and out of repair, while twelve others lived in rooms throughout the city rented by Christ Church. In 1785 the vestry agreed to build a new building on the site of the old one that would accommodate more women who would be supervised by a "prudent matron."[17]

The future of Christ Church Hospital brightened in 1789 with a rather surprising bequest by Joseph Dobbins, formerly a resident of Philadelphia, who at that time was living in South Carolina. For "the use of Dr. Kearsley's bounty to the poor, distressed widows" he presented the churches with property and notes worth $8,825 plus what is now the entire city block from Eighteenth to Nineteenth and Spruce to Pine Streets, which the trustees

FIGURE 22
Christ Church Hospital, 306–308 Cherry Street. Courtesy of the Library Company of Philadelphia.

wisely decided to keep. This gift and the appreciation of Kearsley's bequest eventually allowed the trustees to build a new building behind the original one, increasing to forty the number of women they could accommodate. That building opened in 1819[18] (see Figure 22).

In the 1780s the vestry of the United Churches helped establish another important Philadelphia institution—the Episcopal Academy. The idea for such an academy originated with William White, who believed that every religious society should have "a seminary, in which their youth, at least in the early stages of their education, may be instructed in the principles of religion, agreeably to the views entertained by the society in question." The time seemed particularly favorable because of the takeover of the College of Philadelphia and its Academy by the legislature and their Presbyterian allies.

After studying the issue, the vestry approved the establishment of such an academy in the fall of 1784. By January 1785 a subscription was begun and the "Fundamental Laws of the Academy of the Protestant Episcopal Church in the City of Philadelphia" were established.[19]

The school opened on April 4 in a rented building, with John Andrews, an Episcopal clergyman of some repute, as headmaster. In June 1788 the school moved from its rented location to its own impressive building at Sixth and Chestnut Streets. The future of the school was further brightened in 1787 when the legislature granted a charter to the Academy and provided 10,000 acres of land in Tioga County to support it. By 1789, 137 students attended the Academy.

However, serious problems had already emerged. The trustees had been forced to take out a loan for £2000 to finish the building and in January 1788 had cut faculty salaries. These financial problems might have been overcome had it not been for the reestablishment in 1789 of the College of Philadelphia and its Academy under the original trustees, including White and five other trustees of the Episcopal Academy. Andrews accepted the position of professor and vice provost of the college and two teachers of the Episcopal Academy left with him. By 1790 the Episcopal Academy had ceased to exist and in June of that year the trustees sold the recently built building.

At the same time the Academy ended the trustees began a new venture, free schools to provide rudimentary education to poor Episcopalians, both male and female. In 1789 the schools opened with eighty boys and forty girls. Charity sermons in Christ Church, St. Peter's, and St. Paul's supported the schools successfully for many years. But in 1815 the boys and girls were combined into one school because of low enrollment and in 1818 the free school closed for ten years. In 1828 the school reopened, serving up to sixty students until 1846.

In the meantime the board of trustees, which was still dominated by members of the United Churches, decided once again to establish a classical academy. In 1816 they bought a building on Locust Street and opened both a classical academy and an English school. During this second phase of the academy, which lasted until 1826, the trustees left the day-to-day operation of the schools up to the head teacher who collected the tuition. Unfortunately, an inability to keep teachers, combined with a huge debt on the building, led once again to the closure of the academy.[20] Despite their failures, the trustees had begun a process that would eventually lead to the establishment of an extremely successful educational institution.

Bishop White and his parishioners also took an active role in organizations that reached beyond Episcopalians. White continued to be a trustee of the University of Pennsylvania, attending every meeting until the year before his death. During that forty-five year period, twelve other members of the United Churches also served on the university's board.[21]

White also took an active interest in the education of the poor. After returning from his consecration trip, he suggested that the vestrymen establish Sunday schools like those he had seen in England. Nothing came of this proposal, but in 1791 he enthusiastically joined Benjamin Rush and the Roman Catholic writer Matthew Cary in founding the First Day or Sunday School Society, the first such organization in the country. By May of that year the society was running three schools, with approximately one hundred students in each school. The schools taught reading and writing, as well as the Bible and "morals and manners," in an effort to improve both the education and the behavior of "the offspring of indigent parents." The Sunday School Society also worked to establish free schools in Pennsylvania. In a petition to the Pennsylvania legislature the society maintained that the organization had already demonstrated that the "blessings of illumination among the mass of the people" could be spread through schools established at public expense.[22]

In 1808 White took a leadership role in establishing the interdenominational Philadelphia Bible Society, the first such society of its kind in the country. By this time an intense debate had developed over whether benevolent societies should be interdenominational or strictly denominational. While high church Episcopalians firmly opposed any cooperation with other denominations, White continued to encourage such cooperation. When Bishop John Hobart objected to his participation in a scheme that distributed Bibles without Prayer Books, White's response was characteristically reasoned, moderate and convincing. He argued that he had always believed that when "there can be communications in any laudable design [between denominations] they tend not only to Christian charity, but to reconcile the more sensible and moderate, of other communions to our principles and to our institutions." He then added the most telling point of all: "so far as the increase of our own communion is concerned, we ought not to fear that the making known of the contents of the Bible will be less likely to make people churchmen than any other society."[23]

White also took part in a wide array of humanitarian organizations. Along with Benjamin Rush and Tench Coxe, he participated in the Society for the Alleviation of the Miseries of Public Prisons, founded in 1781, which was influential in gaining a variety of reforms at the Walnut Street Prison. He also was the first to hold services in the prison. White served as president of the Magdalene Society, one of many organizations dedicated to reforming prostitutes, and of the Pennsylvania Institution for the Deaf and Dumb, and he and Robert Blackwell were active in the Philadelphia Dispensary, an outpatient medical facility.[24]

Laymen of the United Churches were also active in benevolent societies. Several members, including William Poyntall, John Dorsey, William Hall and Tench Coxe, served as managers of the Pennsylvania Hospital. A number of Episcopalians, including Rush, Poyntall, Coxe, William Bingham, Joseph Anthony, Jonathan Penrose, William Chancellor, Richard Peters and William Jackson, were members of another predominantly Quaker organization, the Abolition Society.[25]

* * *

The benevolent activity of Christ Church members and its ministers, like that of Protestants throughout the country, increased greatly in the early nineteenth century, even as its character changed. More and more Protestants were involved in strictly religious and denominationally based groups. Throughout the country, among all denominations, the early nineteenth century was a time of frantic activity aimed at advancing Christianity and saving the poor from moral downfall. As denominations adjusted to the religious freedom in the new nation, they realized that the future of a "Christian nation" as well as the growth of their particular denominations required active exertion on their part. With the tremendous westward expansion that followed the War of 1812, such efforts seemed particularly important. Because of the weak state of the Episcopal Church, its missionary and educational efforts were late in developing, but were even more sorely needed. The period from 1814 to 1835 was one of tremendous activity, of reawakening and expansion, a period in which most types of organizations we associate with the Episcopal Church were begun.[26]

While the diocese of New York had taken the lead in missionary activity, with the arrival of Jackson Kemper, Pennsylvania quickly became active in this field. In 1812 Bishop White, with the indispensable aid of Kemper, formed the Society for the Advancement of Christianity in Pennsylvania. This organization, whose aim it was to strengthen existing parishes within Pennsylvania and to serve as a catalyst for the formation of new ones, would be influential in transforming the nature of the diocese of Pennsylvania and its bishopric. The first annual report indicated that members of Christ Church supported this organization enthusiastically. Three members, William Tilghman, William Meredith, and John Perot, served as officers, while 105 pew renters were charter members of the society.[27]

Jackson Kemper served as the first missionary for the society. Exhibiting the energy and zeal that was so characteristic of his life, he spent two months in 1812 visiting churches as far west as Pittsburgh and into what is now West Virginia. He reported back that "the establishment of our Church in the whole western part of the United States will depend in a great measure upon this society." Once again in 1814 Kemper spent more than four months visiting communities as far west as northeastern Ohio. Perhaps surprisingly, both these missionary tours were timed because Kemper was in poor health and overworked; few people would consider months of traveling over bad roads and living under primitive conditions to be a cure for exhaustion![28]

Although hampered by a lack of ministers, the society was still quite successful. Kemper noted that the number of congregations in the diocese increased from twenty-eight in 1812 to sixty-seven in 1828. He did not attribute all these gains to the society, but he argued that "the majority of our congregations . . . owe their existence, their vigour, or their present state, to the Society for the Advancement of Christianity in Pennsylvania."[29]

The society and Kemper also galvanized White, who had concentrated his duties almost entirely on Philadelphia, to assume a more active role as bishop. Because of his increased visits to the country churches, the number of confirmations rose from 61 in 1811 to 581 in 1813. In 1825, at the age of seventy-eight, White, accompanied by Kemper, successfully completed an 830 mile trip to Pittsburgh and Wheeling, his first trip beyond the Alleghenies. In 1826 the two men ventured into northeastern Pennsylvania.[30]

The society also led to missionary activities outside Pennsylvania. In 1816 Kemper and White were influential in founding the Episcopal Missionary Society of Philadelphia, which sponsored missionaries in Ohio and Kentucky. The two also pushed for missionary activity on the part of the national church. Their efforts eventually resulted in the formation of the Domestic and Foreign Missionary Society.[31]

The women of the United Churches, like women throughout the United States, were also extremely active in promoting religious concerns.[32] When it became clear that the Society for the Advancement of Christianity needed tracts, "The Ladies of the Episcopal Churches, with a zeal peculiar to the female sex when works of charity and benevolence are in agitation," formed the "Episcopal Female Tract Society of Philadelphia" in 1816. Forty-eight women from Christ Church can be identified as belonging to this organization in 1830. Within the first year they had published ten thousand copies of tracts which they distributed to organizations and individuals in Philadelphia.[33]

For many years this organization was supported almost solely by women, but in 1830 they were forced to ask for contributions from men. Their pleas combined piety and humility with a certain sense of outrage that was characteristic of later appeals from women's organizations. They bemoaned the fact that when visiting people's homes they had to refuse *"our own citizens* when they extended their hands and raised their imploring eyes for religious and moral assistance." Furthermore, they expressed anger that most children instructed in their Sunday schools later joined other denominations in part because of the lack of Episcopal tracts. At the same time, however, they felt the need to defend their activities, emphasizing that "they acquiesce[d] too cordially in the reasonableness and expediency of St. Paul's prohibitory proclamation that 'he would not suffer a woman to teach' and felt too great a reverence for his command to them 'to keep silence in the churches' to violate the spirit of his injunction." They insisted that they only wanted to be "guided and assisted" in doing the "good works" Paul instructed them to do.[34]

In 1816 the women established the Female Episcopal Benevolent Society to give aid to the poor within their own congregations. This organization continued to serve Christ Church, St. Peter's and St. James even after the separation. Reflecting paternalism and a fear of encouraging indolence, they assured potential contributors that they visited each recipient and therefore represented a "safe channel for charitable contributions."[35] In 1830 the women of Christ Church formed the Ladies' Missionary Society. Unfortunately we have no records for the early years of that organization.

Women made their greatest contribution in the Sunday schools. While the first Sunday schools had been of a nonsectarian variety, shortly after the War of 1812 denominations began to start their own schools; although still aimed primarily at the poor, they emphasized religious instruction rather than reading and writing. In 1814 James Milnor and Jackson Kemper started a school at Commissioners' Hall in the Northern Liberties area, reportedly the first Sunday school officially incorporated by a religious organization.[36]

Within Christ Church it was the women who controlled the Sunday schools. In 1816 "several young ladies" sent out a circular asking for money;

they claimed that "many destitute children were not only receiving no instruction, but on the Lord's day were seen wandering about the street exposed to all the evils of idleness, profanity and vicious intercourse." They planned to alleviate this situation by starting a Sunday school that would teach the children "to read, commit portions of the scripture, catechism, psalms, and Hymns, etc. to memory."[37] A dedicated group of women continued this school for many years, visiting the children when they didn't come, providing clothing for the really destitute (although careful not to encourage "indolence" by such donations), and rewarding the students who behaved well and memorized verses with Bibles and tracts. In 1820 they reported that "the progress of some of our scholars has exceeded our most sanguine expectations," with one girl reciting 3,113 verses from the Bible in one year and another memorizing the entire catechism even though she could not read! The men of Christ Church also joined the Sunday school movement. While their organizational records are not extant, by 1825 the church reported to the diocese that the men's school had four teachers and sixty-five pupils.

While the women took the lead in the parish Sunday schools, the men of the United Churches helped establish the Protestant Episcopal Sunday and Adult School Society of Philadelphia in 1817 to encourage the activities of the Sunday schools in the area and to publish materials for their use. In 1821 the president, William Tilghman, the vice president, Thomas White, son of Bishop White, and the treasurer, William Baker, were all members of Christ Church, as were six of the ten lay managers. By that time the society had grown to include 227 local societies in eleven states and one territory.[38]

The members of the United Churches also concerned themselves with the education of clergymen. Although Bishop White had opposed the idea for the General Theological Seminary in New York, preferring diocesan-based seminaries, once the General Convention of the Protestant Episcopal Church established it he served as an active trustee, attending every commencement and annual examination until 1830, when he was too old to travel. Jackson Kemper was an even more enthusiastic supporter of the seminary, joining the trustees at an early age. When the Board of Agents of the Theological Seminary for the Diocese of Pennsylvania was formed to raise money for the General Theological Seminary, White served as chairman, Kemper as secretary, and nine of the twelve agents were from the United Churches, six of them from Christ Church. In 1821 Philadelphia women, including sixteen from Christ Church, formed the Philadelphia

Female Association in Aid of the Theological Seminary in order to fund a scholarship in honor of Bishop White. By the next year they had raised $1,955. As was so often the case in churches, the women were more effective fund raisers than the men, who, at this point had raised only $1,244![39]

Participation and leadership in these organizations was spread out over a fairly large group of men and women; no individuals or families yet dominated the church's activities. In fact, an analysis of membership in these organizations, including five women's groups and six men's organizations, indicates that participation in religious activities was not a family affair.[40] Of the thirty-six men who could be identified as taking an active role, only seven had female relatives (wives or daughters) who were also active. Similarly, of the fifty-eight active women, only nine had male relatives who were active. While families may have worshiped together, husbands and wives made independent decisions about joining religious organizations.[41]

Among both the men and the women there were small groups of people who were active in several organizations, while most were active in only one. Among the men, ten men were active in four groups, while almost all the others were active in only one.[42] Perhaps because of the amount of work involved in serving on the vestry, ten of the eighteen vestrymen serving in the 1820s were not active in any other activities. The situation for women differed because there was a clear division between the activities of single and married women.[43] As a result of this division, only five women, two married and three single, could be identified as being active in three organizations. However, since some of these organizations listed only officers, this number could be low. Only one of these women, Eliza Bringhurst, had a male relative active in any of the organizations studied. In general, most of the single women were members of both the Missionary Society and the Sunday School Society. Married women tended to be in only one group, but this may be deceptive, since their organizations listed only officers.

*   *   *

While the leadership of Christ Church concentrated on religious and benevolent activities, it could not ignore the political environment. With the return of the federal government to Philadelphia, Christ Church not only elected its members to high office but had the privilege of having the president of the United States, George Washington, as a regular worshiper, although not as a communicant. In 1790 the vestry designated a double pew in the middle aisle, "ten yards from the reading desk," as the "president's pew."[44]

White, however, unlike his colonial predecessors, believed strongly that clergymen should stay out of politics whenever possible. White told his fellow ministers to stay out of the "vortex of civil broils," arguing that "there can be no greater degradation of the ministerial character . . . than when it is employed by a minister of the Gospel, to thrust himself into public councils. Such a man will probably be under the influence of worldly passion." He went on to argue that "if the ministerial office can be at all useful, there is no way in which it may be more so, than in its raising of the harmonizing voice of religion, for the allaying of the jealousies and the resentments which result from the interfering interests and opinions of civil life."[45]

Unfortunately for himself and perhaps for Christ Church, James Abercrombie did not follow his bishop's advice, showing no reticence about speaking out on political issues. A strong Federalist, he preached a sermon during the election campaign of 1800 that associated Thomas Jefferson with atheism and monarchy. The sermon led to a virulent exchange in the newspapers that centered on the issue of clerical involvement in politics. The Democratic-Republican *Aurora* strongly condemned such involvement, accusing Abercrombie of having "prostituted God's holy word to further the cause of a faction." Letters to the Federalist *Gazette*, on the other hand, argued that it was the duty "of the clergy of every denomination, to come forward in defense of that Religious Toleration and INDEPENDENCE, which were the fruits of their zeal at a former period, and which is now threatened to be destroyed."[46] Abercrombie's most blatantly political sermons, which the Democratic press blasted as "seditious," came during the War of 1812. He boldly asserted that "the destructive and unnecessary war in which a blundering and feeble Administration hath involved us, will of all other possible events be most likely to induce, under the plea of necessity and the mask of patriotism, this worst of all evils, this sure precipitation into the gulf of national perdition."[47]

The reaction of White to Abercrombie's forays into politics is unknown, although he must have had misgivings. The *Aurora* specifically exempted White from its attacks on Episcopal clergymen, arguing that he was mortified at the conduct of some of those "political speculators in church politics."[48] During the War of 1812 White expressed concern that any opposition to the war on the part of Episcopalian clergy would lead to attacks on the church, as it did in New England. While many Episcopal clergy in the country shared Abercrombie's opposition to the war, the bishops of the church, including White, felt it particularly important to keep out of politics

Second Street north from Market Street with Christ Church, Philadelphia. Engraved and sold by William Birch and Son, 1800. Courtesy of the Historical Society of Pennsylvania.

Watercolor by William Mason, 1837. Interior before Thomas U. Walter's alterations in the late 1830s. Christ Church Archives.

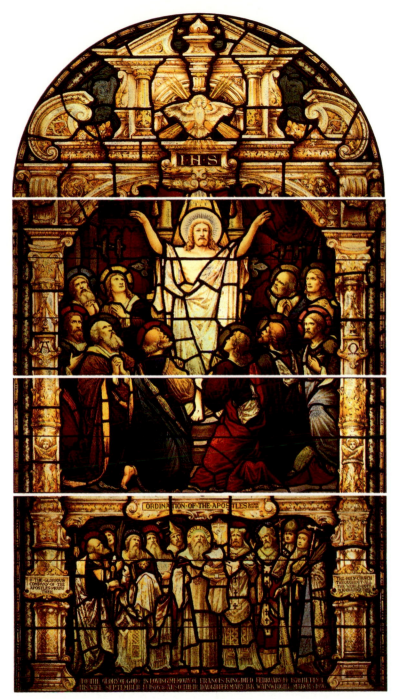

The Risen Christ Commissioning His Apostles. The first in a series of six windows depicting the history of the Christian Church, it has as its sub-subject the apostolic succession. It includes St. Paul and St. Timothy, St. Ignatius holding the book of his epistles on the episcopate, St. Athanasius and Gregory the Great, St. Augustine, St. Anselm and Thomas Cranmer, and Samuel Seabury. Photo by Will Brown.

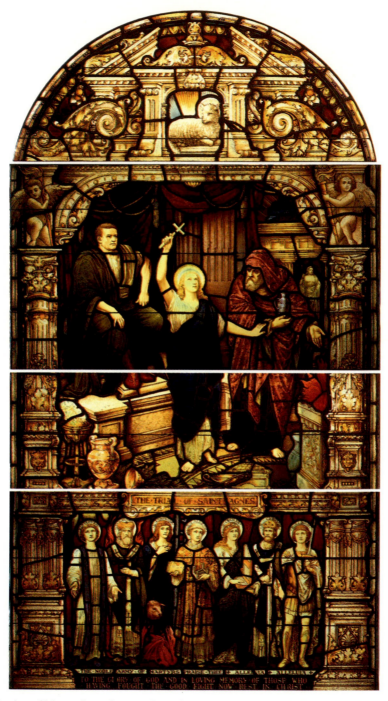

The Age of Martyrdom, the second window, represents the trial of the unflinching maiden Agnes. The sub-subject displays Eastern and Western martyrs of the Church. Photo by Will Brown.

The Conversion of Constantine, the third window, represents the triumph of Christianity, and includes as its sub-subject the crusades. Photo by Will Brown.

The Conciliar Window depicts the Council of Nicaea. The sub-subject depicts the ecclesiastical council in America, particularly the gathering that founded the Protestant Episcopal Church. William White, Samuel Provoost, and William Smith are easily visible. Photo by Will Brown.

The Liberty Window depicts the signing of the Magna Carta with the sub-subject of Jacob Duché offering prayers in the First Continental Congress. Photo by Will Brown.

The American Window depicts the first settlement at Jamestown and the patriots worshiping at Christ Church. Photo by Will Brown.

because of the Church's historic association with England.[49] But evidently White, who hated to impose his views on others, did nothing to stop his controversial assistant.

During the 1790s Abercrombie's sermons probably fit the general political leanings of the United Churches, which appear to have been predominantly Federalist. Among the Episcopalians in one study of the 1800 elite, 31 percent were Federalist and 14 percent were Republican, while the political affiliation of the remainder is unknown. Certainly a prominent Federalist such as William Bingham, who succeeded Robert Morris as senator from Pennsylvania, serving from 1795 to 1801, would have welcomed Abercrombie's remarks. He would have been joined in his approval of Abercrombie by Samuel Meredith, who served as treasurer of the United States from 1789 to 1801, Robert Hare and Francis Gurney, who served in the Pennsylvania legislature, as well as William Tilghman and Thomas Willing, all powerful Federalists.[50]

However, even during the 1790s there were those within the United Churches who supported the Jeffersonian party and such support increased after 1800. Alexander Dallas, who served as the United States attorney for the Eastern District of Pennsylvania and later as the secretary of the treasury under Madison, was an early Jeffersonian, as was Moses Levy, who served in the Pennsylvania legislature. Tench Coxe, who as a Federalist served as assistant secretary of the treasury, had switched his allegiance to Jefferson by the 1800 election, and Benjamin Rush, who still held a pew at Christ Church, was one of Jefferson's most ardent supporters. After 1800 the power of the Federalist party faded rapidly in the city and the state; Republicans won the city races for the legislature for the first time in 1801. Moreover, the War of 1812 was popular throughout Pennsylvania. Thus, while we do not have specific information about the political affiliation of Christ Church members, it is likely that increasing numbers of parishioners disagreed with Abercrombie's positions. It is possible that this contributed to his decreasing popularity.[51]

*   *   *

During White's rectorship Christ Church successfully redefined its focus in the new nation. Following a course in some ways similar to that of the Quakers in the 1750s, the ministers and congregation of the United Churches turned from political involvement to supporting a wide range of religious and philanthropic activities. The number of "firsts" in which Christ Church members and clergy were involved is truly impressive—first interdenominational Sunday school, first Bible society, first church-incorporated Sunday school. Equally impressive was the leadership role White and others took in benevolent activities within the city of Philadelphia. While much of the religious history of the United States in the early nineteenth century focuses on the evangelical denominations, and the Episcopal Church during those early years is often described as "weak" or "convalescing," it is clear that the United Churches were blessed with active and innovative leaders, ready to accept the challenges presented by the new nation.

NOTES

1. Gough, "Toward a Theory of Class and Social Conflict," 285.

2. *DAB*, s.v. Hopkinson, Joseph.

3. Simpson, *Lives of Eminent Philadelphians Now Deceased*, 690–91. *DAB*, s.v. Meredith, William; Tilghman, William; the quotes are from Sidney George Fischer's Diary, May 21, 1858, HSP.

4. *The Autobiography of Benjamin Rush, his "Travels through life" together with his commonplace Book for 1789–1813*, ed. George W. Corner (Westport, Conn.: Greenwood Press, 1970), 165.

5. William White to James Abercrombie, June 20, 1809, in Wilson, *Memoir*, 349; Vestry Minutes, June 4, 1782.

6. William White, *Thoughts on the Singing of Psalms and Anthems in Churches* (Philadelphia, 1808), 10; William White, "Thoughts on the Proposal of Alterations in the Book of Psalms in Metre, and in the Hymns, now before a Committee of the General Convention," in White, *Memoirs of the Protestant Episcopal Church*, 237.

7. Smith, *Life and Letters of the Reverend William Smith*, 2: 221.

8. William White, *Singing of Psalms*, 5–8; Vestry Minutes, April 3, 1785.

9. Bishop White's Communicant's List, Christ Church archives. Richard Shiels found that 64 percent of members in New England Congregational churches were women in 1830, and Terry Bilhartz found that 70 percent of churchgoers in Baltimore in 1830 were female. These figures are not entirely comparable, since many Episcopalians considered themselves members without being confirmed and women were probably more likely to take religion seriously enough to be confirmed. See Shiels, "The Feminization of American Congregationalism, 1730–1835," *American Quarterly* 33 (1981): 46–62; Bilhartz, *Urban Religion and the Second Great Awakening* (Madison, N.J.: Fairleigh Dickinson University Press, 1986), 21.

10. See Vestry Minutes, Dec. 23, 1783, April 30, 1784, Aug. 20, 1785, April 10, 1788, Jan. 22, 1789; Gill, "Christ Church in Philadelphia: Furnishings, The Early Years," 131.

11. Vestry Minutes, Aug. 20, 1785, March 13, 1786, April 23, 1789.

12. Vestry Minutes, June 9, 1794; Pew Rent Books from March 1794. Renting one seat at Christ Church in 1790 would have cost between 0.4 percent and 1.2 percent of the average family's income, depending on which pew they chose. This is based on the fact that a prerevolutionary American family had to have at least £100 a year to live comfortably, while a "genteel" life-style required £200. Similarly, in the 1790s an average artisan's wages would

have been $250 (close to £100), rising to $400 in 1795. See Jackson Turner Main, *Social Structure of Revolutionary America* (Princeton, N.J.: Princeton University Press, 1965), 118; Donald R. Adams, "Wage Rates in the Early National Period, Philadelphia, 1785–1830," *Journal of Economic History* 28 (1968): 406. Billy G. Smith, "Material Lives of Laboring Philadelphians," *WMQ* 38 (1981): 163–202, would argue for lower wages for those he studied, but Adams's rates are probably more accurate for Christ Church artisans who tended to be more skilled.

13. Pew rent books, 1784–1798, First, Second, and Third Presbyterian Churches, Presbyterian Historical Society. First Presbyterian's arrears ranged from 11 to 23 percent while Second Presbyterian's ranged from 10 to 19 percent.

14. Vestry Minutes, April 23 and Sept. 7, 1789; Sept. 29, 1795; July 6, 1796; April 24, 1797.

15. The following history of Christ Church Hospital is based on George B. Roberts, "Christ Church Hospital," *HMPEC* 45 (1976): 90–91.

16. Vestry Minutes, March 19, 1772 and July 1 and July 5, 1773. The Christ Church Hospital Committee reported to the vestry that £2,398 was available for the hospital in 1785.

17. Vestry Minutes, July 29, 1784, Nov. 18, 1785.

18. See Vestry Minutes, April 16, 1789; Roberts, "Christ Church Hospital," 92–93. Unfortunately we know nothing about Dobbins or his relationship with Christ Church.

19. See "The Autobiography of William White," 413–14; "Fundamental Laws" in Charles Latham, Jr., *The Episcopal Academy 1785–1984* (Philadelphia: William T. Cooke, Publishers, 1984), 218. For the early history of the academy see Latham, 20–56.

20. Latham, *The Episcopal Academy*, chap. 4. The trustees are listed on p. 271. Bishop White served as an active president until his death. Of the sixteen other trustees in 1816, two were clergy of the United Churches and ten were laymen of the churches.

21. Cheyney, *History of the University of Pennsylvania*.

22. Brewer, *A History of Religious Education in the Episcopal Church to 1825*, 105–7; Clifford Griffin, *Their Brothers' Keepers* (New Brunswick, N.J.: Rutgers University Press, 1960), 29.

23. William White to John Hobart, Feb. 16, 1811 in Bird Wilson, *Memoir*, 392.

24. See Scharf and Wescott, *History of Philadelphia*, 3: 1829.

25. This information comes from Robert Gough's study of the Philadelphia economic elite in 1800.

26. There are a number of good books on this subject. See, for example, Martin Marty, *Righteous Empire* (New York: Dial Press, 1970) and Robert Handy, *A Christian America* (New York, Oxford University Press, 1984). See Addison, *The Episcopal Church in the United States*, chap. 7, for the situation in the Episcopal Church at large.

27. For a thorough discussion of the society's history, see Donald Russell Gardner, "The Society for the Advancement of Christianity in Pennsylvania," *HMPEC* 23 (1954): 321–252; Society for the Advancement of Christianity in Pennsylvania, *First Annual Report* (Philadelphia, 1813).

28. Stuckert, "Jackson Kemper, Presbyter," 135–38. Kemper's journals for this trip can be found in "Jackson Kemper's Journals and Letters," *HMPEC* 5 (1935): 227–44.

29. "Address by the Rev. Jackson Kemper at the Annual Meeting of the S.A.C. in Pennsylvania, January 7, 1828," in the *Church Register*, Jan. 28, 1828, quoted in Gardner, "The Society for the Advancement of Christianity in Pennsylvania," 323.

30. See Stuckert, "Jackson Kemper, Presbyter," 140–41. White's first attempt to make this trip in 1824 ended when he fell from his carriage and broke his wrist.

31. See Gardner, "The Society for the Advancement of Christianity in Pennsylvania," 338–39; Addison, *The Episcopal Church*, 129–34.

32. For the range of activities in which women were involved, see Nancy Cott, *The Bonds of Womanhood* (New Haven, Conn.: Yale University Press, 1977), chap. 4; Mary Ryan, *Cradle of the Middle Class: The Family in Oneida County, New York, 1790–1865* (New York and Cambridge: Cambridge University Press, 1981), 210–18; Carroll Smith-Rosenberg, *Religion and the Rise of the American City* (Ithaca, N.Y.: Cornell University Press, 1971).

33. *Fifth Annual Report of the S.A.C.*, 1817, 10, quoted in Gardner, "Society for the Advancement of Christianity in Pennsylvania," 339; Female Episcopal Tract Society, *Annual Report*, May 11, 1830, *Protestant Episcopalian* 1, 6 (1830): 234.

34. Female Episcopal Tract Society, *Annual Report*, May 11, 1830, and May 10, 1831, *Protestant Episcopalian* 1, 6 (1830): 234–35; 2, 7 (1831): 273. Nancy Hewitt argues for a much larger level of male support for female charitable work in Rochester, N.Y. See her *Women's Activism and Social Change: Rochester, N.Y., 1822–1872* (Ithaca, N.Y.: Cornell University Press, 1984), 39–69.

35. Managers of the Female Episcopal Benevolent Society, *Eighteenth Annual Report*, 1834 (Philadelphia, 1834).

36. Brewer, *A History of Religious Education*, 151. This school formed the nucleus of St. John's Parish. Anne M. Boylan, *Sunday School: The Formation of an American Institution, 1790–1880* (New Haven, Conn.: Yale University Press, 1988) seems to overemphasize the evangelical connection with denominational Sunday Schools, although she does acknowledge Episcopal participation. See pp. 8–21.

37. Female Sunday School Society, Minute Books, 1816–1833, Feb 13, 16, and 25, 1816, Christ Church Archives.

38. J. Parker Jameson, "The Sunday School in the National Period," *HMPEC* 51 (1982): 187; Protestant Episcopal Sunday and Adult School Society, *Report, 1821* (Philadelphia, 1821).

39. For a discussion of the founding of the General Theological Seminary see Addison, *The Episcopal Church*, 122–25; for White's feelings see Wilson, *Memoirs*, 207. For information on the board of agents see "Minutes of the Board of Agents of the Theological Seminary, 1821–26," Kemper Papers, 5: 145–82. For information on the Female Association see *Episcopal Magazine* 2, 2 (1821): 64 and the *First Annual Report of the Board of Agents,* Dec. 1821 or Jan. 1822 in Kemper Papers, 7: 10.

40. The following paragraph is based on data collected about the Vestry of the United Churches, the Society for the Advancement of Christianity in Pennsylvania, the Protestant Episcopal Sunday and Adult School Society, the General Protestant Episcopal Sunday School Union, the Episcopal Missionary Society of Philadelphia, the Education Society of the Protestant Episcopal Church in Diocese of Pennsylvania, the trustees of the Episcopal Academy, the Female Tract Society, the Ladies Missionary Society, the Female Association in Aid of the Theological Seminary, the Female Benevolent Association and the Christ Church Female Sunday School Society. The numbers are based solely on whether the people had the same last name so may, in fact, be overestimated.

41. Mary Ryan found much greater family participation rates in Utica, N.Y., but her best data came from the Temperance Society. See Ryan, *Cradle of the Middle Class*, 136–38.

42. The prominent lawyer, William Meredith, for example, served as accounting warden and was an officer or trustee of the Sunday and Adult School Society, the Education Society, the Society for the Advancement of Christianity, and the Episcopal Academy. John Read, Judge

William Tilghman, and John Lowber also served as directors of the three societies, but not the Episcopal Academy.

43. The Female Benevolent Association, the Female Association in Aid of the Theological Seminary and the Female Tract Society were predominantly married women, although they allowed single women to join. The Missionary Society and the Female Sunday School Society were almost exclusively single women; after many of the names is the notation "resigned, married." Exactly why this division existed is unclear, since the activities of the organizations were similar. Nancy Hewitt found that the officeholders in all the organizations she studied were predominantly married. See *Women's Activism and Social Change*, 262.

44. See William White to Hugh Mercer, Nov. 28, 1832 in Wilson, *Memoir*, 189; William White to Colonel Mercer, Aug. 15, 1835, ibid., 197, for comments on Washington's church attendance. For the vestry's action, see Vestry Minutes, Nov. 26, 1790. When Adams became president they offered the pew to him. When he indicated that he would rarely use it, the vestry gave the use of it to Bishop White's family. Vestry Minutes, Feb. 28 and April 24, 1797.

45. Wilson, *Memoir*, 285–86, quoting from an unpublished ordination sermon.

46. *Philadelphia Aurora*, Sept. 1, 1800, 3; *Gazette of the United States*, Sept. 10, 1800; see also letters in the *Gazette* on Sept. 6.

47. James Abercrombie, *Two Sermons Preached on . . . July 30 . . . August 20, 1812 . . .* (Philadelphia: Moses Thomas, 1812).

48. *Philadelphia Aurora*, Aug. 28, 1800.

49. Wilson, *Memoir*, 390. For the views of the American bishops in general, which mirrored those of White, see William Gribbin, "American Episcopacy and the War of 1812," *HMPEC* 38 (1969): 25–36.

50. Information on political affiliations come from Robert Gough, "Toward a Theory of Class and Social Conflict"; Richard Miller, *Philadelphia, The Federalist City* (Port Washington, N.Y.: Kennikat Press, 1976), 16, 17, 75.

51. Harry Tinkcom, *The Republicans and Federalists in Pennsylvania 1790–1801* (Harrisburg, Pa.: Pennsylvania Historical and Museum Commission, 1950), 255–56; Victor Sapio, *Pennsylvania and the War of 1812* (Lexington: University Press of Kentucky, 1970).

CHAPTER ELEVEN

THE SEPARATION
OF THE UNITED
CHURCHES

The last two decades of White's life proved difficult and painful for the United Churches, and especially for Christ Church. A serious decline in membership caused nearly catastrophic financial problems, and dissatisfaction among the clergy combined with divisions in the diocese presented the leadership of the United Churches with some painful decisions. Ultimately these problems resulted in the separation of Christ Church, St. Peter's and St. James into three separate parishes, but until the separation occurred the clergy and the parishioners had to endure some difficult times.

The financial difficulties of the United Churches worsened in the nineteenth century and became overwhelming by the 1820s. When Robert Blackwell resigned in 1811, he asked that the vestry settle the debt of $2,899.99 it owed him, reminding the men that the church had been in debt to him for at least $2,000 for the last two years. A year later the churches owed a total of $10,098.90, including $1200 to Blackwell, $1,733.33 to White, and $4,000 from the building of St. James. This was against an average annual income of £2,261.3.5 (approximately $5,000).[1]

In 1813 the vestry attempted to resolve the churches' financial problems. They adopted strict financial rules, including that all funds be kept in the bank! This improved financial management, combined with increased rates for pew rents and fees for burials, allowed Christ Church to pay off all debts and to break even in 1815.[2]

But by 1823 the churches again faced serious financial problems. The churchwardens reported a decrease in revenues of $2,378 since 1816, including $1,715.59 in pew rents, and a deficit of $1,811.55, presumably in part because of the Panic of 1819 and the resulting depression. The vestry's solution was to decrease all salaries by 12½ percent. The vestrymen expressed hope that this would be only a temporary reduction; referring to "the peculiar situation in which the churches now stand, owing to causes too well known" to explain, they hoped they would soon "have it in their power to act in a way more in accordance with their feelings." Unfortunately, things only got worse. The vestry reduced salaries again in 1826, and in 1827 they were still forced to borrow $2,300. In fact, the vestry borrowed money to meet operating expenses every year until the separation of St. Peter's and Christ Church in 1831.[3]

While previous financial crises had been caused by the failure of members to pay pew rents, the crisis of the 1820s stemmed from a decrease in membership. The number of pews rented at Christ Church decreased from 816 in 1813 to 666 in 1820 to 497 in 1828, and similar reductions occurred at the other churches. In 1831 when Kemper resigned, he described the parish as being "in a deplorable state" and Christ Church, in particular, as "sinking." A year later Abercrombie, contemplating the future of the separated churches, remarked that they could not "be lower than they are, without suffering absolute extinction."[4]

It was the condition of the parish rather than the call of greener pastures that caused Kemper to leave Philadelphia. In a poignant essay, "Apology for Leaving Philadelphia," Kemper maintained that he "considered myself for life at Philadelphia," but that "I do not think there is a sufficient interest in me or my ministrations on the part of the government [of the parish] to authorize me to remain here." He complained bitterly not just of the two salary reductions, but of the fact that there was "no communication upon the subject—no sympathy, no regret, no enquiry, whether I could sustain it." Thus, since there was no security for the future, he did not feel he could keep his family in Philadelphia.[5]

The reasons for the decline in the condition of the churches are, no doubt, multiple. The location of Christ Church, the opening of new Episcopal churches, the conflict in the diocese between high church and evangelical factions, all contributed to the church's problems. The most important factor, however, was the failure of the United Churches to adapt their ecclesiastical structure to changes in religion in the nineteenth century.

The location of Christ Church certainly contributed to its financial problems, but the location of the other two churches remained favorable. As we have indicated, more and more of Christ Church's members were moving to the west as the neighborhood around the church became increasingly commercial. However, location could not have been the primary reason for the decline. The area around St. Peter's remained one of the most fashionable in the city and St. James had been built to take advantage of the westward movement of the city, yet both of these churches also faced decreasing membership. Moreover, by 1840, despite still further deterioration in its location, Christ Church had increased its number of communicants to 325, from 120 in 1833.[6]

The erection of three new churches in the central part of the city could also have contributed to the decline. In 1822 St. Stephen's Church, which would join the high church faction, opened at Tenth Street between Market and Chestnut Streets and a year later the evangelicals founded St. Andrew's at Eighth Street above Spruce. Grace Episcopal Church at Twefth Street opened in 1826. This is the only cause for decline openly referred to by the vestry. A report to the vestry maintained that the financial plight began with the "erection of the new Episcopal churches in the city. Before that period a vacant pew in one of the United Churches was rarely met with and commanded a price out of all proportion to such as can now be obtained."[7]

However, while the opening of three chuches must have been unsettling to churches that had previously had only St. Paul's as competition, it could not have been the primary reason for the decline of the United Churches. None of these churches had substantial membership until the late 1820s and the decline of Christ Church began before 1820. Moreover, given the growth in the size of the city, the Episcopal community should have been able to support three new churches. In reality, rather than causing the decline of the United Churches, it is much more likely that the new churches benefited from the United Churches' already-existing problems and, perhaps, took advantage of them.

One of the problems affecting the United Churches was the high church-evangelical divisions within the diocese. From approximately 1822 on, the Diocese of Pennsylvania became the primary battleground between the evangelical and high church factions within the Episcopal church. Unlike New York, which was firmly under Bishop Hobart's control, or Virginia, which was almost completely evangelical, Pennsylvania was much more evenly divided. It was both ironic and tragic that Pennsylvania and particularly Philadelphia were so profoundly affected by the controversies, since Philadelphia Episcopalians had a tradition of tolerating diverse views and Christ Church and St. Peter's had lived peacefully with St. Paul's for many years. While the controversy has often been seen as a contest between the high church ministers of the United Churches and their allies versus the evangelicals led by Benjamin Allen, the situation was far more complex. Bishop White tried for many years to be tolerant of evangelicals, preferring to create a "comprehensive orthodoxy" rather than encourage contesting parties.[8] Even as late as 1829, after the acrimony had reached its height, White defended the evangelical leader Stephen Tyng when Tyng had problems with a minority high church party within his congregation. And, as we have seen, Kemper did not fit neatly into the high church mold either; he referred to himself as "a pretty low churchman in many respects," and continued to have good relationships with many evangelical ministers.[9]

Essentially, the crisis occurred because the moderate positions of White and Kemper were no longer acceptable to militant evangelicals who believed Philadelphia to be fertile ground for recruitment. With the arrival from Virginia of Benjamin Allen as rector of St. Paul's in 1821, peaceful coexistence turned to confrontation. The evangelicals took the lead and Bishop White and his supporters acted defensively. Unfortunately for the peace of the diocese, the evangelical attacks eventually forced White into the arms of the high church group, and exacerbated an already tense situation.

The ecclesiastical battles in Pennsylvania, which began in 1822, climaxed in 1826 with the battle over the election of an assistant bishop. The need for such an assistant, who would eventually succeed White, had long been felt, but the election was finally called because the high church group was confident of victory. However, the evangelicals did not concede defeat; instead they began a struggle for control of the diocese that would last more than a year.[10]

The fight savaged Bishop White. His character was assailed in a way that "cut the mild yet dignified man to the heart." Evangelicals reportedly accused him of not being a "praying man," doubted his piety because he used silver forks, and even questioned his honesty when he had to choose a committee to report on credentials. Exactly how badly things deteriorated can be gauged by White's reply to an attempt to link him to the Evangelicals. When, during a debate, it was suggested that he was a low churchman, White rose to set the record straight. As the term was used in eighteenth-century England, he reportedly argued, it might describe him, but, he went on, "as the word is understood in this country, among us now, you might as well call me a Turk or a Jew."[11]

At the same time that the tactics and rancor of the Evangelicals drove the mild-mannered White, who agreed with many "low church" positions, into the arms of the high churchmen, they also led Kemper and DeLancey to abandon their usually moderate positions. As Kemper put it, he "had (perhaps unusually) high notions of the duty of allegiance to the powers that be," believing he was "bound to support as far as I conscientiously can the views of him, who . . . has the charge & government over me."[12] Similarly, De-Lancey in his pamphlet *Plain Truth* put himself in the camp with those who have "not yet laid aside their veneration for age, their affection for [White's] person, and their respect for his principles."[13]

When the Diocesan Convention took the final vote on the new bishop, the high church candidate Henry Onderdonk of New York won a bittersweet victory. The evangelicals did not accept defeat gracefully and the diocese remained deeply divided for many years. In 1832 a fellow clergyman reported to Kemper that "Church affairs in this City move as usual. The 'great gulf' between the two belligerent parties does not appear to contract."[14] In 1845 the evangelicals finally got their revenge: admitting his addiction to alcohol originally prescribed for medicinal purposes, Onderdonk, who had succeeded White as bishop in 1836, resigned rather than face charges of drunkenness. While this was a personal tragedy for Onderdonk who had labored hard under adverse circumstances, with the consecration of Alonzo Potter, an able, moderate bishop, conditions within the diocese finally improved.[15]

These events had a profound effect on Bishop White and his assistants, but their relationship to the decline in the United Churches is unclear. It is possible that people became disillusioned with Bishop White, who had previously been seen as above party. Some who had joined Christ Church because it was a "middle-of-the road" church may have been disaffected. Others may have merely gotten tired of the dispute and the preoccupation of their ministers with it. A few may have been drawn by the evangelical position, although this type of worship had previously been available at St. Paul's.[16]

Rather than external forces, it was most probably internal weaknesses caused by the yoked nature of the parishes and the failure to assign specific ministers to specific churches, combined with the aging of Bishop White, that led to the decline of the United Churches. The political and ecclesiastical reasons that led to the uniting of Christ Church and St. Peter's in 1761 disappeared with the creation of the Protestant Episcopal Church. No doubt both the decision to unite St. James with the United Churches and the later reluctance to separate the churches were influenced by a desire to keep White as rector of all the churches and a desire to continue to control the Episcopal establishment in Philadelphia. But the yoked nature of the parishes made it difficult for an individual church to provide adequately for its members.[17]

The refusal to put an assistant minister in charge of each of the churches compounded the problems of the yoked churches. While the assistants may have developed a bias toward one church and were occasionally given responsibility for a program at a church, they were never assigned exclusively to one congregation. They rotated their preaching schedule along with Bishop White, generally preaching in each church every three weeks. This rotation system frustrated any attempt to develop a sense of community and rapport among parishioners and ministers. This lack of community no doubt contributed to the vestry's uncaring treatment of the ministers; while the refusal to give Muhlenberg a permanent contract and the decrease in ministerial salaries were caused by financial problems, the way they were handled indicated an unusual lack of attachment to outstanding ministers.

The absence of designated ministerial leadership also made it extremely difficult for any of the churches to maintain the kind of programming that was becoming characteristic of nineteenth-century churches or to address problems in an individual church; for any change to take place the vestry and clergy from all three churches had to agree. In 1828, for example, St. James's Male Sunday School needed a place to meet and the vestry had no money for them. While St. James's members felt they could raise the money, there was no mechanism by which they could do so.[18]

The assistant ministers recognized these problems early. In 1816 Milnor accepted another call because it "appears to open a more advantageous field of usefulness in its restriction to the superintendent of a single congregation than can be afforded in the collegiate charge of several." Similarly, Muhlenberg felt frustrated with his inability to acquaint himself with every parishioner and jumped at the chance to have but one congregation, even though it was a small country parish in Lancaster.[19]

FIGURE 23

The Smyth hatchment. This hatchment was carried before the funeral procession of Frederick Smyth, Chief Justice of New Jersey from 1764 to 1766, who was buried in the Christ Church burial ground. It was funerals such as Smyth's at which Bishop White was allowed to officiate. Located at Christ Church. Photograph by Julia Leisenring.

The aging of Bishop White compounded the problems inherent in uniting three churches. Even when he was younger it had been difficult for White to fulfill his duties as rector of three churches at the same time that he served as the bishop of a large diocese and the presiding bishop of the national church. But by 1820 White was seventy-three years old, and while he remained in good health, he had lost much of his vitality. Kemper bitterly complained that his salary had been decreased because of the need for another assistant (DeLancey) "obtained in consequence of the debility of the Rector—I therefore had to suffer when he became too old to do his duty."[20] While White remained beloved by almost everyone, he became a revered figurehead rather than an active leader. Beginning in 1816 the vestry gradually began limiting the bishop's required role in the churches. Bishop White seemed too devoted to the churches, too concerned with doing his duty to restrict his own activities. In 1816 the vestrymen ruled that White only be asked to do the funerals of the "heads of families being members of the congregation," and in 1818 they relieved White of all duties relating to funerals. (Figure 23 shows a hatchment like those that would have been used for "heads of families.") The rector's responsibilities were still further reduced in 1822 when the vestry "respectfully requested" that he assign the preaching duties to his assistants, "reserving to himself the privilege of preaching for either of them, when and so often, as he may be disposed to do it, but that no duties of that kind will in future be required of him." White, however, continued to preach almost every Sunday up until a month before his death.[21]

The restrictions failed to solve the larger problems of the churches, since assistants were still not assigned specific duties. In what seems like a move of desperation, in 1827 the three assistant ministers, Abercrombie, Kemper and DeLancey, petitioned the *vestry* "to adopt some system of parochial visitation and instruction by the performance of which some of the existing evils of the parish might be remedied." They listed four main evils which involved the "temporal and spiritual prospects of the parish": (1) "the want of Pastoral intercourse with the members of the churches"; (2) "the want of an adequate visitation of the sick and afflicted"; (3) "the want of some systematic instruction for the children and youth of the parish"; (4) "the want of systematic attention to the Sunday schools connected with the Parish." They concluded with a sweeping condemnation of the system, referring to "the utter impossibility of the Assistant Ministers doing their duty as required by their obligations and voices." The vestry, uncomfortable dealing with the assistant ministers' incipient rebellion, referred the entire matter to White. Four months later, White returned a plan that had been approved by the assistants, the details of which are not known. Unfortunately, the resignation of DeLancey and the separation of St. James meant that it was never implemented.[22]

The problems caused by the organizational structure of the United Churches resulted from changes taking place in American religion in the early nineteenth century. Christ Church and St. Peter's had been united for almost sixty years before serious problems developed. But the Second Great Awakening, with its evangelical style of religion and the resulting explosion in church-related benevolent and charitable organizations, changed what people expected of their church. The revival experience moved the emphasis within religion from the institution to the individual. The prayer meeting and the protracted meeting, both of which were used by evangelical Episcopalians, were intensely personal, emotional experiences. Within all churches, not just those experiencing revivals, there came to be more emphasis on lay participation, on the church as a community of people dedicated to changing their lives, the lives of others, and the society in which they lived. Gone were the days when providing Sunday services and catechism for the children was all that was expected of a church. People looked to their minister for personal support as well as for leadership in programs such as the Sunday schools. The yoked structure of the United Churches with no minister solely responsible for one church failed to provide this kind of support.

The opening of new Episcopal churches accentuated the problems that existed at the United Churches, giving the members examples of what a church could provide. As long as St. Paul's was their principal competition, Christ Church, St. Peter's, and St, James could be relatively complacent. But once other churches, both evangelical and high church, were built nearby, the eighteenth-century style church life provided by the United Churches was no longer enough to retain and attract members.

Within this context, the battles in the diocese can be seen as merely exacerbating an already difficult situation. As White and his assistants became preoccupied with the fight over the assistant bishop, they no doubt found it harder to fulfill their parochial duties. And as they were forced into defending a high church position, one of the main characteristics of the United Churches—their moderate, accepting theology—no longer existed. For many members this may have been the last straw.

In 1825 the vestry finally confronted the problems caused by the organizational structure of the United Churches. In March 1824 a group of laymen, predominantly from St. Peter's, had suggested that making the churches "independent for certain purposes" would increase revenue and advance "the usefulness of the clergy." More than a year later, a vestry committee appointed to examine the finances of the churches agreed with that position, arguing that a long term solution to the churches' financial problems could be accomplished by their separation. In so stating, they implicitly acknowledged that it was neither the diocesan divisions nor the formation of other churches that was causing the problems. As a result of this study, the vestry unanimously endorsed a plan of separation and presented it to the congregations in October of 1826, with the stipulation that three-fourths of the members in each of the three churches had to accept it. When the votes were in, the plan failed. Christ Church voted overwhelmingly against it, 109 to 24. St. Peter's narrowly approved it, 60 to 54. Only St. James passed the measure with a large majority, 52 to 23.[23]

Why it was defeated, despite the seemingly obvious need, is uncertain. The vestry later reported that some who favored separation voted against it because of the specific plan.[24] The overwhelming rejection among Christ Church members probably reflected both its status as the mother church and fears for the future because of its less than favorable location. Others may have felt that as long as Bishop White was alive, the churches should stay together. Moreover, those who objected to the yoked status of the churches most strenuously had probably already left the United Churches.

This vote did not put an end to the issue. In 1828 St. James's members sent a strongly worded petition asking for a vote on separation. They expressed "no hesitation" in avowing that the cause of the problems in the churches was "the union of the Churches and that so long as that union subsists, all attempts at a remedy of the evil will prove to be but vexatious and fruitless expedients." As a result of this petition the vestry asked the congregation to vote on a plan to allow just St. James to become a separate parish. This time the plan passed. Christ Church still had the closest vote (63 to 44) but St. Peter's and St. James approved it overwhelmingly (89 to 3 and 126 to 18).[25] Under the plan White would remain as "rector" of St. James, but St. James would selects its own assistant who would actually be in charge. Perhaps letting this newest member of the parish go was easier for Christ Church members.

In 1831, spurred on by the resignation of Jackson Kemper and no doubt influenced by the experience of St. James, the vestry once again voted for the separation of Christ Church and St. Peter's. By this time the need had become apparent to almost everyone. The vote in favor at Christ Church was 66 to 0 and at St. Peter's, 74 to 5.[26]

This vote ended seventy years of association, fifty-three under the leadership of William White. On January 25, 1832 the "late vestry" looked back over those years and thanked God for the "uninterrupted harmony" that had existed between the two churches and expressed satisfaction that the separation was not "occasioned by unpleasant feelings or by discontent," but by "the conviction, that in distinct corporations the interest of the churches will be most effectually promoted."[27] With that, they resolved themselves into two vestries.

White technically remained the rector of both churches, but in reality the assistant minister chosen by each church would take control. The Act of Separation stipulated that this assistant would become rector upon White's death. The act also stated that if neither church chose the current assistant, James Abercrombie, as assistant, he would remain the assistant for both churches, dividing his time between the two churches.

The decision regarding the assistant ministers thus became a touchy issue. In June 1832, after being turned down by DeLancey, who was then provost of the University of Pennsylvania, Christ Church chose John Waller James, the rector of Christ Church, Meadville, Pennsylvania, to be assistant minister "during the lifetime of the present rector."[28] James Abercrombie expected to be named the assistant minister of St. Peter's, but that church succeeded where Christ Church had failed, luring DeLancey away from the University. Rather than having to keep Abercrombie on the payroll, the Christ Church vestry appointed a committee "to ascertain upon what terms an amicable closing of [Abercrombie's] connection with Christ Church . . . may take place." No doubt to the vestry's dismay, Abercrombie rejected such an "amicable closing," refusing to resign unless given his full salary of $1600 for life. Frustrated, Christ Church and St. Peter's finally each agreed to give him $600 a year if he resigned immediately. Facing the inevitable, Abercrombie submitted his letter of resignation, which was accepted without even a pro forma letter of appreciation for his thirty-eight years of service.[29]

While others saw this coming, it was a shock to Abercrombie. Reporting on Abercrombie's illness in 1833, a friend wrote Kemper that he "for some time appeared to be indifferent to life—or rather to prefer death . . . the wound inflicted by those whom he relied on as his best friends, has, since last spring, affected him deeply, though he has openly complained but little." He died nine years later.[30]

Abercrombie's poignant situation was, in part, due to the lack of any provision for a minister's retirement at this time. Christ Church and St. Peter's were already supporting one elderly cleric who could no longer perform his ministerial functions. At a time when they needed to vastly increase the size of their congregations in order to survive, neither church may have had the luxury to keep the seventy-five-year-old Abercrombie on as minister. Yet, one still has to wonder why the vestrymen treated so many ministers so badly.

The separation raised technical issues as well. The Act of Separation stipulated that all debts were divided evenly and the charity funds which belonged to the United Churches in general were to be jointly managed, with half the money going to each church. Christ Church was given ownership of the burial ground at Fifth and Arch Streets, although members of St. James and St. Peter's could be buried there. Christ Church also took title to the property of Christ Church Hospital, but it was to be managed by a committee of three members from St. Peter's and three from Christ Church, elected yearly. The library and the records of the United Churches remained at the mother church, with St. Peter's being guaranteed access to them.[31]

* * *

The final separation of the two churches came with the death of Bishop White on July 17, 1836 at the age of 89. While White had left the day-to-day affairs of the three churches to his assistants after the separation, he continued to preach and visit parishioners up until two weeks before his death. A fall during the night of July 2 led to the "slow failure, one by one of all the springs of life," as a fellow priest put it. He died, as he had wished, on a Sunday, shortly after the Episcopal congregations of the city had raised their voices "in the beautiful supplication of their ritual for a sick person."[32]

The funeral of Bishop White the following Wednesday had been surpassed in Philadelphia only by that of Franklin. The procession, headed by his three assistants who were officiating, and Bishop Henry Onderdonk who gave the eulogy, included representatives of every Christian denomination and every organization with which White had been associated, as well as the mayor and city council. It wended its way past more than twenty thousand mourners and passed stores which had been closed for the day. After a solemn service in Christ Church, he was buried in the family vault in the churchyard. It was hard for many to believe that "that reverend figure, that gray head, so familiar, so honoured, will never be seen in the streets of Philadelphia again."[33]

While tributes to White came in from all over, the response of his fellow bishops was perhaps the most appropriate. They resolved that

the history and character of the deceased prelate are intimately interwoven with that of the church . . . much of the stability of its institutions, they owe to his wisdom; . . . much of what is devout, to his example; of what is harmonious, to his influence; of what is sound or orthodox, to his apostolic teaching.[34]

Christ Church also owed much of its character to Bishop White. Despite its problems, it still stood for moderation, orthodoxy, and stability during a period of rapid change. While White no longer served as a reminder of the church's rich history, the members still had a beautiful building and a legacy of accomplishments upon which to build.

NOTES

1. Vestry Minutes, March 22, 1811, March 16, 1812.
2. Vestry Minutes, Dec. 7 and 21, 1814, Jan. 8 and 11, March 25 and 27, April 3 and Dec. 6, 1815.
3. See Vestry Minutes, Dec. 31, 1823, Jan. 21, 1824, June 1, 1825, Dec. 23, 1825, June 7, 1826, April 23, 1827, April 14 and Dec. 10, 1828, Oct. 7, 1829, June 17, 1831.
4. Jackson Kemper, "Apology for Leaving Philadelphia," June 1, 1831, Kemper Papers, State Historical Society of Wisconsin; James Abercrombie to Jackson Kemper, Jan. 14, 1832, Kemper Papers, 12: 32.
5. Kemper, "Apology for Leaving Philadelphia." The outpouring of regret at Kemper's departure was impressive; see, for example, in Kemper Papers: Thomas White to Jackson Kemper, May 30, 1831, 11: 126; H.M. Davis to Jackson Kemper, May 30, 1831, 11: 130; AJ Cuthbert to the Kempers, [May 1831], 11: 131; E. B. Gibson to Jackson Kemper, June 1, 1831, 11: 134; Teachers of Sunday School at St. Peter's to Jackson Kemper, June 1, 1831, 11: 135; Ann Fleming to Jackson Kemper, Feb. 24, 1832, 12: 1832.
6. See the comments in Oberholtzer, *Philadelphia: A History of the City and Its People*, 2: 102. By 1828 St. James had 181 of 852 seats vacant and St. Peter's had 70 of 751. *Journal of the Diocese of Pennsylvania, 1833* (Philadelphia, 1833).
7. "Report of the Subcommittee appointed to report facts as they deem material and to digest a plan of separation," October 28, 1828, Vestry Records, Committee Reports.
8. The term is David Holmes's. See "The Making of the Bishop of Pennsylvania, 1826–27," *HMPEC* 41 (1972): 239.
9. Charles Tyng, *Record of the Life and Work of the Reverend Stephen H. Tyng and History of St. George's Church* (New York: E. P. Dutton and Co., 1890), 90. Jackson Kemper to Henry Onderdonk, June 14, 1827, Kemper Papers, 9: 58.
10. Holmes's two part article is an excellent summary of the battle over the assistant bishop. (See "The Making of a Bishop," *HMPEC* 41 (1972): 225–62; 42 (1973): 171–97.) He does, however, tend to lump the Christ Church ministers into the high church camp too completely.
11. See Holmes, "The Making of the Bishop," 41: 253 and J.H. Hopkins, Jr., *The Life of the Late Right Reverend John Henry Hopkins By One of His Sons* (New York, 1873), 90. Quote is from Hopkins, p. 101.
12. Jackson Kemper to Henry Onderdonk, June 14, 1827, Kemper Papers, 9: 58.
13. For DeLancey's anonymous pamphlet see William Heathcote DeLancey *"Plain Truth"; A Candid Address . . .* (Philadelphia, 1827).
14. Cooper Mead to Jackson Kemper, April 12, 1832, Kemper Papers, 12: 45.
15. See Holmes, "The Making of a Bishop," 42: 191–92; Robert Mullin, *Episcopal Vision/ American Reality*, 163.
16. Because of the size of Philadelphia and the number of people with the same name, it is impossible to trace the people who left Christ Church.
17. Bishop White reportedly recommended establishing St. James as a separate parish. See "Report of the Subcommittee appointed . . . to digest a plan of separation."
18. "Report of the Subcommittee."
19. Vestry Minutes, June 28, 1816, Nov. 30, 1820; Ayres, *W. A. Muhlenberg*, 55.
20. Kemper, "Apology for leaving Philadelphia," June 1, 1831.

21. Vestry Minutes, June 28, 1816, April 15, 1822. Ward, *Life and Times of William White*, 168.

22. Vestry Minutes, Dec. 5, 1827, Jan. 18, 1828, April 14, 1828; "Report of the Subcommittee . . . to digest a plan of separation."

23. Vestry Minutes, March 3, 1824, Dec. 23, 1825, Oct. 30, 1826.

24. "Report of the Subcommittee. . . to digest a plan of separation." We do not know the specifics of this plan.

25. Vestry Minutes, Oct. 17 and Dec. 3, 10, and 22, 1828.

26. Vestry Minutes, June 17, Sept. 7, and Nov. 16, 1831.

27. Vestry Minutes, Jan. 25, 1832.

28. Vestry Minutes, June 29, 1832.

29. Vestry Minutes, April 23, June 6, Oct. 5, Nov. 5, and Dec. 22, 1832.

30. Cooper Mead to Jackson Kemper, Nov. 13, 1833, Kemper Papers, 11: 145. For hints that the retirement was coming, see Jackson Kemper to Montgomery, June 14, 1831, Kemper Papers, 11: 145. For Abercrombie's bitter yet humorous letter to Kemper see James Abercrombie to Jackson Kemper, Jan. 17, 1834, Kemper Papers, 13: 30.

31. "An Act for Erecting Christ Church and St. Peter's Church in the City of Philadelphia, Into Separate Corporations," in Dorr, *An Historical Account of Christ Church, Philadelphia*, 358–69.

32. The best description of his last days is found in Julian Ward, *Life and Times of William White*, 169–79. The quotes are from pp. 169, 174.

33. Ward, *Life and Times*, 175–178; quote on p. 178.

34. Papers of the Vestry, Christ Church Archives.

CHRIST CHURCH AFTER BISHOP WHITE: THE RECTORSHIP OF BENJAMIN DORR

The separation of the United Churches and the death of William White marked the end of an era in which Christ Church ministers and members had played an important part in the life of the Episcopal Church and the city of Philadelphia. Bishop White was a living reminder of the church's prominent position in politics and society during the colonial and revolutionary era as well as a fine representative of a time when religious leaders of all faiths strove to get along. But the Philadelphia of 1836 was far different from the Philadelphia of 1775 or even 1800, and the pace of change quickened in the next thirty years. White's successor, along with the able lay leadership of Christ Church, had to find a place for the church in the new nineteenth-century industrial city. How successful they would be in carving out a special niche for the church could well determine whether it survived.

We know little about White's immediate successor, John Waller James, who had actually been in charge of the church since the separation and was appointed rector at White's death. He was described as "indefatigable in his clerical duties; mild, dignified and courteous in his deportment," with a "serene and cheerful gravity" that "pervaded his conduct."

FIGURE 24
The Reverend Benjamin Dorr (rector, 1837–1869). Courtesy of the Historical Society of Pennsylvania.

While careful to guard the "distinctive principles" of the Episcopal Church, he regarded "Christians of whatever name as fellow servants of one common master, and his placid temper and conciliatory disposition, secured the respect and esteem of all." Even discounting the stylized rhetoric of an obituary, one would conclude that James, not surprisingly, was cast in a mold similar to that of White and Kemper.[1] Unfortunately, he died in August 1836, only one month after being elected rector. Suddenly, after having the same rector for fifty-eight years, Christ Church now faced its second rector's funeral in less than two months, as it buried James in a vault in the churchyard not far from White.

Despite the deteriorating neighborhood and the church's precarious financial status, its rich past, combined with the strength of its congregation, enabled Christ Church to attract another outstanding minister to guide it in the post-White era. On May 4, 1837 Benjamin Dorr was "instituted into the office of rector" by Bishop Onderdonk, the first time the office of institution had been held in Christ Church.[2] Dorr remained rector for more than thirty years, resigning in 1868 because of ill health (see Figure 24).

Born and raised in Massachusetts, Dorr was educated at Dartmouth College and at the General Theological Seminary in New York. After his ordination in 1820 he led congregations in Lansingburgh and Waterford, Massachusetts. In 1835, when the General Convention reorganized the missionary activity of the church, it appointed Dorr secretary and general agent of the Domestic Committee. Responsible for both raising the consciousness of existing parishes about the importance of missions and selecting the sites best suited for missionary assignments, Dorr traveled over the entire country, preaching in both settled congregations and frontier cities.[3]

Dorr quickly became a beloved figure within Christ Church. In 1838, when he turned down his election as the bishop of Maryland because he thought it was his "solemn" duty as well as his "greatest pleasure and privilege" to remain at Christ Church, the vestry prepared formal resolutions responding to this "very joyous event." Referring to "the harmony of the Vestry, the regularity with which his approving congregation have attended upon the general services of the church, and the increasing number of those who have been led by his teaching and example to come to the Holy Communion," the vestry concluded that "nothing further could or ought to be desired by them in the pastoral relation."[4]

What was it about Dorr that led the vestry of Christ Church, which had not always treated its ministers with such respect, to be so effusive in its praise and so eager to keep him as rector? In many ways Benjamin Dorr was the perfect choice to succeed White, for he combined a missionary zeal, which had been fostered at Christ Church by Kemper and White, with a sincere reverence for history and a moderate, conciliatory personality in many ways like that of the bishop. As his eulogist put it, his character was marked "by no absence of just proportions. . . . He delighted in no turbulence. He dwelt not amid passions." If Dorr did not command the world's attention, he did "without effort, without desire, and even without consciousness, almost universally attract others to" him.[5]

Dorr's moderate personality and theology led him to stay out of the theological controversies that engulfed the Episcopal Church in the 1830s and 1840s. The Tractarian movement, named after the *Oxford Tracts for the Times*, which emphasized the points the Church of England had in common with Catholicism and eventually tried to reconcile almost all Roman Catholic dogma with the Thirty-Nine Articles, caused an uproar among evangelicals in the 1840s that culminated in a heated debate at the General Convention of 1844. Despite Dorr's stature in the national church and his active role in the diocese, he never became involved in these debates. As Dorr put it, when he arrived at Christ Church, the congregation had been walking "in the old paths" and it was his "desire and endeavor, under the divine guidance, to keep steadily in those paths."[6]

Dorr's sermons were similar in style to those of White and Abercrombie. A long-time parishioner admitted that they lacked "the arts of rhetoric" and "the enchantments of elocution," but argued that they were "always distinguished by sound reason, . . . learning, persuasive earnestness." He avoided "perplexed and tangled disquisitions" and "issues of undue emotion." Rather, he "proclaimed with well-weighed reflection and faithfulness, the great call to repentance and salvation" while he "developed and urged the duties of a religious life."[7]

Dorr's writings show both his devotion to the Episcopal Church and his concern for the religious life of his parishioners. The *Churchman's Manual: An Exposition of the Doctrines, Ministry and Worship of the Protestant Episcopal Church in the United States* was "a short treatise to put into the hands of those who had neither time nor inclination to read voluminous works." *Recognition of Friends in Another World* was written to comfort the grieving. Both works went through several editions.

Dorr's fascinating book *The History of a Pocket Prayerbook Written by Itself* was even more popular. Through the book Dorr hoped to "recommend, in a plain and familiar way, the doctrines and usages of his own church," while maintaining "quietness, peace and love, among all Christian people."[8] The "life" of this prayer book begins as a Christmas present for a young girl. It was subsequently owned by a layman who moved west and organized a church, four clergymen in various parts of the country, a Presbyterian man who wanted to learn more about the Episcopal Church, a prisoner, and another young girl.

By telling this delightful tale, Dorr expressed his opinion on a variety of issues. The *History of a Pocket Prayerbook* exuded love for the Book of Common Prayer and for the Episcopal Church. The characters in his book extolled all missionary efforts in a manner reminiscent of Jackson Kemper, especially those initiated by laypeople. The *History* also stressed the importance of family worship, commending a man who gathered his family and servants every morning and evening to read from the Bible and pray the "Family Prayer" from the liturgy and the Lord's Prayer.[9]

Dorr had high standards for the clergy in this book. In describing a parish minister in the *History of a Pocket Prayerbook* he was, no doubt, explaining how he saw his own role. In fact, it is interesting how closely his description of "Mr. P" matches the descriptions of Dorr himself. Mr. P was commended for knowing "how to be cheerful without levity, grave without austerity, dignified without haughtiness, and humble without servility." He labored faithfully "to bring all such as were committed to his charge . . . to that ripeness and perfectness of age in CHRIST. . . ." To do that, he not only preached each Sunday, but followed it up with parochial visits during the week, for "no church can prosper, unless the pastor is acquainted with his whole flock." Mr. P also conscientiously supervised the Sunday School, as well as catechizing the children regularly. He was mindful of the "temporal wants" of his parishioners as well. In the dwellings of the poor "he was always a welcome visiter; for he had been emphatically 'a father to the poor,'" always evidencing an open "hand and heart." Compare that description to the obviously stylized, yet seemingly accurate portrayal of Dorr upon his death: "He led the devotions of his people; he faithfully dispensed the word; he engaged the young by his affectionate interest; he comforted the old by his pious consolations; he visited the sick; he relieved the poor; . . . and won, so far as in him lay, all of every class by sympathy and service to grace and restoration."[10]

Dorr possessed another trait of particular importance for Christ Church: he was a serious student of history, particularly American church history. Christ Church's rich history was, no doubt, one thing that attracted him to its rectorship. He immediately became an active member of the Historical Society of Pennsylvania. Then in 1841 he published *An Historical Account of*

Christ Church, Philadelphia, from its Foundation, A.D. 1695 to 1841. While parish histories would become routine at the end of the nineteenth century, this history was in many ways pathbreaking. It showed an appreciation for American cultural history and the buildings that went with it long before such appreciation had become popular.[11] While his *Historical Account* is primarily a compilation of vestry minutes, Dorr had an excellent sense of what was important. He also exhibited a fine ability to do historical research. For example, his work showed decisively that Christ Church's first building was brick rather than a wooden structure as most believed.[12]

* * *

The vestry had obviously done well in choosing both James and Dorr, for the membership of Christ Church quickly began increasing once the separation of the United Churches occurred. In the first three years of Dorr's rectorship the number of communicants increased from 200 to 318. By 1845 the number stood at 400 and reached a pre-Civil War high of 435 in 1850. Similarly, by 1838 the number of pews rented had increased to 668, from a low of 497 in 1828. By 1844 the number stood at 713. Perhaps surprisingly, given its location, Christ Church recovered its strength sooner than either St. Peter's or St. James. In 1840 St. Peter's reported only 226 communicants while St. James reported 260, and both still lagged behind Christ Church in 1850.[13]

While membership increased at Christ Church, the church never again dominated the diocese. Other churches in center city Philadelphia far outstripped Christ Church in membership throughout the Civil War period. In 1845 St. Andrew's, the evangelical church, had 550 communicants, while Epiphany, located at Fifteenth and Chestnut Streets, was the largest in the diocese, claiming 614 communicants. These two churches, along with Grace Episcopal, would remain the largest churches for the next decade.[14] But while Christ Church was not the largest, the fact that it could attract a sizable congregation, given its increasingly unfavorable location, is impressive.

The increasing size of the city makes it difficult to identify most pew renters, but certain characteristics of the congregation can be established. First, there remained a large, loyal core group that had worshiped at Christ Church for many years. In 1837 when the vestry made an effort to determine who owned pews, they found that 194 people, representing approximately half the sittings rented, belonged to families that had rented pews for twenty years or more. Many of these families, such as the Lardners, Clarks, Glentworths, Bringhursts, Cadwaladers, the Hopkinsons, Conynghams, and Whites, had worshiped at Christ Church since the eighteenth century.[15]

Christ Church continued to have a large number of wealthy and prominent members. Of the ninety-seven members who rented pews in 1844 whose occupations could be determined, twenty-seven were merchants, eleven were gentlemen, eleven were lawyers, and three were doctors; this meant that well over half those identified belonged to the occupations with the highest average income. Included in this group were three members of the Cadwalader family. George, continuing the family military tradition, raised and paid his own voluntary militia and later served as an officer in the Mexican and Civil Wars. George's brother John, a commercial lawyer and a strong Democrat, served in Congress and as a judge. Their cousin Thomas was a gentleman who preferred a private life.[16]

Prominent lawyers also continued to attend Christ Church. William Meredith, the son of the churchwarden who befriended Abercrombie, served on the vestry for nine years and as rector's warden for two years. He held positions as United States secretary of the treasury, attorney general of Pennsylvania and United States district attorney. A whig-turned-Republican, he became the first president of the Union League, an organization founded to support the Union cause during the Civil War. Meredith's colleague at the bar, Charles Jared Ingersoll, also served in Congress and as United States District Attorney.[17] Although Horace Binney had by this time largely retired from courtroom law, he still played a large role in the life of the community and in Christ Church. Also prominent were whig mayors Peter McCall and John Swift, both of whom served on the vestry of Christ Church.

Among the many merchants at Christ Church were Henry Pratt, who was worth more than one million dollars in 1846; Thomas White, the bishop's son, who was prominent in the wine and liquor business; and James Hand, who was in the hardware business as well as a major stockholder in the Pennsylvania Railroad Company. Another member, John Newbold, founded the family banking and brokerage firm. While most of Christ Church elite were in the traditional occupations, manufacturers were also represented. Isaac Davis, a self-made man, owned one of the largest manufacturing firms in Philadelphia.

While we know more about the men of Christ Church, available evidence would suggest that women still made up a majority of the congregation. Women represented 80 percent of the people confirmed during Dorr's rectorship, and 105 of the 300 people renting pews in 1844 were women.[18] This number is impressive since as a rule only single or widowed women rented pews in their own names. In addition, one third of the men who rented pews rented only one seating; one could guess that many were really renting pews for their wives. As we shall see, these women, while unable to serve on the vestry, were responsible for several of the major projects undertaken by the congregation during Dorr's years.

* * *

The Philadelphia Dorr and his congregation served was very different from the colonial and early national city of their predecessors. First, between 1830 and 1860 the population of the city and its suburbs grew threefold, from 189,961 to 565,529. In a development alarming to those concerned for the future of Christ Church, the greatest growth was outside of the city proper, which up until 1854 went from Vine Street to South Street and from the Delaware to the Schuylkill River. In 1854 the government of the original city was consolidated with that of the surrounding areas; only 137,756 out of the new city's total population of 565,529 lived in the old city (see Map 2). The makeup of the increased population was equally disturbing to some; by 1860, 30 percent of Philadelphia's population were foreign-born, with twice as many Irish as Germans. This rapid expansion meant that "citizens . . . lost social knowledge and physical contact with one another," making any traditional sense of community difficult.[19]

The economy, controlled by merchant capitalists, became part of a nationwide economic system with its periodic panics and depressions. Once-proud artisans, whose work was more and more controlled by wholesalers, were particularly susceptible to these economic downturns. Even during good times they saw their hours increase while their standard of living either remained the same or deteriorated. Yet at the same time they saw the rising middle class take advantage of the greatly increased range of consumer products that were available, while the lifestyles of the newly wealthy demonstrated the growing gap between the rich and the poor.

These artisans, eventually joined by unskilled workers whom industrialization had reduced to extreme poverty, participated in a surprisingly successful union movement, culminating in a series of successful strikes in 1835–36. While we do not know how most members of Christ Church viewed the strikers, we do know that when trouble broke out between striking coal heavers and scabs Mayor John Swift of Christ Church sided solidly with management—arresting the strike leaders, imposing stiff fines, and openly expressing the hope that this would defeat the union. The Panic of 1837 and the arrival of thousands of Irish and Germans in the late 1830s and 1840s to compete for jobs ended this phase of the labor movement.[20]

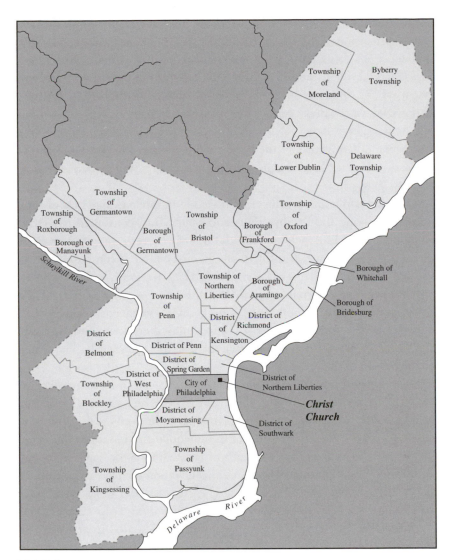

M A P 2
The consolidated city, 1854.

Economic instability and the arrival of thousands of Irish Catholics led Philadelphia to witness one of the largest anti-Catholic, nativist movements in the country. The political arm of this crusade, the American Republican party, founded in Philadelphia in 1837, called for a twenty-one-year period of naturalization, the prohibition of foreign-born people from office holding, and the rejection of all foreign interference in American institutions. The religious dimension of the struggle was exemplified by the American Protestant Association, founded in 1842 by a coalition of fifty Philadelphia clergymen. Pledged to an all-out ideological war on popery, it published tracts and newspapers and sponsored a series of lectures by ex-Catholics. Its primary aim, however, was to make certain that all schoolchildren read the Protestant Bible. As would be the case with all other public controversies, Dorr chose not to become involved on either side of this debate. He did not join the American Protestant Association, but neither is there any evidence that he spoke out against it.[21]

At the same time that Catholics increased in number, evangelical groups, particularly among the Presbyterians and Methodists, continued to extend their dominance of Philadelphia religion. By 1857 there were sixty-two Presbyterian, forty Methodist, and thirty-one Baptist churches compared to fifty Episcopal churches in the newly consolidated city. Revivals, which had been a novel experience for many in the 1820s, became a regular part of the religious life of many churches, including some evangelical Episcopalian congregations. Not only was Christ Church now merely one among more than 250 places of worship, but its style of worship was clearly out of step with the trend in Philadelphia religion.[22]

Religious groups, particularly evangelicals, engaged in an increasing variety of reform movements in the 1840s and 1850s. The problems caused by urbanization, immigration, industrialization, and the westward movement, combined with the evangelicals' belief in millennialism and a general belief in progress, caused Americans to join organizations aimed at converting people, improving individual behavior and alleviating the terrible conditions under which people lived. Among all these causes, the most popular in Philadelphia, as was true elsewhere in the country, was temperance.[23] Neither Dorr nor Christ Church as an institution participated in any of these organizations and unfortunately the records do not allow us to determine in what organizations the members of Christ Church were involved.

By far the most *unpopular* reform movement was abolitionism. Prejudice against blacks ran strong and deep in the Quaker City; the abolitionist William Wells Brown believed that "Colorphobia is more rampant here [Philadelphia] than in the pro-slavery, negro-hating city of New York." While residential segregation was impossible before the days of mass transportation, the 22,000 blacks who lived in Philadelphia in the 1850s were segregated in almost every other respect; they had their own churches, schools, libraries, and voluntary associations. Few Philadelphians endorsed the immediate emancipation advocated by the American Anti-Slavery Society founded in the city in 1833.[24]

The city's increasing social divisions coupled with a cumbersome city government and a weak volunteer militia led to a series of riots from 1834 to 1849 that graphically demonstrated the fragile peace and strong tensions in the City of Brotherly Love in the antebellum era. In 1834 a relatively small group of anti-black rioters beat blacks and destroyed property, including a church. In 1838 a mob burned down Pennsylvania Hall, the newly constructed home of the despised abolitionists, and attempted to burn down a home for black orphans, despite the efforts of John Swift to restore order. Further anti-black rioting occurred in 1842. By far the most spectacular and deadly riots were those in May and July of 1844, pitting the nativists against the Irish, in which two Catholic churches were destroyed and at least twenty people were killed. William Meredith was president of the city's select council, at whose request Horace Binney drew up resolutions asserting the "legal right" to use "any degree of force" against the mob to defend property or life. George Cadwalader attempted to stop the rioting by marshaling his volunteer militia in both May and July, but he was criticized for being too hesitant at first and then, as a result, being too trigger-happy.[25]

While individuals within the church played prominent roles during these turbulent years, Christ Church as an institution, and Benjamin Dorr as an individual, largely stayed out of the public eye. Dorr chose to concentrate on building up the congregation and serving the needs of the new members, and, as we will see, these members preferred to concentrate on traditional forms of benevolence. While Christ Church did not totally turn inward during these years, it did accept a very different role from the one it had had under Bishop White; with neither automatic prominence in the national church nor a rector who was a Philadelphia institution, Christ Church had become a parish church primarily serving the needs of what would today be considered middle and upper middle class Episcopalians.

That the church continued to try to fulfill even that role in its less than advantageous location is significant. By the 1840s First Presbyterian, Second Presbyterian, First Baptist, and Zion Lutheran, all located within a few blocks of Christ Church, had moved to more fashionable neighborhoods. Only the Arch Street Meetinghouse remained.[26] It would appear that unlike the leaders of so many institutions in that age of progress who could think only of the future, the leaders of Christ Church, led by Dorr's vision and his historical knowledge, already recognized the importance of preserving the past.

* * *

A desire to preserve the past did not mean an unwillingness to change and a desire to concentrate on traditional kinds of projects did not mean an unwillingness to take risks. Throughout Dorr's rectorship the leaders of Christ Church continued to show great faith in the future of the church by authorizing major building projects, both for the church and its affiliated institutions. Christ Church, the building, never was a museum, but rather a structure that adapted to changing needs.

The first of many "renovations" actually began before Bishop White died. In 1833, only a few months after becoming assistant minister, John James presented the vestry with a list of improvements in the physical facilities that he felt were needed. While James never stated his motivation, he probably felt these changes would attract members to the old church. In the church building proper he urged that the box pews be replaced by slip pews for "comfort, convenience, appearance and increase in the value of sittings"; that "fixtures for kneeling round the altar" be installed; and that improvements be made in the gallery. The vestry responded almost immediately to James's suggestions, hiring an architect, Thomas U. Walter, who had recently gained prominence by winning the competition to design the Girard College building. Walter's ideas were far more wide-ranging than anything suggested by James and it took the vestry two years to decide which ones to accept.[27]

The changes approved by the vestry combined the utilitarian with current trends in architectural styles. Since Walter believed that the entire "architectural effect of the interior" was injured by the galleries engaging the Doric columns, the galleries were rebuilt behind the columns, with new supports added. Slip pews with thick cushions were installed throughout the church. Stairs at the east end of the church were removed, creating a vestry room and a library, as James had wanted. In keeping with the style of the day, the floor was covered with wood and carpeted. Since this involved covering up grave markers, a plaque was placed in the church listing those who were buried in the aisles. The walls and ceilings were replastered and painted.[28] At the same time the renovations occurred, the vestrymen also authorized two major functional changes. The 1765 organ was replaced with a new one built by Henry Erban of New York, and placed farther back in the gallery with a new organ case, the one still in the church today. A coal-burning furnace was put in a basement excavated under the back row of pews and the tower, replacing the stoves in the back of the church. When completed in 1836, this project, excluding the organ, cost $11,700, forcing the vestry to borrow money from the charity fund.[29]

Despite this indebtedness, in 1837 the vestrymen authorized major repairs to the outside of the church, including the installation of a copper roof, replacing the balustrade and the urns, painting all the woodwork, and gilding the miter, vane, and balls on the steeple. These repairs cost $7,616.99.[30]

Then in the 1850s the church underwent still further remodeling. The blinds and curtains that had covered the Palladian window were removed and "plain enamelled Glass" was placed in the window. The pulpit was moved back to the middle of the chancel and both the pulpit and the pews were stained a "rich walnut." "Classic revival foliage" was also painted on the chancel wall and ceiling[31] (see Figure 25).

The vestry's faith in the church's future, demonstrated by these expenditures, proved correct. Under Dorr's leadership, Christ Church achieved financial stability. The increased number of people renting pews, combined with an increase in the rents charged, allowed the operating expenses to be adequately covered until the late 1850s.

Paying for the capital improvements, particularly those made in the 1830s, provided a bigger challenge, but rather than casually borrowing money, the vestry adopted a different, more aggressive strategy: they required most members of the church either to *buy* their pews or pay an additional yearly fee, equivalent to the interest on the cost of the pew. When it became clear that the records were not able to distinguish who had already paid for a "permanent sitting," the vestry decided that as a general rule anyone whose family had paid pew rents for twenty years would be considered as having a permanent sitting. While this aggressive approach alienated some members, it was successful. Two years later the vestry eliminated the option of paying the yearly fee, requiring most people to buy their pews. Altogether the sale of pews raised $9,557.58. As a result of this strategy and some fortuitous bequests, Dorr could announce in 1862 that the church was entirely free from debt.[32] There were very few other times in the history of the church up to this point when a rector could have made a similar statement!

The vitality of Christ Church under Dorr can also be seen in the organizations and activities of the parish, many of which reached maturity during

FIGURE 25
Benjamin Dorr at the communion table. Shows alterations of the 1850s. Courtesy of the
Historical Society of Pennsylvania.

these years. This was particularly true of the Sunday schools, which had
struggled in the later years of the united parish. At James's suggestion, in
1833 the vestry rented a four-story building at the northwest corner of the
Christ Church lot, which in 1857 it bought and renovated. By 1835 the
Sunday schools could boast 27 teachers and 250 pupils. In 1866 Dorr reported
that for the previous thirty years the Sunday schools had averaged 34 teachers and 250 students, which was just about all the building could accommodate. These schools owed their success to a dedicated staff. The Female

Sunday School had the same superintendent, Anna daCosta, for fifty years, while two other teachers worked for thirty-eight and thirty-nine years. The schools were able to perpetuate themselves in part because pupils grew up to be teachers; Dorr reported that one half of the teachers in 1866 had been scholars at the school in their youth. That is perhaps the best testimony to the effectiveness of this organization.[33]

Under the leadership of Dorr, Christ Church also once again started a parochial day school, something it had not had since the colonial period. The vestry argued that such a school was needed so that children could be taught "in the discipline of the church" and because poor children did not learn how to read in the public schools. Under the direction of twelve women, it opened in 1843 with sixty scholars, including forty who paid. When last mentioned in 1847 it had twenty-eight students.[34]

The women of Christ Church were involved in far more than providing for the education of children. In fact, as had been the case during White's rectorship, the women of the church proved more adept at raising money and more bold in choosing the projects they supported than were the men. Like other women throughout the country, they were active in missionary activities. From 1836 to 1838 the Ladies' Missionary Association (formerly the Ladies' Missionary Society) supported a missionary at Boonville, Missouri, on the request of Jackson Kemper, and they continued to send money to various missionaries throughout the antebellum period. They also helped build an Episcopal church in Huntingdon, Pennsylvania, in memory of their rector, John James, who died there.[35]

Their most ambitious and novel project involved a memorial to William White. In 1846, feeling "no slight emotion of shame" because no attempt had been made to "perpetuate among his spiritual children, a remembrance of his greatness and his virtues," the women decided to build a "free church" in Northern Liberties township as a monument to the bishop. They chose a site on Front Street near Margaretta (now Brown) in an area of "idleness, intemperance, vice [and] . . . godlessness.[36] Rather than envisioning a mission church, one directed entirely toward the poor and supported from outside, they expected this church to be "a blessing to the *whole* neighborhood where it is situated." While the sittings would be free, they expected the church to become self-supporting.

The concept of a church without pew rents, while not unknown, was still considered unorthodox. Horace Binney predicted "consequences from it, not exclusively good" and therefore objected to having Bishop White's name associated with it. Henry Ducachet, rector of St. Stephen's, also attacked free churches as "visionary" experiments that "never succeed well." But despite these objections and the frustrations of slow fund-raising, the women persevered. In July 1846 they agreed to fund a missionary who worked out of a sail loft. Then, on April 4, 1851, the 102d anniversary of White's birth, Bishop Alonzo Potter, who had supported the project from its inception, laid the cornerstone of Calvary Monumental Church. In 1852 the building was completed and by 1860 both the church and a school building constructed next door were entirely free of debt. At this point the women transferred title for both buildings to the vestry of Calvary Church.[37]

While the women of Christ Church were devoted, innovative and, to a certain extent, daring, their work remained in the traditional realm of religious activity. There is no evidence that they ventured into any reform activities aimed at institutions rather than individuals. Their philosophy remained that of the early nineteenth century: they believed that social reform depended on individual conversion rather than on institutional change.[38]

Although information about the membership of women's organizations is difficult to discover, it does appear that the membership of the Ladies' Missionary Association had changed since its inception under White; while it had been made up almost entirely of single women in its early years, in 1847 sixteen of the thirty-seven members listed were married. There also appears to have been an increased tendency for members of the same family to be active, something that had not been the case under White. Nine of these thirty-seven women had relatives who served on the vestry at some point.[39]

The men of Christ Church also concentrated on traditional activities. The most ambitious of these was the erection, in conjunction with St. Peter's, of a new building for Christ Church Hospital. To take advantage of the "country air," the Board of Managers used money from the sale of the lot left by Joseph Dobbins to buy a 126-acre farm near Bala Cynwyd, adjacent to the city line and five miles from downtown. The new building opened in 1861, having cost $155,101.99, considerably more than the $96,000 estimate (see Figure 26). Because the Panic of 1857 sharply reduced the income of the hospital, managers were forced to leave the north wing empty.[40]

The instructions given to the matron by the board of managers in 1864 give an idea of the kind of facility they wanted. They emphasized that they regarded it as "a Christian Family, of which she is the Head." Therefore, she should "regulate exclusively on the principles of the Gospel of Christ." This could be shown "in the practice of more than ordinary forbearance with infirmities, in consideration of the weakness of age and probably previous sufferings:—by the exercise of dignity with humility, and firmness with gentleness: by an unwearied care for the temporal and spiritual needs of each member of the family, avoiding undue partiality towards any one of them."[41] No finer advice could be given to those working with the elderly and infirm!

Members of Christ Church also took an active role in the revitalization of the Episcopal Academy. In 1846 the trustees reopened the Classical Academy and in 1850 they completed an "elegant and spacious brown stone edifice" at the corner of Juniper and Locust Streets. This building, which initially served 154 boys, would be used until the Academy moved to the suburb of Merion in 1921. While Christ Church was not as intimately connected with this third classical academy as it had been with the first two, one of its members, Horace Binney, played an extremely active role, purchasing the land for the new building and serving as a visiting trustee for many years. In addition, Dorr served on the executive committee, while several members, including Francis West, William and James Newbold, Tobias Wagner, and Edward L. Clark, served as trustees.[42]

FIGURE 26
Christ Church Hospital, completed in 1861. Christ Church Archives.

Men from Christ Church also continued to be active in the diocese and in the organizations formed under Bishop White. Philip Nicklin, Francis West, and Henry Watts joined Benjamin Dorr in serving on the Standing Committee of the diocese. Fifteen men served as officers of the Bishop White Prayer Book Society during Dorr's rectorship, while fourteen served on the board of the Society for the Advancement of Christianity. Five of these men—William Wayne, Francis West, Richard Montgomery, William Newbold, and Horace Binney—served in both organizations as well as on the vestry. As was the case during White's time, most men served on only one board; most vestrymen, for example, were not active in any of the other organizations discussed.[43]

Had Dorr stopped in 1857 to look back at his rectorship after twenty years, he could have been proud of his accomplishments. He had taken a struggling church and turned it into a viable parish once again. Christ Church members had greatly expanded the number of church activities and taken bold steps in the area of missions and in remodeling the church building.

* * *

The last ten years of Dorr's service to Christ Church would be far less pleasant than the first twenty. The Civil War, of course, made life difficult for all Americans. The effects of this war on Christ Church, however, were short-term, while the effects of the increasingly disadvantageous location of Christ Church were long term.

During the years of political conflict that culminated in the Civil War, neither Christ Church as an institution nor Dorr as rector took an active part in the controversies. As his eulogist put it, Dorr "was determined not to know anything among his people save Jesus Christ and him crucified." Thus, while his "heart and his prayers were always with his country, and for the triumph and maintenance of her Union," his comments from the pulpit avoided all mention of slavery or of the war. Even in his sermon on January 4, 1861, the day set apart for a national fast, he refused to discuss the specific issues facing the country. He fervently lamented that "the glorious structure which our forefathers reared, and which they and their children thought as enduring as the everlasting hills, is threatened with immediate destruction, by the whirlwind and the storm." But when he came to enumerating the sins that had led to such suffering, he discussed numerous moral failings, but said nothing about slavery. Dorr's position was in sharp contrast, for example, to his fellow Episcopal clergyman Phillips Brooks, the out-spoken anti-slavery rector of Holy Trinity Church.[44]

There is evidence, in fact, that Dorr shared the common prejudices against blacks. When several Philadelphia Episcopalians wanted to give St. Thomas's African Episcopal Church voting privileges in the diocesan convention in 1850, arguing that it would bring peace, not conflict to the diocese, Dorr, as well as the three lay delegates from Christ Church, voted against the proposal.[45]

The only evidence we have that Dorr opposed slavery is a broadside he signed in September, 1863, eight months after the Emancipation Proclamation abolished slavery in the Confederacy. Along with eighty-one other Episcopal clergymen in Philadelphia, Dorr denounced the open letter of John Henry Hopkins, Bishop of Vermont, that had defended slavery. However, even this letter did not take a stand in favor of abolition. Instead it argued that it was not "their province to mix in any political canvass."[46]

Dorr's position paralleled the opinions of many Philadelphians of his day. In 1856, the first year the Republicans ran candidates, the Democrats swept Philadelphia on an openly anti-Negro, anti-abolitionist platform. Even in 1860 Lincoln supporters had to disguise themselves as the "People's Party," making the tariff their main issue. Once war began, however, Philadelphians, for the most part, came to the aid of their union; red, white, and blue bunting appeared on homes, businesses, and streetcars; men could be seen drilling everywhere; and troops were welcomed with open arms as they were transferred to trains in Philadelphia. But as the war dragged on the pro-southern Democrats became bolder, and by the end of 1861 Philadelphia was once again a divided city, with many of the older elite joining those opposed to the war. The Emancipation Proclamation alienated still more people. However, a combination of patriotism and the prosperity that war brought to the city no doubt led a majority of Philadelphians at least lukewarmly to support the union cause. Once the Confederate army was defeated at Gettysburg, the fortune of the "Peace Party" rapidly declined. In part because of fears caused by Lee's invasion of Pennsylvania, Philadelphia experienced no draft riots like those in New York.[47]

Not surprisingly, the parishioners of Christ Church were also divided over slavery and the conduct of the war. William Meredith, for example, urged the north not to give in to secessionist threats as it had in 1820 and 1850. During the war he helped found the Union League as a "refuge for loyalty" and as a way of showing that not all Philadelphia's first families opposed the war. George Cadwalader, whose loyalty was questioned by mobs because of his southern connections, vowed to lead the fight against secession and was eventually put in charge of the city's defenses. However, other Christ Church members showed distinctly southern leanings. Pierce Butler, the transplanted Georgian patrician, was jailed for a month for his openly pro-southern positions. When Charles Ingersoll, the son of Christ Church member Charles Jared Ingersoll, was likewise arrested, it was the Democratic judge John Cadwalader, another member of Christ Church, who issued the writ of habeas corpus, forcing the government to release him. Peter McCall, who served as rector's warden from 1857 to 1862, joined other members of the Philadelphia elite in opposing the Emancipation Proclamation and Lincoln's overall conduct of the war. Moreover, Dorr's assistant, Cameron McRae, who had served Christ Church since 1859, was from North Carolina and resigned his position to return there in June 1861.[48]

While the political opinions within the congregation varied, the women of the church worked hard to help the men at the front. The Dorcas Society, a sewing group that had been formed in 1859 to provide clothing for the poor, turned attention to the outfitting of soldiers. In May 1861 they received a note from Captain E. M. Woodward of Company B who indicated that the clothing they had sent made the mustering of his men "much more agreeable than it otherwise would have been; the men are proud of their improved appearance & it will . . . add to their efficiency in the service." The correspondence of the women's society is full of poignant requests for clothing and other necessities, indicating the desperate situation of many soldiers. In June 1861 a letter lamented that the troops had only bread and coffee to eat and drink and that their families were not being taken care of as promised. It asked the women to send some tobacco since many of the men had "no money to buy any with." The women continued to answer this and other requests throughout the war. In February 1862 Edward Clark reported that "the patriotism that was so strong among the congregation at the start of the 'Revolution' appears to be of equal force in the hearts of the present" people. By 1862 they were sending most of their boxes to hospitals, including 12 boxes to the hospital in Paducah, Kentucky.[49]

Both the dedication and the patriotism of these women were expressed well in a poem, "Knitting for the Army," written by Mrs. Edward A. Souder in November of 1861 in honor of "a venerable lady of Christ Church," which is excerpted here:

All honor to the noble dame.
　　Of fourscore years and seven;
To loyal heart and willing hand,
　　Let honor due be given.
While youth and health the needles fly
　　And knit the livelong day,
We look with loving pride on her,
　　Who soon must pass away . . .
Six pairs of hose; her busy hands
　　Have hastened to prepare;
A happy soldier must he be,
　　Whose feet these good socks wear. . . .[50]

Unfortunately we have no such detailed accounts of the service of the young men of Christ Church during the Civil War. One tragic death is memorialized on the walls of Christ Church: on May 10, 1864, at the Battle of Spotsylvania, William Dorr, the eldest son of the rector, was killed. Dorr had visited his son and dined with the generals at the Headquarters of the Army of the Potomac only two months earlier. William's death was a terrible blow to the aging pastor. He continued to serve Christ Church for several years, but never quite recovered from this loss.[51]

*　*　*

At the same time that the nation was dealing with the secession crisis, Christ Church leaders had to deal with their own problems, problems just as threatening to the existence of the church as secession was to the existence of the nation. For when the church's leaders assessed the church's position in the late 1850s, neither the financial situation of the church nor its location would allow them to be overly optimistic about the future of Christ Church as an independent parish.

The inexorable expansion of the city westward and the tendency toward spatial differentiation, which we have already discussed, continued and intensified in the 1840s and 1850s, with Christ Church located squarely in the manufacturing and wholesale district. A full quarter of the city's manufacturing workers, around 30,000 people, worked in the ward where Christ Church was located. The 100 block of North Second Street, where the church stood, was home to three stove and range warehouses, several hat manufacturers, a liquor store, a grocer, and numerous garment dealers.

Moreover, the people who did live in this area were unlikely to rent pews in Christ Church. In 1850 the blocks immediately surrounding the church were 34.8 percent Irish and only 49 percent native white American (those born in the United States) compared to the city as a whole which was still 70 percent native white. While the proportion of native whites increased to the west and north, what we would today consider middle and upper class Episcopalians no longer lived in this area. In the 1850s the most fashionable district was along Walnut Street west of Seventh and many wealthy Philadelphians were moving west of Broad Street or to the many "satellite communities" in what are now West Philadelphia, Germantown, Mount Airy, and Chestnut Hill.[52]

Christ Church also had to compete with new Episcopal churches located in the fashionable regions. By 1850 there were at least fourteen other Episcopal churches located in what is now center city (see Map 3). St. Andrew's, with 609 communicants in 1860, and St. Luke's, with 610, were now the largest churches. Moreover, St. Peter's, which had been consistently smaller than Christ Church, had entered a period of rapid growth under the Reverend William Odenheimer, recording 480 communicants compared to Christ Church's 350 in 1860.[53]

Despite all these trends, Christ Church remained financially healthy until the late 1850s. Members who had moved to other parts of the city continued to rent pews, although fewer attended weekly services. Interestingly, it was not decreased pew rents but decreased *interments* that led to a shortfall in revenues in the late 1850s. While members were willing to support the church by paying for a pew, it appears they preferred to be buried closer to where they lived. As a result, the revenue from burials, which had reached a high of $2,749 in 1838 and which was usually around $1,000 in the 1840s, fell to $255 in 1857.[54]

Looking to the future, in 1856 the vestry established a committee to report on "the present and probable future condition of the Resources of this Parish." While the report of that committee is not recorded, during the next few years several solutions were proposed, including building a satellite church and building a new church to serve the current membership, while using the old building as a "free mission church."[55]

The immediate solution, however, was to use the church's *past* to ensure its *future*. At the urging of Dorr, the vestry set up an endowment fund and called on people inside and outside of the church to secure the future of the historic structure after the current pew renters had died. A "Circular" appealed to Episcopalians to preserve the "Sacred monument" associated with

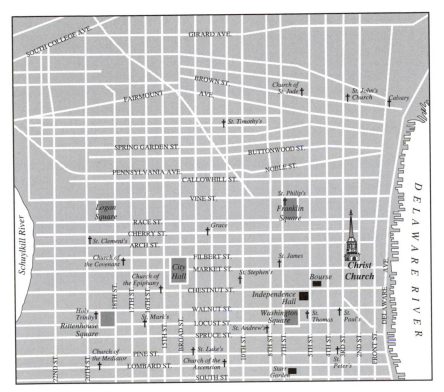

MAP 3
Philadelphia, 1860, with center city Episcopal churches.

Bishop White, the framing of the diocesan and general Church constitutions, the acceptance of the Prayer Book, and many of the early church conventions. The circular then went on to appeal to patriots of all denominations, reminding them of George Washington's and Benjamin Franklin's association with the church and of the seven signers of the Declaration of Independence buried in the church burial grounds. By 1869 this successful appeal had raised $43,000.[56]

This type of discussion about the future of Christ Church occurred again and again during the next century. The basic dilemma—how to preserve an historic structure and remain a viable parish—continued to plague the church. In reality, Christ Church has been able to remain a living parish in a commercial district when other churches moved to the suburbs or closed because its leaders, particularly Benjamin Dorr, were able to tap into its rich history in a way that captured the hearts and minds of Philadelphians. This may be the most enduring legacy of Dorr's rectorship.

*　*　*

Dorr's death in 1869 followed several years of ill health; while never resigning, he had given up regular ministerial duties in 1867 and in 1868 he relinquished his salary. His death marked the end of an era at Christ Church. Dorr served longer than any other rector except White. Like White, he had set the direction the church would take for years to come. He had not only breathed life into a struggling parish, but he had played a large part in ensuring that it would live on after his death and the death of his parishioners. To further ensure that goal he bequeathed five thousand dollars to the endowment fund of Christ Church, as well as one thousand dollars to the parish school. While other ministers of Christ Church played a larger role in the history of the national church, none were more important to the local church's history than Benjamin Dorr.

NOTES

1. Dorr, *Historical Account of Christ Church, Philadelphia*, 256; Vestry Minutes, Aug. 1836. *Poulson's*, Aug. 22, 1836.

2. Vestry Minutes, March 9, May 4, 1837; Dorr, *Historical Account*, 257–62.

3. John William Wallace, *A Discourse Delivered before the Historical Society of Pennsylvania, October 27th, 1870, Commemorative of the Reverend Benjamin Dorr, D.D.* (Philadelphia, 1870), 10–13, 19–21.

4. Vestry Minutes, June 5 and Sept. 27, 1839.

5. Wallace, *Discourse*, 39, 20.

6. Benjamin Dorr, *Memorials of Christ Church, Philadelphia. Two Sermons Preached in Said Church, April 27 and May 4, 1864. One the 135th Anniversary of Laying the Corner-Stone of the Present Building; The Other the 25th Anniversary of the Rector's Institutions* (Philadelphia: Collins, 1862). For a discussion of Tractarianism see Addison, *The Episcopal Church*, 152–63.

7. Addison, *The Episcopal Church*, 42.

8. Benjamin Dorr, *Churchman's Manual, An Exposition of the Doctrines, Ministry and Worship of the Protestant Episcopal Church in the United States* (Burlington, N.J.: J. H. Powell Missionary Press, 1835), vii; *The History of a Pocket Prayerbook Written by Itself* (Philadelphia: George W. Donohue, 1844), ix; *Recognition of Friends in Another World*, 8th ed. (Philadelphia: H. Hooker, 1864).

9. Dorr, *History of a Pocket Prayerbook*, 65, 22.

10. Dorr, *History of a Pocket Prayerbook*, 72–79; Wallace, *Discourse*, 40.

11. Morgan Dix's *A History of the Parish of Trinity Church in the City of New York* did not appear until 1898 about the same time as C. P. B. Jeffery's history of St. Peter's, *The Provincial*

and Revolutionary History of St. Peter's Church, Philadelphia 1753–1783 (n.p., n.d.). See Michael Kammen, *Mystic Chords of Memory: The Transformation of Tradition in American Culture* (New York: Knopf, 1991), for a description of the slow development of a true historic consciousness. Church histories and the historical celebrations that went with them became common in the last quarter of the nineteenth century.

12. Dorr, *Historical Account*, 7–14. Watson accepted Dorr's version in his revised edition of *Annals of Philadelphia.*

13. Confirmation Register, Christ Church Archives; Christ Church Pew Rent Books, Christ Church Archives; *Journal of the Diocese of Pennsylvania* 1835–1860 (Philadelphia, 1837–1860).

14. *Journal of the Diocese of Pennsylvania*, 1835–1860.

15. List located in the Reports to Vestry Concerning Pews, Accounting Wardens' Records, Christ Church Archives.

16. For most of this information on the elite of Christ Church I am indebted to Lee Benson, whose students at the University of Pennsylvania compiled massive amounts of information on the 1844 elite in Philadelphia.

17. Irwin F. Greenberg, "Charles Ingersoll: Aristocrat as Copperhead," *PMHB* 93 (1989): 190–91.

18. Only a handful of these women appear in the City Directory, so it is impossible to draw any conclusions about them.

19. Michael Feldberg, *The Philadelphia Riots of 1844: A Study of Ethnic Conflict* (Westport, Conn.: Greenwood Press, 1975), 13; Warner, *Private City*, 51, 57.

20. Warner, *Private City*, 63–76; Bruce Laurie, *Working People of Philadelphia 1800–1850* (Philadelphia: Temple University Press, 1980), especially chap. 1.

21. Feldberg, *The Philadelphia Riots of 1844*, 64, 87; Vincent P. Lannie and Bernard C. Diethorn, "For the Honor and Glory of God: The Philadelphia Bible Riots of 1844," *History of Education Quarterly* 8 (1968): 44–106.

22. Bell, *Crusade in the City*, 193.

23. For a discussion of reform movements in Philadelphia, see Bell, *Crusade in the City*, 95–106; Othniel Pendleton, Jr., "The Influence of the Evangelical Churches upon Humanitarian Reform: A Case Study Giving Particular Attention to Philadelphia, 1790–1840" (Ph.D. diss., University of Pennsylvania, 1947); Elizabeth Geffen, "Philadelphia Protestants React to Social Reform Movements Before the Civil War," *Pennsylvania History* 30 (1963): 192–202.

24. See Elizabeth M. Geffen, "Industrial Development and Social Crisis, 1841–1854," in Weigley, *Philadelphia, a Three Hundred Year History*, 352–54; Russell F. Weigley, "The Border City in Civil War, 1854–1865," in ibid., 385–87. The quote is from Weigley, "The Border City," p. 386, quoting William Wells Brown, *The American Fugitive in Europe*, p. 312.

25. Warner, *Private City*, 125–27; Feldberg, *Philadelphia Riots*, chap. 5, 6, 7; Charles Chauncey Binney, *The Life of Horace Binney with Selections from His Letters* (Philadelphia: J. P. Lippincott, 1903), 235–41.

26. Scharf and Wescott, *History of Philadelphia*, 2: 1229–1446.

27. John Waller James to Vestry, April 15, 1833 in Vestry Minutes, April 15, 1833; Vestry Minutes, Sept. 4, 1833; April 7 and May 7, 1834; Jan. 25, 1836.

28. See Vestry Minutes, Jan. 25, 1836, Sept. 17, 1836. Permission was obtained from all the descendants of those buried in the aisles who could be located. For Walter's plans, see his letter in Dorr, *Historical Account of Christ Church*, 338–43.

29. Vestry Minutes, June 25, 1833, Dec. 7, 1836.

30. Vestry Minutes, Dec. 5, 1838.

31. Peterson, "The Building of Christ Church, Philadelphia," in *Catalog of the Antique Show*, 142.

32. The vestry spent most of its time from 1837 to 1842 on the pew situation. In particular see Vestry Minutes, Sept. 22, 1837, Jan. 18, Feb. 19 and April 8 and 28, 1839, May 7, 1840; Dorr, *Memorials of Christ Church*, 47.

33. John James to Vestry, April 15, Sept. 4, 1833; Vestry Minutes, April 8, Dec. 1, 1857; Benjamin Dorr, *Elisha's Fountain or the Waters Healed* (Philadelphia, 1866), 44–47. The annual statistics are given in the annual *Journal of the Diocese of Pennsylvania*.

34. Managers of Parochial Day School to Vestry, 1847, Vestry Correspondence.

35. Ladies' Missionary Association, Secretaries' Correspondence, 1825–1860, Christ Church Archives.

36. Ladies'Missionary Association, *Seventeenth Annual Report* (Philadelphia, 1847), 4–5; *Eighteenth Annual Report* (Philadelphia, 1848).

37. Horace Binney to Anna DaCosta, Aug. 8, 1846; H. W. Ducachet, to Anna DaCosta, Feb 6, 1846, Correspondence, Ladies' Missionary Society; Ladies' Missionary Association, *Twenty-Fourth Annual Report* (Philadelphia, 1854).

38. For a discussion of the wide array of activities in which church women became involved, see Mary Ryan, *Cradle of the Middle Class*, 105–45. For a discussion of the different categories of benevolence activities see, for example, Anne M. Boylan, "Women in Groups: An Analysis of Women's Benevolent Organizations in New York and Boston, 1797–1840," *Journal of American History* 71 (1984): 497–523.

39. Ladies' Missionary Association of Christ Church, *Seventeenth Annual Report* (1847); Vestry Records. Because of name changes it is impossible to know whether the single women active during White's rectorship had stayed active after they married, or whether these were new members.

40. Minutes, Board of Managers of Christ Church Hospital, Feb. 2, 1852, Jan. 3, 1853, Sept. 5, 1853; Roberts, "History of Christ Church Hospital," 93–95; *Report of the Managers of the Christ Church Hospital on the Completion of the New Building at Belmont* (Philadelphia, 1864).

41. Roberts, "Christ Church Hospital," 94–95.

42. Charles Latham, Jr., *The Episcopal Academy*, 61–86.

43. *Journal of the Diocese of Pennsylvania*. Society for the Advancement of Christianity, *Annual Report*, 1836–44 (Philadelphia, 1836–1844); Bishop White Prayerbook Society, *Annual Report*, 1834–1867 (Philadelphia, 1834–1867).

44. See Wallace, *Discourse*, 33; Benjamin Dorr, *The American Vine, A Sermon Preached in Christ Church, Philadelphia, Friday, January 4, 1861, on Occasion of The National Fast* (Philadelphia: Collins, 1861), 13, 16, 17. For a discussion of Phillips Brooks's views on slavery, see Alexander Allen, *Life and Letters of Phillips Brooks*, 3 vols. (New York: Dutton, 1901), 1: 373–74, 418, 428, 446–47, 450.

45. *Journal of the Diocese of Pennsylvania*, 1849, 1864.

46. *The Voice of the Clergy* (Philadelphia, 1863).

47. Weigley, "The Border City in Civil War 1854–1865," 384–13.

48. See William Dusenberre, *Civil War Issues in Philadelphia, 1856–1865* (Philadelphia: University of Pennsylvania Press, 1965), esp. pp. 100, 111, 144, 157–58, 170; Weigley, "The Border City in Civil War 1854–1865," 402–3; Vestry Minutes, April 29, June 5, 1861.

49. Capt. E. M. Woodward to Mr. Edward Clark, May 29, 1861, Thomas Crozier to Edward

Clark, June 2, 1861, Edward Clark to Surgeon, Feb. 27, 1862, Correspondence, Dorcas Society, Christ Church Archives.

50. Found in the Correspondence of the Dorcas Society, Christ Church Archives.

51. The burial records indicate the deaths of three young men in 1861, one in 1863, one in 1864 and five in 1865. Only two list any military title. Wallace, *Discourse*, 34–39, includes Dorr's letters to his son recounting his visit to the Headquarters.

52. Warner, *Private City*, 59, gives the data for Ward Six, which in 1860 extended from Vine Street to Chestnut, and from Front to Seventh. This was almost identical to the parish boundaries that were eventually set for Christ Church. The information on the area surrounding Christ Church and the ethnicity figures come from the Philadelphia Social History Project, a data base established at the University of Pennsylvania under the guidance of Lee Benson, which has computerized the business directory of 1850. Information on Chestnut street as well as the residential information is taken from Elizabeth Geffen, "Industrial Development and Social Crisis, 1841–1854," in Weigley, *Philadelphia*, 310–12.

53. *Journal of the Diocese of Pennsylvania*, 1850–1860. St. James, which had peaked at 376 communicants in 1843, had only 250 by 1860.

54. *Circular to the Congregation of Christ Church, Philadelphia and to all friends of the Church here and elsewhere* (Philadelphia, 1864) refers to the difficulty of members attending services. Financial summaries are given in the April vestry minutes for each year. The report of the Committee on Financial Condition, Vestry Committee Record, Christ Church Archives, discusses the fall in burial fees.

55. Vestry Minutes, Dec. 3, 1856; Endowment Committee Minutes, Vestry Committee Records, Christ Church Archives.

56. *Circular to the Congregation of Christ Church*, May 1864; Wallace, *Discourse*, 29–30 discusses the endowment fund and Dorr's role in it.

CHRIST CHURCH STRUGGLES TO SURVIVE IN THE LATE NINETEENTH CENTURY

At Benjamin Dorr's death in 1869 the future of Christ Church was not yet secure, despite the leadership's successful endowment campaign and its emphasis on the historical importance of the church. Only exceptional leadership and considerable luck would keep the church alive in an ever-changing neighborhood, and for much of the last half of the nineteenth century Christ Church appeared to have neither. (For a contemporary picture of Christ Church and its surroundings see Figure 27.) Dorr's successor, Edward Foggo, accomplished many things, but his rectorship was characterized by controversy and decline and he resigned in 1891 because he hoped someone else could succeed where he had failed. In turn, Foggo's successor, C. Ellis Stevens, while an extremely able clergyman who drew new people to the old church, generated even more controversy and ultimately was forced to resign. By 1900 Christ Church's continued existence was in doubt.

Edward Foggo and C. Ellis Stevens served Christ Church during a period of rapid change and controversy in American religion and within the Protestant Episcopal Church in particular. Two themes dominated the history of American Protestantism in the late nineteenth century-responding to

FIGURE 27
"Christ Church and the celebrated Carpet Hall," showing the buildings around Christ Church at the end of the nineteenth century. Courtesy of the Library Company of Philadelphia.

the new science and dealing with the increasing poverty in America. At the same time, the Episcopal Church had to deal with the Anglo-Catholic movement.

Beginning in the 1870s Protestant churches had to deal with repercussions from new scientific theories, particularly Darwin's theory of evolution, which seemed to undermine the creation story and, by implication, much of the Old Testament. While many conservatives steadfastly opposed evolution, branding it anti-Christian, others developed a liberal theology that incorporated much of the new science without undermining the basics of Christianity.[1]

Protestants during the Gilded Age also began to grapple seriously with the increasing poverty and inequality resulting from the industrial revolution. Even many conservatives began to believe that all was not well with the social and economic order in the United States. "Conservative social Christianity" argued for a more active role for the churches in alleviating the suffering of the poor. Never challenging the basic economic assumptions, proponents of this approach called on employers to raise wages voluntarily as a "Christian act" and called on churches to help the poor by such activities as comsumers' cooperatives and savings banks.[2]

By the 1870s a group of influential people began to call on Christians to go beyond individual philanthropy and voluntary acts to work for change in the economic system of the country. While rejecting socialism, they called for a "new social spirit based on Christian love." The social gospel movement they established rejected the traditional laissez-faire attitude toward business and worked for a wide range of reforms; many came to endorse the dreaded labor union movement. Perhaps surprisingly, the Protestant Episcopal Church was the first major denomination to respond favorably to these doctrines. In 1883 the General Convention commented that in recent years "this Church has been awakened to increased practical sympathy with the worker and suffering classes; victims of social wrong, of unequal laws, of intemperance in drinks and an unscrupulous traffic in them, and sometimes of merciless wealth." In 1887 a group of New York Episcopalians founded the first social gospel Organization, the Church Association for the Advancement of the Interests of Labor.[3]

At the same time that Protestant churches were dealing with evolution and with the social gospel movement, the Episcopal Church had to deal with the serious divisions caused by the Anglo-Catholic movement. Direct theological descendants of the high church supporters that had caused such problems for the Pennsylvania diocese during White's bishopric, Anglo-Catholics after the Civil War went much further in their identification with the Roman Catholic church. Among their more controversial beliefs and practices

FIGURE 28
The Reverend Edward Foggo (rector, 1869–1890). Christ Church Archives.

were their emphasis on the "Real Presence in the Eucharist," their use of prayers for the dead, and their belief in sacramental confession with priestly absolution. As had been the case with the High Church movement, Philadelphia became one of the centers of controversy over Anglo-Catholicism.[4]

While there is no evidence that Christ Church was affected by the disputes over evolution, it was directly affected by the Anglo-Catholic contro-versies and, because of its location in the city, its leadership had to, at least by their actions, take a stand on the debate over what to do with the urban poor.

The first rector to be required to deal with these issues was Edward Foggo (see Figure 28). As assistant minister under Dorr, Foggo had assumed most of the rector's duties several years before Dorr's death. Born in Ber-muda, Foggo had graduated from the General Theological Seminary at the age of nineteen, one of the youngest men ever to receive a degree there. After serving as rector of Christ Church in Bordentown, New Jersey, Foggo came to Christ Church in Philadelphia in 1861, where he served on a year-to-year basis.[5] In 1868, probably because he had officially begun assuming all the duties of the rector, Foggo asked to be named permanent assistant minister, declaring that he would resign if he were not so appointed. Foggo's request generated intense controversy, in part because it positioned him so clearly as Dorr's successor. Eighty-two members wrote an impassioned plea on Foggo's behalf, but twelve other members urged the vestry to do nothing "inexpe-dient" that would "divide the congregation." The vestry itself was divided. Despite the pleas of so many members, at first the vestry voted to accept Foggo's resignation. Only after Dorr argued that it would be difficult to find an appropriate assistant "under the peculiar circumstances in which the parish was placed" did the vestry elect Foggo as permanent assistant minis-ter, and even then the vote was seven to four, the minimum needed for such an election.[6]

This vote proved to be the first of many crucial issues in the late nine-teenth century on which the vestry was deeply divided. As a result of these divisions, the vestry never exercised the kind of courageous leadership needed to save Christ Church.

We know less about Edward Foggo, who was elected rector by a ten-to-one vote in 1869, than about any other rector of Christ Church after the eighteenth century. This is no doubt in part because, while he was "a man of strong character," he was "reserved and undemonstrative." His obituary indicated that "he was less widely known than his learning and goodness entitled him to be." Yet when he retired in 1891, after serving Christ Church for thirty years, the vestrymen wrote a warm letter, speaking of their "un-abated friendship" and "affectionate good will," and thanking him for "the unrepining and undaunted constancy with which" he served the church.[7]

Foggo's rectorship included several important accomplishments, notably a major construction project. In 1870 the vestry agreed to build a new parish

FIGURE 29
Christ Church, showing attached schoolhouse. Christ Church Archives.

building to replace the small schoolhouse. After efforts to buy land adjacent to the church proved unsuccessful, the vestry decided to construct a building connected to the northwest corner of the church. This involved building a crypt over the old tombs, something which bothered many. Others were bothered by the damage done to the appearance of the church building, but Foggo argued that "living souls were of more consequence than the appearance of the ancient Structure"[8] (see Figure 29).

The "living souls" served by Christ Church reached a high of four hundred communicants in 1880. They continued to be predominately women; 41 percent of the 138 pew renters were women, up from 35 percent during

Dorr's years, and women made up 68 percent of the confirmands during Foggo's rectorship. The church also continued to draw primarily from center city Philadelphia. Three quarters of the pew renters still lived in center city, with almost a quarter living within the designated parish area—between the Delaware River and Sixth Street and Chestnut and Vine. Public transportation was not yet good enough to allow the congregation to be too widely scattered. In 1881 Dr. Chester Murray, who lived at Eighteenth and Chestnut Streets, gave up his pew because he lived too far from the church! The occupational distribution for the thirty-two members for whom this information is available (all men) indicates that Christ Church continued to draw middle and upper middle class men; six were lawyers, four were doctors, and eight were merchants or manufacturers.[9] Obviously, conclusions based on so few people can only be suggestive.

Christ Church still attracted outstanding men to serve on its vestry. Two descendants of Bishop White served the church. Thomas H. Montgomery, who was prominent in insurance, and William White Wiltbank, a distinguished lawyer and a judge of the Common Pleas Court of Philadelphia, both served as vestrymen for more than twenty years. These men were joined on the vestry for twenty years by Dr. John DaCosta, whose family had been active in Christ Church throughout Dorr's rectorship. Specializing first in mental and nervous disorders and later in surgery, Dr. DaCosta became professor of surgery at Jefferson Medical College and wrote extensively in his field. Another longtime vestryman, Edward Coates, the descendant of an early Quaker family, founded the insurance company of Edward H. Coates and Company. Prominent in philanthropic, educational, and artistic circles in Philadelphia, he served as president of the Pennsylvania Academy of the Fine Arts, as manager of the Pennsylvania Hospital, and as vice president of the Insurance Corporation for the Relief of Widows and Orphans of Clergymen of the Episcopal Church in the Commonwealth of Pennsylvania.[10]

For Christ Church to survive, the leadership would have to reach out to the surrounding neighborhood, which changed dramatically between 1850 and 1880. (See Figure 30 for the neighborhood near Christ Church.) In 1850 the parish area was still peopled predominately by "native white Americans" (those born in the United States); only the blocks immediately surrounding Christ Church contained less than 50 percent native whites. But by 1880 the population of all but a few blocks within the parish was at least two-thirds immigrant or first generation American, at a time when 55 percent of the citywide population fell into these categories. Among these immigrants the

FIGURE 30
Second Street, north of Market, c. 1876, showing steeple of Christ Church. Courtesy of the Historical Society of Pennsylvania.

Irish predominated, but there were many Germans as well.[11] And while Philadelphia lacked the extreme tenement conditions that plagued New York, poverty and deprivation still characterized the lives of many of Christ Church's neighbors.

The response of Foggo and Christ Church to these conditions fell within the bounds of conservative social Christianity. Never recognizing the need for general reform, Foggo concentrated on serving the needs of individual members of Christ Church. Despite these limitations, it is true that Foggo did reach out to the neighborhood more than Dorr had done. By 1879 Foggo and the laity had expanded the Sunday school to 400 pupils, compared to the average of 250 under Dorr. Christ Church actually had the highest pupil/communicant ratio of any downtown Episcopal church, and only the Church of the Epiphany and St. Andrew's served more students.[12] Foggo also re-established the parish school, which must have ended its brief run in the 1840s. While not encouraged by those who felt the public schools did a competent job, it continued throughout the nineteenth century, reporting fifty pupils in 1886. In addition, Foggo also started a night school for young men. In 1869 the vestry reported that they had "learned with interest of the marked zeal and success with which the parish and night schools of the Church are being conducted by the Rector." They expressed their "cordial approval" and hoped his labors would prove "abundantly fruitful." Christ Church also addressed the needs of girls. The women of the church re-established the Sewing School, a project that had been suspended during the Civil War, and by 1879 an industrial school, which taught domestic skills, served eighty-three people.[13] Unfortunately there are no records extant for these laudable efforts.

Foggo also initiated regular house-to-house visitation, through which he felt he met the needs of anyone "with the slightest claim on the Parish." Foggo even established a soup kitchen one winter. Although hundreds were provided for, Foggo did not consider the project a success, for the "worthy poor were too self-respecting to come forward, and the throng of others frightened them away." He therefore had to send the meals to many of them. Despite this patronizing attitude, Foggo did begin the social outreach that became such an important activity of Christ Church in the early twentieth century.[14]

In 1867 Foggo began free Sunday evening services in order to encourage the people in the neighborhood to take advantage of the spiritual as well as the charitable activities of the parish. One person told him that she had lived within the "sound of the bells for over forty years but had never been in the Church doors, as she had heard that poor people were not allowed in the pews there." In 1877 the church opened afternoon services to anyone.[15]

Christ Church members also supported charitable activities outside the neighborhood. Members actively supported the Episcopal Hospital, which opened in 1862 at Front Street and Lehigh Avenue, providing the money for the hospital chapel, endowing both a fund for the chaplain, and a free bed for the use of the Parish. The church also continued to be actively involved in the management of Christ Church Hospital. As the property became less isolated, the trustees were able to sell some of its land in 1888 and increase the number of residents from forty to fifty. They also decided to hire a full time chaplain, rather than relying on the rectors of Christ Church and St. Peter's. While providing better service for the residents, it did distance the hospital from the churches.[16]

Christ Church reestablished its relationship with Calvary Monumental Church during Foggo's rectorship. Because the members of Calvary could no longer sustain their church, which was increasingly surrounded by railroad warehouses, in 1870 the Christ Church vestry resumed responsibility for it. Once again the Ladies' Missionary Association provided the money. In 1881 the women finally decided that it was no longer "practicable" to carry out a mission at that location and agreed to move the church to West Philadelphia. With the money received from the sale of the land, the church was moved brick by brick and re-erected at Forty-first Street and Oregon Avenue. At this point the vestry of Calvary Monumental resumed control. In 1946 Calvary merged with the African-American congregation of St. Michael and All Angels located at Forty-third and Wallace Streets; the two congregations chose to use the Calvary Monumental church building, so it remains today as a monument to Bishop White.[17]

Foggo and the vestry also took good care of their own church building. Once again, Christ Church experienced a period of extensive repair and remodeling. In 1869 the outside of the church was painted with brown sand paint to simulate sandstone then in vogue and the steeple ornaments were gilded. Then in the early 1870s the vestry turned attention to the inside of the church. The increasing influence of the high church, Anglo-Catholic segment of the Episcopal Church, with its emphasis on the altar and deemphasis on the pulpit, affected almost all Episcopal churches, even Christ Church with its steadfastly low church orientation. In 1870 the vestry had the pulpit removed from the chancel to the north pillar and the communion table placed against the eastern wall. The next year Foggo, who believed that the "honest four-legged" table given by Gostelowe was not in harmony with the building, presented the church with a "suitable Altar made of oak" that was placed over the little table. "Suitable Altar cloths and stoles for the Church seasons" were also presented as gifts. This was the first time a rector of Christ Church had worn a stole. With the altar table against the wall, Foggo, like most priests at the time, said at least some of the communion service with his back to the congregation.[18]

Shortly after Foggo assumed the rectorship, the leadership made other changes unrelated to the new liturgical emphasis. The church once again used the old baptismal font, in which William Penn had been baptized. At the same time the vestry placed a cover over the Gostelowe font so it could be used as a credence table, the first ever placed in Christ Church. The vestry also returned the chandelier to its original position. A colored glass window in honor of Bishop White was placed in the Palladian window in place of the "dingy looking old one." Foggo's dream of having a leaded stained glass window there was never fulfilled.[19]

All these changes and improvements served as only a prelude to the major restoration project undertaken in the 1880s. The centennial of the nation, celebrated in Philadelphia in 1876, and the general increased interest in history led Foggo and others in the congregation to look with disfavor on the changes that had been made in the church in the 1830s and 1850s. Planning was begun in 1880 and by November 1882 the restoration, under the direction of architect George Hewitt, was complete. The carpet was taken up from the aisle floor, once again revealing the gravestones beneath. The walnut-stained pine pews were replaced with oak slip pews "in old style" without upholstery. The pulpit was moved to what was considered its original position in front of the chancel arch, a little north of the middle aisle. The "Washington door" at the east end was reopened, serving once again as the entrance to the south gallery. The "western doors" on the north and south side were moved east one bay to their original position and a cross aisle connected them. The western stairways to the gallery built in 1836 were removed and a new stairway in the "South East room" was built to replace the one removed in 1836. The church was painted a "plain tint" to replace the gray paint there at the time. This major work was paid for by generous contributions from former members of Christ Church and from those who had "a simple desire to see . . . an old landmark revived"[20] (see Figures 31 and 32).

The interest in refurbishing and restoring the church came at a time when Christ Church hosted a number of historical celebrations. In 1870, Bishop White's remains were removed from the family vault and placed under the chancel floor in an impressive ceremony commemorating the one hundredth anniversary of his ordination as a deacon.[21] The church held another impressive ceremony to mark the one-hundredth anniversary of his consecration as bishop in 1887. Christ Church also hosted the celebration of the centennial of the formation of the Protestant Episcopal Church in 1883.

*   *   *

While Christ Church members made a valiant effort to serve the neighborhood at the same time that they took care of what was becoming a national

FIGURE 31
Interior of Christ Church, looking east, showing restorations and "colored glass window."
Edward Jones, 1899. Courtesy of the Historical Society of Pennsylvania.

treasure, the rectorship of Edward Foggo was ultimately characterized more
by controversy and decline than by positive accomplishments.

It was, in fact, the church's most ambitious effort to assure its survival—
the erection of a chapel—that led to the greatest controversy. Even before
Dorr's death the vestry of Christ Church, fearing that as members moved out
of the parish area they would "for the convenience of their families" join

FIGURE 32
Interior of Christ Church, looking west. Edward Jones, 1899. Courtesy of the Historical Society of Pennsylvania.

other churches, had approved the erection of a chapel west of Broad Street, but the project was not implemented.[22] In 1874 G. Wolsey Hodge, an assistant minister who had been hired in 1871 to take charge of Calvary Monumental Church, asked permission to hold services in the "western section of the city," offering to relinquish his salary while involved in this project. Fearful that the project might prove to be a drain on the limited resources of the mother church, the vestry agreed to Hodge's proposal only after resolving that it had no "pecuniary responsibility in the premises."[23]

The vestry did, however, help Hodge raise money for the new church. In a flier reminiscent of the request for contributions to the endowment fund, Foggo, Hodge and a committee of the vestry explained the precarious financial position of Christ Church, arguing that the endowment probably could not be increased by much, and that if Christ Church were left in the hands of those who lived in the vicinity "who would be unable to sustain it, it could not be long before this consecrated possession was sacrificed to its commercial value." A chapel built in the newer section of town was the answer both to the financial problems of Christ Church and to the desire of older members to continue their association with the Church.[24] Thus, rather than being a missionary effort, as were many chapels, Christ Church Chapel was an effort to ensure the future financial stability of the mother church.

Under the guidance of Hodge, the chapel proved successful. In 1876 the congregation, which included sixty communicants, built a small gothic church on Pine Street above Nineteenth street. Patterned after St. George's Chapel, Windsor, it was described as "by no means imposing exteriorly, though strikingly pretty" on the interior[25] (see Figure 33). At the consecration service, Bishop Stevens hoped that "by this plan . . . much which Christ Church has lost by this westward movement may be recovered; that the dispersed families, and even the children's children" might be once again associated with Christ Church. Thus, when the "demands of commerce" in the area of Christ Church led to "contracting the light of this 'morning star of our Church in this commonwealth,' it will find a new life and a new dawning here."[26]

Two characteristics set the new chapel apart from its mother church and from most other churches. It was a free church, open to all who wanted to attend. In fact, it did not even have pews, using only movable chairs. While this plan had been denounced when the women established it at Calvary Monumental in the 1850s, by the 1870s Bishop Stevens wholeheartedly endorsed it. Admitting that it would take years to end the current pew rental

CHAPTER THIRTEEN

FIGURE 33
Christ Church Chapel, Pine Street above Nineteenth Street. Christ Church Archives.

system, he argued that "the House of God should not be sold off in strips and square feet to men who can afford to outbuy others." In addition, Christ Church Chapel was open all day for prayer and meditation, a practice that was adopted at the mother church in 1877. Commenting on the crowded living conditions in the city, Stevens argued that there were many, and not all of the lower classes, who had no private place for reading and prayer and who, as a result, neglected that important aspect of their religious life. Christ Church Chapel would provide such a place.[27]

Within a year of its opening the chapel had established a thriving, active congregation. As of May 1878 102 families with 161 communicants attended the chapel. By 1879 the congregation had grown so large that a temporary addition to the building was added, doubling the size of the chapel's seating capacity to 400. Despite the original aim of the chapel, its members did not come primarily from families with connections to Christ Church. Of the 675 parishioners on the parish rolls from 1874 to 1880, only 14 could be identified as having been or having a relative who was a pew holder at Christ Church.[28] Presumably people chose the chapel because of its location and its ministry and not because of its connection with Christ Church.

This connection with the mother church was, from the beginning, a bit unusual. In February 1876 the vestry delegated the management of the chapel to a board made up of six vestrymen and six members of the chapel to be chosen by the six vestrymen. The resolution stated that their actions were "subject always to the approval and control of the Vestry of Christ Church" and that no acts were binding on the vestry unless approved by it.[29] However, during the first four years of the chapel's history neither Foggo nor the vestry showed any interest in it. No regular reports were made; no financial statements were received. The board of managers did not even inform the vestry when it built a new building or later enlarged it. Because of his duties at Christ Church, Foggo visited the chapel only a few times before 1880.

Moreover, from its inception Foggo allowed the chapel to pursue a style of worship that was "higher" than that of the mother church. The chapel immediately adopted a surpliced choir and later introduced the choral service. It offered communion weekly and held two services daily, compared to Christ Church, which still had monthly communion and weekday services on Wednesday and Friday.[30]

Such neglect seems at odds with the goal of establishing the chapel as the savior of, if not the succcessor to, the mother church. It appears that the leaders of Christ Church were purposely trying to distance themselves from the chapel in case it did not succeed. However, in the event that the chapel were financially successful, then the mother church would be happy to call on it for help in times of need.

Despite the laissez-faire attitude of Christ Church, in 1880 the future looked bright for the chapel and, indirectly, for Christ Church. The number of people worshiping in the chapel exceeded the number attending the mother church, as did the contributions, and while the chapel had a $22,000 mortgage, it had never had to ask the mother church for money.[31]

Beginning in January 1880, however, a controversy began that would rock both the chapel and the mother church, a controversy that would be played out in the local newspapers and in the courts, as much as in the vestry rooms of the two churches. The source of the problem was Henry Percival, hired as the rector's assistant, a position that served at the pleasure of the rector, in 1878. Percival, who was independently wealthy, agreed to work without pay. Already well known for his "advanced" Anglo-Catholic views when he was hired at the chapel, after leaving the chapel he became rector of the Church of the Evangelist and in 1890 he founded the Anglo-Catholic St. Elizabeth's Church in Philadelphia.[32] He later founded a religious society, the Communion of the Holy Savior, to further his extreme views which included acceptance of all the proclamations of the Roman Catholic church's Council of Trent except papal infallibility.[33] Because of Percival's unorthodox beliefs Bishop Stevens had actually advised Hodge against hiring him. Foggo later indicated that he, too, had been hesitant, but had agreed to the hiring because Percival had given assurances of "his loyal adhesion to myself as Rector and to the general polity of the parish."[34] That Percival had a different view of what "loyal adhesion" meant would soon become apparent and should not have surprised Foggo.

The problems began in December 1879, when a chapel parishioner asked Foggo to transfer her membership to Christ Church because Percival had urged her daughter to make confession to a priest before receiving her first communion. When the mother protested that her husband would not approve, Percival allegedly suggested that she not tell her husband about it. On investigation, Foggo determined that Percival had indeed repeatedly taught the expediency of confession and circulated devotional books advocating it, and that Percival understood from Hodge that he was at liberty to express these views. Foggo also charged that Percival had refused communion to a girl because she would not go to confession, a charge Percival later denied, and that he had sent a parishioner to another minister rather than to the rector for counsel. On January 2, 1880 Foggo confronted Hodge. His conversation convinced him that Hodge supported Percival and would not require that the "rector's assistant" change his behavior. As a result, the next day Foggo fired Percival, without even interviewing him, and asked for Hodge's resignation.[35]

Foggo could fire Percival, since he was a "rector's assistant," but he could not fire Hodge, who was a duly installed assistant minister. Instead he relied on a promise that Hodge had made at the time of his election that if "any difficulty should arise" between the two ministers he would immediately resign. Hodge acknowledged the promise, but argued it was made long before he was put in charge of a separate church. He reluctantly tendered his resignation, but made it effective when a replacement could be found. Foggo, piqued at Hodge's independence, returned the resignation, insisting that it be unconditional and effective January 19. Hodge, arguing that Foggo's refusal to provide for the work of the chapel pressed his promise of resignation beyond all bounds, appealed to the vestry. In his letter to that body, he argued that he had not been told of the charges against him and that it was unfair to dismiss him before a new minister was named.[36]

The vestry met to consider the issue on January 8. In the first of a series of actions that indicated frustration with, if not outright disapproval of Foggo's actions, the vestry set up a committee to investigate the situation, rather than dismissing Hodge immediately, as Foggo wanted. On February 4 the vestry met to vote on the committee's recommendation that Hodge's resignation be accepted. On the one side stood their rector of eleven years. On the other stood the board of managers which included six vestrymen, arguing that "the present prosperity of the chapel is mainly due to the energy, devotion and self sacrificing services of the Minister in charge" and that his resignation "would seriously and disastrously affect the welfare of the chapel." Uncertain and divided, the vestry, on a vote of six to five, barely defeated a motion to sever all connection with the chapel. However, in the end, by a vote of eight to three, they decided they were not willing to "make an issue with the rector," and voted to accept Hodge's resignation effective March 10, thus allowing time to find a replacement.[37]

The following Sunday Hodge went public with his problems. In an impassioned speech, which was printed in full in the *Philadelphia Inquirer*, he informed his congregation of his forced resignation. He argued that it was unjust that "the spiritual home of those who have found one here in this free church . . . should be disrupted and destroyed, and a clergyman forced away . . . by a body of men, scarcely any of whom ever come here." Immediately after the announcement, the congregation met to protest Hodge's dismissal and asked the vestry to reconsider its actions. If that were not done, they "demanded a separation from the said corporation."[38]

The vestry met on February 18 to reconsider the situation and once again narrowly defeated a motion to allow the secession of the chapel. Instead, arguing that the charter did not allow the vestry to give up property without a congregational vote, they put the issue before the pew renters of the mother church, the only group allowed to vote. After much lobbying, covered heavily in the press, the pew renters voted fifty-three to sixteen not to allow the chapel to separate from the mother church. Interestingly, a newspaper reported that a majority of the vestry voted in favor of the separation.

For its part, the chapel congregation did not even wait for the vote before it formed a separate church, the Church of the Holy Communion, and applied for a charter.[39] And when Bishop Stevens's efforts to mediate failed, the chapel's board of managers decided to take physical possession of the chapel.[40] Consequently, on March 11, when Foggo arrived at the chapel with its new minister, he found the doors barred and two men outside ready to ensure that they did not get in. The spectacle of a rector locked out of a church caused a sensation in the press. "Holding the Fort . . . Sentinels Guarding the Building Against Intrusion—An Amusing Condition Of Affairs . . ."; "A Chapel As A Fortress"; "Barred Out" the headlines read. Interviews with those inside, where the vestry room was filled with "a heap of mattresses and bed clothing" and where five men were "comfortably ensconced," indicated that the chapel congregation had forty men willing to sleep in the chapel until the issue was decided.[41] By the time the Christ Church vestry met on March 17, compromise was no longer possible. While the chapel members insisted that they had merely changed the name of their church, neither the bishop nor the vestry recognized the new charter. The vestry did inform those occupying the chapel that they could leave, since Christ Church would not try to possess the building except through legal channels. Legal proceedings were begun on April 6.[42]

By the time the issue reached the courts in June 1880, both sides had adopted extreme positions. Hodge argued that the chapel, from its inception, was "an independent and distinct congregation" whose only connection with Christ Church was its name, which the congregation was now more than willing to give up.[43] On the other side, the counsel for the vestry of Christ Church convincingly demonstrated that the chapel was always intended to be a part of Christ Church. In fact, the bishop approved its construction only because it was intended as "a chapel entirely under the control of the Rector, Churchwardens and Vestrymen of Christ Church . . . for the accommodation of a portion of the parishioners of Christ Church living at a distance from the old edifice." Christ Church's lawyers also tried, less successfully, to show financial involvement in the chapel, producing affidavits from people who gave to the chapel fund only because it was associated with Christ Church.[44]

On June 23 the court ruled in favor of Christ Church, basically accepting the entire argument of its lawyers. The court argued that no convincing evidence for the independence of the chapel could be found. In fact, Hodge's actions, including his own resignation and the acceptance of Percival's dismissal, indicated that he accepted the subordinate status of the chapel.[45]

This legal opinion ended one of the saddest episodes in the history of Christ Church. Hodge went on to become rector of the Church of the Ascension and became a prominent minister in the diocese. Most of the parishioners followed either Hodge or Percival to their new churches.[46] This left Christ Church with a rather hollow victory: a building with a $22,000 mortgage and few parishioners.

Surprisingly, however, within a few years the chapel had been revived. In November Foggo appointed W. P. Lewis to take charge of the chapel, and he immediately began rebuilding the congregation. By April 1882 he had enrolled 120 new communicants and by 1886 the total stood at 165. In 1885 the newspaper reported that worshipers could scarcely find accommodations. These members made major improvements to the building. In 1883 the interior of the chapel was renovated and two houses which had been used for the Sunday school were combined, creating a more functional parish building. The chapel also received a new organ, described as one of the finest in the city, given by D. C. Wharton Smith in memory of Philip F. Wharton. Two years later two Tiffany windows were added. Despite the expense of these improvements, by 1886 the chapel's mortgage had been retired, at which time Bishop Stevens performed an impressive consecration ceremony.[47]

At the same time that a new minister began to rebuild the congregation, the vestry of Christ Church clearly defined the governing structure of the chapel. The board of managers was given "care, custody, and control of all buildings," but could not "alienate, convey or encumber" them. Board members could appoint any officers that they felt necessary, but ultimately they were subject "to the Authority of Christ Church and to such direction and control as the proper authorities thereof may at any time direct or prescribe." In a break with the past, they were required to make a report to the vestry each Easter Monday.[48] Christ Church Chapel was still to be independent, but not too independent.

Despite the success of Lewis, by 1894 the future of the chapel was once again in doubt. This time the problem was financial—resulting from too many churches in its vicinity. Thus when the much older and larger Church of the Epiphany, which was located at Fifteenth and Chestnut Streets, proposed uniting with the chapel, the board of managers as well as 95 of the 120 communicants who responded to a questionnaire (out of 190 sent out) endorsed the merger. Despite this support, and the offer from Epiphany to pay the mother church $60,000, the vestry of Christ Church refused to approve the merger. Judge Thayer "spoke feelingly of the Connection between Christ Church Chapel and Christ Church, of the growth and prosperity of the former, of her possibilities of future assistance to Christ Church and of the legal impediments to any severance."[49] While Thayer's description may not have been accurate—the connection had never been close and the possibilities for future assistance did not look good even in 1894—the result was the same as it had been in 1880; the wishes of the chapel congregation had been thwarted. Epiphany then chose to merge with St. Luke's, creating a church that continues to serve center city.

The vestry's failure to endorse the wishes of the chapel did not lead to secession this time, but it did lead to the resignation of W. P. Lewis. Lewis resigned in February 1895, citing as his reasons the nature of the relationship between the chapel and Christ Church, the difficulty of obtaining help from the laity, and the financial condition of the chapel. While the vestry tried to convince Lewis to stay by appointing him vicar, a more secure position than rector's assistant, and pursuing a laissez faire course in the relations between the two churches, he refused to reconsider, this time citing his health. The vestry, on the recommendation of the board of managers, then chose Edward Riggs to replace him.[50]

The vestry's refusal to accept the $60,000 for the chapel is especially surprising given the financial situation of Christ Church at the time. While the membership of Christ Church, as reported to the diocese, actually did not decline much during Foggo's rectorship, pew rents, which represented the church's main source of income, decreased from $2,974.44 in 1870 to $1,012.75 in 1890.[51] The church was kept afloat by the interest on the endowment fund. Unfortunately, even this revenue was decreasing due to lower interest rates.

To help ensure the future of the church the vestry decided once again to launch a major campaign to raise the endowment fund. Recognizing that their goal of $150,000 could only be reached by going beyond the parish, in 1891 the vestry established the Memorial Endowment Association of Christ Church. Showing how important they thought Christ Church was, they included among the ex officio members the presiding bishop of the Episcopal Church, the bishops of the thirteen original states, and the governor of Pennsylvania. Active members would include anyone giving money and willing to help raise more. While it is unclear whether this organization was ever active, it did foreshadow similar efforts in the twentieth century.[52]

At the same time that Christ Church struggled financially, it was also hurt by the death of many members who had been the backbone of the church. In 1871 Edward L. Clark, who had been a warden since 1858, died. The vestry so appreciated the work he had done that they established a scholarship at St. Paul's Episcopal School in Concord, New Hampshire in his

FIGURE 34
Market Street at Delaware Avenue. Photo by W.N. Jennings. The area one block away from Christ Church was the center of a variety of activities, as well as the eastern terminus of the Market Street trolley line. Courtesy of the Free Library of Philadelphia.

honor; his son was the first recipient of these funds, which are still distributed by Christ Church. The 1880s saw a far greater loss of leadership. In the two-year period, 1886–87, four vestrymen died. And these leaders were no longer being replaced by younger men. The women reported a similar loss of membership. In 1871 the members of the Ladies' Missionary Association lamented the death of "several of the very ones who in our eyes could least be spared," including their president, Mrs. Mary King. As they saw "one by one the older members . . . dropping from the list," they were equally mindful that their losses were "not at once supplied by others pouring in."[53]

While the vestry saw the only hope for the church in increasing the endowment, Edward Foggo felt that another rector might be better able to bring new people into the failing parish. (See Figure 34 for the area around the church.) In December 1890 he announced his resignation effective in October 1891, "with the hope that one may be found who is able to create greater interest in this difficult and important work." The vestry accepted his resignation with regret, recalling his "devoted and urgent labors for good as the young Rector of this Parish, full of zeal and courage in the work when it was new, and of the unrepining and undaunted constancy with which, since then, you have remained at your post." The vestry unanimously elected him rector emeritus, a position he held until 1894.[54]

* * *

In September 1891 the vestry chose Charles Ellis Stevens to succeed Foggo as rector of Christ Church (see Figure 35). After having studied at Yale and the University of Pennsylvania, Stevens received his degree from Berkeley Divinity School in New Haven, Connecticut. He then held a variety of positions on Long Island. He served as rector of the Church of the Ascension in Brooklyn and as examining chaplain to the bishop of Long Island and chairman of the boards of the diocesan church extension. He was then appointed archdeacon of Brooklyn, a position responsible for developing new parishes. This experience in promoting church growth should definitely have been an asset in his new job.[55]

Stevens had a much more varied background than any other minister who served Christ Church. In addition to his divinity degree, he held a Ph.D. in history and political science from the University (now College) of Wooster in Ohio. He continued to pursue his interest in these subjects after being ordained, publishing in various journals and serving as a guest lecturer on constitutional history and law at several universities, including the University of Pennsylvania. In 1888 he received honorary degrees of Doctor of Laws from Wooster and Doctor of Civil Law from King's College, Canada.[56]

His most important academic contribution actually came after his election to the rectorship of Christ Church. In 1894 he published *Sources of the Constitution of the United States Considered in Relation to Colonial and English History*, a major study of the background of the Constitution. Building on the work of others of his time who were emphasizing the historic continuities of the Constitution, he traced the development of American government from "its earliest distinguishable forms" through English and American colonial history. The work was very favorably received in both the United States and Europe.[57] As a result, he was elected a Fellow of the

FIGURE 35
The Reverend Charles Ellis Stevens (rector, 1891–1904). Christ Church Archives.

Society of Antiquaries in Edinburgh, and of the Royal Geographical Society of London, and an officer of the Academy of France. He was knighted by Maria Cristina, queen regent of Spain, and granted the decoration of the Royal Order of Isabella the Catholic in recognition of services to political science. King Charles II of Portugal similarly created him knight commander of the Royal Military Order of Christ.[58] This serious interest in the early history of the United States should also have suited him well to be rector of Christ Church.

In addition to his other interesting characteristics, Stevens was also a poet. In 1897 he published *The Romance of Arenfels and Other Tales of the Rhine*. In the title poem, a knight is separated from his true love, Hilda, when he joins the crusades. On his return, after languishing in Moslem jails, he finds Hilda's family homestead destroyed and her family and friends nowhere to be found. This romantic ballad has an ending befitting its author; the knight is reunited with Hilda when he goes into a church to pray.[59]

One aspect of his background, however, did not seem to suit Stevens for Christ Church—his high church, Anglo-Catholic sentiments. In addition to his studies at Berkeley, he also received a bachelor of divinity degree from Nashotah Seminary in Wisconsin, the bastion of high church sentiments, and served as an associate editor of *The Living Church*, one of the publications of the high church group. Why Christ Church would choose a minister with such leanings so soon after the controversy surrounding Hodge and Percival is unclear. The members may have had assurances from Stevens that he would not change the worship service, for there were no complaints about his liturgical practices during his thirteen years at Christ Church.[60]

The first ten years of Stevens's rectorship were quite successful. In 1892 he reported that 167 new communicants had been added, bringing the total to 515. The following years saw steady, but unspectacular growth, so that in 1903 he could report 602 communicants, almost 300 more than Foggo reported in 1889. In 1903 he presented forty-five people for confirmation, more than in any year since 1840.[61]

In 1892 the *Handbook of Christ Church* indicated that the congregation was not only large but active. In addition to the Sunday school, the Dorcas Society, Mothers' Meeting, Cooking and Industrial Class and Ladies' Missionary Association, which had existed for some time, the women were now involved in the Altar Guild, the Almoners' Guild, St. Agnes' Guild, the Coal Club, St. Paul's Society, and the Girls' Friendly Society. Of special interest was the Christ Church Hospital Society, a woman's auxiliary to the hospital that listed fifteen "visitors." The men of the church could join the Brotherhood of St. Andrew, the St. Philip's Society, and the St. Luke's Society for Medical Charity. Unfortunately we have no records indicating what these organizations did, but it is clear that Christ Church parishioners did more than just attend church on Sunday.[62]

Members of Christ Church continued to be active in the diocese as well.

Men from Christ Church served on the Diocesan Committee on Parochial History and as trustees of the Christmas Fund, the Episcopal Residence, and the Home of the Merciful Savior for Crippled Children. They represented Christ Church on the boards of the Bishop White Prayerbook Society, the Corporation for the Relief of Widows and Children of Clergymen, and the Episcopal Academy. Three members also served as managers of the Churchmen's Missionary Association for the Seamen of the Port of Philadelphia. The women were also active outside the parish; Christ Church women continued to serve as managers of the Bishop White Parish Library Association, the Female Prayerbook Society, the Female Episcopal Benevolent Society of Philadelphia, and the Episcopal Female Tract Society.[63]

While the membership of Christ Church was increasing, the congregation continued to have financial trouble. Despite an increase in giving, for many years the church balanced the budget only by special appeals at Easter.[64] Attempts to increase the endowment fund had raised only $10,000 rather than the original goal of $150,000.

In 1894 Stevens and the vestry endorsed a new and much more successful way to raise money: they established a plan to encourage people to give "memorial windows." In keeping with the historic nature of the church, the vestry approved a plan for the nine large windows on the main floor to represent events in the history of the church from the life of Christ through the founding of the Anglican and then the Protestant Episcopal churches. Unlike most memorial gifts, those giving windows would have to contribute approximately $5,000 beyond the cost of the window; this money would be put in a fund for the upkeep of the building. By the end of Stevens's rectorship four windows had been installed and the window endowment fund stood at almost $24,000.[65] (See color plates.)

Far more significant than gifts for memorial windows was the bequest of Henry Elder, who died in 1902. At the death of his two children, two-thirds of his estate, which at the time of his death was valued at more than $300,000, would go to Christ Church. While this money was not received by the church until 1928, its promise gave the vestry much cause for optimism.[66]

Memorial windows also introduced a distinctly nineteenth-century look to the Georgian interior. The windows were in keeping with the large stone altar that had been given to the church in 1895 by the daughter of Dr. Buchanan, the last of the clergymen ordained by Bishop White to survive (see Figure 36). The colonial Gostelowe table was put inside the new stone altar.[67]

FIGURE 36
The Buchanan altar. Christ Church Archives.

The worship service also changed during Stevens's tenure. In 1892 the
General Convention approved the first major revisions in the Book of Common Prayer in one hundred years. Fittingly, while the convention was com-
pleting work on the new book in Baltimore, four bishops journeyed to Christ
Church on consecutive Sundays to deliver historical discourses on the Prayer
Book, "intended to go forth in published form, as, in some sort, a popular
introduction to the new Book." They were published, with an introduction
by Stevens.[68] While the changes were not great, they indicated the direction
the church was going, for most were restorations of things that had been

included in the more "catholic" Prayer Book of Edward VI and had been dropped "during periods of Protestant domination." The one significant change, the official decision that morning prayer and the Holy Communion could be separate services, had actually been made by the presiding bishop earlier. By 1892 Christ Church had instituted a separate weekly communion service, while keeping its monthly service which combined communion with morning prayer.[69]

Not only were the stained glass windows in keeping with the liturgical changes, the decision to have them represent historical events was also in keeping with the increasing emphasis on the early history of the church. Stevens seemed far more interested in promoting Christ Church as a historic monument than Foggo had been. In 1892, shortly after Stevens arrived, the Christ Church Historical Association was established. Open to anyone who was interested in the church, it aimed to preserve the historical objects and records and commemorate the historic events associated with the church. Among the more interesting projects of this group was a plaque placed in the church to honor Richard Welton, the nonjuring bishop who had caused such problems for the church during the colonial period. Although the issue of his nonjuring status obviously was of little consequence in the 1890s, his behavior hardly merited commendation. Presumably it was his title as "bishop" that was the "special reason for commemorating" him.[70]

Interest in the church's history reached its height in 1895 with the celebration of the two-hundredth anniversary of the parish. The primary service featured two processions, including the vestries of the three churches that made up the United Churches, the Standing Committee of the diocese, the trustees of diocesan institutions, the provost of the University of Pennsylvania, seventy clergymen, and three bishops. Ozi W. Whitaker, Bishop of Pennsylvania, gave an address on "Christ Church and the Diocese of Pennsylvania," while William Stevens Perry, retired Bishop of Pennsylvania and the Episcopal Church's historiographer, gave a speech on "Christ Church and the National Church." The Historical Association published the proceedings of all the services and distributed them to libraries and churches throughout the country.[71]

Stevens also urged community groups to take an interest in Christ Church. He encouraged them to hold services in the church and invited visiting dignitaries to worship in the church, attempting to make it a "favorite place for patriotic and popular occasions."[72] In so doing, Stevens hoped to expand the number of people actively concerned about the future of the church. This use of Christ Church by groups unassociated with the parish became a regular part of life at Christ Church in the twentieth century and did, as Stevens no doubt hoped, serve as an important source of fund-raising.

Stevens also took the lead in the effort to protect Christ Church from fire. The parish building built by Foggo greatly increased the danger to the church if one of the many factories—which were within a few feet of the parish building—were to catch fire. Within the first year of his rectorship Stevens suggested that a new parish building be erected, but since that seemed impossible, other measures had to be taken. In 1902 Stevens convinced the city to widen American Street from Church Street to Filbert, thus providing a buffer between the church and the adjacent buildings.[73]

* * *

If one looked at Stevens's record in 1903 one would conclude that, under the circumstances, his rectorship had been a success. As of April 1903 Christ Church could report 602 communicants, a Sunday school with 386 pupils, and 45 confirmations during the previous year. While income from offerings had dropped in the previous couple of years, the church still had a balanced budget and an endowment of more than $91,000, approximately $37,000 of which had been added under Stevens. The Elder estate held the promise of more than doubling that endowment.[74]

Yet within a year the vestry had forced Stevens to resign his rectorship and the church faced a crisis situation. The details of the controversy involving Stevens's dismissal are unclear. While a newspaper article referred to attendance falling off and the weakened financial condition of the church, it is doubtful that these were the cause of the problems. Despite much more serious problems in 1891, the vestry had urged Foggo *not* to resign.[75]

Rather, the controversy seems to have been a personal dispute between the rector and the vestry. Stevens was charged with playing an inappropriate role in the vestry election of April, 1901 when John DaCosta and C. Francis Wood, long-time members, were not reelected. Clearly trying to make amends, Stevens wrote to the vestry in June "in reference to his action at the time of the election of the Vestry," stating his "personal and unqualified desire so far as in me rests, and my suggestion (subject to the wishes of the vestry) that Dr. John DaCosta and Mr. C. Francis Wood" be reelected to the vestry. This letter did nothing to help the situation. In December of that year Stevens once again wrote to the vestry, upset because the "customary peacefulness of this parish . . . has been threatened or disturbed by certain results of the last election" and that he had "been held to be associated . . . in a manner liable to give cause for question." In the interest of peace he refused to defend himself, instead expressing his "apology as between gentlemen, to any and all persons who may under whatever conditions have felt aggrieved by me personally or officially." He asked that his apology be "received and reciprocated in the same heartily generous spirit in which it is offered."[76]

DaCosta and Wood were reelected to the vestry in 1902, but relations between the rector and the vestry worsened. In May of that year two vestrymen conveyed to Stevens the desire of the vestry that "at a fitting and convenient time hereafter it would seem to be best that the existing relations between the Rector and the Parish should be terminated." When Stevens did nothing about this suggestion, the vestry became more direct; in November 1903 the group informed Stevens that they intended to ask for his resignation at the next meeting. Stevens still refused to resign to save face, so the vestry resolved that "Whereas in the judgment of this Vestry the relations existing between the Rector and the Parish have been seriously impaired," Stevens be requested to resign his rectorship effective April 30, 1904.[77]

Stevens, however, did not give up the fight. Arguing that "sufficient reason" had not been given and that "the overwhelming majority of the parishioners" wanted him to stay, he still refused to resign. Instead he asked that any difficulties be resolved by the proper ecclesiastical authorities. The vestry, for its part, did consult these authorities, but it was not to "resolve difficulties." Uncertain whether the charter of Christ Church gave the vestry the right to dismiss a rector, in February 1904 they wrote to the bishop, formally asking him to dissolve the pastoral connection. As a result, once again Christ Church's relationship with a minister was on the front page of the papers.[78]

At the same time that the vestry wrote to Bishop Whitaker, it wrote a letter to all pewholders requesting that the vestry election on April 4 be a referendum on Stevens's dismissal. At that time, forty of the fifty-one pew holders voted, unanimously reelecting the same vestry. Stevens, seeing the inevitable, on April 11 finally resigned his position effective May 4, before the bishop had taken any action.

While the pewholders backed the vestry, other members of the congregation supported Stevens. Arguing that the vestrymen "imperfectly represented" the congregation and that they had, in fact, "long attended services but slightly," Stevens and his supporters argued that most parishioners who actually attended church wanted him to stay. To show their support, right before the crucial vestry election in 1904 his supporters published a simple document, entitled "A Record," outlining the accomplishments of Stevens. Discussing the "depleted condition in which the Rector found this parish" and the "grave dangers" that overhung it, they argued "it is not too much to say that none in the honored succession of our Rectors has ever done a more beneficent work for Christ Church." Charting the statistics for 1903 versus 1892, which showed impressive gains in membership, they outlined the many accomplishments of Stevens's years which we have already discussed.[79]

The charges that the vestry no longer represented the congregation may well have been true. Under the outdated charter, only men who rented pews for three years could vote for or be elected to the vestry; as a result that body had no representatives from among the neighborhood people that Stevens recruited. As we will see in the next chapter, even Louis Washburn, who had the full support of the vestry, complained about their lack of involvement in the religious life of the church. Similarly, the vote of the pewholders was, no doubt, equally unrepresentative of the congregation as a whole. However, in reality, the support of even a majority of the congregation mattered little if the influential members were against the rector. In May 1904 Stevens severed his relationship with Christ Church, dying two years later. It is indeed sad that such a distinguished man should have ended his career so ignominiously.

*   *   *

It was also sad for Christ Church, which entered the twentieth century at one of the lowest points in its history. Given the precarious situation of the church and the unseemly treatment of Stevens, it is not surprising that it took the church three years to find a new rector. But this gloomy situation should not hide the most important accomplishment of the late nineteenth century: Christ Church had survived as a functioning parish. Between 1870 and 1905 four Episcopal churches in center city had moved and four had merged or closed.[80] All these churches except St. Paul's had been in more favorable locations than Christ Church. Aided by the increasing emphasis on history and on historical sites, Christ Church had been able to use its historic position as a means to attract money at the same time that it continued to serve its local neighborhood. This is a formula that would be followed in the twentieth century with much more success.

NOTES

1. For a brief summary of this controversy, see Sydney E. Ahlstrom, *A Religious History of the American People* (New Haven, Conn.: Yale University Press, 1972), 763–84.

2. Henry F. May, *Protestant Churches and Industrial America* (New York, 1949), 163–169; quotes are from pp. 163, 164.

3. May, *Protestant Churches and Industrial America*, 170–203; the quotes are from pp. 181, 183. For a detailed discussion of the Episcopal Church's response to labor see Spencer Miller and Joseph Fletcher, *The Church and Industry* (New York: Longmans Green, 1930).

4. Chorley, *Men and Movements in the American Episcopal Church*, 315–39.

5. *Evening Bulletin*, March 9, 1898, p. 3.

6. Vestry Minutes, Nov. 4, 12, 25, 1868.

7. Vestry Minutes, Nov. 10, 1869, Oct. 6, 1891; *Journal of the Diocese of Pennsylvania*, 1898, 70. Minutes, Oct. 6, 1891.

8. Edward Foggo, *A Sketch of the Work in the Parish of Christ Church By the Reverend Edward Foggo* (Philadelphia, 1897), 7.

9. *Journal of the Diocese of Pennsylvania*, 1881; Pew Rent Books, Christ Church Archives. The increase in the number of women renting pews may merely mean that it was more acceptable for women to rent pews themselves. Pew Rent List for 1880, 1881; *City Directory of Philadelphia* 1880 (Philadelphia, 1880).

10. Oberholtzer, *Philadelphia: A History of the City and Its People*, 3: 181–82, 429–30; *Encyclopedia of Pennsylvania Biography*, ed. Frederic Godcharles (New York: Lewis Historical Publishing Company, 1914), 8: 30–34.

11. The information about the Christ Church area is from the Philadelphia Social History Project. The overall Philadelphia information is found in Theodore Hershberg et al., "A Tale of Three Cities: Blacks, Immigrants and Opportunity in Philadelphia, 1850, 1880, 1930, 1970," in *Philadelphia: Work, Space, Family and Group Experience in the Nineteenth Century*, ed. Theodore Hershberg (New York: Oxford University Press, 1981), 468. Citywide the Irish accounted for 27 percent of the population and the Germans 16 percent in 1880.

12. Christ Church had a 1.09 student/communicant ratio, almost double what it had had under Dorr. St. Peter's, in contrast, was 0.52 and St. Luke's, which had had the highest in 1846, was now 0.73. *Journal of the Diocese of Pennsylvania* 1879.

13. Foggo, *A Sketch of the Work in the Parish*, 9. Many other Episcopal Churches also had small "parish schools," including St. Peter's and St. James. See *Journal of the Diocese of Pennsylvania*, 1870–1890; Vestry Minutes, Dec 1, 1869; *Abstract Concerning Christ Church for the Diocesan Year ending April 30, 1879.*

14. Foggo, *Sketch of the Work in the Parish*, 7–10, 20. The charity funds that financed this work totaled $20,864 in 1886, generating $1,200 in annual income; see *Abstract Concerning Christ Church for the Diocesan Year ending April 30, 1886.*

15. Foggo, *Sketch of the Work in the Parish*, 10; Vestry Minutes, April 18, 1877.

16. Miss Hollingsworth provided money for the chapel, while Wilhelmina and Washington Smith endowed the bed and the fund for the chaplain. See Foggo, *Sketch of the Work in the Parish*, 19–21; Roberts, "Christ Church Hospital," 95; Vestry Minutes, April 16, 1884.

17. Foggo, *Sketch of the Work in the Parish*, 7, 17; Ladies Missionary Association of Christ Church, *Annual Reports*, 1871, 1874. Calvary was actually run by a board of managers, six from Christ Church and six from Calvary, but the women kept it financially afloat. See Vestry

Minutes, Dec. 9, 1870, April 21, 1871, June 6, 1877, Dec. 7, 1881, March 5, 1884. For a brief history of the church, see J. Wesley Twelves, *History of the Diocese of Pennsylvania of the Protestant Episcopal Church* (Philadelphia: Diocese of Pennsylvania, 1969), 159–60.

18. Vestry Minutes, Dec. 1, 1869, June 1, Dec. 7, 1870, April 11, 1871; Foggo, *Sketch of the Work in the Parish*, 12–13. See George M. DeMille, *The Catholic Movement in the American Episcopal Church* (Philadelphia: Church Historical Society, 1941), for a good discussion of how what had been considered scandalously high church came to be accepted by the end of the nineteenth century.

19. Foggo, *Sketch of the Work in the Parish*, 12–13; Vestry Minutes, Dec. 2, 1871.

20. See Vestry Minutes, Feb 1, 1882; *Christ Church: Repairs and Restoration, February 1, 1882*; Foggo, *Sermon on the Restoration of the Interior of Christ Church, Philadelphia, November 11, 1882* (Philadelphia, 1882).

21. Vestry Minutes, Nov. 30, Dec. 7, 9, and 23, 1870.

22. Vestry Minutes, Jan. 9 and 18, 1867.

23. Vestry Minutes, Feb. 4, 1874.

24. *An Address to all who have been at any time Connected with Christ Church or who may be interested in it* (Philadelphia, 1874); Christ Church Archives.

25. Unidentified newspaper articles, Christ Church Archives.

26. William Bacon Stevens, *Free and Open Churches: A Sermon Preached at the Opening of the Chapel of Christ Church* (Philadelphia, 1877), 5.

27. Stevens, *Free and Open Churches*, 6–7, 9–10.

28. A summary of the Parish Register is found in the Archives of Christ Church. These names were compared to the pewholders from 1861 to 1875.

29. Vestry Minutes, Feb. 9, 1876.

30. Yearbook of Christ Church Chapel, 1877–78; E. A. Foggo, *History of Recent Events in Christ Church Parish* (Philadelphia, 1880), 6.

31. Affidavit of G. Wolsey Hodge, *Christ Church et al. vs. The Church of the Holy Communion et al.*, Court of Common Pleas No. 1 for the City and County of Philadelphia, March term, 1880, No. 163, Affidavits of Defendants.

32. The Church of the Evangelist was located on Catherine Street, between Seventh and Eight Streets. Henry Percival became rector in 1880. In 1886 the old building was torn down and a church of Italian Basilican style was built; it now serves as the Fleisher Art Museum.

33. Charley, *Men and Movements in the Episcopal Church*, 336, 353, 356.

34. Foggo, *History of Recent Events*, 6–7; Chorley, *Men and Movements in the American Episcopal Church*, 336, 353, 356; DeMille, *The Catholic Movement*, 163–170.

35. Foggo, *History of Recent Events*, 8, 9, 13.

36. Hodge to Foggo, Jan. 8, 1880, in Foggo, *History*, 11; G. Wolsey Hodge to the Vestry, Jan. 5, 1880; *Christ Church Statement* (Philadelphia, n.d.), n 3.

37. Vestry Minutes, January 8, 1880, Feb. 4, 1880; Board of Managers of Chapel to Vestry in Vestry Minutes, Jan. 19, 1880.

38. "Christ Church Chapel," *Philadelphia Inquirer*, Feb. 9, 1880, p. 1.

39. Vestry Minutes, Mar 1, 1880. The vote was 53 to 16 against. For coverage of the election in the papers see "The Polls Open," "2nd Day of Balloting," *Philadelphia Inquirer*; "Church and Chapel: The Vote on the Question of Separation Began at Christ Church," *Philadelphia Times*, Feb. 27, 1880, p. 2; "Church and Chapel: Vote Against the Separation of Christ Church Chapel from the Parish," *Philadelphia Inquirer*; "Rector and Curate, Christ Church and the

Chapel Again," *Philadelphia Times*, Feb. 24, 1880. Copies of these articles, most without dates, appear in a scrapbook in the Christ Church Archives.

40. Stevens's compromise, presented on March 3, would have made the chapel a semi-independent body; see William Stevens to Dr. Anthony Stocker, March 10, 1880, Papers of Bishop William Stevens, Archives of the Diocese of Pennsylvania (herein Stevens's Papers). While the Board of Managers cooperated with the Bishop, Foggo did not even agree to call a vestry meeting until eight days after Hodge's resignation took effect. The entire mediation process can be followed in letters found in the Stevens's Papers. Particularly revealing are a series of unpleasant letters between Stevens and Foggo while Stevens was in Atlantic City recovering from an illness. Stevens was to meet with the Vestry on March 9, but there is no record of that meeting. See William Stevens to Edward Foggo, March 2, 4, 7, 1880; Edward Foggo to William Stevens, March 3, March 4, 6, 1880, Stevens's Papers.

41. "Holding the Chapel," *Philadelphia Times*, March 11, 1880; "Barred Out," *Philadelphia Press*, March 12, 1880, p. 2; "A Chapel as a Fortress," *Philadelphia Record*, March 12, 1880; "Holding the Fort," newspaper clipping, n.d., n.p., Christ Church Archives.

42. Vestry Minutes, March 17, 1880; William Stevens to Committee of Christ Church Chapel, March 22, 1880, Stevens Papers; Vestry Minutes, April 6, 1880; for a statement of the Chapel's position see Petition of Christ Church Chapel to Bishop, Easter Tuesday, 1880, Stevens's Papers.

43. Affidavits of Defendants, *Christ Church et al. vs. Church of the Holy Communion et al.*; G. Woolsey Hodge, Admiral Fairfax, and J. Edward Carpenter, *A Reply to Certain Personal Reflections, Contained in the Speech of One of the Counsel for the Complainants, in the Case of Christ Church vs. The Church of the Holy Communion* (Philadelphia, 1880), 10.

44. *Christ Church et al. vs. Church of the Holy Communion et al.*, Arguments of William W. Wiltbank, Esq. and Henry Rawle, Esq.; Hodge, Fairfax and Carpenter, *A Reply*, 15–16.

45. Hodge, Fairfax and Carpenter, *A Reply*, 94–110.

46. Foggo, *A Sketch of the Work in the Parish*, 18–19.

47. Vestry Minutes, Dec. 5, 1883; *Church News* article, n.d., "Christ Church Chapel," *Philadelphia Register*, n.d., unidentified newspaper article, May 4, 1885, Christ Church Archives; Vestry Minutes, April 11, 1882; *Abstract Concerning Christ Church, April 30, 1886*; Foggo, *Sketch of the Work of the Parish*, 19; Vestry Minutes, March 28, 1883, March 30, 1886; "Chapel Consecrated," newspaper clipping, n.d., Christ Church Archives.

48. Vestry Minutes, May 6, 1881.

49. See Vestry Minutes, June 6 and Oct. 11, 1894. The vestry set up a committee to study the issue, but discharged it without action on May 3, 1895. Thayer's quote was from June 6.

50. Vestry Minutes, Feb. 25, March 8 and 20, and May 3, 1895.

51. In 1888 the number of communicants stood at 332, down only 44 from 1870; Foggo, *A Sketch of the Work in the Parish*, 6–7. The communicant figures are in the *Journal of the Diocese of Philadelphia*, 1870, 1880. In 1870 138 people rented pews; this decreased to 58 in 1890; see the Pew Rent Books, Christ Church Archives.

52. See Report of the Endowment Committee, March 7, 1890, Vestry Records; Accounting Warden's Journals, 1870–1890; Vestry Minutes, April 30, May 5, Oct. 1, 1890, March 31, April 23, May 20, Oct. 9, Nov 20, Dec. 2, 1891.

53. Vestry Minutes, Mar 30, 1875, June 8, 1871; for the vestry's tribute to Clark see Minutes, Dec. 20, 1871. Ladies Missionary Association of Christ Church, Philadelphia, *Forty-Second Annual Report* (Philadelphia, 1871).

54. Vestry Minutes, Dec. 3, 17, 1890.

55. C. Ellis Stevens, *Stevens Genealogy* (New York: privately published, 1904), 86–87.

56. Stevens, *Stevens Genealogy*.

57. The influential historian James Harvey Robinson asserted that Stevens was "the first to represent the subject in a complete and satisfactory form" and that it was "a really important addition to our historical literature." See James Harvey Robinson, review of *Sources of the Constitution of the United States* by Charles Ellis Stevens, *Annals of the American Academy of Political and Social Science* 4 (1893–94): 999.

58. Stevens, *Stevens Genealogy*, 86–87.

59. C. Ellis Stevens, *The Romance of Arenfels and Other Tales of the Rhine* (New York: G.P. Putnam's Sons, 1897). The book contains several other romantic poems as well as a section of "Musings," short verses on a variety of subjects.

60. Rev. Rex Perry, to author, July 27, 1988; Obituary of C. Ellis Stevens, unknown newspaper, Christ Church Archives.

61. *Abstracts Concerning Christ Church* (1892, 1893, 1894, 1895); *A Record*, 1903, Christ Church Archives.

62. *Handbook of Christ Church, Philadelphia*, 1892 (Philadelphia, 1892), 51–54.

63. *Handbook*, 29–34.

64. *Abstract Concerning Christ Church* (1889, 1892); see *Christ Church Easter Offerings, March 15, 1895*.

65. See Vestry Minutes, June 6, Oct. 11 and Dec. 5, 1894 for a discussion of the plan. The first window represented Christ commissioning his apostles. The second represented the Age of Martyrdom, showing the girl Agnes on trial. The third window showed the vision of Constantine, who stopped martyrdom in his kingdom, and the knights of the crusades. The fourth window represented the Council of Nicaea *and* the first ecclesiastical council in America, showing those who founded the Protestant Episcopal Church. See *Handbook of Christ Church*, 1912, 108–12; *Abstract Concerning Christ Church* (1900).

66. Vestry Minutes, April 1, 1902. Unfortunately, nothing is known about Elder's connection with Christ Church.

67. Vestry Minutes, Dec. 23, 1895, Feb. 12, 1897.

68. C. Ellis Stevens, ed., *The Genesis of the American Prayerbook* (New York, 1893). The quote is from p. ix.

69. DeMille, *The Catholic Movement*, 196; *Our Common Prayer* (Philadelphia: Episcopal Diocese of Pennsylvania, 1984), 18; *Handbook of Christ Church, Philadelphia*, 1892, 45–47.

70. Christ Church Historical Association, Minutes, Christ Church Archives; Vestry Minutes, Jan. 18, April 12, 1898.

71. *Memorial of the 200th Anniversary of the Founding of Christ Church, Philadelphia, 1695–1895* (Philadelphia, 1895); Christ Church Historical Association, Record Book.

72. "Reverend Dr. Stevens Defies Vestry," *Philadelphia Press*, Feb. 19, 1904.

73. Vestry Minutes, Feb. 13, 1901, April 1, 1902.

74. *Abstract Concerning Christ Church* (1903).

75. "Reverend Dr. Stevens Defies Vestry."

76. Vestry Minutes, April 9, June 5, Dec. 4, 1901.

77. Vestry Minutes, Dec. 16, 1903; Vestry to Bishop Whitaker, Feb. 23, 1904, in Vestry Minutes, Feb 23, 1904.

78. Vestry Minutes, Feb. 22 and 23, 1904; "Rev. Dr. Stevens Asked to Resign," *Philadelphia*

Bulletin, Feb. 18, 1904, p. 1; "Rev. Dr. Stevens Defies Vestry"; "Dr. Stevens' Case to Go to Bishop," *Philadelphia Press*, Feb. 21, 1904, 1; "Bishop Asked to Remove Stevens," *Philadelphia Press*, Feb. 25, 1904, p. 1; "Bishop Whitaker Has Stevens Case," *Philadelphia Press*, Feb. 26, 1904; "Says Vestry Can Dismiss Rector," *Philadelphia Bulletin*, Feb. 20, 1904, p.4.

79. "Rev. Dr. Stevens Defies Vestry," *Philadelphia Press*, February 19, 1904; *A Record*, 1904, Christ Church Archives.

80. St. James, the Church of the Ascension, the Church of the Atonement, and Calvary Monumental moved; the Church of the Mediator and St. Paul's closed; the Church of the Epiphany and St. Luke's merged.

CHAPTER FOURTEEN

REVIVING AN
URBAN CHURCH:
THE RECTORSHIP OF
LOUIS WASHBURN

With the forced resignation of C. Ellis Stevens, Christ Church had reached the low point of its 208-year history. The departure of so distinguished a man as Stevens, combined with the decreasing number of people renting pews and the deteriorating nature of the neighborhood made the future of the church look bleak. Yet within ten years the church had become once again a thriving, vibrant parish. Taking on the challenges of the surrounding neighborhood rather than bemoaning their existence, the new rector, Louis Washburn, seemed to pull the church into the twentieth century almost singlehandedly. In the process he changed the image of Christ Church within the neighborhood and in the city as a whole.

Prior to Washburn's arrival, however, Christ Church would go through several difficult years. In fact, for a while many must have questioned whether they would ever find a new minister. Between 1904 and 1906 the vestrymen seriously considered at least three candidates, offering the position to two men who declined the job.[1] During this futile search the assistant minister, R. Hebre Barnes, carried on as best he could.

Christ Church's difficulty in attracting a rector no doubt stemmed from the negative image it had in the community. As a newspaper article put it, for many years it had been "regarded by the general public simply as an historic shrine to be visited by the curious or patriotic pilgrim to our city."[2] Despite the efforts of Stevens and Foggo to minister to the surrounding neighborhood, they had not been successful in projecting a positive public image of the church or in attracting members who could support the church financially. Moreover, any minister would obviously think twice about accepting a position from which his predecessor had been forced to resign for no obvious or compelling reason.

Despite these problems, in June 1907 the Reverend Louis Cope Washburn of Rochester, New York accepted the position of rector of Christ Church, thus ushering in a remarkable era in the history of the church (see Figure 37). Dr. Washburn was born in Pottsville, Pennsylvania, one of fifteen children of an itinerant minister who preached to the many coal miners in the area. Raised in this poverty stricken region, Washburn had a natural affinity for those less fortunate than himself. After receiving his bachelor's degree from St. Stephen's College in New York and his master's from Trinity College, Connecticut, Washburn attended Berkeley Divinity School. He later received honorary doctorates from Hobart College and the University of Pennsylvania. On ordination in 1885 he became rector of St. Peter's Church in Hazleton, Pennsylvania, not far from where he grew up. He then moved to St. Paul's Church in Rochester, New York. In 1895, he was selected as the archdeacon of Rochester, the same church development position Stevens had held in Brooklyn. While serving in that position, Washburn held a summer rectorship in Maine, where he met people from Christ Church who vacationed there.[3]

In the thirty years Dr. Washburn remained at Christ Church, he became an institution, not just within the congregation, but in the city as well. When he retired, tributes poured in from all over the city and from people in all walks of life. Not since Bishop White had a rector of Christ Church been so widely known and widely loved. While he is remembered today for the buildings he built and the programs he started, to the people who knew Washburn it was the very personal, one to one relationships he established that made him such a beloved figure. Again and again the tributes on his retirement described him as the "one who has always been ready to do the deed for the one in need." "Did someone need medical care, or hospitalization, or clothing, or food; sympathy, advice, or a good 'straight from the

FIGURE 37
The Reverend Louis Cope Washburn (rector, 1907–1937). Christ Church Archives.

shoulder' talking to, Dr. Washburn gladly and willingly stopped whatever he might be doing and gave his time and best attention."[4] Such sentiments were expressed by the poor residents of the neighborhood as well as the wealthy vestrymen and community leaders.

Washburn also had a crusading, demanding side to his personality; while he gave much, he also asked much of his congregation. A fine speaker who possessed a "vibrant, clear voice" and was "impressive" in the formal setting of an Episcopalian service, Washburn used his sermons and his written messages to challenge his congregation.[5] An advocate of the social gospel movement, which was at its peak at the time Washburn arrived at Christ Church, Washburn insisted that his congregation put their faith into action. He regularly took the side of the oppressed and supported the rights of labor, even when speaking before middle class, establishment organizations. In a service for the Sons of the American Revolution he spoke of those who were "dangerously deaf . . . to the current demand for an equitable sharing of industrial prosperity," and in a service marking the Fourth of July he praised the spirit that was "drafting a new Declaration of Independence against all oppression and corruption . . . and singing battle hymns of deliverance from economic and social slaveries."[6]

While the social gospel movement encountered serious resistance in the 1920s and progressive movements in general fell on hard times, Washburn did not change his approach. He denounced the "money-mad generation" who were "living like spendthrifts on the accumulated spiritual inheritance from the past." He reminded his parishioners that "friendship, peace, self-control, love, joy and faith" were not available at the "bargain counters" and he condemned those who were contented with what they had accomplished: "the real Christian should have the motto "push on" and never be self-satisfied."[7] With this as his motto it is not surprising that he accomplished much during his rectorship.

* * *

Washburn faced major challenges when he arrived at Christ Church. While Stevens had increased the number of communicants to 600 by his outreach into the neighborhood, the number of pew renters, who still represented the chief source of revenue and leadership for the church, continued to decline. As a result, the church had particular trouble recruiting men to serve on the vestry. In fact, since there were never more than eight vestrymen at a meeting, before the vestry chose a new rector it had to change the bylaws to require only eight votes, rather than ten out of twelve.[8]

Furthermore, the geographic position of the church continued to deteriorate as commercial and industrial buildings replaced housing within the parish. While only 3,522 people lived within the parish boundaries (Delaware Avenue west to Seventh Street and from Vine Street south to Walnut) in

1912, nearly 60,000 people worked in the area. The largest number worked in offices and in the 1,761 stores that lined the streets, but much manufacturing also occurred. "The largest number of Jewish clothing sweat-shops congested in one place in the city" were located on the upper stories of buildings along Market Street from Second to Seventh Street, and several thousand people worked in the shoe and leather industry. Several sugar refineries were located in the area immediately surrounding Christ Church.[9]

The small number of people who did still live in the parish were not likely to become pew renters of Christ Church. In 1912, according to a parish survey undertaken by the church, only 14 percent or 502 people were known to be Protestant while 36 percent were identified as Catholic and 29 percent were "Hebrew." These people, 40 percent of whom were foreign born, largely Russian, lived in tenements, often in substandard condition. The survey found 124 privy wells within the parish limits and commented that, while 9,000 had been removed from within the city in recent years, only three had been removed in this area. Large numbers of idle men could be seen because of the "great number of cheap lodging houses and missions" to the west of the parish. The parish contained sixty-five saloons, and the "largest and vilest cabaret in the city" was in the immediate vicinity of the church. Moreover, "excursion steamer speak-easies" unloaded hundreds of "intoxicated persons every Sunday night" during the summer within two blocks of the church.[10] Not only did this neighborhood seem unlikely to yield pew renters for Christ Church, but it was hardly a welcome environment for middle and upper class Episcopalians coming from the suburbs (see Figure 38).

Washburn had a plan for dealing with these problems even before he accepted the position at Christ Church. On being offered the job he wrote the vestry outlining his conditions for acceptance. He defined the "present and prospective problem of the Parish" as "both the preservation of the historic shrine and also the making it an increasing influence for Christ amongst more of the people of the neighborhood." In order to achieve these goals he insisted that a major effort be made immediately to build a substantial parish house to replace the dangerous, outmoded building attached to the church. Second, he called on the vestry to abolish the pew system and establish a "free church." While the vestrymen enthusiastically endorsed the parish house, they had more trouble with abolishing pew rents, since the charter allowed only those who rented pews to vote for the vestry. The vestry eventually passed a resolution agreeing to support "all measures consistent with the Charter that may encourage general attendance upon the services."[11]

FIGURE 38
226 South Second Street. This photograph of an area within five blocks of Christ Church illustrates the conditions faced by those Christ Church wished to serve. Urban Archives, Temple University.

The two goals expressed in his letter to the vestry—a desire to preserve the physical building and to glory in its history *and* an equally strong desire to make the church an influence for good in the present—would guide Washburn's actions throughout his rectorship. No rector before or since had more interest in the long history of Christ Church. But neither has any rector been any more concerned with making the congregation live in the present and accept social responsibility for the people living around the church. One further goal of Washburn's should be mentioned: he was always extremely concerned with ministering to the spiritual needs of those who were already members of Christ Church, a goal that included urging them to put their faith into action.

*   *   *

From the time of Benjamin Dorr, the leadership of Christ Church had viewed the changing nature of the neighborhood as a *problem*, a discouraging situation that could eventually lead to the destruction of the church. In sharp contrast, Washburn saw the neighborhood as a wonderful *opportunity*, as a reason for the continued existence of Christ Church. Because his enthusiasm was contagious and his dominant and electric personality hard to resist, he was, indeed, able to turn Christ Church into the center of social services for the neighborhood and a leader in the citywide efforts to help the poor.

While Washburn was not the first rector of the church to reach out to the community, his philosophy differed from that of both Foggo and Stevens and, perhaps because of this different philosophy, he was more successful in gaining support for his programs. Essentially, Washburn was a proponent of the social gospel movement while Foggo's and Stevens's beliefs fell under the rubric of "conservative social Christianity." Foggo and Stevens concentrated on helping individual members of the congregation. Moreover, their attitude was condescending; Foggo was upset when the "worthy poor" did not come to his soup kitchen; Stevens stated that "relief is adequately given . . . to the church attendance poor." He added that the church "preferred that no one else help them without consultation," seeming to indicate a desire that the poor not receive too much aid.[12] In contrast, proponents of the social gospel movement, as we have discussed, attempted to reform certain aspects of society in addition to aiding individuals; for example, efforts were made to *improve* the basic living conditions of the poor, such as bad housing and poor sanitary conditions, rather than merely dealing with the poor health that resulted from them. It was into this category that Washburn would fall. As we will see, he not only established a "mission" or "settlement" house, but he also lobbied the city to improve the conditions in the parish.

While Washburn's programs were not original, they were impressive and especially well timed. By the 1920s many churches that had at one time been active in the social gospel movement had abandoned their mission activities. In contrast, the outreach efforts of Christ Church were first fully developed in the 1920s. As a result, the church was in an excellent position to move swiftly to help its neighbors when the Great Depression hit.

Washburn believed that building a proper parish house was the essential first step in serving the needs of the Christ Church neighborhood. Moreover, removing the Sunday school building that was attached to the church and moving the heating system to the new building would greatly decrease the chance of fire and restore the original beauty of the church. However, the struggle to complete the building was long and often discouraging. After borrowing $15,000, the church finally constructed the first two floors in 1911 and tore down the old parish house, but the building was not completed until 1922[13] (see Figure 39).

When it was finally finished the building, referred to as the Neighborhood House, was one of which all could be proud. The main floor contained offices and meeting rooms as well as a kitchen, while the second floor consisted primarily of the large "Sunday school room," complete with stage. The third floor had a gymnasium, and the basement included room for an industrial school and bowling alleys. The roof was finished in a way that allowed "rooftop sings" for many years. Not surprisingly, the Neighborhood House quickly became a hub of activities involving both church people and those living in the immediate neighborhood.

Washburn assembled a fine staff to assist him in his efforts to reach out to the neighborhood. In 1908 he created a new position, the parish visitor, which Miss Hannah Cowell held for twenty-one years. As the title suggests, Cowell visited the families in the neighborhood and met their needs as best she could. While we know little about her, her reports in the church newsletter show a caring and industrious woman, doing the best she could to help the less fortunate. In 1932 Cowell was replaced by Miss Gertrude Fritzinger.[14]

An assistant minister aided Washburn and the parish visitor, working particularly with the men and boys. For a number of years a succession of young men served in this position for a year or two until they could get their own parish. But in 1926 W. Roulston McKean began a fifteen-year associa-

FIGURE 39
Neighborhood House. Christ Church Archives.

tion as assistant minister. Deeply loyal to Christ Church, he stayed on even when he was not appointed to succeed Washburn. Described as a "wonderful pastoral priest" who got along with everyone, his "homey," quiet style contrasted well with Washburn's more crusading, dominating personality.[15]

Helen Washburn, the rector's daughter, also played a crucial role in reaching out to the neighborhood; she began working in the Sunday school almost immediately after she arrived with her father, and was named the church's first director of religious education in 1927. Helen Washburn devoted her life to the education of the church's children. "Endowed with a brilliant mind, a nobility of purpose, and a great cheerfulness of heart, she shared generously with all. The earnest desire to serve and help others seemed of the very essence of her soul, while her merriment and laughter warmed and uplifted the hearts of all around her." Never marrying, she held prominent positions at both the diocesan and national level. But it was at Christ Church that she made her greatest impact.[16]

A discussion of the staff would not be complete without mention of Harvey Mertz, the ever present sexton of Christ Church. Mertz had met Washburn while working on the railroad in Buffalo, New York. When Mertz visited Christ Church, Washburn persuaded him to give up a much better paying job to become sexton, a position he held for fifty years. Mertz had wanted to be a priest when he was young and on joining the staff at Christ Church he soon became far more than a sexton. A gruff but sociable man, Mertz had immediate rapport with the people of the neighborhood, providing another bridge between those of modest means and the wealthier pewholders of Christ Church. In the later years of Washburn's rectorship, Mertz began to function as almost another parish visitor.[17]

While many people contributed to the success of Washburn's vision, the centerpiece of the church's outreach was the Sunday school. The church school, under Helen Washburn's care, grew substantially at a time when most center city church schools were faltering. In 1932 she reported having 676 children in the school, almost a threefold increase from the time her father arrived. Most of these children were not Episcopalians. In 1931 Washburn reported that of the 146 families in the church school only 32 had a parent who was a communicant of Christ Church. Most of the remaining 114 belonged to Eastern Orthodox churches, primarily Russian Orthodox. While their parents went to a Russian service (probably St. Nicholas's Russian Orthodox Church at 813 North Seventh Street) most of the children, who were English speaking, came only to Christ Church.[18]

The relationship between Christ Church and the Russian Orthodox community was influenced by the efforts of Anglicans worldwide to strengthen ties with Eastern Orthodox churches. Helen Washburn expressed her goal in this regard well: "Our effort here is to help those who come to us, to understand somewhat the unique position of these two Communions, to appreciate the contribution of the Eastern Orthodox Church in history, and to offer them spiritual nurture in their new and changing environment." And while Helen Washburn helped the children, her father aided their parents; when St. Nicholas's church was unable to pay its mortgage, Washburn raised the necessary money.[19]

Helen Washburn's commitment to these immigrant children did not stop with the classroom. She regularly visited with the parents in their homes, consulted with the public school teachers, and, when necesary, accompanied the children to juvenile court. She and the other teachers also made certain that the physical needs of the children and their families were met. In fact, in 1932 she reported that the Sunday school was swelled by people who knew that Christ Church was good to "its own people who are in need." While she reminded the congregation that the Sunday school was mainly concerned with "things of the spirit, . . . with character growth, with developing the creative power of religion in human life," she could not ignore the human suffering she saw firsthand.[20]

Helen Washburn was not just a kindhearted Christian, she was also an innovative teacher. Rather than lecturing from a teacher's manual, she asked her teachers to give "opportunity for the child to learn by practice in a social group." Realizing that there was far more to religion than learning the catechism, she recalled that the success of the school was found "chiefly in the growth in individual lives and personal relationships—when two people who have quarreled learn forgiveness in the name of Christ, when the non-cooperative learn cooperation . . . when the problem child, through understanding friendship, is helped to purposeful living." In order to provide for such experiences, Miss Washburn inaugurated a student council in 1930. Made up of a representative from each grade above sixth, it was responsible for all activities of the Sunday school. For several years it published an extremely well done newsletter[21] (see Figure 40).

Miss Washburn's broader views of the goals of the Sunday school also led her to develop some innovative units for the children to study. In 1936 the entire school engaged in a study of African Americans that culminated in a program on Race Relations Sunday in which the boys and girls shared what they had learned. They concluded that they should "be friendly" with blacks, "not fight," "work for justice for the race," and "see that they get equal opportunity." Since the number of blacks in Philadelphia had increased from 63,000 in 1900 to almost 220,000 in 1930, and blacks were rapidly becoming the majority group in the area north of Vine Street from which Christ Church had traditionally drawn members, this unit was particularly important.[22]

The following year the Sunday school studied the issue of "peace," concluding, among other things, that "a person cannot be a real follower of Jesus Christ unless he believes in Peace and helps in every way he can to promote it," and that "it is necessary to elect peace-minded Congressmen and to write to them when neutrality legislation is before Congress." Then in 1938 the school focused on "Christian Unity," visiting churches of different denominations and studying about Christians throughout the world.[23] With this kind of activity it is not surprising that both the diocese and the Baptist Church wanted to send their teachers to Christ Church for training.

By 1912 the Neighborhood House had become the center for much more than the Sunday school. A lunch room provided inexpensive lunches for 150 women working in the area each day. Four basketball teams used the gym. The Neighborhood Meeting, a men's group, met every Sunday evening and a dancing class was held on Mondays. The Young Men's Club of Christ Church, a group for men of at least sixteen years of age, and its "junior group" for younger boys also met there. This group was first organized in 1907 by Edward Lowber Stokes, a vestryman who devoted himself for many years to the needs of the neighborhood boys. Starting with boys from the choir and the Sunday school, the group became a flourishing organization. In the 1920s the Reverend W. Roulston McKean greatly expanded the work among the boys.[24]

Christ Church also sponsored programs that enabled underprivileged children to escape the city during the summer. Each year around one hun-

FIGURE 40
High school Sunday school class. Eleventh grade girls in foreground sew layettes for Indian Mission. Christ Church Archives.

dred boys and girls attended camps, while approximately fifty mothers and children escaped the city for a week or two. In addition, dozens of people were escorted on one-day excursions to parks within the city. For those children who remained in the city, the Neighborhood House housed a daily vacation Bible school for six weeks each summer. Not officially a parochial activity, it did serve up to two hundred neighborhood children.[25]

These wide-ranging activities served as a way for Christ Church staff members to find out about the basic physical and spiritual needs of the people in the neighborhood, for at the same time Washburn expanded the activities sponsored by the parish, he also expanded the individual aid or "charity" distributed. Washburn took care of many of the individual needs himself. Visiting the neighborhood people in their homes regularly, he distributed food or clothing along with whatever spiritual solace he could provide. People still remember the pair of shoes or the basket of food provided for them personally by Washburn. He was, of course, aided by his able staff. In 1932 the parish visitor reported having made more than one thousand home visits in the previous year.[26]

The women of the church provided invaluable assistance as well. Each fall the Dorcas Society, the sewing society established during Dorr's rectorship, provided the neediest Sunday school children with a set of new clothing. The Girls' Friendly Society also sewed clothing which was distributed by the parish visitor, while the leader of the Mothers' Meeting kept in touch with needy people in the parish, giving aid where necessary, and encouraging the families to save by buying the stamps that they sold.[27]

With the onset of the Depression, the needs of the neighborhood obviously intensified. Philadelphia, whose manufacturing base had been weakening throughout the 1920s, ranked third in unemployment among nineteen major cities in 1930. By 1933, 11.5 percent of whites, 16.2 percent of blacks and 19.1 percent of foreign born Philadelphians, the group primarily served by Christ Church, were unemployed. Having abandoned any form of public relief in 1879, the city was forced to depend largely on private philanthropy to cope with this massive challenge. While the Lloyd Commission, a group organized by private citizens, and its successor, the Bureau of Unemployment Relief, received nationwide praise for their efforts to relieve the unemployed, resources never equaled the demand. The $3 million dollars contributed by the city was gone by the end of 1930 and the $5 million raised privately in 1931 lasted three months. Despite the infusion of state money in 1932, by the summer of that year 57,000 families were once again without

FIGURE 41
Bread line during the Great Depression. Christ Church Archives.

any regular aid; for ten agonizing weeks they had to fend for themselves as best they could.[28]

Christ Church was one place to which they could turn. In September 1932 the church supplied 1,000 articles of clothing, 500 pairs of shoes, and 800 grocery orders, as well as numerous cash grants. Members prepared between eighty and one hundred Thanksgiving and Christmas baskets each year with food provided by area banks, and beginning in 1929 the church started a bread line at the Neighborhood House (see Figure 41). People from the neighborhood lined up to receive one of the 125 loaves of bread distributed daily. In 1935 the church decided to make this bread line a religious experience by giving out a card with the picture of Jesus feeding the five thousand with each loaf.[29]

Medical needs were often as urgent as the need for food and clothing. In 1930 Hannah Cowell reported that the "present season is one of unusual sickness. Undernourishment, exposure and anxiety sap the vitality . . . and our errands to the hospitals and calls for the visiting nurses, and supplying of medicines and comforting ministrations are continuous." The free bed at the Episcopal Hospital endowed by Washington Smith in the late nineteenth century must have been especially useful during these years. Miss Cowell expressed well the aim of all of these efforts: "With the giving of material aid, our prayer and effort is to awaken their better natures, and to help them to realize that after all there is a God who cares, and that it is He who is really reaching out to them through us."[30]

During Washburn's years Christ Church also reached out to those who worked but did not live in the area. In 1908 the church inaugurated a series of weekday services during Lent. Held Monday through Friday, they averaged 140 people a day. Organized by the Men's Club of Christ Church, a group that came together once a year for this purpose, they initially were presided over by bishops and prominent clergymen from near and far. In later years the clergymen were joined by prominent laymen, and by the young men of Christ Church, who actually delivered the sermons. These services were an important part of Washburn's efforts to open Christ Church to everyone in the vicinity who needed or wanted its ministrations.[31]

Washburn and McKean were also active in a number of relief agencies outside the parish boundaries. A particularly special relationship existed with St. John's House, a diocesan settlement house located in the area north of Vine Street where many Christ Church members lived. In 1933, when the diocese stopped funding this mission, Christ Church extended its support and in 1935, when the settlement house closed, Washburn announced that the people they served were now "our people." As a result, Miss Loman, a staff member from St. John's, temporarily joined the staff of Christ Church.[32] In addition, Washburn served as president of the board of the Galilee Mission, an organization dedicated to the rehabilitation of men, particularly alcoholics. He also served as an honorary vice president of the Seamen's Church Institute, an interdenominational organization that provided food and shelter and a wide range of services to sailors.[33]

Perhaps Washburn's most important extraparochial contribution was the founding of the East Central Social Agency in 1932. This organization brought together all organized groups working for the social betterment of the people in the district between Market Street and Girard Avenue and between Delaware Avenue and Broad Street. It provided crucial coordination of relief services during the Depression years.[34]

Like other believers in the social gospel movement, Washburn and his staff went beyond providing relief to individuals and attempted to improve the basic living conditions in the neighborhood. When his attempts to recruit the help of private foundations failed, he turned to the city. The vestry sent a letter to the director of public welfare, urging him to "provide tolerable living conditions for those who ought to be kept in residence in this section." At the same time Gertrude Fritzinger wrote a letter to the mayor and city council on behalf of the parish council.[35] While there is no evidence that any of this had any effect, the efforts were, nevertheless, laudable.

* * *

While Washburn had tremendous energy and an able staff, he could not have accomplished many of his programs without the aid of laypeople. The congregation of Christ Church continued to be small in comparison to those of many other churches; the number of communicants stood at 487 when Washburn arrived and remained between 450 and 500 during most of his tenure. In comparison, St. Mark's and St. Luke and the Epiphany, both center city churches, each had well over 1,000 communicants.[36] But given its neighborhood Christ Church was fortunate to keep enough members to have a legitimate congregation.

A 1912 membership list, the only one surviving from these years, gives some idea about the composition of the congregation. As had been the case in the nineteenth century, the congregation was predominantly women; 63 percent of the communicants were women. The geographic dispersal of the congregation was, however, in sharp contrast to the nineteenth-century situation. Sixty-two communicants, or 12 percent, lived within the established parish boundaries, between Vine and Walnut Streets and the river and Seventh Street (see Map 4). In addition seventy-five people, or 15 percent, lived in the area immediately north of Vine, an area no longer served by an Episcopal church. So the church did have a core of people living within walking distance of the church. But the remaining members, almost three-quarters of the congregation, were spread out all over the area, with 11 percent living in West Philadelphia and 10 percent living in the suburbs.[37]

The occupational distribution of the congregation had also changed since the nineteenth century. Among the eighty-three people for whom occupations could be found, there were no lawyers, three doctors, and four manufacturers. Replacing the high status occupations that had predominated in the first half of the nineteenth century and were still quite common in 1880, were industrial workers, two policemen, two firemen, six "drivers," and a variety of skilled or semiskilled tradesmen. The church's claim that it was no longer a wealthy congregation seems to have been an accurate one.[38]

The nature of the congregation changed still further as Washburn's social

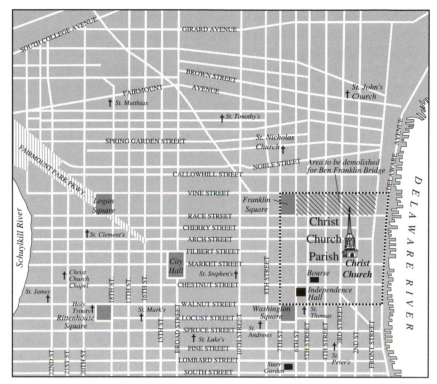

M A P 4
Philadelphia, 1914, with center city Episcopal churches.

service and outreach programs developed. Under Washburn's leadership, Christ Church became a "free church," where neighborhood people of modest means and no prior affiliation with the generally affluent Episcopal church felt comfortable worshiping. This can be seen by both the addresses and prior religious affiliations of his confirmands. Between 1915 and 1924, 31 percent of those confirmed had been baptized in a non-Episcopalian church. Of those 27, or 10 percent of the total confirmed, were Lutheran, while 19, or 8 percent, were Roman Catholic. The number of converts increased in the next decade, with 120 of 260 confirmands, or 46 percent, coming from a non-Episcopal background. Of these converts, 38 percent were Roman Catholic or Eastern Orthodox. Not surprisingly, these new members, especially the converts, were more likely to live in the immediate area than the members in 1912. Between 1915 and 1925, approximately 60 percent of confirmands for whom we have addresses lived in the parish or in the area north of Vine. The work of Washburn and his many helpers was obviously having an impact on the surrounding neighborhood.[39]

The communicants continued to be disproportionately women, but the percentage of women decreased. During Washburn's tenure 56 percent of the confirmands were female, whereas 63 percent of the confirmands under Stevens and 68 percent under Foggo had been women. Perhaps the men's programs initiated by McKean led men to feel more comfortable at Christ Church.

The Christ Church congregation during Washburn's years, then, could be roughly divided into two groups. One group, the middle and upper class members, included those who continued to belong because of family connections or interest in the historical nature of the church, as well as those drawn by Washburn's message of Christian responsibility. The second group, poor and working class people from the area, felt increasingly comfortable at Christ Church as Washburn tried successfully to rid it of its elitist and antiquarian image.

It is an unfortunate irony that Christ Church completed its Neighborhood House and began its outreach programs at almost the same time that the "neighborhood" was rapidly disappearing. In preparation for the construction of the Delaware (now Benjamin Franklin) Bridge, the city demolished the five blocks between Front and Sixth Streets and between Vine and Race Streets in 1923, essentially wiping out the residential section of the Sixth Ward (see Map 4). As a result, the population of this ward, in which Christ Church was located, decreased from 4,078 in 1920 to 1,635 in 1930 to 855 in 1940.[40] Many of these people moved to the working class neighborhoods of northeast Philadelphia, from where they commuted to the downtown church.

The membership statistics for Christ Church reflected this destruction of the neighborhood. By 1926 the total membership had fallen to 398. The number rose to 467 by 1930, but these new members were increasingly coming from outside the parish. Between 1928 and 1932, 72 percent of the new members were from outside the Christ Church area. This situation would only intensify in the 1940s and 1950s.

While Washburn attracted new members, he had much more difficulty attracting men to serve on the vestry. Even after the vestry changed the bylaws to allow any man paying $5.20 a year through the envelope system to qualify, Washburn continued to bemoan the lack of "qualified men." Between 1910 and 1918 six vestrymen died, and three more died in the 1920s.

The situation was so bad in 1930 that only ten men rather than the usual twelve were elected.[41] This shortage should not be a surprise. Since the vestry dealt primarily with the business affairs of the church, and since it had traditionally attracted older, successful men, the new members, most of whom were young and many of whom were first generation American, would not have felt comfortable and were, no doubt, not welcome. Since the middle and upper class members increasingly lived at some distance from the church, serving on the vestry was a burden.

Because of this situation, Washburn had to accept a vestry that contained men who were not even members of Christ Church and who, while dedicated to preserving the church, were not actively involved in the day-to-day work of the parish. Only six of the twelve vestrymen appear on the communicants list in 1912. Washburn showed continual concern for this situation. In 1911 he told the vestry that it had been "helpful to have some of you in attendance at the Sunday morning services" and hoped that in the future he would "have this measure of cooperation from you all regularly." That hope was obviously not fulfilled, for in 1921 he again expressed a hope of "enlisting a larger measure of cooperation in our worship and work on the part of all." In 1923 he became so upset that he threatened to resign if he was not "assured of the close cooperation of the vestry in the work of the church."[42]

The men who were willing to serve on the vestry included many with historic connections to the church. Some, like John C. DaCosta, Jr. and Thomas Seeds, Jr., had grown up in the church. Clement and John C. Newbold were members of the prominent Philadelphia banking family in Philadelphia who had been members of Christ Church since the rectorship of Benjamin Dorr. Other vestrymen traced their ancestry to the colonial church. Several descendants of Bishop White served during Washburn's years, including William White, a lawyer who served as accounting warden until 1916; his father, J. Brinton White, who served until his health forced his retirement in 1913; and George Robbins, who began his long association with the church in the 1930s. Dr. Thomas Bradford was descended from William Bradford, the colonial printer, and Richard Peters, a civil engineer and district judge for thirty years, was a descendant of another Judge Peters, the nephew of Christ Church's rector. Allen Childs, whose father was secretary for the diocese, also traced his roots to the colonial Pennsylvania church, while Thomas and William Rudolph Smith traced their ancestors back to both the Reverend William Smith and John Moore, one of the founders of Christ Church.[43]

Two vestrymen are worth particular mention. Alfred Craven Harrison used much of his fortune gained in the sugar refining business to support philanthropic endeavors. Having rented a pew at Christ Church in 1904 to show his interest in preserving the structure, by the 1920s he was almost singlehandedly supporting the budget of Christ Church. He also responded generously to specific appeals, giving ten thousand dollars for the wall around the graveyard, for example.[44] Edward Lowber Stokes, founder of the investment firm of Edward Lowber Stokes and Company, and a two-term Republican congressman, was generous with both his time and his money. He served on the vestry of Christ Church from 1913 to 1940 and, unlike most vestrymen, he was extremely active in the church. He gave generously to the fresh air fund that sent neighborhood children to camp in the summer and, as we have mentioned, worked tirelessly with the boys in the neighborhood.

The day-to-day help that Washburn needed to run his programs came not from the vestrymen but from the women of the church.[45] The leadership of Christ Church acknowledged the importance of women in 1924 by establishing the all female parish council. Serving as almost a parallel vestry, the parish council had primary responsibility for furnishing the Neighborhood House, coordinated the celebration of the sesquicentennial and kept track of the relief efforts being conducted by the church. Perhaps most surprising, it also had responsibility, with the help of the *young* men of the church, for the Every Member Canvass which was begun in 1919. Such financial matters were traditionally the responsibility of the vestry.[46]

The Every Member Canvass proved to be crucial to the survival of Christ Church. During the first fourteen years of Washburn's rectorship, the parish ran a deficit every year, despite relatively low expenses; only the endowment income of $4,454 allowed the church to function. But the introduction of the Every Member Roll Call in 1919 led to "a veritable revolution" in the church's financial situation. Washburn had introduced the envelope system shortly after his arrival, but it did not succeed until the system of visitation, with its pledges of income, church attendance, daily intercessions, and parish work, was introduced. As a result of this, 1920 was the first year that the church did not have a deficit. In 1924, 242 out of the 490 members made a financial pledge.[47] The financial situation of the church was further improved by the large contributions made by Alfred Craven Harrison; in 1927 he provided $15,000 of the $23,000 pledged!

Despite the precarious financial situation of Christ Church, Washburn asked his members to pledge two-thirds of their money to extraparochial causes. While not everyone followed his guidelines, the results are still impressive, in part because Harrison always followed the two-thirds guideline; in 1923, for example, $10,464 was pledged for parish support while $11,089 was pledged for "beyond the parish." As a result, Christ Church was always among the top contributors to the diocese.[48]

Harrison's death in 1927 could have been disastrous for the church. Pledges increased $3,000 in 1928, but this hardly filled the gap. Fortunately for the church, and for the people accustomed to its generosity, at approximately the same time Harrison died, the church finally received the entire Henry Elder estate, which had been willed to the church in 1902 pending the life interest of several relatives. It totaled $240,000 and generated approximately $28,000 in annual income.[49] From that point forward, Christ Church's programming was largely dependent on endowment income.

The Great Depression made the endowment even more important. Pledges dropped precipitously, reaching a low of $5,300 in 1935, and despite a reduction in salaries, the church had a deficit from 1930 until the end of Washburn's tenure. However, despite the small contributions the members were able to make, they still gave more than half to benevolence; in 1930 the congregation pledged $2,637 to the parish and $4,452 to causes beyond the parish.[50] Washburn's insistence on helping others had so changed the priorities of the parish that benevolence remained the top concern of those pledging, even during years when the parish itself could not make ends meet.

* * *

Despite Christ Church's financial uncertainties, numerous improvements were made both inside and outside the old church during Washburn's years. The vestry and Washburn continued their plan to place eight stained glass windows depicting the history of the church in the sanctuary. In 1910 Mrs. John Creth endowed the "American window" in memory of her husband, a long-time vestryman. The fifth window to be placed in Christ Church, it depicted the first permanent settlement at Jamestown and, as a sub-subject, showed the patriot congregation worshiping at Christ Church. Then in 1925 Mrs. Helen Belfield provided the "Liberty" or "Magna Carta" window in memory of her husband, Mr. T. Broom Belfield, another long-time vestry-man. This window showed the signing of the Magna Carta and Duché offering a prayer before the First Continental Congress[51] (see color plates).

Other repairs and improvements to the inside of the church came in the 1920s. The inside of the church was painted a light buff, with a sky blue ceiling. The pews, which up until this time had been dark wood, were painted white with a mahogany rail. One interior improvement suggested by Washburn was not done: despite the rector's repeated assertions that the decreasing availability of gas made lighting the church difficult, the vestry refused to install electric lights in the church![52]

The condition of the organ presented a more challenging problem. In 1912 Washburn reported that nearly nine-tenths of the pieces the organist played had to be adapted for the "mechanical and musical limitations" of the 1837 organ. At the rector's urging, a major reconstruction of the instrument took place in 1921.[53] In 1934 Mary Louise Curtis Bok offered the church a more permanent solution: the organ from the home of her father, the wealthy publisher, Cyrus H. K. Curtis, who had been a pewholder at Christ Church for thirty years. Despite the perilous financial situation of the church and the country, the vestry agreed to borrow $20,000 to have the organ installed. This magnificent instrument, which is still in use, was dedicated on May 29, 1935.[54]

Parishioners and visitors had ample opportunity to benefit from these improvements. Morning prayer, Holy Communion, and evening prayer were observed each Sunday. Morning prayer was observed on Wednesdays and Fridays from October to July and Communion was celebrated on all festivals and saints' days. Altogether, there were 327 services per year, approximately sixty more than had occurred under Rector Stevens.[55] But while the number of services increased, Christ Church stood firmly in the low church tradition.

Major improvements had to be made to the outside of the church building because of fire and the threat of fire. (Figure 42 shows how boxed-in the church was.) In May 1908 the church steeple was struck twice by lightning. While the heroic work of the sexton and firemen, combined with rain, saved the church and parish building from destruction, the top portion of the steeple had to be rebuilt. Then in 1923 the Compston Paper Box factory caught fire, damaging the sexton's house next to the church. Had Harvey Mertz not sounded the alarm immediately, the church building could have been destroyed. As a result of this close call, the vestry authorized the installation of a water-curtain sprinkler system that would bathe the building and lower half of the steeple in water in case of fire.[56]

To further protect the church from fire, as well as to beautify the area around it, Washburn and members of the vestry decided to persuade the city to widen both Filbert and Church Streets and to condemn the buildings to the north of the church and make "an open park around the church." After several years of lobbying, their plan was at least partially accepted. In May 1929 the buildings were torn down, and Robert Morris Memorial Park, or "Morris Park" as it is generally referred to, was created and put under the jurisdiction of the Fairmount Park Commission. At the same time, the city widened Filbert Street. Christ Church was now protected on the north and west, and the view of the church was greatly enhanced (see Figure 43).[57]

The final improvement to the property during Washburn's years came in 1932 when the vestry agreed to build a structure to provide lodgings for the sexton near to the church. Constructed on the lot north of the Neighborhood House, it contained a boardroom on the first floor and an apartment upstairs. The vestry named it "Washburn House" in honor of the rector's twenty-fifth anniversary at Christ Church.[58]

*   *   *

As we have seen, from Dorr's time on, Christ Church functioned on two levels—as a local parish church and as an historic monument. Washburn seemed particularly comfortable with this dual emphasis; while he had tremendous concern for the people of the neighborhood, he had a serious interest in the history of the church as well. In addition, Washburn inaugurated the tradition of giving speeches and invocations to historic groups throughout the city. These activities gave the church a visibility it had lacked under Foggo and Stevens.

The most significant historical celebration during Washburn's years was for the church's 225th anniversary in 1920. Taking this opportunity to showcase the church and build support for its programs, Washburn, aided by the vestry, the parish council and the newly revived Christ Church Historical Association, planned an elaborate, year long celebration. Two lasting contributions came out of that celebration. The "Compton Tablet," which remains on the church's wall, was given by the Colonial Dames to honor Henry Compton, the bishop of London who was responsible for the paragraph in the Pennsylvania charter guaranteeing Anglicans a minister when they asked for one (see Figure 44). More important, Washburn himself paid for the publication of the scholarly papers presented at the anniversary, along with other valuable papers given earlier. Together, this *Symposium* constituted the first attempt at a scholarly history of Christ Church.[59] The book also contained the first full catalog of the Bray Library given to the church during the colonial period, including which volumes remained. At the same time Washburn removed this valuable collection from storage.[60]

FIGURE 42
Christ Church prior to the construction of Morris Park, hemmed in by buildings. Christ Church Archives.

Christ Church members also helped found the Historical Association of the Protestant Episcopal Church (now located in Austin, Texas). This organization, dedicated to studying all aspects of the Protestant Episcopal Church, had its first headquarters in the Neighborhood House, and Allen Childs, a vestryman of Christ Church, served on its executive board.[61]

In addition, Christ Church played a role in the national commemorations that were held in Philadelphia, particularly the sesquicentennial of the Declaration of Independence. Christ Church joined with the diocese in sponsor-

FIGURE 43
Christ Church after the demolition of buildings and the establishment of Morris Park.
Christ Church Archives.

ing a booth at the World's Fair, which included a scale model of the church building (see Figure 45). At the church, volunteer guides passed out 70,000 brochures to the crowds of visitors, which averaged a thousand a day. On the Fourth of July, at an impressive service attended by a wide array of dignitaries, a tablet honoring the seven signers of the Declaration of Independence buried in Christ Church burial ground was unveiled. The following day President Coolidge visited the church "in the presence of a great concourse," passing through the "President's Door."[62]

FIGURE 44
*Henry Compton tablet,
given by the Philadelphia
Chapter of the Colonial
Dames of America in
honor of the 225th anni-
versary of Christ Church.
The tablet was unveiled
in June 1921. The design
was patterned after tablets
in English churches dat-
ing from the late seven-
teenth century, when
Compton lived. Photo-
graph by Louis W.
Meehan.*

Washburn used the historic commemorations as opportunities to call his listeners to act for the present good, not merely to bask in past glory, for, as he put it, "the backward look . . . is but to provide solid footing for present duty, and incentive for further accomplishment." When speaking to the Sons of the American Revolution annual service commemorating Washington's winter at Valley Forge, Washburn, showing his social gospel leanings, re-

FIGURE 45
Diocesan exhibit at the Sesquicentennial. The scale model of Christ Church can be seen at the right of the picture. Christ Church Archives.

minded them that it is possible that we "may be so engrossed glorying in our spendid inheritance of Civic and religious freedom and universal suffrage that we shall be dangerously deaf . . . to the current demand for an equitable sharing of industrial prosperity." Similarly, at a union service on the Fourth of July he argued that the same Spirit of God that brought forth the Declaration of Independence was now "drafting a new Declaration of Independence against all oppression and corruption. . . . It is making the heart of the multitude to sing thunderously battle hymns of deliverance from economic and social slaveries."[63] This use of the history of Christ Church to further much larger goals than historic preservation was a new thrust for the parish.

* * *

Washburn and the members of the congregation continued to be involved in activities throughout Philadelphia. Three vestrymen from Christ Church and three from St. Peter's still served as the board of management for Christ Church Hospital. The first three decades of the twentieth century were reasonably prosperous ones for the hospital. The sale of land combined with bequests allowed the hospital to increase the number of residents from sixty-seven in 1920 to eighty in 1927.[64] The lives of these residents were made more pleasant by the establishment of a "Ladies' Committee," which must have been patterned after the women's auxiliary during Stevens's rectorship. Women from Christ Church and St. Peter's, later joined by women from other churches, held monthly teas or parties, arranged for Christmas presents and birthday cards for the residents, visited the women, and refurbished the house in a variety of ways. This group continued to function until 1985.[65]

Christ Church Chapel did not fare nearly so well as the hospital. In 1929, after years of decline, the chapel finally closed, one of six center city churches to close or move between 1905 and 1930. Surrounded by several large, prosperous churches, and faced with a declining population in the center city area, the chapel had reported financial problems as early as 1906, but the board of management and the vestry let it stay open until the death of the long time vicar, James Nisbett.[66] At that point a survey of the fifty-one communicants indicated neither the level of concern nor the financial means necessary to keep the chapel open. The building was sold to a Christian Scientist congregation, which still worships there. The memorial windows were transferred to the chapel at Christ Church Hospital.[67]

The closing of Christ Church Chapel at a time when the mother parish was doing exceptionally well was the final irony in the rocky and, at times, sad history of that institution. Founded with the idea of providing financial insurance for the mother church, the Christ Church vestry had prevented the chapel from becoming independent and from merging in order to keep that insurance. Yet by the 1920s, perhaps to most people's surprise, the mother church was better off both financially and in terms of members than was the chapel. The population's continuous move to the suburbs had created an excess of churches in the once fashionable neighborhoods in center city, and the chapel could not compete with such large and wealthy churches as Holy Trinity on Rittenhouse Square. The mother church, on the other hand, was saved by its history and made useful by the work of Washburn. In the end, the only financial contribution the chapel made to Christ Church was at its closing; the church used the $60,000 received from the sale of the building to erase the deficit during the Depression!

While the closing of the chapel was both ironic and sad, it was fitting that it happened during Washburn's years, for it had been founded by those who saw the neighborhood as a liability rather than an opportunity and wanted to follow the former members of Christ Church to their new homes rather than develop new members. Such a philosophy was anathema to Washburn. In 1933, when a diocesan committee studying center city churches suggested that some should close and others move to the suburbs, Washburn, along with Gilbert Pember, rector of St. Michael's in Germantown, objected strongly. Referring to seaboard cities where the church had "an enviable record for downtown anchorage and serviceableness, through generations of change and chance," they declared: "The times call with increasing insistence in every country for the Christian Church to make a clearer manifestation of its determination and ability not to seek its own, but to sacrificially serve."[68] Unfortunately, the convention did not follow their recommendations.

While the convention did not always do as Washburn wished, he was the first rector of Christ Church since Dorr to play a prominent role in the diocese. He served on the Standing Committee, the most important committee in the Diocese, from 1918 until his retirement. He also served as a trustee of the Protestant Episcopal Church (later the Church Foundation). Perhaps most important, he served as Vice President of the Episcopal City Mission from 1926 until his retirement, after having chaired its Committee on Consumptive Department.[69]

Given Washburn's concern for people of all faiths, it should not be surprising that he took a leadership role in the Philadelphia Federation of Churches. He joined the organization, which was founded the year before he arrived in Philadelphia by an interdenominational group of people interested in the social gospel movement, shortly after he arrived and continued active participation for thirty years. His was, as one eulogist put it, "a Catholic soul." Because he was serving as an honorary vice president at the time of his death, the federation sponsored a memorial service in his honor.[70]

*   *   *

While Washburn focused his work on the parish and the diocese, the church was, of course, also affected by far larger events, most especially the onset of World War I. Christ Church sent fifty-four men to fight, while the chapel sent twenty-one; one Christ Church member died.

The rector and vestry of Christ Church felt that they had a special responsibility to support the war effort because of their standing as the "Patriots' Sanctuary." Four days after the United States entered the war, on

April 10, 1917, the vestry met, "as custodians of this patriotic shrine," to "pledge anew our loyal support . . . to our Government in defence of the sacred principles for which the country is now called to arms." They rededicated themselves "to this supreme task in the spirit of the Revolutionary Fathers who knelt in this Sanctuary" and offered their buildings for use as needed.[71] The sign hung outside the church asked Philadelphians to come into the "Patriots' Sanctuary" and pray for:

Our Country and those in Authority
Our Enlisted Men and the Allies. . . .
The Wounded and the Dying and those who mourn.
The Forgiveness of our Enemies, and all who would have Might make Right. . . .
The Will of God and the Spirit of Christ.
A Just and Lasting Peace.[72]

Washburn himself made a contribution to the war effort, serving as a chaplain at Camp Meade. More important, as chairman of the Diocesan Commission on War Work, he compiled the little devotional book, *A Prayerbook for Soldiers and Sailors*, tens of thousands of which were distributed.[73]

With the end of the war, Christ Church welcomed its soldiers back with a "Benediction and a New Challenge": "Grant unto us that we may use the fruits of victory nobly, and show ourselves worthy of Thy gift of peace." Washburn, like other Episcopal leaders, believed that the best way to end war was to spread Christian ideals. He argued that war could not be avoided until men stopped living as "educated beasts" and formed a "true brotherhood of fraternity and religious idealism."[74] He therefore supported the peace efforts of the 1920s and 1930s, including disarmament.

* * *

When Washburn retired in 1937 at age 77 and died a year later, the tributes that poured forth evidenced both the breadth and the depth of his following. All the organizations with which he was associated expressed their appreciation for his contributions and regret at his retirement. But a recent confirmand gave perhaps the best tribute of all: she dedicated herself to continue Washburn's work "as a token of my gratitude . . . for teaching me in six weeks . . . what I had been trying to find out all my life—that true happiness is found only in the love and service to God our Father and love and service to our neighbors."[75] No better summary of Washburn's rectorship could be found!

NOTES

1. See Vestry Minutes, June 4, Nov. 2, Dec. 20, 1904, April 25, Oct. 18, 1905, Jan. 18, March 7, May 24, and June 6, 1906.

2. "Old Church in New Era of Activity," *North American*, March 11, 1913. At the service to mark Washburn's twenty-fifth year, Bishop Tait similarly referred to his having "lifted [the church] out of the museum class"; newspaper clipping, unknown source, scrapbook, Christ Church Archives.

3. A Service in Honor of Louis Cope Washburn, S.T.D., And of Dedication in his Spirit to the Cause of Church Unity held Under the auspices of the Philadelphia Federation of Churches in Christ Church, Philadelphia, Sunday, October 16, 1938, *Program* (hereafter Memorial Service for Washburn) contains a biography; Louis Cope Washburn, grandson of the rector, interview with author, Philadelphia, June 15, 1987.

4. *Christ Church Reporter*, 6th Year, no. 21 (1937), 4.

5. Ibid., 3, 4.

6. Louis Washburn, "The Washington Sanctuary—The Source of His Power," in Louis Washburn, *Christ Church, Philadelphia: A Symposium*, 237; Louis Washburn, "A Fourth of July Address," in ibid., 132.

7. See Paul Carter, *The Decline and Revival of the Social Gospel* (1958; reprint, Hamden, Conn.: Archon Books, 1971). The social gospel did not die in the 1920s, but many proponents encountered stiff resistance from parishioners. Louis Washburn, "The Call of Lent," n.d., Christ Church Archives; "Rector Denounces Mummy Christians," *Evening Bulletin*, May 6, 1936, p. 3.

8. Vestry Minutes, June 7 and Oct. 18, 1905, May 24, 1906. Twice in 1905 they did not have the seven members necessary for a quorum.

9. Christ Church, *Social Survey of the Parish* (Philadelphia, 1912), 10–12.

10. Ibid., 12, 29–30, 33–39.

11. Louis Washburn to Dr. William Ashton, March 15, 1907, in Vestry Minutes, March 21, 1907, April 2, 1907.

12. *A Directory of the Charitable, Social Improvement, Education and Religious Associations and Churches of Philadelphia*, prepared by the Civic Club of Philadelphia (Philadelphia, 1903), 344.

13. Vestry Minutes, Jan 7, April 2, May 10 and Dec. 17, 1907; Oct. 19, 1908, April 13, July 7 and Nov. 15, 1909; July 7 and Sept. 10, 1910; March 26, May 19, 1920, May 31 and Oct. 19, 1922; *Handbook of Christ Church*, 1912, 72–73; Committee on the New Parish House, Minutes, Vestry Committee Records, Christ Church Archives.

14. The *Christ Church Newsletter* came out each Advent in the 1930s. The parish visitor included a report each year.

15. Jane Jordan O'Neill, interview with author, Philadelphia, August 5, 1986.

16. *Helen Carpenter Washburn, 1892–1946* (privately published, 1946), 17–28; the quote is from p. 28.

17. Jane O'Neill, interview, with author; Louis Washburn, interview with author, Philadelphia, June 15, 1987; Amelia Lingham, interview with author, Philadelphia, June 17, 1987.

18. See Parish Council Minutes, December, 1932, Christ Church Archives. In 1905 St. Mark's had 935 in its Sunday School and St. Luke's had 580, compared to 272 at Christ Church. By 1935 St. Mark's had 13, St. Luke's had 109. See *Journal of the Diocese of Pennsylvania*, 1932, 1935 (Philadelphia, 1932, 1935). For information on the ethnic makeup of the school, see *The Voice*, Advent 1931 (a newsletter sent out yearly).

19. *Christ Church Newsletter*, Advent 1931; Parish Council, Minutes, May, 1931; V. Rev. A. P. Gougnin to Louis Washburn, June 9, 1937, Christ Church Archives.

20. *Christ Church Newsletter*, Advent 1932.

21. *Helen Carpenter Washburn*, 14; *Christ Church Newsletter*, Advent 1931. For the Sunday School newsletter see *Christ Church Reporter*, 1931–38.

22. *Christ Church Reporter*, 5th Year, Epiphany 1936, no. 17; Arthur Dudden, "The City Embraces Normalcy," in Weigley, *Philadelphia: A Three Hundred Year History*, 588; Lloyd Abernethy, "Progressivism," in ibid., 561.

23. *Christ Church Reporter*, 6th Year (1937) no. 22; 7th Year (1938), no. 26; *Helen Carpenter Washburn*, 14–15. Helen Washburn described the unit on "Christian Unity" in her book, *A Church School Looks at Christian Unity: A Seven Week Study by All the Classes in the Church School* (Philadelphia: privately published, 1939).

24. *Handbook of Christ Church*, 1912, 102–4.

25. Ibid., 106–7; *The Voice*, 1930, 1932.

26. *Christ Church Newsletter*, 1932.

27. Christ Church, *Social Survey of the Parish*, 17–18; *Christ Church Newsletter*, 1932.

28. Bonnie Fox Schwartz, "Unemployment Relief in Philadelphia, 1930–1932: A Study of the Depression's Impact on Voluntarism," *PMHB* 92 (1969), 86–108; Margaret Tinkcom, "Depression and War, 1929–1946," in Weigley, *Philadelphia: A Three Hundred Year History*, 612.

29. Parish Council Minutes, Dec. 1931, March 1935; *The Voice*, 1930, 1932; *The Evening Bulletin*, Sept. 5, 1932.

30. Both quotes are from *The Voice*, 1930.

31. See *Handbook of Christ Church*, 1912, 98–100.

32. Vestry Minutes, May 27, 1930; Parish Council Minutes, Feb. 16, May 1932; Feb, April 1933; April 1935. For a description of St. John's House see *Social Service Directory of Philadelphia*, 1919, comp. Leon Stern (Philadelphia: Council of Social Agencies, 1919), 233.

33. *The Galilee Mission, The Church's Greatest Life Saving Station, Extracts from Annual Report, 1915* (Philadelphia, 1915). *Seamen's Church Institute of Philadelphia, Prospectus* (Philadelphia, 1920).

34. "Resolution of the Protestant Episcopal City Mission," "Resolution of the East Central Social Agencies," Jan. 26, 1937, Christ Church Archives; Parish Council Minutes, April 1935; *Social Service Directory of Philadelphia*, 1938 (Philadelphia: Council of Social Agencies, 1938), 62.

35. Vestry Minutes, April 7, 1931; Feb. 15, 1932; Parish Council Minutes, Feb. 16, 1932. These letters seemed to have been spurred on by a wave of crime in the area.

36. *Journal of the Diocese of Pennsylvania*, 1910–1935.

37. *Handbook of Christ Church*, 1912, 136–48.

38. The information was obtained by comparing the membership list in the *Handbook*, 1912 with the *City Directory for Philadelphia* (Philadelphia, 1912).

39. List of Confirmations, Christ Church Archives.

40. "$6,000,000 Realty Taken for Bridge," *Evening Bulletin*, Dec. 6, 1923; "Bridge Wipes Out 6th Ward," ibid., June 11, 1921; U.S. Department of Commerce, Bureau of the Census, *Fifteenth Census of the United States: Metropolitan Districts* (Washington, D.C.: U.S. Government Printing Office, 1932).

41. Vestry Minutes, Oct. 13, 1915, Jan. 11, 1922, Jan. 18, 1926.

42. Vestry Minutes, May 8, 1911, Oct. 12, 1921, Oct. 18, 1923; see also Jan. 11, 1922.

43. Most of this information is gleaned from the Vestry Minutes at the time of the vestrymen's retirement or death. See Vestry Minutes, Jan. 11, 1911, June 4, 1913, Oct. 13, 1915, March 3, 1916, May 24, 1921, Oct. 19, 1922, Oct. 21, 1935.

44. Vestry Minutes, June 21, 1927, Sept. 17, 1927; Godcharles, ed., *Encyclopedia of Pennsylvania Biography*, s.v., Harrison, Alfred Craven.

45. The increasing involvement of women in Christ Church occurred at a time when one study has found the involvement of women in Minnesota churches *decreasing*. See Joan R. Gunderson, "Parallel Churches: Women and the Episcopal Church, 1850–1980," *Mid-America* 69 (1987): 87–97.

46. See Parish Council Minutes, 1924–1937.

47. *Abstract Concerning Christ Church*, 1912; Vestry Minutes, June 3, Oct. 19, 1908; Oct. 14, 1914, Oct. 13, 1915, Jan. 12, 1916, Jan 10, 1917, Dec. 17, 1924.

48. Vestry Minutes, Jan. 11, 1922; Dec. 17, 1924; Oct. 25, 1928; *Journal of the Diocese of Pennsylvania*, 1915, 1920, 1925, 1930. Parish Council, Nov. 15, 1927.

49. Vestry Minutes, Dec. 17, 1928; Dec. 18, 1929; Parish Council Minutes, Dec. 20, 1927.

50. Vestry Minutes, Dec. 18, 1931, Jan. 18, Oct. 17, Dec. 19, 1932, Jan. 16, Oct. 16, Nov. 27, Dec. 18, 1933; Dec. 17, 1934; Feb. 18, Nov. 18, 1935; Jan 20, April 3, Nov. 16, 1936; Jan. 18, Feb. 15, 1937. "Budget for 1930," Vestry Minutes, Dec. 18, 1929. For national statistics on church giving during the Depression see Samuel C. Kincheloe, *Research Memorandum on Religion in The Depression* (New York, 1937, reprinted New York: Arno Press, 1971). Kincheloe concludes that, in real dollars, giving increased from 1930 to 1932 and declined from 1932 to 1935. Even taking into account the declining value of the dollar, Christ Church's decline began in 1929 and continued through 1936.

51. The best description is found in *Handbook of Christ Church*, 1912, 108–12. See also Vestry Minutes, Dec. 17, 1924; Jan. 26, 1925.

52. See Vestry Minutes, Jan. 11, 1922; June 21, 1923; Washburn, *Christ Church: A Symposium*, 312–13.

53. Washburn's comments were made in the *Handbook of Christ Church*, 1912, 60–61.

54. Vestry Minutes, June 14 and Oct. 24, 1934; May 30, 1935.

55. *Journal of the Diocese of Pennsylvania*, 1894, 1915.

56. Vestry Minutes, May 26, June 3, Dec. 2, 1908; Nov., 1923.

57. See Vestry Minutes, Mar. 14, April 3, 1923; May 31, June 21, Nov. 21, Dec. 22, 1927; "City Plans Garden at Christ Church," *Evening Ledger*, May 2, 1929, copy in Christ Church Archives.

58. Vestry Minutes, Feb. 15, March 29, April 25, May 16, Sept. 19, Oct. 17, Nov. 21, Dec. 19, 1932.

59. Washburn, *Christ Church, Philadelphia: A Symposium*, 177–81. Dorr's history had been little more than a summary of the vestry minutes. Washburn's volume included articles on such unusual topics as the church's relationship with Indians and blacks and a discussion of women in colonial America.

60. Washburn, "The Library," in Washburn, *Christ Church: Philadelphia: A Symposium*, 157–67. Most of the work for this list was done by Austin Baxter Kemp, who was doing a dissertation on "Colonial Libraries in America."

61. *Handbook of Christ Church*, 1912, 113–18.

62. Vestry Minutes, July 6, Sept. 27, 1926. The Coolidge visit was, of course, widely reported in the press.

63. Washburn, *Christ Church, Philadelphia: A Symposium*, 14; Washburn, "The Washington Sanctuary—The Source of His Power," in ibid., 237; Washburn, "A Fourth of July Address," in ibid., 132.

64. Roberts, "Christ Church Hospital," 97.

65. Ibid.; Christ Church Hospital *Annual Report*, 1933; Ladies Committee, Minutes, Christ Church Archives.

66. "Special Appeal" of Christ Church Chapel, 1906, Christ Church Archives, reported a falling off of contributions for the previous two years and indicated a gap between expenses and income of approximately $400. Another Appeal was sent in 1920, showing a gap of almost $1800. See letter from James Nisbett, Frank Wirgman, and William Montgomery to members, Nov. 1, 1920, Christ Church Archives.

67. In 1922 Washburn expressed impatience about the Chapel situation and asked the vestry not to "let sleeping dogs lie." In 1925 he suggested to Nisbett that the work of the Chapel be transferred to the hospital, with Nisbett being the chaplain. Initially after Nisbett's death there was a group of thirty people who petitioned to keep the chapel open. But the inability to attract a minister seems to have dissuaded many of them. See Vestry Minutes, Jan. 11, 1922; Jan. 11, 1926. For the decision to close the chapel see Chapel Board of Management Minutes, Christ Church Archives, March 12, Oct. 16, 1929; Christ Church Vestry Minutes, Jan. 21, Feb. 18, April 18, Oct. 21, Dec. 18, 1929; Jan. 13, 1930; April 22, May 27, 1930.

68. *Journal of the Diocese of Pennsylvania*, 1933, 357–62; quotes are from pp. 361 and 362.

69. See *Journal of the Diocese of Pennsylvania*, 1907–1938. Resolution of the Philadelphia Protestant Episcopal City Mission on the retirement of Dr. Washburn, Christ Church Archives.

70. "Extract from the Address by Dr. E.A.E. Palmquist at Memorial Service for Dr. Louis C. Washburn, Sunday, October 16, 1938," Christ Church Archives.

71. Vestry Minutes, April 10, 1917.

72. Louis Washburn, "The War to End War," in Washburn, *Christ Church, Philadelphia: A Symposium*, 54.

73. Ibid., 55; Vestry Minutes, Dec. 11, 1917.

74. Washburn, "The War to End War," 56; "Says Nation Needs Religious Idealism," unidentified newspaper article, Christ Church Archives; for a discussion of the views of the Episcopal Church on peace, see Robert Miller, "The Social Attitudes of the American Episcopal Church During Two Decades, 1919–1939," *HMPEC* 25 (1956): 178–79.

75. *Christ Church Reporter*, 6th Year (1937), no. 21, 4.

FROM DEPRESSION TO POSTWAR BOOM: CHRIST CHURCH ADJUSTS TO CHANGING TIMES

Louis Washburn's retirement left a large void for his successor to fill; he had become, after all, a Philadelphia institution. But he also left an active church with a real purpose, an institution that had successfully combined appreciation for its past with service in the present. Unlike the situation when Washburn arrived, Christ Church in 1938 was an attractive assignment, a church that could easily find an active, energetic minister. The two rectors who led Christ Church during the next seventeen years both fit that description. While the neighborhood continued to deteriorate, with even the businesses moving out, the church retained a sense of purpose, a reason for remaining more than a museum. As had been the case under Washburn, that sense of purpose continued to combine a strong sense of the church's historical roots with a desire to minister effectively to both its members and its neighborhood.

* * *

To continue the work of Washburn the vestry chose Edward Felix Kloman, who was at the time serving as assistant to the rector of Grace Church in New York City (see Figure 46).

FIGURE 46
The Reverend Felix Kloman (rector, 1938–1949). Christ Church Archives.

The son of a clergyman, Kloman had been educated at the University of Virginia and the Episcopal Theological Seminary in Virginia. He thus began the connection between Christ Church and the low church tradition in Virginia that still continues. Ordained by the bishop of London, Kloman's first job was as a missionary to Liberia, a position that illness forced him to give up in 1927.[1]

Like Washburn, Kloman was, above all, a deeply committed Christian whose primary goal was to bring the true meaning of the gospel to as many people as possible. To Kloman, the gospel's true meaning included putting one's faith into action. Responding to those who felt religion did not make enough difference in their lives, he suggested that that was because they had not yet experienced the Holy Spirit. "A humanistic religion," he asserted, "lacks power. The Holy Spirit brings power to the followers of Christ." Once a man has accepted the Holy Spirit, "he has a new outlook on life, a new idea of God, a new conception of the universe, a new sense of values, a new estimate of human nature and a new sense of obligation. . . . For him, 'thou shalt' has replaced 'thou shalt not.' " "From Christ will come the unlimited vigor, the complete self-dedication, the team work and inspiration that is needed" to build a "new world."[2] Kloman personified these ideals himself. The word used most often to describe him was energetic. He worked his volunteers so hard they affectionately nicknamed him Simon Legree, but they accepted it because Kloman worked himself even harder.

While Kloman was serious and formal in public services, in person he could be extremely informal, sometimes making it hard for strangers to believe he was a minister. Following his father's advice that a minister should hold other jobs to learn what the world was like, Kloman's first job was as a taxi driver. Perhaps it was that experience that allowed him to make friends easily with young people and particularly with the businessmen in the neighborhood. When the owner of the Tap Room, a bar that stood on the block next to Christ Church, suggested that Kloman bring the vestry over after a meeting, the rector readily agreed. So the distinguished vestrymen of Christ Church sat around a table drinking martinis at a bar usually frequented by sailors and other itinerants. Such openness was typical of Kloman, who believed that the church should embrace everyone who lived or worked in the parish.[3]

Kloman's openness led him beyond the parish boundaries to minister to the city at large. He expanded Washburn's practice of giving invocations at various ceremonies around town, thus increasing the awareness of Christ Church among city leaders. He also took a leadership role in the diocese, serving on the executive committee from 1942 to 1948.[4]

While Kloman was as eager as Washburn to find new ways to serve both his parishioners and the neighborhood of Christ Church, the services he provided were largely defined by crises beyond his control—the last years of the Great Depression and World War II. Thus, while Washburn came in with a specific plan for the church that he wanted to implement, Kloman found himself, out of necessity, reacting to events rather than controlling them.

Kloman was not only constrained by events, he was also handicapped by the increasing geographic dispersal of his members. While no membership lists are available, one can get a sense of the dispersal by looking at the "district meetings" Kloman set up in 1942 in an attempt to increase the sense of community among members. Of the ten districts, one encompassed the area from the river to Broad Street and north to Girard Avenue, indicating how few people lived in the vicinity of the church. In contrast, five districts were located in north and northeast Philadelphia, one in west Philadelphia, and one in the suburbs.[5] Kloman himself lived in Mount Airy, a residential area of northwest Philadelphia.

With more and more of the parishioners of Christ Church moving away from the area, finding volunteers, particularly men, to help in the work of the parish became even more difficult. The vestrymen continued to be a distinguished group of men, many of whom had served under Washburn, but, as had been the case earlier, they took little part in the organizational or worship life of the church. Instead of relying on the vestrymen, Kloman recruited men just out of college to become "vestry assistants." Starting with men who had had some association with Christ Church, like William White, Jr., whose father was on the vestry, and Francis Van Dusen, who had had the Clark Scholarship at St. Paul's School, he used these young men to bring in other interested young people. Kloman expected these vestry assistants to help in the social service programs of Christ Church at the same time they were being groomed for future service on the vestry.

After surveying the parish to determine what needs were not being met, the vestry assistants concentrated their efforts on the boys' club begun by Washburn. While the neighborhood was shrinking, there were still enough boys to attract thirty or forty to such activities as weekly basketball games, picnics during the summer, and a camp that met three days a week at the Neighborhood House during July. The vestry assistants were also each assigned to help a current vestryman with committee work. While World War II disrupted this program, the plan had its desired effect. Men such as William White, Francis Van Dusen, Sydney Lea, Horace Churchman, Robert Tresher, and John Whitney all later served long terms on the vestry.[6]

While the vestry assistants addressed the needs of neighborhood boys, the parish visitor provided needed activities for girls. Jane Jordan, a young woman just out of high school, accepted the position in 1938 and remained until World War II. She established the Sunshine Club, a program that attracted between ten and thirty neighborhood girls after school and on weekends to play basketball and go on various outings. A trip to a restaurant where they could order anything they wanted was an exciting experience for most of these young women.[7]

The importance of the Sunday school in the life of the church and the community decreased dramatically in the 1940s. Helen Washburn resigned as director of religious education in 1939 in order to allow Kloman to choose his own director, but continued to work in the church school until her death in 1946. Unable to afford to pay a successor (Washburn had served with no pay), Kloman and McKean supervised the school. The number of children had already begun to decline before Washburn's resignation; of the 244 pupils registered in 1939, more than 150 were in the "correspondence group." This decline continued as more and more people moved out of the area; by 1945 the total number was down to 95, with about half that number attending each Sunday.[8]

The services provided for the adult population also underwent some changes, as social service agencies within the city took over most of the direct aid to the poor. The parish visitor continued to visit the sick and help meet the physical needs of the congregation, but Christ Church no longer engaged in much direct philanthropy. Instead, Jordan served as a source of information, referring the people to the appropriate city agencies. She also started a project aimed at improving the quality of life for the poor: *Pleasure Through Leisure* was a highly successful newsletter that listed free amusements, hobbies and clubs within Philadelphia.[9]

Despite the dispersal of the congregation, the women of Christ Church continued to participate in a variety of activities. The Mothers' Meeting, the Girls' Friendly Society, which by this time was made up primarily of older women, the women's auxiliary, and the altar guild all continued to meet during Kloman's tenure. The Ladies' Committee of Christ Church Hospital remained active, although increasingly women from other churches joined in this effort. In addition to hosting teas in their homes for hospital residents, they began meeting monthly at Christ Church, combining business with a program, thus serving a social function for the women. As had been traditional in Christ Church, the women continued to raise much needed money.

In 1939 the women instituted the "Fair of Old Philadelphia," a successful money-making event that continued throughout the 1940s; set in 1695, this novel undertaking combined history, religion, and carnival. The women also sponsored the Lenten lunches, served for thirty-five cents every Wednesday and Thursday after the noonday service to hundreds of neighborhood businessmen and women.[10]

Kloman's rectorship saw the development of several new groups within the church. The Joseph Volunteers did maintenance work around the church, while the Guild of Mary did the "kind of work that women can do so well—visiting, writing, mending. . . ." On the social side, the Young People's Fellowship sponsored a weekly dance, while the Bishop White Club provided activities for "Older Young People and Young Married" people. The Golden Age Club, organized for older people in the neighborhood, welcomed people of all races and creeds. While church attendance may not have been large, Christ Church was still a vibrant parish.[11]

Kloman, like Washburn, believed that "the function of a church in its community" was to interest itself "not only in the spiritual development of its neighbors, but also in the well being of the neighborhood." Because the residential area around Christ Church had almost disappeared by the time he arrived, Kloman turned his attention to the people who worked in the neighborhood and to the condition of the commercial buildings. Bothered by the filthy streets and the generally unpleasant environment that characterized the "old city area," in 1941 Kloman called together a small group of men who worked in the neighborhood to see if they could effect some change. Foremost among them was David Grossman, whose furniture and rug warehouse was at Second and Market Streets. The result was the formation of the Old Christ Church Neighborhood Businessmen's Association. Although initially skeptical of the idea, Grossman, a Jew, agreed to serve as the secretary of the Association and over the years became a loyal friend of Christ Church.[12]

The association took as its stated purpose "the bringing together of the businessmen of the oldest business district in America for better acquaintance with each other and cooperation for the good of all in the neighborhood." Meeting monthly for lunch, by 1945 the organization had grown to 250 men from "all walks of life" and a variety of religions. George Whidden, an executive of the Corn Exchange National Bank, expressed well the most basic accomplishment of the organization: "Men who had been in business down here from thirty to fifty years and yet knew each other by face only today call one another by their first names." When one of them was in need, the others would come to his aid; when Grossman's warehouse burned down, Whidden responded within an hour, asking what his bank could do, even though Grossman did not bank there.[13]

In addition to providing social gatherings, the organization hoped to improve "the neighborhood, . . . revitalizing the historical aspect of the surroundings, and restoring, as near as possible, the atmosphere prevailing at that time [the Revolution]." They planned to have colonial architecture throughout the community by restoring some buildings and constructing colonial façades on others. While these lofty goals were shelved during the war, never to be achieved, the association did do less dramatic things for the neighborhood. Its members worked to clean up the streets, as Kloman had wanted, and they tried to help the people who still lived on those streets. Where possible, they created jobs for the unemployed. In other cases, they negotiated with landlords not to evict people, and cosigned loans when needed. They also took over direction of the war chest, raising contributions from $3,800 a year to $13,000, and increasing the sale of War bonds from three hundred fifty thousand dollars to more than two million dollars within their district.[14]

While the Association was not sponsored by or directly affiliated with Christ Church, the members were quick to come to the church's aid when needed. In 1947 the Neighborhood Businessmen's Association gave the church two badly needed bells, made from metal captured from the Germans, Japanese, and Italians during the war and dedicated "in memory of the men from this oldest business neighborhood in the United States of America who served in World War II."[15] The Neighborhood Businessmen's Association had less tangible benefits for Christ Church as well. Its members, coming from a variety of backgrounds and living in various parts of the city and suburbs, could spread a positive message about the church. The fact that businessmen of all faiths cared so much about the church said a great deal to even the casual observer.

*   *   *

Kloman, like Washburn, was always keenly aware of the world beyond Christ Church, a world that rapidly was becoming engulfed in war. In 1938, when others were still choosing to ignore the conflicts in Europe, Kloman challenged his congregation to think globally. Reflecting on the fact that air travel would soon annihilate distances between men, he asked whether man was ready for this: "Has man the strength of character that alone can make peace and goodwill possible on this little planet? As we are thrown closer together the world over . . . will we see each other as brothers, workers together in God's world?" Much of the answer, he argued, depended on "the sincerity and depth of religious experience of those who call themselves Christians." The following year, as the war in Europe grew more menacing, he argued that "the challenge to us today in our relative safety and security in the United States is to so draw close to God that we may play our part in bringing about a lasting peace established on the basis of His principles."[16]

Thus Kloman had already prepared Christ Church for a special role once the United States became engaged in World War II. The leaders of Christ Church believed that the "Shrine of the Patriots," or the "Cathedral of Democracy," should serve as a spiritual beacon during the war. In 1943, at the suggestion of Kloman, the church dedicated the "United Nations Chapel." Erected in the box pew at the northeast corner of the sanctuary, it

FIGURE 47
The United Nations Chapel, dedicated in 1943. Christ Church Archives.

was "set aside for the use of those who enter the Church to pray for relatives and friends serving in the Armed forces of the United Nations and for the winning of a just and righteous peace" (see Figure 47). Kloman reminded the members that "from colonial days on those who fought against tyranny and oppression have sought here from Almighty God—and found—the wisdom, the strength and the courage to sustain them." Thus by dedicating the chapel the church carried on "the heritage left to it by those who have worshiped here in the past." The dedication ceremonies were attended by the bishop coadjutor, and the mayor, the secretary of the Philadelphia Federation of Churches, as well as representatives from eighteen countries.[17]

Throughout the war the church also served a variety of more typical functions. It tried to support its members who served in the armed forces as well as the families they left behind. The "Ivy League" club, a box-lunch program for families of those in the service, met regularly. Christ Church also opened its doors to servicemen stationed in the area. Various activities for the Coast Guard, merchant seamen, and the military police took place in the Neighborhood House, while the church welcomed servicemen to both regular and special services. In order to serve civilians, Christ Church volunteered to serve as an air-raid shelter.[18]

Kloman's approach to World War II went beyond patriotism to dealing with the underlying causes of the conflict. Recognizing that the kind of racial and creedal prejudices that led to atrocities such as those committed in Nazi Germany were present to some degree everywhere, he worked to help his parishioners recognize these prejudices and deal with them. In particular, he reached out to the Jewish community, some of whom were already friends of Christ Church as a result of the Neighborhood Businessmen's Association. A special and long lasting relationship was established with Mikveh Israel, the first synagogue in Philadelphia. Although the Jewish congregation had moved from its old city location on Cherry Street to Second and York in north Philadelphia, Christ Church still felt a special bond with it. After all, the vestry had urged the city in 1740 to let both Catholics and Jews establish places of worship, and in 1782, when Mikveh Israel was close to foreclosure, members of Christ Church contributed generously. Kloman renewed this relationship in 1943 by helping to establish a joint dinner that is still held yearly by the two congregations. After the war, Kloman urged the Jewish congregation to rebuild its synagogue in the downtown location, a goal that was eventually achieved in the 1970s.[19] In addition, each armistice day the Neighborhood Businessmen's Association sponsored a "prayer for peace" service, which Kloman led jointly with a rabbi, often Rabbi D. A. Jessurum Cardozo from Mikveh Israel.

Kloman showed great compassion for blacks as well. As thousands of African Americans moved to northern cities to work in the defense industries, racial tensions increased greatly. In 1943 several race riots occurred, the most serious one being in Detroit, where it took six thousand federal troops to bring order after thirty hours of rioting. While Philadelphia avoided rioting, racial tensions led to the only major labor strike during the war; in 1944 the streetcar and bus operators walked off their jobs after the War Manpower Commission forced the Philadelphia Transportation Company to hire blacks as motormen and conductors. Federal troops had to be brought in to get the trolleys and buses running again.[20]

Showing concern for this increase in racial tensions, Kloman asked his congregation to admit their racial prejudice openly and then begin to deal with it. In his prayer at the "Day of Prayer for Peace" service in 1943 he asked "God's forgiveness for our selfishness, our bitterness, our indifference, and our injustice to each other. We have been blind to what was happening outside our gates, we have acted as though the color of a man's skin in some way affected his right to freedom." A few months later he asserted that it was of the "utmost importance that we of Christ Church Parish should confess our failure individually and corporately to do all that we might have done to understand and appreciate others as members of a common family. Having made that confession we will go on to conquer our racial and group prejudices by the grace given us by Jesus Christ." To deal with the practical issues of the day, the vestry of Christ Church met with representatives of the Federation of Churches in 1943 and agreed with their suggestion to keep the church open as a "sanctuary" where "oppressed members of either race could go when disturbances take place."[21]

Given the high ideals shown during the war, it is not surprising that Christ Church welcomed the formation of the United Nations in 1945. The Sunday before the San Francisco Conference met to found the organization, the church prayed for God's guidance and blessing on the meeting. Kloman reminded his parishioners that members of the conference could not achieve the desired result alone. "Upon the peoples of the world rests the responsibility to establish by their faith in Almighty God the spiritual foundation upon which any organization or world order and peace must rest." In the summer of 1945, after the United States ratified the charter, Christ Church hosted the United Nations Council of Philadelphia for a special service of thanksgiving. Services on United Nations Day continued to be a regular feature of Christ Church for many years. In March of 1946 the parish meeting unanimously passed a resolution supporting the United Nations.[22]

* * *

Christ Church celebrated its 250th anniversary in 1945. The end of the war brought victory, but it also brought great uncertainty about the future of the nation and the world. Christ Church considered itself to be the "Nation's Church." It believed that it had played an important role in the founding of the nation and in nurturing the democratic ideals World War II was fought to preserve. Yet far more than the nation as a whole did, Christ Church faced an uncertain future; while it welcomed the nation's return to peace, it did not share in its prosperity. The anniversary gave the church a chance to revel in its past before taking a serious look at its future.

The anniversary celebration focused on the ideals of Christ Church rather than on narrow, antiquarian history. In 1941 the committee in charge reported that the main theme should be "religious tolerance and religious progress of all religions throughout the world." The committee further suggested that "as a part of this large general objective the duty of Christ Church to aid in the religious and physical improvement of all of Philadelphia and particularly in the community in which it is located" should be emphasized. The celebration four years later reflected this theme. The church produced a booklet that outlined the church's history and extolled its many valuable treasures, but the focus was on monthly lectures on such topics as "The Government and the Peace," "Employment and the Peace, " "Religious Cooperation," "The Church and the Community," and "Unity— Whence and Whither." The celebration ended in November with the lord bishop of Derby leading the anniversary service and with a parish family dinner.[23]

While the end of the war and the 250th anniversary brought celebrations, the situation of Christ Church seemed to present more problems than opportunities. For the previous sixteen years, including all Kloman's years in Philadelphia, the church had been responding to national crises and the path it needed to take seemed obvious. With the return of peace and prosperity, the "Nation's church" needed once again to take stock of its situation and decide on its future direction.

In many respects, the situation looked bleak, not just for Christ Church but for Philadelphia as a whole. Between 1930 and 1940, the population of the city had declined by 0.8 percent, while the counties around it had grown by 7 percent. Of more concern to Christ Church, the part of the city that had been within the original city limits—the downtown section—now had fewer people residing in it than had been there in 1810. And the people who lived there were largely those who could not afford to move out. By 1930 the downtown residential districts were characterized by "poverty, low skills and low status." In 1950 more than 70,000 structures in the city lacked indoor bathrooms or were dilapidated, and, despite the population decline, over-crowding was a serious problem. The title of an article in *Business Week* in 1942 expressed the overall situation well: "Philadelphia's Ills: Diagnosis by Real Estate Specialist Calls for Surgery and Rigorous Rehabilitation to Cure Bad Case of Big-City Blight." Years of corrupt, conservative government had resulted in an infrastructure badly in need of repair and basic services badly in need of improvement.[24]

The situation Christ Church faced immediately after the war seemed as ominous as that faced by the city as a whole. With the acceleration of move-ment to the suburbs, Christ Church members moved farther and farther away from the church. At the same time the nature of the business commu-nity surrounding the church was changing, as warehouses and manufac-turers gradually either moved or closed; thus the number of people who worked in the area declined. As a result of these changes, the church elimi-nated evening prayer and the Tuesday and Friday noonday services in 1946, leaving only one on Wednesdays. Attendance at the Lenten services also de-creased, with only the Wednesday service remaining large. While attendance at Sunday morning services remained about the same, the number of mem-bers gradually declined. From 1945 to 1950 the number of communicants de-clined from 592 to 537, with 107 members transferring their membership.[25]

The most serious problem, as usual, was money. After finally wiping out the deficit from the Depression, in 1943, the church once again faced serious financial problems in 1947. When pledges for only $11,354 were received to cover a budget of more than $40,000, the vestry decided that in lieu of the sermon one Sunday in January "there [would] be a meeting of the congrega-tion to discuss the finances of Christ Church and the place of Christ Church in the community." While the immediate results of this meeting are un-known, two years later there was a deficit of more than $1,500.[26] Clearly the leadership of Christ Church had to take a close look at the situation the church faced and come up with some creative solutions.

Determining the future of Christ Church became more urgent in 1949 with the resignation of Kloman to become rector of St. Alban's Church in Washington, D.C., a church with almost four times as many members as Christ Church.[27] Perhaps significantly, this was the first time that any rector of Christ Church had resigned to go to another church.

The vestry, encouraged by Kloman, took his resignation as an opportunity to examine seriously the future course of Christ Church. Some even questioned whether there was a reason to keep the church open as a parish; perhaps the church building should become a museum. If it were to stay open, should it merely try to concentrate on being a parish church and not worry about the visitors and its national reputation? If so, then the vestry would recruit a young minister. Or should it continue its wider role in Philadelphia and the nation? If it should, where would the money come from? Christ Church had reached a crucial point in its 254-year history.

After serious discussions the vestry decided to *expand* the role Christ Church would play in the nation, bringing its message not just to those who came to visit the church but to all those who would listen on the radio or read newspapers—to become, more emphatically, the "Nation's Church." In so doing the vestrymen were shifting the church's delicate balance more in the direction of Christ Church as historic structure than it had been during Kloman's rectorship. The vestry committed itself to raising the funds from outside sources to accomplish this goal. The parish ministry would not be neglected, but the vestry believed that Christ Church had a responsibility to speak out, to make Christianity a vital force in the world.[28]

In one sense the campaign to establish the importance and widen the influence of Christ Church had already begun. In 1947 Congress designated Christ Church as a national shrine. Such a designation not only brought symbolic prestige, it also meant that the government would take over the church building if its parish ministry ended. Then in 1949 Christ Church entered into its official relationship with the National Park Service, becoming part of Independence National Historic Park. This arrangement actually grew out of the continued concern over the fire danger faced by the church; this time the leadership focused on the buildings to the south of the church, between Church Street and Market. In 1947, under the leadership of Judge Lewis Van Dusen, president judge of the orphans court of Philadelphia and a warden of Christ Church, the vestry joined forces with the Colonial Society of Pennsylvania to lobby for creation of a block-sized park south of the church. Because of the timing of the drive, the group hoped to make the park part of the Independence Hall project. As a result of the support of Charles E.

Peterson, the architect for Independence Park, a massive lobbying campaign, and a masterful presentation by Judge Edwin Lewis, the moving force behind Independence Park, before a congressional committee, a park for Christ Church was included in the legislation creating Independence Park.[29]

It took twenty years and another lobbying campaign before this park was completed, but as a result of the initial legislation, in 1949 Christ Church entered into an agreement with the National Park Service.[30] Under this agreement Christ Church agreed to maintain the building in its original condition, as nearly as possible, and to allow the public and the National Park Service access to the building whenever it did not conflict with the religious uses of the building. In return the Park Service agreed to provide technical expertise to help in the protection and restoration of the building, to provide an appropriate marker attesting to the church's national stature, and, when funds were appropriated, to acquire the two buildings directly south of the church. While the agreement with the National Park Service may not have seemed very significant at the time, in the long run it would be extremely valuable to Christ Church. As the Independence Park project became a reality and the number of visitors increased vastly, so too did the visibility of Christ Church. In this respect, the original desire to protect the church from fire took on much greater significance.

* * *

The leadership of Christ Church wanted it to be far more than a stop for tourists visiting Independence Hall. They intended the church to be a nationwide influence for spiritual good, a beacon to light the way through what they saw as troubled times.

The person the vestry chose to lead them in this endeavor was E. A. deBordenave, or "Froggy," as everyone called him, a young minister from Virginia. DeBordenave, who was recommended by the bishop, had up until this time confined his non-wartime service to the diocese of Virginia. DeBordenave had been rector of St. Paul's Church in Alexandria prior to the war. After serving as a navy chaplain in the Pacific, he returned to become assistant to the bishop of Virginia, dean of the church schools for the diocese. At the time of his call to Christ Church he was also serving as rector of St. John's Church in Tappahannock.

Described as a "live wire," a "real Virginia Cracker," and a lot of fun, deBordenave like his predecessor loved people, always finding time to talk with them. He was well liked by the businessmen in the neighborhood. But he had an even greater affinity with young people, particularly those of college age. DeBordenave was an evangelical in the original sense of the word, desiring to proclaim the gospel to all the world. It was this interest in spreading the influence of Christianity throughout the land that led him to Christ Church. Only his belief that Christ Church could play a major role in the nation as a whole could have convinced him to leave his native Virginia and devote the "best years of his ministry" to the Philadelphia church.[31]

Before launching any specific plan, the vestry, under the leadership of deBordenave, spent a year intensively studying exactly what role the church should play. The vestrymen decided that Christ Church should work in three areas. Two—church unity and inter-racial understanding—continued the earlier thrusts of Washburn and Kloman. The third was new—"the field of National, state and local government and community business and civic activities." The aim was to "spread Christian principles through emphasis on Christ Church's position in the days when the leaders of the government believed that religion and Christianity were important."[32]

The end result of this study was a program known as the United Spiritual Action or USA campaign, launched in November 1951. Behind this campaign was the belief that evil was "overpowering humanity with two integrated forces—tyranny and moral degeneracy." Abroad, fascism, nazism, and communism were devastating the lives of millions of people. Communism seemed a threat to America as well. This threat was much greater because, as a USA brochure put it, "moral degeneracy, like cancer, is destroying the fiber of [American] society . . . Corruption infests every phase of life. Deceit, concealment, bribery, slander and murderous force are accepted means, not only to attain evil purposes but in the service of worthy ends." The answer to fighting these evils was not to be found in "vague ideals" like "the American Way of Life" or "democracy," since most people did not know what they meant and had forgotten the "roots that gave them power." Rather, the answer lay in reaffirming the fundamental truths on which this nation was founded, truths that could only be found in the "Judeo-Christian tradition." A false religion—communism—could only be overcome by another religion—"a true one." The history of Christ Church, the leadership felt, uniquely qualified it to put forth "a spiritual call to arms" to the nation as a whole, to inspire Americans to strengthen their faith just as it had given spiritual strength to the Continental Congress. All Americans needed to realize, as deBordenave put it, that they "cannot have what Independence Hall symbolizes without having what Christ Church symbolizes."[33]

Thus on November 13, 1951 the Christ Church congregation launched the USA campaign by adopting the "Christ Church Declaration." This declaration affirmed that

the foundation of the American political, economic and social system, and the basis for any enduring society, is the truth that
God acknowledges every man as His son and each man has the right and duty to establish this relationship by the best means open to him. Therefore, each man has the obligation . . . to do all in his power to aid his fellow man in achieving this relationship.[34]

It went on to assert that "this truth is the only force powerful enough to defeat the evil confronting us." Therefore, they pledged themselves to do everything in their power "to persuade men to commit themselves, their lives and their fortunes, according to this truth.

Out of this declaration came four fields of activity in which the church felt it should be involved: (1) to remind everyone that God is the basis of all of America's laws and way of life and to call all Americans to renew their faith; (2) To further the worldwide ecumenical movement aimed at uniting Christian churches; (3) to "foster mutual understanding, respect and cooperation between Christianity and Judaism, breaking down the barriers that separate men and emphasizing the common points in their differing faiths"; and (4) to "strengthen government, business and education in their manifold contributions toward the good life for mankind."[35]

The USA campaign fit in well with the mood of the country in general. A tremendous revival in interest in religion occurred following World War II, and there was a growing consensus that in order to be truly patriotic one had to be religious. A nation shaken by the destructive power of the bomb and obsessed with the threat of the atheistic communists naturally turned to religion. Thus a prayer room with a window depicting George Washington praying was constructed in the Capitol, and the phrase "under God" was added to the Pledge of Allegiance. As President Eisenhower put it, "Our government makes no sense unless it is founded on a deeply felt religious faith—and I don't care what it is."[36]

The church proposed to accomplish the goals of the USA campaign through a variety of avenues. The 250,000 visitors who stopped at Christ Church would be greeted by paid guides who would interpret the church's history in a manner aimed at increasing the visitors' spiritual and historical awareness. As part of this effort to open the church even more to the public,

FIGURE 48
People gather to sign the "Christ Church Declaration." Christ Church Archives.

major renovations to the physical structure were planned. The church would also be used as a platform for prominent speakers on a variety of subjects. More important, Christ Church would, for the first time, attempt to reach out to those who never came near the church or its neighborhood. It would serve as a publishing agency for "inspirational writings" and would distribute speeches and other promotional material to schools, churches and trade union papers. In addition, it would use radio and television to spread its message.[37]

This ambitious project got off to a promising start in March 1952 with a large meeting at the Franklin Institute and a luncheon at the Bellevue Stratford Hotel co-sponsored by William Schnader, a prominent Republican lawyer, and Albert Greenfield, the Democratic real-estate entrepreneur and banker (see Figure 48). Former United States Senator George Wharton Pepper agreed to serve as honorary chairman of the campaign, and the first advisory committee, formed to help the church determine how best to put the Declaration into practice, was headed by the Honorable Owen J. Roberts, former associate justice of the United States Supreme Court. He was joined by Judge Harold Medina, Harold Dodds, the president of Princeton University, General George C. Marshall, Governor John S. Fine of Pennsylvania, Dr. John Shryock, director of Johns Hopkins Institute of Medical History, movie and radio star Robert Montgomery, and industrialists Edwin Cox, Henning Prentis and William K. Ruffin. Not surprisingly, given this distinguished list of supporters, the Declaration and the USA campaign received widespread publicity. The declaration was read before Congress and broadcast to many nations behind the iron curtain.[38]

Assessing the success of the campaign is difficult; however, it is clear that the more concrete goals were achieved. For the first time since Washburn's era, the church building underwent major repairs and renovations. The entire interior of the church was redecorated, using what was determined to be the original "stone" color, with colonial blue over the chancel and gallery. Most important, thirty years after Washburn first suggested it, the open gas lights were replaced with electricity. The forty-two-year-old coal heating system was replaced with an oil one. The organ underwent $20,000 worth of repairs, most of which was underwritten by its donor, Mary Louise Curtis Bok, now Mrs. Efrem Zimbalist. Three of the bells, including the two given by the Neighborhood Businessmen's Association, were recast to achieve a true tone. This was largely financed by the businessmen. All the exterior bricks were repointed and the entire church was repainted.[39]

The painting of the steeple and tower clearly produced the most spectacular, if unwanted, publicity for the church. Cameramen from all the major media who had gathered to take publicity pictures of the painting of the church instead photographed a near tragedy when a ladder snapped, stranding two men at the top of the spire. Pictures of a man hanging onto a window ledge graced the front page of all the local newspapers![40] (see Figure 49).

The campaign also achieved its goal of attracting more visitors to the church. These visitors were greeted by two paid guides who provided tours from 9 to 5 each day of the week. Many more special services were held, including annual services for the Negro Masonic Service, the Society of the War of 1812, the Colonial Society, the Baronial Order of Magna Carta, the Benjamin Franklin Post of the American Legion, and the 315th Infantry Association, to name a few (see Figure 50). Many outstanding laymen spoke at these services, including Governor Theodore R. McKeldin of Maryland, who was made an honorary vestryman, Mayor Joseph Clark, District At-

FIGURE 49
*Photograph of the ladder
that snapped, stranding a
man (barely visible) at the
top. Christ Church Ar-
chives.*

torney Richardson Dilworth, George Wharton Pepper, and columnist Mar-
quis Childs; these speakers attracted large crowds and reached thousands
more on radio and television.[41]

DeBordenave and his staff made a major effort to spread the message of
the declaration through the printed media as well. Leaflets were put in all
midcity hotels, schools, colleges, YMCAs and travel agencies. *The Story of
Christ Church*, a greatly expanded and improved guide book, was produced
to be sold to tourists and distributed to libraries. Innumerable press releases
were sent to newspapers and magazines. Within a six-month period in 1953

FIGURE 50
E. A. deBordenave (rector, 1950–1955) and verger Harvey Mertz lead procession into Christ Church. Christ Church Archives.

the press activity included 1,472 releases sent to 452 newspapers and magazines, 39,278 pieces of educational material distributed, 19 pictures printed in newspapers with 114 articles, 17 telecasts and 12 radio broadcasts. All of these publicity pieces tried both to promote Christ Church and to further the theme of "freedom's dependence on religion."[42]

No doubt deBordenave himself was the most effective means of promoting Christ Church and the USA campaign. Using USA money to hire an assistant to carry on much of the day-to-day activities of the parish, deBordenave spoke to any organization that would invite him. He met regularly with the Neighborhood Businessmen's Association, which continued to be a vital organization; deBordenave seemed to enjoy it as much as Kloman had. Expanding on Washburn's and Kloman's practice of giving invocations and benedictions, deBordenave presented speeches to civic, professional, and charitable organizations in the Philadelphia area on a variety of subjects. Never directly promoting either Christ Church or religion, he used his homey, southern style to get his message across subtly. These efforts were aided by a public relations director, Lucille Clark, and by his own involvement in a host of organizations. He was a board member of the Philadelphia Convention and Visitors' Bureau, vice chairman of the Philadelphia Housing Association, on the Citizens' Committee for City Planning and the Citizens Charter Committee, Chaplain to the Philadelphia Reserve Fire Force, and President of the Elfreth's Alley Association. He also continued the traditional involvement of Christ Church rectors in charitable work, serving on the boards of the Episcopal City Mission and the Evangelical Society as well as the Society for the Advancement of Christianity in Pennsylvania.[43]

In keeping with the nationwide goals of the USA campaign, deBordenave was active in a number of national religious organizations. He was a board member of the national departments of Christian Education and Christian Social Relations for the Episcopal Church, the Evangelical Educational Society, and the Hood Conference. He also served as editor of the *Protestant Episcopal Standard*, a low church publication that was headquartered in the Neighborhood House for a while. He was particularly interested in the Episcopal Evangelical Fellowship, serving as vice president. DeBordenave also spoke at a number of religious conferences in the mid-Atlantic and southern states. Through these speeches he attempted to achieve the larger goal of the campaign, deepening the spiritual involvement and strength of Americans.[44]

This goal was also addressed by deBordenave's numerous appearances on college campuses. His background in education qualified him well for the many speeches he gave and conferences he led at colleges throughout Pennsylvania and surrounding states. While some of these events were merely one-hour speeches, more commonly he was invited by the Student Christian Movement to lead a two day conference. DeBordenave seemed in his natural element staying up to all hours of the night helping young people explore and deepen their faith.[45]

The USA campaign and deBordenave's efforts to publicize Christ Church clearly "put Christ Church on the map" on a national level. Never before had the church had such nationwide publicity. By the end of deBordenave's short stay, the long process, started by Washburn, of establishing Christ Church as a major historical attraction and symbol was successful. Further efforts would be aided by the rise of the Independence Mall area and the resurgence of Society Hill, but the basic groundwork had already been laid before these movements had gotten very far. By 1955 Christ Church had established itself as the most historically important church in Philadelphia and one of the most important in the nation. While much of this was based on fact, it was also a result of a very successful public relations campaign, a campaign that was in many ways driven by necessity. The physical location of Christ Church, leading to a loss of members and financial difficulty, forced it to rely on its history for survival.

It is interesting to compare the stature of Christ Church as an historical attraction with other churches in Philadelphia. St. Peter's, which shared much of the history that Christ Church emphasized and whose members were as important in the early years of the country as were the members of Christ Church, was experiencing a number of internal problems during the years of Christ Church's rise to national stature. Moreover, its location was even less advantageous than that of Christ Church; while Christ Church was surrounded by respectable businesses, St. Peter's came to be surrounded by flophouses and brothels. Thus it never established itself as a major tourist attraction or patriotic symbol. The Presbyterians, who were in reality more important than the Anglicans to American independence, had torn down their first churches and thus did not have the physical structure to accentuate their history. Gloria Dei, or Old Swedes Church, had the building, but not the important members to publicize. The Quakers' pacifism left them with a far less dramatic story to tell, despite their importance in Pennsylvania history. With an extremely impressive building and a history to match it, Christ

Church had little competition in Philadelphia for the title of the "Nation's church."

* * *

At the same time that the leadership of Christ Church was running a nation-wide campaign, it was equally interested in running an active local parish. DeBordenave was as concerned with challenging his congregation as he was in awakening the nation. While the USA campaign had a strong anticommunist element, deBordenave was quick to condemn the "poison" of McCarthyism, the symptoms of which were "distrust, suspicion, distortion of our forms of justice, assumption of guilt before proof is furnished a jury, violations of civil liberties and the acceptance of distorted facts as being completely true," all of which it was the Christian's responsibility to stop. If one accepted the basic premise of the USA campaign, that God intended all people to be free, then all Christians had to "set their hearts and minds and strength against" this tyranny. DeBordenave was not afraid to criticize both political parties the Sunday before election day in 1952; he condemned them for manifesting "the pride of power" that leads them to "self-righteousness" rather than "self-criticism" and thus "blinds them to obvious fallacies and obvious injustices" and deceives the public.[46]

Moreover, just as he challenged college students to search and grow, he tried to make members of his congregation deepen their spiritual life by study and searching. Shortly after arriving, deBordenave informed his congregation that since most Episcopalians were woefully ignorant of their religion, he planned to preach a series of sermons explaining its basic precepts. To help people grow still further the Explorers Group was formed; originally designed for "young people" and later opened to everyone, the group met weekly with the rector to study their faith.[47]

The rector also encouraged the already existing groups within Christ Church. Although their numbers were small, the Girls' Friendly Society, Altar Guild, and Mary Volunteers continued to meet regularly. The Young People's Fellowship managed to average fifteen teenagers at their weekly meetings, and the Golden Age Club, which attracted neighborhood people, continued to be a large and active group. While there were few young people to serve in the neighborhood, there still was a basketball team and a small, but active Sunday School.[48]

DeBordenave was aided in these activities by a number of able staff members. Two assistants, William Eckman and later Eric Allen, did much of the day-to-day work of the parish when deBordenave was out of town. Harvey Mertz, who retired as sexton in 1950, continued on as parish visitor and verger. Charles Mitchell, a candidate for orders, who had previously worked as a state police officer, took over as custodian and assisted the rector with the boys' clubs and Young People's Fellowship.

The members of Christ Church also continued their involvement in Christ Church Hospital; in fact, changes in the administrative structure during deBordenave's years actually increased that involvement. Having decided that the running of such an institution was not necessarily suited to six vestrymen, in 1951 the board of managers created an operating committee to handle more of the day-to-day decisions, reserving the more major decisions to itself. This Operating Committee, which consisted of twenty-one people, included three women, thus increasing the role of women in running the women's home. It also included deBordenave; prior to this time the rector of Christ Church had no official role in the hospital. In 1952 the Ladies' Committee was invited to attend the meetings of the Operating Committee, still further expanding the role of women.[49]

Other important changes occurred at the hospital in the 1940s and 1950s. The method most patients used for payment gradually changed; in 1944 the board decided that a woman no longer had to contribute all her property to the institution in order to be admitted. Anyone with less than $15,000 in property could enter and pay a monthly fee. Moreover, as the Pennsylvania Department of Public Assistance and Social Security began to provide for older people in need, a majority of residents soon became recipients of this aid.[50] The board also hired a professional social worker to evaluate all applicants. While the admissions committee continued to visit each applicant in her home, the members felt the need for more detailed information than had been provided by the Episcopal City Mission.

Neither the continuing activities of Christ Church members nor all deBordenave's outreach led to increased membership for Christ Church, but it did lead to increased attendance at the services. The number of communicants remained stable during his five-year tenure and the average number of confirmands remained between fifteen and twenty, the same as during the last years of Kloman. But the number of people attending morning prayer and communion increased from a total of 7,800 people in 1950 to more than 11,500 in 1954.[51]

The USA campaign also at least temporarily increased the financial stability of the church. While the campaign failed to achieve its fund-raising goals, during the three years it existed it allowed Christ Church to achieve financial prosperity, something that seemed a faint dream in the late 1940s. Pledges remained fairly stable, but since the salary of the assistant minister, the guides, one custodian, upkeep on the church, and heat and lights during the week were all paid out of USA campaign money, it was possible for the church to have a surplus of more than five thousand dollars in 1953. While the heating system and some of the organ repairs had to be paid for with borrowed money, the total income from 1950 to 1954 exceeded expenditures by $13,835.[52]

In 1955 deBordenave announced his decision to resign the rectorship to return to his native Virginia. Having suffered a massive heart attack in 1954, he no longer felt physically able to perform the extremely strenuous duties required of any rector of Christ Church. In February 1955 he left Philadelphia to become rector of a rural parish in Middleburg, Virginia. He left behind a church that had successfully made the transition from the social service orientation of the Washburn-Kloman era to a more high-profile, leadership role. This role was, in part, mandated by circumstances; the neighborhood that Christ Church served had ceased to exist. However, it also fit in well both with the renewed emphasis on religion in the 1950s and the tremendous interest in developing Independence Park and showcasing Philadelphia's history. Christ Church still had problems; it still had a small, widely scattered congregation that did not contribute large amounts in pledges, a physical plant that required massive amounts of money to maintain, and an immediate neighborhood that continued to remain commercial long after the residential resurgence had begun in other areas of Center City. But it seemed to have found a proper niche for itself in the postwar era.

NOTES

1. Letter from Olivia Kloman, wife of Felix Kloman, to author, n.d. [1986].
2. Rector's Message, *Christ Church Newsletter*, Sept. 21, 1947, August 21, 1938, Sept. 23, 1945, Oct. 8, 1944.
3. William White, interview with author, Philadelphia, August 5, 1986.
4. *Journal of the Diocese of Pennsylvania*, 1942–1948. William White, interview with author, June 13, 1986; Jane O'Neill (née Jordan), interview with author, Philadelphia, June 14, 1986.
5. Christ Church, *Leaflet*, April 19, 1942. The *Leaflet* was a weekly newsletter started by Kloman.

6. The survey is discussed in the Vestry Minutes, June 20, Sept. 26, Oct. 25, 1938 and Nov. 20, 1939. The activities are discussed in the *Leaflet*, June 18, July 30, 1939; Sept. 16, 1940. William White, interview with author, June 13, 1986; Jane O'Neill, interview with author, June 14, 1986; Vestry Minutes, Oct. 17, 1938.

7. Jane O'Neill, interview with author, June 14, 1986.

8. For the vestry's tribute to Helen Washburn see Vestry Minutes, Oct. 16, 1939. For information on the Sunday school see ibid., Sept. 18, Oct. 17, Dec. 18, 1939; *Leaflet*, Oct. 5, 1941, *Journal of the Diocese of Pennsylvania*, 1940, 107, 135. Christ Church still had a larger Sunday school than most center city churches. St. Luke and the Epiphany, for example, with a membership of 779, had only 33 in the Sunday school.

9. Jane O'Neill, interview with author, June 14, 1986; *Leaflet*, Feb. 5, 1939.

10. Christ Church Hospital Ladies' Committee, Minutes, 1940s, Christ Church Archives; Vestry Minutes, Feb. 20, June 19, 1939; *Leaflet*, May 7, 1939; *Leaflet*, May 10, 1948. A copy of the program of the 1940 Fair is located at the HSP. It made $1,100 in its first year. Jane O'Neill, interview with author, June 14, 1986.

11. The Joseph Volunteers and the Guild of Mary were introduced in the *Leaflet*, Nov. 14, 1948. The other activities are described in the *Leaflet* throughout the Kloman years.

12. "The Old Christ Church Neighborhood Business Men's Association," *Southern Churchman* 111, 43 (Oct. 27, 1945): 3.

13. Ibid., 4; Christ Church Neighborhood Business Men's Association, Brochure, Christ Church Archives.

14. Christ Church Neighborhood Businessmen's Association, Brochure, 3; "The Old Christ Church Neighborhood Business Men's Association," 3–4; Jane O'Neill, interview with author, June 14, 1986.

15. "Our Good Neighbor—Old Christ Church," *The 3-3 News, Girard Trust Corn Exchange Bank* (c. 1952), 17.

16. *Leaflet*, July 24, 1938, p. 1, September 17, 1939.

17. *Leaflet*, Feb. 21, 1943.

18. Vestry Minutes, Feb. 16, May 18, June 15, 1942, Feb 23, March 22, April 26, 1943; *Leaflet*, Sept. 27, 1942, May 16, 1943.

19. Discussed in an article in the *Evening Bulletin*, Feb. 9, 1952. For the founding of Mikveh Israel and its financial problems, see Edwin Wolf and Maxwell Whiteman, *The History of the Jews of Philadelphia from Colonial Times to the Age of Jackson* (Philadelphia: Jewish Publication Society of America, 1956), 115–45.

20. Margaret Tinkcom, "Depression and War, 1929–1946," in Weigley, *Philadelphia*, 644–45. For information on the Detroit riots, see Harvard Sitkoff, "The Detroit Riot of 1943," *Michigan History* 53 (Fall 1969): 183–206.

21. *Leaflet*, Nov. 11, 1943, Feb. 13, 1944. Vestry Minutes, June 28, 1943.

22. *Leaflet*, June 10, 1945, March 10, 1946.

23. Vestry Minutes, June 16, 1941; *Two Hundred Fiftieth Anniversary of Christ Church*, Program, Christ Church Archives.

24. Warner, *Private City*, 171; "Philadelphia's Ills: Diagnosis by Real Estate Specialist Calls for Surgery and Rigorous Rehabilitation to Cure Bad Case of Big-City Blight" *Business Week*, Feb. 7, 1942, pp. 35–36.

25. Service Record Books, Christ Church Archives. In 1938 the Lenten services were all about equally attended, averaging 112 people at the weekday services. By 1947 the average was

down to 65, with the Wednesday service attracting more than the other four put together. See also List of Confirmations, Christ Church Archives. Kloman listed transfers in and out in his register; *Journal of the Diocese of Pennsylvania*, 1945, 1950.

26. Vestry Minutes, Jan.5 and 27, 1947; Sept. 22, 1947; Jan. 25, 1949.

27. Vestry Minutes, June 19, 1949.

28. William White, interview with author, June 13, 1986.

29. See Vestry Minutes, April 28, 1947; Joint Committee on Christ Church and Other Historic Sites, Minutes, May 13, 1947, Christ Church Archives. For a thorough treatment of the creation of Independence National Historic Park see Constance M. Greiff, *Independence: The Creation of a National Park* (Philadelphia: University of Pennsylvania Press, 1987). Peterson's role is described on p. 54. Lewis was originally skeptical of including the Christ Church park, but eventually supported it. His testimony is discussed on pp. 66–67. Discussion of the massive lobbying campaign, orchestrated primarily by Judge Van Dusen, can be found in the minutes of the Joint Committee on Christ Church and Other Historic Sites. The actual bill is reproduced in these minutes.

30. Joint Committee on Christ Church and Other Historic Sites, Minutes; Vestry Minutes, April 28, 1947; March 30, Oct. 25 1948, Nov. 22, 1949; Frank Worthington Melvin, "The Miracle of Christ Church Park: Report to the Council of Colonial Society of Pennsylvania," *The Colonial Society of Pennsylvania, Christ Church Park Edition* (Philadelphia, 1958), 6–7.

31. Cyane deBordenave, wife of the Reverend E. A. deBordenave, to author, April 20, 1986.

32. The vestry commissioned the John Price Jones Corporation to study the mission of the church. Unfortunately its report cannot be found. The report of the committee that considered it is found in the Vestry Minutes, Feb. 1, 1951.

33. *A Declaration by Christ Church in Philadelphia* (Philadelphia, n.d. [1952]), *A Program of Action for the Nation's Church* (Philadephia, n.d. [1952]), 6; *Beacon*, Jan. 1, 1952. (The *Beacon* replaced the *Leaflet* as the church's newsletter.)

34. *A Declaration by Christ Church in Philadelphia, November, 1951* (Philadelphia, 1951).

35. Ibid., p. 13.

36. See Winthrop Hudson, *Religion in America*, 3d edition (New York: Scribner's, 1981), 384; Sydney Ahlstrom, *A Religious History of the American People*, 950–60; Martin Marty, *The New Shape of American Religion* (New York: Harper, 1959), 6–30. The quote is from *Christian Century* 71 (1954), quoted in Ahlstrom, 954.

37. *Report on the United Spiritual Action Program at Christ Church in Philadelphia, March 15, 1953.*

38. "Historic Christ Church Issues a New Declaration," *The Witness*, May 15, 1952, p. 1; "Christ Church Is Organizing National Spiritual Call to Arms," *Evening Bulletin*, March 4, 1952; "Christ Church Program Ready," ibid., March 30, 1952; see also the *Philadelphia Daily News*, April 4, 16, 1952; *Philadelphia Inquirer*, March 5, 12, 27, 1952. Copies of these are all located in the Christ Church Archives, without page numbers.

39. *A Report on the United Spiritual Action Program at Christ Church in Philadelphia, March 15, 1953.*

40. Lucille Clark, interview with author, Philadelphia, August 2, 1987.

41. *A Report of Christ Church in Philadelphia, 1950–1954* (Philadelphia, 1954).

42. *Beacon*, Feb. 14, 1954, p. 5.

43. *A Report of Christ Church in Philadelphia, 1950–54* .

44. Ibid. See, for example, Vestry Minutes, Nov. 24, 1952, which describes a conference of

fifty-five people from ten colleges in West Virginia. The Vestry Minutes of March 23, 1953, discuss other conferences. For a discussion of his involvement with the Hood Conference see the *Beacon*, June 1, 1952.

45. See the *Beacon*, Jan. 15, 1953, pp. 1–2, for a detailed discussion of a college conference. For mention of the numerous colleges to which he went to see, for example, Vestry Minutes, Nov. 24 and Dec. 15, 1952 and Mar 23, 1953.

46. "A Word from the Rector," *Beacon*, June 15, 1953, p. 1; "The Well Spring of Freedom," sermon preached at a service commemorating the signing of the Magna Carta, June 14, 1953, reprinted, *Beacon*, June 15, 1953, p. 3; *Beacon*, Dec. 1, 1952.

47. *Beacon*, March 21, 1954.

48. See the *Beacon* for the five years of deBordenave's rectorship.

49. Roberts, "Christ Church Hospital," 99; Board of Managers Minutes, March 19, 1951; Minutes of the Operating Committee, April 23, 1951, Feb. 18, 1952.

50. Roberts, "Christ Church Hospital," 98.

51. Communicants are found in the *Journals of the Diocese of Pennsylvania*, 1950–1954. Attendance figures are summarized in *A Report of Christ Church in Philadelphia, 1950–1954*.

52. *A Report of Christ Church in Philadelphia, 1950–1954*.

CHAPTER SIXTEEN

CONTINUITY IN CHANGING TIMES: THE RECTORSHIP OF ERNEST HARDING

Having successfully come through hard times and skillfully orchestrated a major change in the role the church played in the community, the vestry and congregation of Christ Church were in a good position to solidify that change. De-Bordenave had made a major effort to make Christ Church known throughout the country and to increase the emphasis on its historic influence. But five years was not enough time to institutionalize that role, and the USA campaign, with its emphasis on fighting communism, was more successful as a short-term crusade than as a long-term identity for the church. If Christ Church were going to be successful in establishing itself as the "Nation's Church" in the long run, the next rector would have to modify the anticommunist focus of deBordenave while keeping much of the public relations activities in which he had been engaged. At the same time the rector would have to increase the size of the congregation.

Ernest Harding, the person the vestry chose to accomplish these demanding tasks, was in many ways very different from deBordenave, but like his predecessor he seems to have been the right man at the right time (see Figure 51). By choosing Harding, the vestry replaced a true Virginia

FIGURE 51
The Reverend Ernest Harding (rector, 1955–1977) in pulpit. Christ Church Archives.

gentleman with a Scottish New Englander who was proud of both his ethnic heritage and his regional loyalty. Born and raised in Boston, Harding had graduated from Virginia Theological Seminary in 1935. From that year until his appointment to the rectorship of Christ Church he had served at the Church of the Messiah and Incarnation in Brooklyn, first as assistant and then as rector.[1]

Unlike the rectors discussed up until this point, Harding is well remembered by many current members of the church, and what is most striking about those remembrances is their similarity. Described as "a whirlwind" who, like Kloman, exhausted all those around him, a twenty-four-hour day seemed about twenty hours too short for him. Disarmingly charming when he wanted to be, a tremendous storyteller with a great sense of humor and an enticing twinkle in his eye, his warmth and kindness drew people to him. His sense of caring and a real gift for the "pastoral function" led many to think of him as a second father. A lifelong bachelor, Harding loved a good party and eagerly joined a number of social organizations. He was equally comfortable socializing with Philadelphia blue blood families and eating cheesesteaks with teenagers in South Philadelphia. This ability to mingle fit with his broad ranging interests; he loved music, the theater, gardening, traveling, cooking; he collected prints and antiques. Yet he was at the same time a humble person. Despite being a "militant low churchman," Harding believed strongly in formality and tradition. He had a real presence in the pulpit; as one person put it, "he looked the part of a priest." A "superb communicator," he delivered well thought out, practical sermons.

His ability to be formal when needed combined with his charming personality and his love of people made him an ideal representative of the church in the community. He served as chaplain of any organization that requested it, including the St. Andrew's Society, the Pennsylvania State Society of the Cincinnati, and the 325th Infantry Association of Philadelphia. He also served on the boards of a wide array of both religious and secular institutions, ranging from the Episcopal Evangelical Society to the American Museum of Jewish History. He was, as we will see, also extremely active in the diocese. All of these activities, combined with his work at Christ Church, led to his being honored with an honorary doctorate by his alma mater, Virginia Theological Seminary, in 1958.[2]

Above all, Harding was a deeply pious, devoted priest. He noted with dismay that "many take much more seriously the requirements of secular clubs and groups than they do those of the Christian Church," something of which he himself could never be accused. He called on his parishioners to accept the duties of a Christian: to worship every Sunday, to dedicate their unique talents to God's purposes, to pray daily, and to give money and time to the church.[3] The joy Harding found in a Christian life was well expressed in an Easter message:

Just to be alive is our opportunity to have the power of laughter and tears; to sound the depths of love; to take part in a game where the farthest stars are the goal; to be conscious of the infinite need about us, of our ability with the help of God to satisfy that need; yes, more to be aware of life ablaze with the Presence of God and to enter into companionship with Him—who wants a greater opportunity than this?[4]

Harding's charm combined with his good political sense led people to overlook his stubborn side and allowed him to accomplish controversial things. When he wanted the 1895 stone altar removed, for example, he casually mentioned that he might fall off the step some time during the liturgy; the vestry thus saw it as an issue of safety, rather than one of aesthetics. Similarly, as we will see, the vestry agreed with his request to remove the colored glass from the Palladian window despite the disapproval of many parishioners.

It would take such an extraordinary man to keep Christ Church alive and well, for the immediate neighborhood continued to deteriorate and the population base would take many years to be reestablished. In 1964 the diocese conducted a parish survey of every parish. It "arbitrarily" assigned a much larger area to the Christ Church "parish area" than the church had previously accepted, including areas north of Vine Street and all the way to South Street, and from the Delaware River to Broad Street, including the area around St. Peter's. Yet despite this large area, the entire population was only 11,394, only 177 of whom were Episcopalian. Moreover, as had been the case for decades, the ethnic and educational information available indicates that they were unlikely to *become* Episcopalian: 37 percent were nonwhite, mostly black, and the average educational level for the eight census tracts ranged from 6.8 to 9.0 years, compared to the median in Philadelphia of 9.6.[5]

Only Society Hill offered hope that Christ Church might once again become a real "parish church." Beginning in the 1950s the city undertook by far one of the largest urban renewal projects in the country in the vast area from Delaware Avenue to Sixth Street and South Street to Chestnut. For more than one hundred years this area had housed most of Philadelphia's population, but as the people moved west it had become a combination of commercial warehouses, dilapidated housing, and flophouses. Rather than tearing these deteriorating structures down, as was done in New York and other eastern cities, Philadelphia decided to restore those dating back to the eighteenth century. The city acquired all significant historic structures and resold them to private citizens for restoration.[6]

Harding believed that Christ Church should identify itself with this rebirth in center city in its early stages by having the rector live in the neighborhood. As a fund-raising brochure stated, "the present renewal of a residential area in Old Philadelphia is a challenge that the Church cannot ignore. Christ Church believes that its Rector should reside, as in the eighteenth and nineteenth centuries, among the people the Church will serve." Thus on his arrival in Philadelphia Harding rented an apartment in Society Hill, despite its still rather run-down character. Then in 1960, at his request, the vestry purchased a large eighteenth-century town house—the so-called "Wharton house" at 336 Spruce Street—to serve as a rectory (see Figure 52).

"One of the notable eighteenth-century dwellings remaining in the Old City," the four-story house still retained its "panelled walls, exquisitely turned mantels, cornices and a superb staircase," but needed major renovation. With the help of L. Arnold Nicholson, a vestryman who was active in Society Hill renovations, Christ Church painstakingly restored this home to its original charm and elegance, spending more than $70,000 in addition to the $30,000 purchase price.[7] While this seemed to some at the time to be an extravagant use of money for a small parish, the tremendous increase in property values in the area turned it into a wise investment. More important, the faith in Society Hill was justified. By 1964, 4.3 percent of the church's membership—twenty-five people—lived in Society Hill, one of only two census tracts that contained more than twenty members.[8]

While the long-term hope of Christ Church may have been in center city, the membership continued to be small. The number of communicants actually declined from 534 in 1955 to 407 in 1960, as people moved to more distant suburbs and many long-time members died. That alarming trend was reversed in the early 1960s, as the number of communicants gradually climbed to 460 by 1969. While this was not a large congregation, it did compare favorably with other center city churches.In fact, only St. Luke and the Epiphany had a larger number of communicants, and several, including St. Peter's, with only 173 communicants and six children in the Sunday School, were struggling to survive.[9] (See Figure 53.)

Christ Church members came from an increasingly wide geographic area (see Maps 5 and 6). While 4.3 percent now lived in Society Hill and an additional 8.3 percent lived in other parts of center city, members could be

CONTINUITY IN CHANGING TIMES

FIGURE 52
Wharton house, 336 Spruce Street, purchased for the rectory of Christ Church. Photograph by Louis W. Meehan.

FIGURE 53
Congregation with Ernest Harding at the lectern. Christ Church Archives.

found in every county of the diocese. In addition, almost 30 percent lived in New Jersey, their trip to Christ Church made possible by the same bridge that had displaced so many of the church's earlier members. Within the city, the other large concentration of members occurred in northeast Philadelphia; some of these members had moved there when the Benjamin Franklin Bridge was built. Not surprisingly, Christ Church also drew well (thirty-seven members, or 6.4 percent) from the Main Line area. Overall, of members responding to the diocesan survey, 62 percent reported that it took them more than thirty minutes to get to church. It is not surprising then, that only 20 percent of the baptized membership attended services every Sunday, compared to the national average of 50 percent.[10]

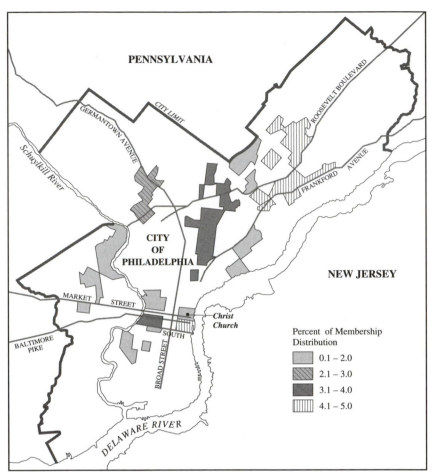

M A P 5
Christ Church membership distribution within Philadelphia, 1964.

The 1964 survey found that "the largest proportions of the membership" were "found in the age ranges above fifty, with an exceedingly large proportion of this membership being women." The age range with the smallest percentage of members was, unfortunately, that between twenty-five and thirty-five. People of that age tended to live in suburban areas and attend a church in their community where their children could go to Sunday school and they could benefit from a wide range of activities. The occupational distribution of the congregation is not surprising, given the age and sex of the congregation. The most common categories of occupations were clerical

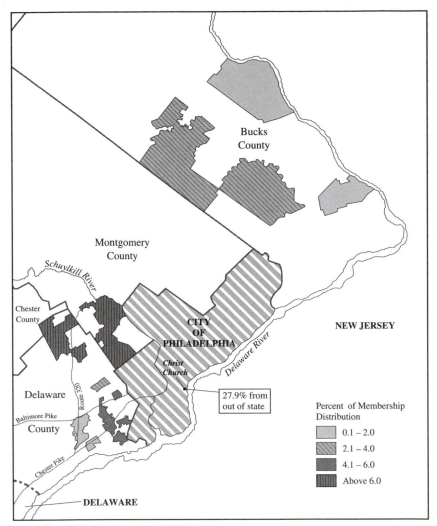

Within the map:

Bucks
County

Montgomery
County

Schuylkill River

Chester
County

CITY
OF
PHILADELPHIA

NEW JERSEY

*Christ
Church*

Delaware River

Delaware

Route 320

Baltimore Pike

County

Chester Pike

27.9% from
out of state

Percent of Membership
Distribution

0.1 – 2.0

2.1 – 4.0

4.1 – 6.0

Above 6.0

DELAWARE

MAP 6
Christ Church membership distribution outside Philadelphia, 1964.

workers, professional people, retired people, and craftsmen, in that order.[11] Despite the preponderance of older people, 35 percent of those responding to the survey had been members less than ten years, indicating that Harding was attracting new members.

Christ Church continued to attract outstanding people to serve on the vestry and, significantly, these vestrymen were chosen more and more from within the congregation. Because of Christ Church's dual role as national shrine and parish church, both the rector's warden and the accounting warden of Christ Church had unusually demanding duties to perform. Several outstanding men served in those capacities during Harding's rectorship. William White, a descendant of the bishop, served as rector's warden from 1956 to 1965. A prominent lawyer, White also served as chancellor of the diocese, the principal legal officer of the diocese. When White resigned in 1965 Harding appointed Henry Watts, a member of the New York Stock Exchange since 1929 and a former chairman of the board of governors of the Exchange. The equally demanding position of accounting warden was filled from 1953 to 1968 by James H. Stevenson, the owner of a business a few blocks from Christ Church who was active in the Neighborhood Businessmen's Association. For the next five years L. Arnold Nicholson, an associate editor of the *Saturday Evening Post* who had been influential in the renovation of the rectory, handled that position. Besides his role as accounting warden and as a manager of the Christ Church Hospital, Nicholson spent endless hours making certain that the Christ Church burial ground was in good repair, a job that became much more demanding as vandalism increased in the 1970s (see Figure 54). Nicholson was succeeded as accounting warden by Frank Dyer, the executive vice president of Philadelphia National Bank.[12]

In 1972 the vestry of Christ Church took a major step forward by nominating a woman to join its membership, a move that had been delayed by Harding's opposition to women serving in the clergy or on the vestry. The rector finally gave in to pressure from the congregation and allowed his good friend Bertha von Moschzisker to be elected to the vestry. An expert on fine art prints, von Moschzisker had served as director of the Print Club for twenty-six years. In the late 1970s and 1980s she would use her connections to coordinate a unique fund raising effort; she persuaded a number of artists to create prints and even books that were sold by Christ Church. In so doing, she not only helped support Christ Church but also contributed to the development of church art.[13]

While Christ Church still recruited outstanding members for its vestry, it had more difficulty recruiting and keeping assistant ministers. After hiring several lay people to help him in a variety of ways, in 1966 Harding finally succeeded in hiring C. Jon Widing, a recent graduate of Philadelphia Divinity School. Widing, who was known for his deep concern for all members of the congregation, took over the Sunday school, as well as assisting Hard-

FIGURE 54
Christ Church burial ground, in constant need of repair as its age and vandalism increase. Photograph by Louis W. Meehan.

ing with preaching and parish visiting. Also during this time, Dabney Carr, the executive secretary of the Episcopal Evangelical Education Society, assisted Harding with worship and led Bible study groups. When Widing and Carr left in 1970, the vestry hired Michael Mohn, a member of Christ Church who had worked there as a seminary student. Mohn's tenure lasted a little more than a year, at which time the church once again had trouble finding an assistant.[14]

In September 1973 James Shannon, a recent seminary graduate who had worked in the Peace Corps, took over as assistant, remaining until Harding's retirement. Both because of Harding's age and because a special rapport developed between Harding and Shannon, Shannon probably played the most active role of any of the assistants during Harding's tenure as rector. Described as "a little dynamo," Shannon exhibited the same energy level Harding had when he was younger and was, in fact, probably a great deal like the rector had been as a young man.[15]

A discussion of the staff under Harding would not be complete without mention of Harvey Mertz. From 1952 until 1967, when he finally retired at the age of 91, fifty-one years after being hired by Washburn, Harvey Mertz served officially as verger of Christ Church, leading the procession every Sunday morning, greeting old friends and visitors, and leading tours through the church (see Figure 50). Harvey Mertz was truly an institution at Christ Church, providing a sense of continuity for older members and a sense of history for more recent ones. Everyone connected with Christ Church during these years remembers Mertz fondly.[16]

* * *

Despite Christ Church's rich history and status as a national shrine, the first priority of Harding and his lay leaders had to be the same as it is for all ministers: the worship life of the church. During Harding's tenure, Christ Church underwent the most important changes in its worship since the acceptance of the American Book of Common Prayer in 1789. Some of these changes were imposed by the national church and some were decided on by the vestry and Harding.

The most important change made by Christ Church involved the music. At the time Harding arrived, Christ Church still had a choir made up of men and boys. For much of the twentieth century these boys had been recruited from outside the congregation, usually from the neighborhood, lured by the promise of free camp in the summer and other outings during the year (see Figure 55). But by the 1950s there were few boys left in the neighborhood and the vestry found that the camping experience was "not much of an incentive . . . any longer." An attempt to recruit boys from the renowned Choir School of St. Peter's failed because Christ Church was unable to pay

FIGURE 55
Francis Murphy leads a boys' choir in the loft at Christ Church. Changing demographics made its continuation impossible. Christ Church Archives.

the partial scholarships needed. Even the addition of women and girls, something that had been strongly opposed by the vestry, failed to solve the problem.[17]

Thus in 1962, after six years of study, the vestry finally decided to hire a professional choir. Believing that Francis Murphy, a mathematics teacher who had served as organist and choirmaster for twenty years, could not adequately handle a group of professional musicians, the vestry asked him to resign. While dismissing such a long-term employee was not easy, the vestry felt it had no choice. To replace Murphy, Christ Church hired a young organ student from Curtis Institute of Music, Walter Hillsman, and authorized him to hire six voices for the choir. A year later the music was reported to be "superb." Hillsman stayed only two years. He was replaced by another student at Curtis Institute, John Binsfeld. Unlike Hillsman, Binsfeld did not consider Christ Church to be a temporary assignment. Thirty years later he is still the organist at Christ Church, having devoted most of his life to improving the quality of music at the church.[18]

The musical program initiated by Hillsman and greatly expanded by Binsfeld, with the open encouragement of Harding, had a major impact on the life of the church. Almost overnight the music of Christ Church went from being an embarrassment to being a factor that drew people to the church. People came to the church to hear a special program and, impressed by more than the music, came back, some becoming members. Others who came to a service because of Christ Church's historical significance were so impressed by the service, including the music, that they too returned.[19]

This exceptional musical program was expensive to maintain. By 1967 the music budget, exclusive of the organist's salary, was $10,000 and in future years, despite increases, the budget often had a deficit. The major drain was not the salary of the choir members but the organ itself. While the Curtis organ was an exceptionally fine instrument, its upkeep at times has seemed overwhelming. In 1965 a new console was purchased and five years later the organ required $100,000 worth of repairs, $40,000 more than a new organ would have cost. Despite arguments by some vestry members that the church could not afford the luxury of such a fine organ when there were so many pressing social issues, those favoring the old instrument always prevailed. They believed that the organ "was an effective missionary force that brought people into the church" and that a historic parish had "an obligation to restore and preserve the past in the finest way" it could.[20]

Approximately ten years after the music of Christ Church changed dramatically, equally important changes in the service were initiated by the national church. In 1967 the General Convention, after seventeen years of study, authorized the Standing Liturgical Commission to prepare a major revision of the Book of Common Prayer. The result was a gradual transformation of Episcopal worship. A new Liturgy of the Lord's Supper, which increased the participation of the people and used contemporary English, was introduced for trial use in 1967 and followed in 1970 by *Services for Trial Use*, a reworking of the entire book. After six years of trial and much controversy, in 1976 the General Convention adopted the Proposed Book of Common Prayer. a decision that was confirmed in 1979.[21]

A major feature of the new Book of Common Prayer was the inclusion of three "Rites," or three different versions of the communion service. Rite I was in the traditional language that Episcopalians had used since the first

Anglican Prayer Book of 1549, while Rite II used contemporary English. Rite III, which was not authorized for use in the principal Sunday service, provided for a kind of flexibility previously unknown in Episcopal services; allowing a variety of Bible readings and secular literature and music, it was intended to be used only with "careful preparation by all the worshipers so that all may understand what takes place."[22] But no matter which rite a congregation chose to use, there were major changes in the order things were presented, in the content of the services and in the language.

The reaction of Harding and the Christ Church congregation to the new liturgy probably paralleled that of many Episcopalians. In 1969, when the church first used the new liturgy for Holy Communion, the vestry reported "tremendous opposition." By 1971, when the "Trial Service" was used, "the Eucharist was generally liked but there was a definite feeling that the simplification of the old service did not always convey its meaning." To Harding, the 1928 Prayerbook, which was adopted while he was in college, was the new Prayerbook. But by the time the book was officially adopted, Harding at least had reluctantly come to accept the changes. He reported to the congregation: "At the start I was much opposed to the new book, but the more I use it, and come to know it, the better I like it." But Christ Church remained conservative in its liturgical preferences. Not only did Harding choose to use only Rite I, the version closest to the 1928 Prayerbook, but for those who could not even go that far, the 1928 Prayerbook remained in the pews; the weekly bulletin gave page references to *both* books![23]

While the Harding era saw major changes in the Sunday services, the organizational life of the church saw continuity and, eventually, decline. Until the late 1960s the women of Christ Church maintained a fellowship group that continued to provide volunteers for luncheons and coffee hours. It also continued to raise much needed money, often taking advantage of the historic nature of the church. In 1959, Mrs. L. Arnold Nicholson worked with the women of Gloria Dei and St. Peter's churches to sponsor a highly successful walking tour of the churches and fifteen historic homes in the area. Also in the early 1960s a group of women began making "Betsy Ross Dolls." These dolls, dressed in handmade authentic-looking revolutionary era costumes, were made by women from a variety of faiths, and received a great deal of publicity. By 1978 one seamstress, Mrs. George Sealing, had made 1,773 dolls! Financially as well as aesthetically successful, by 1978 the women had made $12,000 from this effort.

With the continued aging and dispersal of the congregation, and with the nationwide decrease in the popularity of churchwomen's organizations, it is not surprising that by the end of the 1960s the women's organizations of Christ Church were no longer very active. What remained were task oriented groups: the altar guild continued to take care of the altar and vestments; the garden committee kept the gardens around Christ Church in good repair; and women could always be counted on to serve lunch or dinner when needed.[24]

Another newer organization, the Christ Church Neighborhood Businessmen's Association, continued to thrive for many years. Ernest Harding was at his best when socializing with businessmen of all creeds who shared his concern for Christ Church. In 1965 the association could boast of 205 members, with at least 80 attending its monthly luncheons. This group continued to raise funds for Christ Church projects and developed a strong interest in scouting during these years.[25] But by the end of Harding's rectorship even this organization had declined precipitously; businesses continued to move out of the area, businessmen retired, and the organization was hurt because it never opened its fellowship to business*women*.

Because the number of children available for Christ Church programs during these years was even smaller than the number of men and women, the Sunday school was struggling when Harding arrived. In 1956 a survey of the names on the Sunday school roster found that the list "was so out of date that people on it were grown and had children." The school itself was described as being in "bad shape," with its one trained teacher leaving. The situation improved dramatically with the appointment of Mrs. Peter Dexheimer as part-time director of religious education; Mrs. Dexheimer had previously worked in the diocesan department of religious education. But the numbers continued to remain small; by 1960 the number of children enrolled stood at fifty. A few years later Widing was able to increase the number of children registered to seventy-eight, but the average attendance remained around thirty.[26]

In 1973 Christ Church, under the leadership of Jim Shannon, tried a new and daring approach to the problem of a small Sunday school. Together with St. Peter's Episcopal Church and Old Pine Street Presbyterian Church, Christ Church set up the "Church School Without Walls." The Sunday schools of the three churches were merged into one and the children met at each church for five or six weeks at a time. This unique, ecumenical solution to the problems of inner-city churches continued until the end of Harding's rectorship. Although it may have been born out of necessity, it provided the children with a rich experience in keeping with the general ecumenical tendencies of the times.[27]

*   *   *

While the number of organizations at Christ Church declined, both clergy and members of the church continued to be involved in a variety of activities within the diocese and within the city. Christ Church Hospital remained a time consuming project for certain vestry members. One of the remarkable aspects of the vestry of Christ Church was its ability to find people willing to devote large amounts of time to the hospital. During much of Harding's rectorship Horace Churchman, an attorney, played a particularly large role, serving as president of the board for many years.[28]

Important changes occurred during these years in the physical plant, the name and the organizational structure of the hospital. In the hundred years since the "new" building opened, major changes had occurred in both the age of its residents and the kind of care given to the elderly. The average age of Christ Church Hospital residents in 1961 was over eighty, and many of these women needed extended care. To meet their needs a new infirmary wing, Kearsley House, opened in 1962, allowing the hospital to provide up-to-date convalescent care to its residents.[29] Having already violated Kearsley's will by naming a wing after him, in the late 1960s the board decided to give him even more recognition. Since the name of Christ Church Hospital had caused confusion for many years, the board changed the name of the institution to "Kearsley Home."

In 1975, after five years of study, the organizational structure of the Kearsley Home was changed dramatically. Because of concerns about the long-term financial health of the home, the vestry of Christ Church, later joined by the vestry of St. Peter's, decided to incorporate Kearsley Home as a separate institution. This major step, separating three organizations that had been tied together for two hundred years, relieved the churches of any fiscal responsibility for the home. In the process, the board was expanded to twenty-one people, and members were allowed from any Episcopal church in the diocese. While the initial impetus for the change was financial, the ultimate decision made sense from an organizational standpoint as well. Given the complexity of running a home for the elderly in the 1970s, limiting membership on the board to the vestries of Christ Church and St. Peter's was no longer wise. This change in structure, combined with the admission of women to the board in 1973, allowed for the full utilization of available talent.[30]

Christ Church also continued to play an important role in the diocese. The church had always had a special position in the Diocese of Pennsylvania because of its role as the "mother church" and because William White served as the first bishop of Pennsylvania. Its position was enhanced by the lack of a designated cathedral. As Christ Church put more and more emphasis on its history and became known nationally, its stature in the diocese also increased. Further influence came from the positions held by representatives of Christ Church. Sydney Lea, a successful businessman who had served as a vestry assistant under Kloman and as a vestryman since right after World War II, had begun serving on the executive committee of the diocese in 1953, and in 1958 Harding joined him. In 1965 Harding was elected to the Standing Committee, later serving as president. In addition, as we have indicated, William White served as chancellor of the diocese.

Christ Church's leadership role in the diocese took on new importance during Harding's rectorship as the church in general and the Philadelphia diocese in particular grappled with a series of difficult social issues. The 1960s and 1970s were turbulent but exciting times for the nation as a whole and for churches in particular. Poverty in America was "rediscovered," and churches at both the national and local levels groped for ways to help the poor. The civil rights movement, which had been widely supported by the Episcopal Church during its early years, took a new, more unsettling turn in the late 1960s. First, riots ravaged many ghetto areas. Then the "Black Power" movement, with its assertion that blacks should control their own destiny and its call for economic as well as legal equality, replaced the earlier emphasis on integration for many blacks. Many Episcopalians were particularly upset by the "Black Manifesto," issued by the Black Economic Development Conference in 1969, which demanded that the churches and synagogues of America pay $500,000,000 in "reparations" to the black people.[31] As the civil rights movement accelerated, opposition to the war in Vietnam also increased. Many church people were torn between their sympathy for those who had conscientious objections to the war and their abhorrence of the massive, at times violent demonstrations, the burning of draft cards, and other forms of civil disobedience they saw all around them. If this were not enough, the society in general, and the Episcopal Church in particular, had to deal with the demands of women for equality.

Robert DeWitt, the crusading bishop of the Diocese of Pennsylvania from 1964 to 1972, forced Episcopalians under his care to confront these issues from a religious perspective. Believing that the church was meant to be "prophetic" and that the role of the bishop was "not to represent his *people*, but to represent God *to* his people," DeWitt quickly became a controversial figure. He believed that "if you care at all about people, you have to care about issues—poverty, war, injustice." Consequently, he took a leadership role in the civil rights issues. Appropriately, given Bishop White's earlier efforts to contest Stephen Girard's will, DeWitt championed the cause of those who wanted Girard College open to blacks. Encouraging the clergy to picket the institution, he refused to stop until the issue was brought to the courts, which eventually did open the school to blacks. He was also a vocal opponent of the Vietnam War, joining twenty-three other clergy in 1968 in calling for a bombing halt and "every other means of de-escalation in order to terminate the undeclared war in Vietnam as soon as possible." And he openly supported the ordination of women to the priesthood; after his retirement he participated in the noncanonical ordination of eleven women in Philadelphia in 1974.[32]

Not surprisingly, DeWitt's actions elicited strong opposition within the diocese. Of particular concern to many was DeWitt's hiring of David McIver Gracie as an urban missioner. Gracie, a priest who had been involved in civil rights activities in Detroit, actively supported the antiwar movement and "Black Power" groups, including the Black Panthers. In many ways he served as a lightning rod for those opposing DeWitt's policies. One such group, the Committee for the Preservation of Episcopal Principles, worked strenuously against the bishop and in 1968 convinced the diocesan convention to cut funding for most of his controversial programs.[33] Many congregations decreased their contribution to the diocese and some, including Trinity Church on Rittenhouse Square, eliminated it altogether, causing a major fiscal crisis. While some congregations were united in their disapproval, others were deeply divided over DeWitt's policies; like the society as a whole, individual churches often had to deal with opposing factions, each of whom felt very strongly that their beliefs were the only acceptable ones for Episcopalians. For churches that had prided themselves on allowing great diversity of opinion, this was a truly painful period.

Because of Christ Church's highly visible position in the city and its leadership role in the diocese, the attitude of its leaders toward the issues in general and toward DeWitt in particular was particularly important. Knowing that any opposition on his part would be quickly picked up by the press, but also knowing that he presided over a conservative congregation, Harding chose to say nothing in public but to give support quietly for DeWitt's positions. While not as politically liberal as DeWitt, he did believe that the general direction of the bishop's policies was correct. Moreover, he was extremely loyal to the diocese and to the position of bishop. On DeWitt's retirement, Harding argued that DeWitt had been "a faithful prophet and Bishop in a most difficult period of the life of our world and the church. He has stirred many of us to a new and vital realization of our duty as followers of Christ whether we agreed with him or not. His courage and calmness through these troublesome years has been a shining example to us all." As a result of these beliefs, when DeWitt needed a platform to state that "he would not resign in the face of public protest, Harding willingly provided Christ Church and a New Year's Eve service for that purpose." He also allowed DeWitt to hold a peace vigil service at Christ Church in 1973. These symbolic gestures, which were, of course, covered by the press, gained added significance because of Christ Church's stature as the "mother of the diocese."[34]

While Harding quietly supported DeWitt, he did not expect all within his congregation to agree with the bishop's stands. Given the generally older, conservative makeup of the congregation of Christ Church in the 1960s and 1970s, it is not surprising that opposition was expressed. In 1967 the vestry discussed clerical involvement in civil disobedience, and some "expressed concern over the trend which Episcopal leadership appeared to be taking." Two years later a member wrote the vestry objecting to the bishop's stand on the Black Manifesto. Many more members no doubt objected in less formal ways. Harding was neither surprised nor upset at these reactions, but attempted to make certain that objections to specific policies did not lead to rejection of the Episcopal Church as a whole, or to the kind of "financial blackmail" in which some churches engaged. An article in the *Beacon* faced the issue head-on, urging members to continue their contributions. It answered those wanting to withhold money as a protest this way:

If we truly love the church . . . it is our Christian duty to criticize and seek to bring about a change. The truly loyal person stands fast in his faith in God and continues both his criticism and his support. One thing binds us all together . . . and that is our loyalty to our Lord Jesus Christ and His work that can only be done through our love and support of him.

At the same time, the leadership of Christ Church provided a "way out" for those who strongly objected; members could designate their pledges for use inside or outside of the parish. This allowed Christ Church to continue supporting the diocese at the same time that it allowed individual members to record their protests.[35]

In some ways Christ Church seemed like a calm island amid a stormy sea during this period, continuing the long-standing middle-of-the-road, non-political stand that had been advocated so many years before by Bishop White. But in reality, Harding's ability to keep the church from *opposing* DeWitt, and his willingness to let DeWitt use the church for services, increased the "respectability" and perhaps the acceptance of the bishop's controversial programs.

While not all Christ Church members supported DeWitt, they were concerned about the social problems they saw around them. In 1970 the church supported an experimental ministry among the young people who congregated in Rittenhouse Square, a ministry that led to the founding of Voyage House, an ecumenically supported home for runaways. Christ Church, along with the nine other churches in old Philadelphia, also attempted to help some of the older people in center city Philadelphia. In 1973, at the urging of social worker Jean DeGraff and with the leadership of Jim Shannon, the Coffee Cup, a "club" for senior citizens, was opened in a storefront. Serving coffee, pastries, fruit, and cheese five afternoons a week, it provided a place for companionship and inexpensive food. Within a year it had begun to offer meals at noon, serving 1,100 in a six-month period. While such senior citizens' centers later became common when federal money became available, the Coffee Cup, which still exists, was one of the first in Philadelphia. In addition to giving money, Christ Church also provided a number of volunteer workers.[36]

* * *

Harding faced two tasks when he became rector—building up the congregation and institutionalizing the church's role as a national shrine. Harding took at least as much pleasure in promoting the historical nature of Christ Church as he did in serving the needs of his parishioners. In fact, no rector before or since loved the history of the church or reveled in its pageantry more than Ernest Harding. He studied the history, loving to recount stories to whomever would listen; he joined historical societies, serving as the presi-

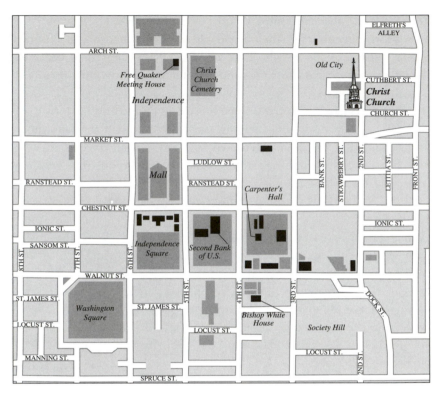

M A P 7
Independence Historic Park, 1970s.

dent of the Colonial Philadelphia Historical Society; and he worked hard to preserve the buildings so closely associated with that history.

Unlike deBordenave, Harding promoted the church's history for its own sake rather than using it to promote a particular cause. This was in part possible because deBordenave had done his job so well; the massive publicity generated by the USA campaign meant that Christ Church already had a national reputation. Harding's apolitical "history for history's sake" approach also fit in well with the restoration of Independence Hall and the resurgence of interest in colonial architecture. It was no longer necessary to tie Christ Church to any particular cause, and in the long run, it was better not to do so. (See Map 7 for the Independence Historical Park in the 1970s.)

Anyone associated with Christ Church during Harding's years remembers the wide array of special historical services held in the church with Harding's encouragement. While these services had actually begun during Washburn's days and expanded greatly under deBordenave, Harding took them to an all time high; at times it seemed like there was something to commemorate and a special group to commemorate it almost every Sunday. Groups that had annual services included the Society of the War of 1812, commemorating the writing of the "Star-Spangled Banner"; the First City Troop, which rode to the church on horseback in full dress to commemorate the death of George Washington; the St. Andrew's Society, which held a pilgrimage to the grave of James Wilson; the Colonial Society of Pennsylvania, commemorating the anniversary of the founding of Pennsylvania; the National League of Masonic Clubs, which held an annual service in honor of Benjamin Franklin; and the Magna Carta Society, with all its beautiful flags bedecking the sanctuary[37] (see Figure 56). These services gave Christ Church enormous publicity, since they were wonderful photo opportunities for the

FIGURE 56
Christ Church decked out for the annual service in honor of the Magna Carta. Christ Church Archives.

CHRIST CHURCH

PHILADELPHIA

FIGURE 57
Christ Church seal, designed by Dr. Howard Bowditch, a genealogist of Boston. Christ Church Archives.

local press, and produced tremendous goodwill; these organizations proved to be fertile ground for fund raising.

In keeping with this emphasis on history and pageantry, Harding had a coat of arms designed for the parish. It combined swords from the coat of arms of the bishop of London, three roundels argent (round silver dots) from the coat of arms of William Penn, and a miter at the top, representing Bishop White (see Figure 57). While the founders of Christ Church may have found the positive memorial to William Penn a bit disturbing, it represented well Christ Church's relatively easy acceptance of religious freedom during the colonial period.[38]

Just as Harding and the congregation had to struggle to maintain a balance between an emphasis on history and an appreciation for the needs of the present in the programming of the church, they also had to decide how much to modernize the church building. Shortly after Harding arrived, the church took two major steps into the twentieth century. In 1957 a public address system was installed. And in 1958 the outside of the tower was illuminated for the first time, a gift of Howard Story of the Poor Richard's club. For a church that had installed electricity only a few years before, these were major steps![39]

The other improvements during the early years of Harding's era were geared toward returning more of the eighteenth century charm to the building. After considerable discussion and dissension, the plain wooden Gostelow communion table was removed from within the stone altar where it had been encased, and returned to use. Harding also had the Gostelowe baptismal font, which had been used as a credence table, restored.[40]

The Palladian window presented even more of a problem than the altar. The "colored glass" window, which had been installed in the nineteenth century, had deteriorated to the point of being dangerous. Yet Harding's plan to remove it and restore the plain glass window beneath it did meet with some resistance. In 1960 Harding's wishes were finally met. Mrs. Thomas Graham gave the money in memory of the relationship between Mikveh Israel and Christ Church. Unfortunately, the mattress factory across the street was a far less pleasant view for the congregation than the Delaware River must have been for their eighteenth-century ancestors. In fact, at times the congregation could see workers eating their lunches on the fire escape, peering down on the church service below! Shades of "smoked glass" and red drapes were both tried to hide the view, but by the late 1960s the window was plain, as it had been in the eighteenth century. When parishioners objected, Harding reminded them that Christ Church was part of the city and could not set itself apart. A compromise solution was found after Harding died; sometime in the 1980s a tree was planted outside the window, a tree that now almost totally covers it[41] (see Figure 58).

These improvements were minor compared to the repairs that had to be made in the 1960s. In 1963 the church members learned that the copper roof needed to be replaced. In the end, the new roof, with new structural supports, reshingling of the tower, and a total repainting of the church inside and out cost $125,000—the most expensive restoration project since 1838. Then in 1968 the ceiling over the galleries had to be replastered, with new steel girders built in. While the finances of Christ Church had improved greatly since Harding arrived, with pledges increasing from $13,690 in 1955 to more than $30,000 in 1960, a congregation that could contribute less than a third of the amount needed for the annual operating budget could certainly not pay for $125,000 in repairs.[42]

The solution that Harding proposed to meet the financial needs was in many ways similar in design and rationale to deBordenave's USA campaign. Believing that there were people who would be willing to contribute to the upkeep of the building as a national shrine, but not to the religious life of the

FIGURE 58
Christ Church chancel after the removal of the colored glass window and the restoration of the Gostelow altar. Christ Church Archives.

church, in 1965 the church, in cooperation with the National Trust for Historical Preservation, established the Old Christ Church Preservation Trust, a "non-profit, non-sectarian, publicly supported, charitable foundation." According to the charter, half of the board of directors had to come from outside the church and its funds could be used only for the "preservation of the Church structure and Burial Ground as monuments of national concern," not for the operational needs of the parish. While the Trust originally intended to raise an endowment of $450,000, the continuing need for repairs led it to become oriented more toward raising money for particular needs.[43] It has proved to be an invaluable fund-raising organization for Christ Church.

Harding and the vestry continued to be concerned about the area immediately surrounding Christ Church. Since the park Congress authorized south of Christ Church had never been funded, the church was still surrounded by factories and wholesale establishments. Just how much a problem this could be was demonstrated in 1963 when Harvey Mertz and Amelia Lingham, Christ Church's cleaning woman, discovered a fire in a warehouse behind the Neighborhood House. Its early detection combined with the church's sprinkler system, which was used for only the fourth time in its history, once again saved the historic church.[44]

DeBordenave had continued Kloman's efforts to obtain a park, but the National Park Service had other priorities. Recognizing this, Harding and several vestrymen decided that much more direct action was needed if the block-sized park was ever to become a reality. They convinced Colonel Frank Worthington Melvin of the Colonial Society of Pennsylvania once again to champion the cause in Congress. After a monumental effort, for which he was given the Christ Church Distinguished Service Award, in 1958 Melvin successfully shepherded a bill through Congress authorizing the purchase of the entire block to the south of Christ Church.[45]

After five years of delay, in 1963 the buildings, with the exception of one whose owner held out, were finally razed and in 1965 Wilson Park was officially opened. For the first time in its history Christ Church was not hemmed in by buildings. With Morris Park on one side and Wilson Park on the other, the church not only was protected from fire but also provided a fitting respite from the frantic pace of the city for residents and tourists alike. But even though sitting on one of the benches in the park and gazing up at the beautiful eighteenth-century structure can be a renewing experience, one should remember that it is a far different picture from the one that the parishioners of Christ Church would have seen in the eighteenth century when buildings surrounded the church on all sides.

* * *

It was truly fitting that the nation's bicentennial took place near the end of Harding's rectorship, for no-one could have appreciated Christ Church's role in the Revolution more fully than this now elderly priest who had spent the last twenty years reveling in the church's history. Harding and the vestry were determined that if Christ Church were going to be a part of this national celebration, they were going to do it right.

Planning for the church's part in the bicentennial began in earnest in 1972. John Hannum, a United States District Judge with a keen interest in American history, took the lead. He would later be joined in the leadership role by Jim Shannon, who coordinated efforts with the other churches in the area. From the beginning everyone involved had a number of concerns. They were determined that the church building should be in first-class condition, but were also concerned for the physical safety of the church and those who visited it. At that time Philadelphia officials were expecting forty million people to descend on the city, with as many as 16,000 visitors a day touring Christ Church. There were real concerns about whether the two-hundred-year old structure could stand that level of attention. At the same time, Christ Church representatives were concerned that an accurate, consistent, and professional interpretive program be provided for those visitors. It was clear to all that the bicentennial preparation would be a massive undertaking.[46]

Planning in 1974 and 1975 continued on three fronts—the physical needs of the church, the presentation of a proper interpretive program for visitors, and the funding of both these efforts. With a grant from the National Park Service, Charles Peterson, who had been involved in the early planning of Independence Park, and the engineering firm of Keast and Hood did the first comprehensive study of the needs of the building. This two-volume report suggested $268,000 worth of improvements that should be made. Of these, the main project involved strengthening the galleries. The painting of the interior of the church and certain improvements at the burial ground were later added to the physical needs. All of these improvements were accomplished by 1976.[47]

The National Park Service also provided assistance with the interpretive program. A comprehensive proposal submitted by the Park Service was accepted by the vestry in 1974 and subsequently implemented by Sandra Thornton, the executive director hired by the Preservation Trust to help with fund-raising and interpretation. A graduate student from the University of Pennsylvania did massive amounts of research into the church and its members in 1776, gathering information about everyone she could on the 1778 pew list. Her research resulted in a new pamphlet, "Christ Church in the Crisis Years," which dramatically and accurately described the church's role in the Revolution. Scripts were prepared for guides outlining both the architectural and historical significance of the church, emphasizing, of course, the revolutionary era.[48]

As a result of all this planning, Christ Church was in excellent shape to face the bicentennial year. The crowds proved to be far smaller than predicted; 394,696 visited the church during the year. But they were presented with a well maintained church and a professional interpretive program presented by fourteen paid guides, including three at the burial ground. Clergy from various churches in the diocese conducted evening prayer every night at five o'clock from May 30 through September 4, and a wide range of special programs were held throughout the year. While 1976 was not the blockbuster tourist year that had been predicted, Christ Church did present its message of the key role religion played in the Revolution to a large number of people.[49] In a sense, the bicentennial was the final chapter in the establishment of Christ Church as a premier tourist attraction, as a true "national shrine," a process which had been under way since 1950.

*　*　*

By 1977 at the close of the bicentennial, Ernest Harding was sixty-nine years old, slightly hard of hearing, and generally not in good health. While Jim Shannon had carried on many of Harding's duties, developed new programs and in many ways kept the church going, signs of deterioration were occurring: church attendance had dropped from a high of 15,538 in 1972 to 13,590 in 1975, and with it, plate income had decreased. After 1972 pledges also began declining,and in 1974 the church was forced to take $18,900 from the principal of its endowment to meet operating expenses.[50] Much of this situation had nothing to do with Harding; church attendance in general was declining in the Episcopal Church in the 1970s and in center city churches in particular, and inflation was wreaking havoc with everyone's budget. However, it was true that Harding no longer attracted new members as he had in his early years. As had been the case with White and Dorr, Harding stayed as rector, in part at the urging of his congregation and in part because of his love of Christ Church, after his health prohibited him from fully performing his duties. Harding and the congregation eventually had to face the inevitable. When Shannon announced his plans to leave, Harding also announced his retirement, effective at the end of 1977. On his retirement he was elected rector emeritus of Christ Church, honorary trustee of the Old Christ Church Preservation Trust, and honorary chaplain of the Independence Hall Association.[51] Harding died in 1984.

* * *

For many who worshiped at Christ Church, as well as many more Philadelphians who may have never stepped foot in the building, Harding *was* Christ Church, in a way that Bishop White and Louis Washburn must have been looked upon in their day. While he did not initiate major new programs as Washburn and deBordenave had, he was an ideal person to perpetuate the dual role of Christ Church as active parish and national shrine. His ability to draw new people into the church as well as his ability to raise money allowed Christ Church to continue to exist and prosper in an age when mainstream churches in far better locations were falling on hard times. While the congregation and, consequently, the activities of the church had declined during his later years, Harding left to the new rector a church that was in good shape physically, with a large endowment, a national reputation and a fiercely loyal body of supporters.

NOTES

1. Bertha von Moschzisker, "Ernest A. Harding, An Appreciation at the Time of His Retirement," *Preservation Post* 1, 2 (Christmas 1977): 1.
2. Ibid., 4; *Beacon*, June 1, 1958. The Right Reverend Robert L. DeWitt in a letter to the author, April 23, 1989, refers to him as a "militant low churchman."
3. *Beacon*, October 1974.
4. *Beacon*, April 10, 1966.
5. Diocese of Pennsylvania, "Parish Survey, Christ Church," 1964, 1–5, in Archives of the Diocese of Pennsylvania, Philadelphia.
6. Richard Wurman and John Gallery, *Man-Made Philadelphia* (Cambridge, Mass: MIT Press, 1972), 53–54.
7. Vestry Minutes, May 15, Sept. 19, Dec. 19, 1960; Sept. 11, 1961; *Christ Church Rectory: A Project to Restore an Historic House for the Use of an Historic Church*. David Van Pelt gave ten thousand dollars toward the project. The Wharton House was built in 1790 and occupied by several prominent merchants before being bought by Samuel Rowland Fischer for his daugh-

ter, Deborah Wharton. Mrs. Wharton, wife of Quaker gentleman and philanthropist William Wharton, lived there for seventy years, raising ten children, one of whom, Joseph Wharton, is best remembered for his endowment of the Wharton School of Finance and Commerce at the University of Pennsylvania.

8. "Parish Survey, Christ Church," 1964, CS 11,12. Christ Church benefited from a series of problems at St. Peter's that led new residents of the area to choose Christ Church over St. Peter's, which was much closer. Allen Heavens, clerk, St. Peter's Church, interview with author, Philadelphia, August 3, 1987.

9. *Journal of the Diocese of Pennsylvania*, 1970, 186. (Data for St. Luke and Epiphany give the same number for "total baptized persons" and communicants.) Overall, Episcopal churches in central Philadelphia had a 6.6 percent decline between 1955 and 1960, much smaller than the decline in Christ Church, but the overall decline continued from 1960–63 (−2.7 percent) while Christ Church began to gain members. "Parish Survey of Christ Church," CS 13, 17.

10. "Parish Survey of Christ Church," CS 7, 10–12.

11. Ibid., CS 13, 17.

12. The 1974 *Beacons* carried profiles of the vestry members.

13. *Beacon*, Oct. 1975.

14. Vestry Minutes, Mar 16, 1966, Nov. 22, 1965; Feb. 16, 1970; *Beacon*, Oct. 15, 1967, Jan. 18, April 19, 1970; Jon Widing, taped memoirs of his years at Christ Church.

15. Vestry Minutes, Jan. 16 and Feb. 28, 1972, Feb. 26, 1973.

16. "The Ultimate Transplant: A Whole Man," *Philadelphia Daily News*, Dec. 13, 1967, copy in Christ Church Archives; *Beacon*, April 3, 1966.

17. Vestry Minutes, Oct. 8, Dec. 19, 1956; Jan. 28, Feb 18, June 17, Dec. 16, 1957; Feb. 17, 1958; *Beacon*, Dec. 7, 1958.

18. Vestry Minutes, Jan. 15, Feb. 18, June 18, 1962; April 16, Oct. 14, 1963; June 18, 1964. Robert Gill, interview with author, July 30, 1987. Dr. Gill was member of the vestry and the music committee in 1962.

19. Survey of current members conducted by the author, Fall, 1986.

20. Vestry Minutes, Oct. 23, 1967, March 30, Oct. 23, 1970; Sept. 21, Nov. 16, 1970; *Beacon*, March 7, 1971.

21. Betty Gray, "Episcopalians Shape a New Liturgical Life," *Christian Century* 93 (September, 1976): 731–32; Charles P. Price for the Standing Liturgical Commission of the Protestant Episcopal Church, *Introducing the Proposed Book* (New York: Church Hymnal Corporation, 1976), 9–15.

22. Ibid.

23. Vestry Minutes, April 7, May 19, 1969, Oct 18, 1971; *Beacon*, March 1977.

24. Vestry Minutes, Nov. 17, May 18, June 15, Oct. 27, 1959; October 8, 1962; *Beacon*, May 17, 1959, May 19, 1963; Sept. 21, 1970; "Parish Survey of Christ Church,", K-19,20; "Dollars for Dolls," *Preservation Post* 2, 1 (1978): 1–2. The first tour netted a total of $4,800.

25. "Parish Survey of Christ Church," K-17.

26. Vestry Minutes, March 4, May 14, June 18, Nov. 19, 1956; Jan. 28, Feb. 18, Dec. 16, 1957; Oct. 20, 1958; Feb. 15, 1960; Feb. 20, 1961; Oct. 8, Dec. 17, 1962; Feb. 2, Nov. 25, 1963; Oct. 17, 1966; March 27, April 17, Nov. 20, 1967; March 19, 1968.

27. Vestry Minutes, June 18, 1973, *Beacon*, Summer, 1977; James Shannon, interview with author, New York, August 1, 1987.

28. These men were elected at the organizational meeting in April of each year.

29. Minutes of the Board of Managers, 1961–62; Roberts, "Christ Church Hospital," 101. Horace Churchman played a major role in the fund raising efforts. Much of the cost was covered by a legacy from Sarah Russell and a generous contribution from Mrs. H. S. Valentine.

30. Vestry Minutes, Dec. 21, 1970; May 17, 1971; April 15, Nov. 17, 1975. The woman was from the vestry of St. Peter's.

31. See John L. Kater, Jr., "Experiment in Freedom: The Episcopal Church and the Black Power Movement," *HMPEC* 48 (1979): 67–81.

32. For a discussion of DeWitt's position on Vietnam see Trevor Wyatt Moore, "In Unity and Godly Love," *Christian Century* 85 (Sept. 11, 1968): 1140–41 and "Episcopal Bishop Under Attack," *Christian Century* 87 (November 11, 1970): 1363. For a good summary of the problems involved in the noncanonical ordination of women, see "Episcopal Agony over Ecclesiastical Disobedience," *Christian Century* 91 (Sept. 4, 1974): 812–14. For an excellent discussion of overall conflict in the Episcopal Church in the 1970s see Earl H. Brill, "The Episcopal Church: Conflict and Cohesion," *Christian Century* 95 (Jan. 18, 1978): 41–47.

33. Brill, "Episcopal Church: Conflict and Cohesion," 41–47.

34. The quote is from the *Beacon*, Nov. 19, 1972. DeWitt "was always confident" of Harding's support. Robert DeWitt letter to author, April 23, 1989; James Shannon said essentially the same thing.

35. *Beacon*, October 26, 1969; Vestry Minutes, October 27, 1969.

36. Vestry Minutes, May 18, June 15, Nov. 16, Dec. 21, 1970; April 16, June 18, 1973; *Beacon*, Jan. 17, 1971, May 27, 1973, March 1974; James Shannon, interview with author, Aug. 1, 1987; Bertha von Moschzisker, interview with author, Philadelphia, June 13, 1986.

37. These services, as well as many others, are listed each year in the *Leaflet* and the *Beacon*.

38. Vestry Minutes, October 19, 1958. The coat of arms was designed by Dr. Howard Bowditch, a genealogist of Boston.

39. Vestry Minutes, Nov. 7, 1956; Jan. 16, 1957; Oct. 20, 1958; "Christ Church Tower to be Illuminated for First Time," *Evening Bulletin*, Jan. 12, 1959, copy in Christ Church archives.

40. Vestry Minutes, June 16 and Oct.5, 1958.

41. *Beacon*, July 1956; Oct. 5, 1958; Vestry Minutes, Jan. 18, Feb. 15, March 21, Nov. 21, 1960. Information about the view and the planting of the tree was provided by Bruce Gill, curator of Christ Church.

42. Vestry Minutes, Jan. 18, March 21, May 15, Dec. 19, 1960; Jan. 16, Feb. 20, 1961; Feb. 2, Oct. 14, 1963; Mar. 30, 1964; Sept. 16, 1968; Arnold Nicholson, "Historic Christ Church in Philadelphia Faces Problems," *Today Magazine, Philadelphia Inquirer*, n.d., Christ Church Archives.

43. Vestry Minutes, June 8, 1964, Jan. 11, June 21, Dec. 20, 1965; Isadore M. Scott, "The Intent of the Trust," *Preservation Post* 1, 1 (1977): 1, 2.

44. Amelia Lingham, interview with author, Philadelphia, June 9, 1987.

45. Frank Worthington Melvin, "The Miracle of Christ Church Park," 6–10; Vestry Minutes, Sept. 15, Dec. 15, 1958.

46. See for example, Vestry Minutes, Feb. 26, March 19, Oct. 19, Nov. 11, 1973; Jan. 21, Feb. 26, 1974.

47. The architectural and engineering studies are located in the Archives of the Independence National Historical Park. For the vestry's reaction see Vestry Minutes, June 2; 1975, March 1, 1976.

48. The results of the research done by Pam LaJeunesse are in file boxes in the Christ Church Archives. I have used these materials in Chapter 7. Copies of the scripts can also be found in the archives. This work was funded from a variety of sources. The Pew Family Trusts provided $100,000 while the Pennsylvania Historical and Museum Commission provided another $20,000. Pennsylvania National Bank funded two guides and a variety of other sources gave small amounts. See Vestry Minutes, Jan. 21, June 2, Sept. 15, Nov. 17, 1965.

49. *Beacon*, Jan.,1977; Vestry Minutes, March 1, 1976.

50. *Beacon*, Oct., 1974.

51. *Preservation Post* 2, 1 (1978): 5.

CHAPTER SEVENTEEN

CHRIST CHURCH ENTERS ITS FOURTH CENTURY

While it is always hard for a congregation to replace a long-time rector, and especially hard when he is as revered as was Ernest Harding, in many ways the timing of Harding's retirement was propitious for Christ Church. Not only had the church declined in membership and in programming in Harding's later years, the situation it faced had also changed. The public relations campaign that began under deBordenave and climaxed with the Bicentennial had fully ensconced Christ Church as a major tourist attraction and, as a result, the continued existence of the church building was secure. However, the other role of Christ Church—that of parish church—was not as solid. If Christ Church were to remain a viable parish, the next rector would have to concentrate on building up the parish.

The task of building the congregation was made easier by changes that were occurring in center city Philadelphia in the late 1970s. The residential renaissance that had begun in Society Hill in the 1950s had expanded in all directions by the late 1970s, and, while the Old City area surrounding Christ Church was one of the last areas to succumb to "gentrification," by the late 1970s and increasingly in the early 1980s

FIGURE 59
The Reverend James Trimble (rector, 1977 to present).

warehouses and refineries were being converted into apartment buildings. The commercial district did not disappear, but the area was gradually developing the kind of diversified look it had in the colonial period. For the first time since Washburn's rectorship, there was hope that Christ Church could once again become a neighborhood church.

So, when the vestry members set about choosing a replacement for Harding, they were looking for someone cast in a slightly different mold. The new rector should, of course, be a good preacher, have a strong sense of history, get along well with outside organizations, and be capable of taking a leadership role in the diocese as Harding had. But just as important, he should be capable of building up the parish by appealing to young people and families.[1]

To provide this leadership the vestry chose James Trimble, who for fourteen years had taught at and served as the chaplain of the Episcopal Academy (see Figure 59). While he had not been a parish rector since he served as rector of Redemption Parish in Southampton, Pennsylvania prior to moving to the academy, the vestry believed that his work with youth, his obvious interest in education, his warmth, and his commitment to Christ Church as an active parish made him the ideal choice to build up the congregation. Since he already was active in the diocese, having served on the Standing Committee and as a delegate to the General Convention, the vestry knew he would continue Christ Church's leadership in that arena. Trimble began his duties at Christ Church in January 1978.

* * *

While the events of the last fifteen years fall in the realm more of current events than of history, a few brief comments about Trimble's rectorship and the future of Christ Church as it reaches its three-hundredth birthday are appropriate.

The history of Christ Church in the 1980s could probably best be described as one of continuity mixed with subtle but important changes. Christ Church remains a bastion of low church Episcopalianism, where differing theological and social views are tolerated. It is still a place where excellent preaching and fine music are expected and achieved. When the congregation was surveyed in 1986, these three characteristics—the music, the preaching and the tolerance—were the reasons most often given for joining the church.[2] There has been one important change in the service: on Trimble's arrival, the 1928 Book of Common Prayer was removed from the pews. In addition, Trimble began using Rite I and Rite II on alternate Sundays, thus giving Christ Church parishioners their first opportunity to become accustomed to the liturgy in contemporary English.

The church continues to play an important role in the diocese. Trimble has served as the president of the Standing Committee and as chair of the deputation to the General Convention on six occasions. He also serves on the board of trustees of the Episcopal Hospital and as an officer of the Episcopal Community Services. Bishop Lyman Ogilby valued Christ Church's role in the diocese so highly that he wanted to move the diocesan headquarters to the Neighborhood House. He also considered designating Christ Church as a cathedral. For a variety of reasons, neither of these proposals became reality.[3]

Christ Church's relationship with the Kearsley Home also continues to be important. While the home is now a separate legal entity, three vestry members continue to serve on its board and Christ Church continues to take an active role in the home's development. Trimble also serves on the board of trustees. During the last ten years the major fiscal problems of the home have been alleviated and a large new wing was built with money from the low-income housing program of the federal government. In 1993 the board undertook a twelve million dollar fund-raising effort to build new apartments and to expand the nursing unit. These projects assure that Kearsley's original goal of providing care for the poor will continue to be carried out in an age when that care has become extremely expensive.[4]

Another theme in the history of Christ Church—the need for major renovation projects—has also continued. In 1984 the church and the Preservation Trust embarked on the biggest project ever: a $750,000 restoration of "the Philadelphia Steeple," the only eighteenth-century steeple left in the city. The two-hundred-foot steeple was still supported by its original wooden posts, some of which, it was discovered, had deteriorated so badly that they were now hollow in the middle. The project, which included reinforcing the steeple structure with steel and timber, repainting and repointing, insulating and fireproofing, as well as shoring up the floor beneath the organ chamber in the tower below, was finally completed in 1988. Shortly thereafter an additional $200,000 was expended to restore the fence and wall around the church, including the original ironwork.[5]

Against this backdrop of continuity, there have been important changes during Trimble's rectorship. One such change occurred in the interior of the church. When the stained glass windows were removed to be cleaned, the sun streaming through the clear glass windows and the breeze blowing through windows that could now be opened, convinced the leadership not to put them back. While this decision was not without controversy, it did move the church one step closer to its eighteenth-century appearance. As soon as money is available, the church leadership intend to install these windows in the Neighborhood House or in another location where they can be appreciated by many without interfering with the eighteenth-century appearance of the church.

More important, as the vestry had hoped, Trimble has given his first priority to building up the parish. Believing that the future of the church as an active parish required an outstanding Sunday school, he hired John Midwood, one of his assistant chaplains at Episcopal Academy, as assistant and put him in charge of the Sunday school. The Church School Without Walls, while a unique effort, did not seem to be serving the needs of Christ Church any longer; the church provided most of the teachers but very few of the students. Midwood, who was married with a child of his own, set to work to build a successful Sunday school program for Christ Church. While all Trimble's goals have not been accomplished, by the late 1980s Christ Church could boast of the largest Episcopal Sunday school in center city Philadelphia. Midwood and Trimble also worked hard to improve the adult education program which had waned during Harding's last years.[6]

When Midwood left in 1984 to become rector of a parish, Trimble chose to involve the Christ Church congregation directly with one of the most important changes taking place in the Episcopal Church as a whole: with vestry approval, he hired a woman—Miriam Acevedo-Naters—to be his assistant. In 1984 she became the first Hispanic woman to be ordained as a priest in the Episcopal Church. That ordination, fittingly, took place in Christ Church, where the first black man had been ordained almost two hundred years before.

The General Convention of the Protestant Episcopal Church had in 1976 finally affirmed the right of women to be ordained to the priesthood, but the controversy surrounding this issue did not die. Twenty-seven bishops signed a "covenant" refusing to recognize women as priests; in October 1977 Presiding Bishop John M. Allin announced that he himself could never accept the ordination of women. In order to keep peace, the bishops adopted a "conscience" clause, allowing bishops to refuse to ordain women if their consciences forbade it. This victory for the conservatives did not stop more than 10,000 Episcopalians from seceding and founding various organizations such as the Anglican Church of North America.[7]

While Christ Church had never officially reacted to the decision to ordain women, and certainly did not condone the secession of some sister parishes, many members did have trouble dealing with women as priests. Acevedo-Naters had to deal with both open opposition—those who would not receive communion from her—and more subtle disapproval. While this was hard for her and for the congregation, Trimble felt it was an important step for Christ Church, the "mother of the Episcopal Church," to take.

At the same time that some were unable to accept Acevedo-Naters, others warmly welcomed her. During her four years as assistant she attracted a devoted following especially, but not exclusively, among the women. She reestablished a woman's group that had been dormant for many years and reached out especially to the older women, some of whom had been members since Washburn's rectorship.[8]

When Acevedo-Naters left in 1987 to become vicar of St. Mary's Episcopal Church on Bainbridge Street in Philadelphia, David Laquintano, a former Baptist minister who had become an Anglican while studying in Wales, became assistant. A fine preacher and an experienced minister, he took over the duties of the rector when Trimble spent three months studying at Cambridge University.

Laquintano's departure to become rector of a church in Williamsport, Pennsylvania gave Christ Church the opportunity once again to welcome a female assistant. Wendy Watson took the position on an interim basis in the fall of 1989 and was followed by Jean Salin-Miller, who stayed from the spring of 1990 to the fall of 1993. This time the congregation was ready; neither Watson nor Salin-Miller experienced opposition based on her sex; Acevedo-Naters's pioneering stay had laid the groundwork for the acceptance of women clergy at Christ Church.

Salin-Miller, a graduate of Virginia Theological Seminary, which had a long connection with Christ Church, was a former banker, having served as vice president of the Tulsa National Bank. She brought the efficiency learned in a business environment to her new job. She worked hard to set up small groups within the parish so that the still widely dispersed members could get to know each other. While not all the groups were successful, her efforts to get people to make and serve sandwiches for the homeless at the St. Mary's soup kitchen at St. Mary's, Bainbridge, where Acevedo-Naters was vicar, did become an ongoing activity.[9]

The soup kitchen is only one example of the ways Trimble and his assistants have encouraged Christ Church parishioners to increase their benevolence work outside the parish. The rector's discretionary fund, which is made up of income from the "Charity Fund Endowment," gives thousands of dollars each year to a variety of causes, ranging from Episcopal Community Services to scholarships for students. The outreach committee, which was started by Trimble and is responsible for raising its own funds, has greatly expanded the projects the church supports, giving money to the homeless, to black students in South Africa, and to poor churches, as well as continuing to support the Coffee Cup. To broaden the horizons of the church, Trimble has insisted that the proceeds from any fund-raising event the church members hold must be given away.[10]

More recently, following the lead of the General Convention's call for churches to make capital funds available for the poor, rather than merely giving charity, Trimble took a leadership role in convincing the diocese to establish the Episcopal Fund of the Delaware Valley within the Community Investment Fund. This fund provides loans to low income people to buy homes and start businesses. Christ Church has contributed $100,000 in loans to the fund, while the diocese gave $500,000. Altogether the Episcopal Fund now has $2.8 million to lend.

Trimble has also been active in the Philadelphia Interfaith Action Coalition, an organization based on Saul Alinsky's principles of community empowerment. Currently this group has raised $4.5 million in loans to build two thousand houses for low income people; the first four hundred will be built in West Philadelphia.

While the church has reached out to the community in new ways, Trimble's rectorship witnessed the end of one of Christ Church's earlier efforts to be involved in the neighborhood—the Neighborhood Businessmen's Association. With the retirement of many of its members and the removal of more and more businesses, the association had trouble getting people to come to its meetings. So, at Trimble's suggestion, the association ended its distinguished and unique existence. However, Christ Church still remains active in the neighborhood, particularly through the Old City Civic Association.

With all of the changes in the neighborhood in the last sixty years, the leadership of Christ Church realized it was time for the Neighborhood House to undergo major changes. After all, it had been years since the gymnasium had been regularly used for basketball and few remembered bowling in the basement. The vestry commissioned a study, completed in 1993, to determine how best to use this space to serve the congregation and the neighborhood. Final decisions about this space depend on the availability of funding.

As Trimble put more emphasis on Christ Church as an active parish, he subtly de-emphasized its role as a national shrine. Tourists, of course, still flocked to the church. However, Trimble refused to join any patriotic organizations except one and served on only one historical association—the board of the the Independence Hall Association. While patriotic groups still held special services at the church occasionally, these services became the exception rather than the rule.

This does not mean that Trimble lacked interest in the church's history, only that he saw the church's role differently than did Harding. The best example of Trimble's views are the conferences Christ Church has sponsored. For the Bicentennial of the Constitution, at Trimble's suggestion and largely through his initiative, the church held a conference in October 1987 on religion and the Constitution, entitled "Religion and the Public Good," featuring prominent historians and religious figures. This ecumenical three-day conference, sponsored and in part funded by the Preservation Trust, explored five areas: religion's influence on the writing of the Constitution; the role of religion in public life; church, state, and religious freedom; religion in a pluralistic society; and religion and the public good from a Third World perspective. The papers delivered at this conference were published.[11] Another conference, on the future of the Episcopal Church, was held in 1989.

Thus it is not surprising that when the church looked at ways to celebrate the three-hundredth anniversary of its founding, it chose to look both backward and forward. In addition to two major celebrative services, complete with original music, the church plans to sponsor a three-day conference entitled "The Soul of America in a World of Violence: A Religious Response." Like Washburn, Trimble believes that the urban church cannot isolate itself. Rather than focusing on the events of the past, Trimble's vision, like deBordenave's, has been to use Christ Church's visibility and historical importance to address important issues of the present and the future.

How successful have Trimble and the laypeople of Christ Church been in achieving their primary goal—building up a parish church? In some ways the best answer to that question is a comparison of the 1964 parish study with a more recent analysis of pledging units. Although the group used in the diocesan study included more than just those who pledged, the comparison provides a general idea of the changes. While only 50 percent of the 1964 group lived in Philadelphia and almost 30 percent outside the state, 73 percent of the 242 people who pledged in 1989 lived in the city and only 8.6 percent lived in New Jersey. More important, 23 percent lived in the area between Delaware Avenue and Broad Street and Callowill and Pine Streets, compared to 6.1 percent living in a similar area in 1964 (see Map 8). The congregation of Christ Church is still scattered; in 1989 pledgers could be found in thirty-seven of Philadelphia's fifty-two zip codes and many suburbs

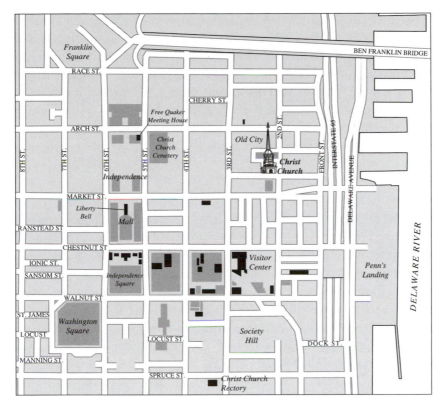

MAP 8
Area surrounding Christ Church, 1980s.

as well. Everyone agrees that more work still needs to be done in attracting center city residents. But progress toward regaining Christ Church's role as a true Parish church is being made.[12]

As the church began to draw from the neighborhood, the character of the congregation also began to change. The number of working class members declined, as those who joined during Washburn's era have died or moved away. At the same time, young, affluent professionals who live in center city joined Christ Church. Of those responding to the survey of the parish in 1986, 54 percent had incomes above $50,000 and had at least a college education. While still attracting a variety of people, including a small number of minorities, Christ Church fits the description of an upper middle class church far more today than it did in the colonial period.

These members continue to represent the broad range of political and ecclesiastical views that have been present throughout the church's history. Of the seventy-nine who answered a survey in 1986, 24 percent disapproved of the present Book of Common Prayer, while 63 percent approved of it (the remainder did not answer). When asked to describe the political orientation of Christ Church, thirteen said it was conservative, twenty said it was active in social issues, while eleven said it was middle of the road. As one person wrote, "the church seems to be able to steer a course somewhere between the far right and the far left and meet needs and opportunities in appropriate ways as they arise."[13]

*   *   *

What does the future hold for Christ Church as it enters its fourth century? Perhaps the best thing the rector and congregation of Christ Church could do to assure the church's future is to follow the examples set by previous rectors and congregations, for when one looks back over the history of Christ Church, a number of themes emerge of which the church should be proud. Christ Church has a tradition of accepting diversity and scorning rigidity or exclusivity of any kind. From the time of Richard Peters, the church has been willing to accept divergent beliefs within the congregation and as a result, it has been largely unaffected by the many theological battles that have plagued the Episcopal Church over the last two hundred years. This acceptance of diversity combined with the low church tradition epitomized by Bishop White has allowed those not raised in the Episcopal Church to feel comfortable as members of Christ Church. Similarly, since colonial days, Christ Church has been a leader in accepting other faiths as equal. Because of both the colonial experience and the ecumenical spirit exemplified by Bishop William White, it was fitting that Louis Washburn should have played an active role in the Philadelphia Federation of Churches. This ecumenical spirit was extended to include an unusually friendly relationship with the Jewish community during World War II. The church has also shown concern for blacks at a time when it was not yet popular to do so; the school for blacks set up by William Sturgeon was a model for others throughout the colonies. And while Benjamin Dorr did not take a leadership role when slavery was the burning issue. both Louis Washburn and Felix Kloman urged their congregations to show concern for blacks at a time when it was not yet popular to do so. Thus it was appropriate that Ernest Harding show at least tacit support for Bishop Robert DeWitt's programs in the 1970s, even though the congregation was rather conservative. While Christ Church itself has always been a primarily white, middle of the road to conservative institution, toleration and concern for others has been an ever present theme in its history.

This concern for others has led in the last century to an emphasis on social service and a desire to be of use to the neighborhood around the church. While Louis Washburn personifies this theme for most who know Christ Church, it was begun by Edward Foggo and expanded by C. Ellis Stevens. The changing neighborhood led E. A. deBordenave and Ernest Harding to downplay this facet of the church's history, but recently James Trimble and the outreach committee are reviving it in new ways.

The current congregation and all those that follow it must also, of course, continue to grapple with the dual role of Christ Church—that of a national shrine and a parish church. While this balancing act is a difficult one, the leadership of Christ Church over the years has evidenced an amazing ability to know which theme needed to be emphasized when. Louis Washburn, who came to Christ Church when it was considered no more than a museum, knew that he had to put most of his energies into building up the parish church, while not forgetting, of course, the historical aspect. Felix Kloman continued this theme, focusing on the crises of the present. But by the 1950s it was apparent to both E. A. deBordenave and Ernest Harding that the usefulness of the church—and possibly its future—depended on accentuating its history. Now, once again, the emphasis has been rightly placed on the parish church. But throughout this period, no rector has concentrated on one aspect to the total exclusion of the other.

Finally, as with all churches, Christ Church needs to continue to minister to the needs of its members. The United Churches demonstrated what happens when the spiritual needs of the church's members are not met. Benjamin Dorr established a truly caring rectorship at Christ Church, and this tradition has been followed by all rectors who came after. Even when the members of the congregation were so dispersed that caring for their needs meant spending hours on the road, the rectors have continued to see this as their primary function. While the rich history of Christ Church has allowed it to survive financially, its reason for being has always remained the spiritual development of its members, so that they can serve God.

It is by following these themes that Christ Church can best use its history to assure its future and play a meaningful role in the lives of its members and in the city for another three hundred years.

NOTES

1. Vestry members interviews with author; Peter Hearn, Philadelphia, Aug. 4, 1987; Henry Watts, Philadelphia, Aug. 7, 1986; Frank Dyer, Philadelphia, Aug. 6, 1987.

2. Survey of current members of Christ Church conducted by author, Fall 1986.

3. Rev. James Trimble, interview with author, Philadelphia, Aug. 4, 1987.

4. Ibid.

5. "Trust Seeks $750,000 for Steeple Project," *Preservation Post* 4 (Fall 1984): 1–3.

6. Rev. James Trimble, interview with author, Aug. 4, 1987; Peter Hearn, interview with author, Aug. 4, 1987; Bruce Gill, interview with author, Philadelphia, June 13, 1986; Robert Gill, interview with author, July 30, 1987; Henry Watts, intreview with author, Aug. 7, 1986; Frank Dyer, interview with author, Aug. 6, 1986.

7. Noreen Carter, "The Episcopal Story," in *Women of Spirit: Female Leadership in the Jewish and Christian Traditions*, ed. Rosemary Radford Ruether and Eleanor McLaughlin (New York: 1979), 356–72; "Episcopal Bishops Eke Out a Fragile Peace," *Christian Century* 94 (Nov. 2, 1977): 996; "A Case of Woman Trouble," *Time* 110 (Oct. 17, 1977): 80; "Anglican Secessionists Consecrate Four Bishops," *Christian Century* 95 (February 15, 1978): 149–51.

8. Rev. James Trimble, interview with author, Aug. 4, 1987; Rev. Miriam Acevedo-Naters, interview with author, Aug. 2, 1986.

9. Rev. James Trimble, telephone interview with author, December 14, 1993.

10. Rev. James Trimble, interview with author, Aug. 4, 1987, Dec. 14, 1993; Bertha von Moschzishker, interview with author, June 13, 1986. Von Moschzisker served as chair of the Outreach Committee for many years.

11. The origins of this conference are discussed in the *Beacon*, Summer 1988, 1–2.

12. "Parish Survey, Christ Church, 1964"; Pledging units by zip code, 1989.

13. Survey of current members of Christ Church, Fall 1986.

BIBLIOGRAPHY

Interviews and Personal Communication

Acevedo-Naters, Miriam, Assistant to the Rector, Christ Church, interview with author, Philadelphia, August 2, 1986.

Clark, Lucille, former Public Relations specialist, Christ Church, interview with author, Philadelphia, August 2, 1987.

DeBordenave, Cyane, letter to author, April 20, 1986 and March 30, 1989.

DeWitt, Robert, letter to author, April 23, 1989.

Dyer, Frank, vestry member, Christ Church, interview with author, Philadelphia, August 6, 1987.

Gill, Bruce, curator and member, Christ Church, interview with author, Philadelphia, June 13, 1986.

Gill, Robert, vestry member, Christ Church, interview with author, Philadelphia, July 30, 1987.

Hannum, John, vestry member, Christ Church, interview with author, Philadelphia, August 6, 1986.

Hearn, Peter, vestry member, Christ Church, interview with author, Philadelphia, August 4, 1987.

Heavens, Alan, clerk and vestry member, St. Peter's Church, interview with author, Philadelphia, August 3, 1987.

Kloman, Olivia, letter to author, n.d [1986].

Lingham, Amelia, cleaning woman, Christ Church, interview with author, Philadelphia, June 9, 1987.

O'Neill, Jane, former parish visitor, Christ Church, interview with author, Philadelphia, June 14, 1986.

Perry, Rev. Rex, letter to author, July 27, 1988.

Snaidman, Mrs. Frank, former parishioner, Christ Church, telephone interview with author, June, 1986.

Shannon, James, former Assistant to the Rector, Christ Church, interview with author, August 1, 1987.

Trimble, James, Rector, Christ Church, interview with author, Philadelphia, August 4, 1987; telephone interview, December 14, 1993.

Van Dusen, Francis, former vestry member, Christ Church, interview with author, Philadelphia, August 2, 1987.

VonMoschzisker, Bertha, vestry member, Christ Church, interview with author, Philadelphia, June 13, 1986.

Washburn, Louis, grandson of rector of Christ Church, interview with author, Philadelphia, August 5, 1988.

Watts, Henry, vestry member, Christ Church, interview with author, Philadelphia, August 7, 1986.

White, William, former vestryman, Christ Church, interview with author, Philadelphia, June 13, 1986.

Widing, C. Jon, former Assistant Minister, Christ Church, taped answers to written questions, April 1986.

Manuscripts and Unpublished Sources

Board of Trade Papers, Proprietors; transcripts. Historical Society of Pennsylvania.
Christ Church Archives.

> Accounting Warden's Journals, 1708–1880
> Accounting Warden's Cashbooks, 1880–1976
> Accounting Warden's Letterbook, 1892–1902.
> Baptism records of Christ Church and St. Peter's, 1715–1776.
> Burial records of Christ Church, 1832–1976
> Calvary Monumental Church, Account Book, 1848–1871.
> Charity Fund Records, 1793–1814.
> Christ Church Chapel Board of Management Records, 1876–1929; Parish Registers, 1879–1929
> Christ Church Historical Association. Minute Book, Record Book.
> Christ Church Hospital Board of Managers. Minutes, 1804–1942.
> Christ Church Hospital Ladies' Committee. Minutes.
> Collection Records, 1765–1772, 1785–1799, 1803–1814, 1834–1867.
> Confirmation Register, 1835–1976.
> Corporation. Correspondence and Other Records.
> Dorcas Society. Correspondence, 1861–1863; Record Book, 1859–1913.
> Dorr, Benjamin. Correspondence, 1844–1853.
> Female Sunday School Society. Minute Book, 1816–1833; Attendance Register, 1816–1821.
> Joint Committee on Christ Church and Other Historic Sites. Minutes.
> Ladies' Missionary Association. Correspondence of Secretary, 1825–1860.

Male Sunday School. Receipt Book, 1847–1853.

Parish Council. Minutes, 1912–1939.

Pew Rent Books, 1776–1957.

Protestant Episcopal Association of Christ Church for the Promotion of Christianity. Minute Book, 1833–1836.

Service Record Books, 1938–1976.

Vestry of Christ Church. Minutes, Committee Records and Correspondence, 1717–1761, 1834–1976.

Vestry of United Congregations. Minutes, Committee Records and Correspondence, 1761–1834.

Women's Auxiliary. Minutes, 1949–1957.

Women's Missionary Society. Minute Book, 1908–1915, 1925–1937; Secretary's correspondence

Washburn, Louis. Correspondence, 1910–1935.

Coombe Family Papers. Historical Society of Pennsylvania.

Coxe, Tench. Papers. Historical Society of Pennsylvania.

Dreer Autograph Collection. Historical Society of Pennsylvania.

First Presbyterian Church. Pew Rent Books, 1784–1798. Presbyterian Historical Society.

Fischer, Sidney George. Diary. Historical Society of Pennsylvania.

Fulham Papers. American Colonial Section, Lambeth Palace Library, volumes 7 and 8, microfilm, Van Pelt Library, University of Pennsylvania; transcripts, Library of Congress.

Gratz Autograph Collection. Historical Society of Pennsylvania.

Independence National Historic Park, Archives.

Kemper, Jackson. Papers. State Historical Society of Wisconsin

Lambeth Palace Papers. Three volumes relating to the American colonies; transcripts, Library of Congress.

Logan, James. Papers, Historical Society of Pennsylvania.

Meredith, William. Papers. Historical Society of Pennsylvania.

Norris, Issac. Papers. Historical Society of Pennsylvania.

Parish Survey of Christ Church, 1964. Archives of the Episcopal Diocese of Pennsylvania, Philadelphia, Pennsylvania.

Penn Papers. Historical Society of Pennsylvania
> Official Correspondence.
> Private Correspondence.
> Saunders Coats, Additional Letter Books.
> Thomas Penn Letter Books.

Perry, William S. "Life of William White." Typescript, Rare Book Room, University of Pennsylvania.

Peters, Richard. Papers. Historical Society of Pennsylvania.

Peterson, Karin. "Christ Church, Its Congregation Between 1750 and 1760." Seminar Paper, University of Pennsylvania, 1975.

St. Paul's Episcopal Church. Vestry and Register, 1766–1772. Archives of the Episcopal Diocese of Pennsylvania, Philadelphia, Pennsylvania.

Second Presbyterian Church. Pew Rent Books, 1784–1798, Presbyterian Historical Society.

Smith Family Papers. Historical Society of Pennsylvania.

Smith, William. Manuscripts. Archives of the Protestant Episcopal Church, Austin, Texas.

Smith, William. Papers. Historical Society of Pennsylvania.

Smith, William. "State of the American Church presented to Archbishop Drummond, Bishop of London and others May, 1762." Copy in Christ Church archives.

Society Autograph Collection. "Record Book of the Acts of Cummings as Commissary." Historical Society of Pennsylvania.

Society for the Propagation of the Gospel in Foreign Parts. Letters and Journals, microfilm, Library of Congress.

Stevens, Bishop William, Papers. Archives of the Episcopal Diocese of Pennsylvania.

Third Presbyterian Church. Pew Rent Books, 1784–1798. Presbyterian Historical Society.

Trustees of the University of Pennsylvania. Minutes. University Archives.

Wallace Papers. Historical Society of Pennsylvania.

White, William. Manuscripts. Archives of the Protestant Episcopal Church, Austin, Texas.

Court Records

Application for approval of the Charter of the Church of the Holy Communion. Court of Common Pleas No. 2, December Term, 1879, no. 639. Petition and Exceptions Against Approval.

The Rector, Churchwardens and Vestrymen of Christ Church et al. against the Rector, Churchwardens and Vestrymen of the Church of the Holy Communion et al. Court of Common Pleas No. 1 for the City and County of Philadelphia, March Term, 1880, No. 163.

> Affidavits of Defendants.
>
> Complainants' Affidavits.
>
> The Arguments of Wm. W. Wiltbank Esq. and William Henry Rawle, Esq. to which is Added The opinion of the Court, delivered June 23rd, 1880 and the Decrees.

Newspapers

American Weekly Mercury. Philadelphia. 1720–40.

Daily News. Philadelphia. April 4 and 16, 1952.

Evening Bulletin. Philadelphia. March 9, 1898, June 11, 1921, Dec. 16, 1925, Sept. 3, 1932, May 6, 1936; Feb. 9, March 4, 30, 1952; January 12, 1959.

Evening Ledger. Philadelphia. May 2, 1929.

North American. Philadelphia. March 11, 1913.

Pennsylvania Gazette. Philadelphia. 1729–40; Sept. 18—Nov. 14, 1768; Jan. 5, Feb. 24, March 3, 17, 31, 1779.

Pennsylvania Journal and American Weekly Advertiser. Philadelphia. March 25, April 22, May 20, June 10, June 17, 1756; March 24–July 7, 1768.

Philadelphia Aurora. August 28, September 1, 1800.

Philadelphia Bulletin. February–March, 1880, February, 1904.

Philadelphia Inquirer. February–March, 1880, March 5, 12, 27, 1952.

Philadelphia Press. February–March, 1880; February, 1904.

Philadelphia Register. February–March, 1880.

Philadelphia Times, February–March, 1880

Preservation Post. 1977–1984.

Printed Sources

Abbey, Charles J. and John H. Overton. *The English Church in the Eighteenth Century*. 2 vols. London: Longman's and Green, 1878.

Abercrombie, James. *Charge delivered after a public examination of the Senior Class of the Philadelphia Academy*. Philadelphia: Smith and Maxwell, 1807.

——. *Lectures on the Catechism*. 2d ed. Philadelphia: Smith and Maxwell, 1811.

——. *A Sermon on the Liturgy of the Protestant Episcopal Church*. Philadelphia: Smith and Maxwell, 1808.

——. *Two Sermons, the First Preached on Thursday, July 30, the second preached on Thursday, August 20, 1812*. Philadelphia: Moses Thomas, 1812.

Abernathy, Lloyd M. "Progressivism, 1905–1919." In *Philadelphia: A Three Hundred Year History*. Ed. Russell F. Weigley. New York: W.W. Norton and Company, 1982, 529–64.

Abstracts Concerning Christ Church for the Diocesan Year Ending April 30. Philadelphia, 1879, 1886, 1892–1895, 1900, 1903, 1912.

Adams, Donald R. "Wage Rates in the Early National Period, Philadelphia, 1785–1830." *Journal of Economic History* 28 (1968): 404–17.

Adams, John. *Diary and Autobiography*. Vol. 2. Ed. L. H. Butterfield. Cambridge, Mass.: Belknap Press of Harvard University Press, 1961

Addison, James Thayer. *The Episcopal Church in the United States, 1789–1931*. New York, 1951. Reprint, Hamden, Conn.: Archon Books, 1969.

Ahlstrom, Sydney E. *A Religious History of the American People*. New Haven, Conn.: Yale University Press, 1972.

Allen, Alexander. *Life and Letters of Phillips Brooks*, 3 vols. New York: Dutton, 1901.

An Address of Thanks to the Wardens of Christ Church and St. Peter's and the Rev. W— S—h, D.D., Provost of the College and Tool to the P—r and Jacob Duche AM &

MVD from F—A—n DD and Jn E—g in their own Name and in the Name of all the Presbyterian Ministers in Pennsylvania. Philadelphia: Anthony Armbruster, October 26, 1764.

An Address to all who have been at any time Connected with Christ Church Or who may be interested in it. Philadelphia, 1874.

Andrews, Doris Elizabeth. "Popular Religion and the Revolution in the Mid Atlantic Ports: The Rise of the Methodists 1770–1800." Ph.D. diss., University of Pennsylvania, 1986.

"Anglican Secessionists Consecrate Four Bishops." *Christian Century* 95 (Feb. 15, 1978): 149–51.

Armstrong, Anthony. *The Church of England, the Methodists and Society, 1700–1850*. Totowa, N.J.: Rowman and Littlefield, 1973.

Armstrong, Edward, ed. *Correspondence between William Penn and James Logan*. In Historical Society of Pennsylvania, *Memoirs*, 9 and 10 (1870, 1872). Philadelphia: The Society, 1870, 1872.

Ayres, Ann. *Life and Works of William Augustus Muhlenberg*. New York: Harper and Brothers, 1880.

Barclay, Robert. *Barclay's Apology in Modern English*. Ed. Dean Freiday. Elberon, N.J.: Privately printed, 1967.

Barratt, Norris S. *Outline of the History of Old St.Paul's Church*. Philadelphia: Colonial Society of Pennsylvania, 1917.

Barton, Thomas. *Unanimity and Public Spirit*. Philadelphia: Franklin and Hall, 1755.

Beardsley, E. Edwards. *History of the Episcopal Church in Connecticut*. 2 vols. New York: Hurd and Stoughton, 1866.

Bell, Marion L. *Crusade in the City: Revivalism in Nineteenth Century Philadelphia*. Lewisburg, Pa: Bucknell University Press, 1977.

Bell, Whitfield J., Jr. *John Morgan: Continental Doctor*. Philadelphia: University of Pennsylvania Press, 1965.

Bilhartz, Terry. *Urban Religion and the Second Great Awakening*. Madison, N.J.: Fairleigh Dickinson University Press, 1986.

Binney, Charles Chauncey. *The Life of Horace Binney with Selections from His Letters*. Philadelphia: J. P. Lippincott, 1903.

Bioren, John, ed. *Journals of the General Conventions of the Protestant Episcopal Church in the United States of America; from the year 1784, to the year 1814 inclusive*. Philadelphia: John Bioren, printer, 1817.

Bishop White Prayerbook Society. *Annual Reports*. 1834–67. Philadelphia, 1834–67.

Bolton, Sidney G. "The Anglican Church of Colonial South Carolina 1704–1754: A Study in Americanization." Ph.D. diss., University of Wisconsin, 1973.

Bonomi, Patricia. *Under the Cope of Heaven: Religion, Society and Politics in Colonial America*. New York: Oxford University Press, 1986.

Boylan, Anne M. *Sunday School: The Formation of an American Institution, 1790–1880*. New Haven, Conn.: Yale University Press, 1988.

——. "Women in Groups: An Analysis of Women's Benevolent Organizations in New York and Boston, 1797–1840." *Journal of American History* 71 (1984): 497–523.

Brewer, Clifton. *A History of Religious Education in the Episcopal Church to 1835.* New Haven, Conn.: Yale University Press, 1924. Reprint, New York: Arno Press, 1969.

Bridenbaugh, Carl. *Cities in the Wilderness: The First Century of Urban Life in America, 1625–1742.* New York: Knopf, 1955.

——. *Mitre and Sceptre.* New York: Oxford University Press, 1962.

Bridenbaugh, Carl and Jessica Bridenbaugh. *Rebels and Gentlemen: Philadelphia in the Age of Franklin.* New York: Oxford University Press, 1942.

Brill, Earl. "The Episcopal Church: Conflict and Cohesion." *Christian Century* 95 (1978): 41–47.

Brinton, Howard H. *Friends for Three Hundred Years.* Philadelphia: Pendle Hill Publications, 1964.

Brobeck, Stephen. "Changes in Composition and Structure of Philadelphia Elite Groups 1756–1790." Ph.D. diss., University of Pennsylvania, 1972.

——. "Revolutionary Change in Colonial Philadelphia: The Brief Life of the Proprietary Group." *WMQ* 33 (1976): 410–34.

Bronner, Edwin H. "Village into Town, 1701–1746." In *Philadelphia: A Three Hundred Year History.* Ed. Russell F. Weigley. New York: W.W. Norton and Company, 1982, 33–67.

Bronson, William W., comp. *Inscription in St. Peter's Church Yard.* Camden, N.J., 1879.

Brunhouse, Robert. *The Counter-Revolution in Pennsylvania 1776–1790.* Harrisburg, Pa.: no publisher, 1942.

Bucke, Emory S., ed. *The History of American Methodism.* New York and Nashville: Abington Press, 1964.

Bultmann, William A. "The Society for the Propagation of the Gospel in Foreign Parts and the Foreign Settler in the American Colonies." Ph.D. diss., University of California at Los Angeles, 1951.

Burnett, Edmund C., ed. *Letters of the Members of the Continental Congress.* 8 vols. Washington, D.C.: Carnegie Institution of Washington, 1921–36.

Burr, Nelson. *The Anglican Church in New Jersey.* Philadelphia: Church Historical Society, 1954.

Butler, Jon. *Power, Authority, and the Origins of American Denominational Order: The English Churches in the Delaware Valley 1680–1730.* American Philosophical Society, *Transactions* 68 (1978).

Buxbaum, Melvin H. *Benjamin Franklin and the Zealous Presbyterians.* University Park: Pennsylvania State University Press, 1975.

Byrnes, Don Roy. "The Pre-Revolutionary Career of William Smith, 1751–1780." Ph.D. diss., Tulane University, 1969.

Carter, Noreen. "The Episcopal Story." In *Women of Spirit: Female Leadership in the Jewish and Christian Traditions*. Ed. Rosemary Radford Ruether and Eleanor McLaughlin. New York: Simon and Schuster, 1979, 356–72.

Carter, Paul. *The Decline and Revival of the Social Gospel*. 1958. Reprint, Hamden, Conn.: Archon Books, 1971.

"A Case of Woman Trouble." *Time* 110 (Oct. 17, 1977): 80.

The Catalog of the 1981 Antiques Show: A Benefit for the Hospital of the University of Pennsylvania. Philadelphia: Privately printed, 1981.

Chandler, Thomas Bradbury. *An Appeal to the Public in Behalf of the Church of England in America*. New York: James Parker, 1767.

Cheyney, Edward Potts. *History of the University of Pennsylvania, 1740–1940*. Philadelphia: University of Pennsylvania Press, 1940.

Chorley, E. C. *Men and Movements in the American Episcopal Church*. New York: Charles Scribner's Sons, 1946.

Christ Church. *The Beacon*. 1952–78.

Christ Church Easter Offerings, March 15, 1895. Philadelphia, 1895.

Christ Church. *Leaflet*. 1938–51.

Christ Church. *The Voice*. 1930–1932.

Christ Church Hospital. *Annual Report*. 1933. Philadelphia, 1933.

Christ Church Hospital Board of Managers. *Report of the Managers of the Christ Church Hospital on the Completion of the New Building at Belmont*. Philadelphia, 1864.

Christ Church Newsletter. 1931–32, 1938, 1944–47.

Christ Church Rectory: A Project to Restore an Historic House for the Use of an Historic Church. [1960].

Christ Church Reporter. 1932–37.

Christ Church Statement. Philadelphia, n.d.

Circular to the Congregation of Christ Church, Philadelphia and to all friends of the Church here and elsewhere. Philadelphia, 1864.

Coombe, Thomas. *A Sermon Preached Before the Congregation of Christ Church and St. Peter's, July 20, 1775*. Philadelphia: John Dunlap, 1775.

Cott, Nancy. *The Bonds of Womanhood*. New Haven, Conn.: Yale University Press, 1977.

Cross, Arthur. *The Anglican Episcopate and the American Colonies*. New York: Harvard Historical Studies, 1902.

Cummings, Archibald. *The Danger of Breaking Christian Unity in Two Sermons Preached at Christ Church in Philadelphia*. Philadelphia: Andrew Bradford, 1737.

——. *An Exhortation to the Clergy of Pennsylvania at Philadelphia, September 24, 1729*. Annapolis, Md.: W. Parks, 1729.

——. *Faith Absolutely Necessary but Not Sufficient to Salvation Without . . . Good Works*. Philadelphia: Andrew Bradford, 1740.

Cummings, Hubertis. *Richard Peters: Provincial Secretary and Cleric, 1704–1776*. Philadelphia: University of Pennsylvania Press, 1944.

Dallimore, Arnold A. *George Whitefield: The Life and Times of the Great Evangelist of the Eighteenth Century Revival*. London: Banner of Truth Trust, 1970.

Davies, Horton. *Worship and Theology in England*. Vol. 3: *From Watts and Wesley to Maurice, 1690–1850*. Princeton, N.J.: Princeton University Press, 1961.

A Declaration by Christ Church in Philadelphia, November, 1952. Philadelphia, 1952.

DeLancey, William Heathcote. *"Plain Truth": A Candid Address . . . .* Philadelphia, 1827.

DeMille, George M. *The Catholic Movement in the American Episcopal Church*. Philadelphia: Church Historical Society, 1941.

Dexter, Franklin, ed. *Extracts from the Itineraries and Other Miscellanies of Ezra Stiles*. New Haven, Conn.: Yale University Press, 1915.

Diamondstone, Judith. "The Philadelphia Corporation 1701–1776." Ph.D. diss., University of Pennsylvania, 1969.

Diocese of Pennsylvania. *Journals of the Diocese of Pennsylvania*. Philadelphia: Published by the Diocese, 1833, 1835–1869, 1879, 1894. 1898, 1907–1938, 1940, 1970.

A Directory of the Charitable, Social Improvement, Education and Religious Associations and Churches of Philadelphia. Prepared by the Civic Club. Philadelphia, 1903.

Dix, Morgan. *A History of the Parish of Trinity Church in the City of New York*. 4 vols. New York: Putman, 1898–1906.

Doerflinger, Thomas M. *A Vigorous Spirit of Enterprise*. Chapel Hill: University of North Carolina Press, 1986.

"Dollars for Dolls." *Preservation Post* 2, 2 (1978): 1–2.

Dorr, Benjamin. *The American Vine: A Sermon Preached in Christ Church, Philadelphia, Friday, January 4, 1861, on Occasion of The National Fast. . . .* Philadelphia: Collins, 1861.

——. *Churchman's Manual: An Exposition of the Doctrines, Ministry and Worship of the Protestant Episcopal Church in the United States*. Burlington, N.J.: J. H. Powell Missionary Press, 1835.

——. *Elisha's Fountain or the Waters Healed*. Philadelphia: 1866.

——. *A Historical Account of Christ Church, Philadelphia from Its Foundation In 1695 to 1841*. Philadelphia: R.S.H. George, 1841.

——. *History of a Pocket Prayerbook Written by Itself*. Philadelphia: George W. Donohue, 1844.

——. *Memorials of Christ Church, Philadelphia. Two Sermons Preached in Said Church, April 27 and May 4, 1864. One the 135th Anniversary of Laying the Corner-Stone of the Present Building; The Other the 25th Anniversary of the Rector's Institutions*. Philadelphia: Collins, 1862.

——. *The Recognition of Friends in Another World*. 8th edition. Philadelphia: H. Hooker, 1864.

Dubbs, J. H. *History of the Reformed Church in Pennsylvania*. Lancaster, Pa.: New Era Press, 1902.

Duché, Jacob. *The American Vine: a sermon, preached in Christ-Church, Philadelphia, before the honourable Continental Congress, July 20th, 1775*. Philadelphia: J. Humphreys, Jr., 1775.

———. *The Duty of Standing Fast in our Spiritual and Temporal Liberties, a sermon, preached in Christ-Church, July 7th, 1775*. Philadelphia: J. Humphreys, Jr., 1775.

Dudden, Arthur P. "The City Embraces 'Normalcy.'" In *Philadelphia: A Three Hundred Year History*. Ed. Russell F. Weigley. New York: W.W. Norton and Company, 1982, 566–600.

Dunbar, John, ed. *The Paxton Papers*. The Hague: Martinus Nijhoff, 1957.

Dunn, Mary Maples and Richard Dunn. "The Founding, 1682–1701." In *Philadelphia: A Three Hundred Year History*. Ed. Russell F. Weigley. New York: W.W. Norton and Company, 1982, 1–32.

Dusinberre, William. *Civil War Issues in Philadelphia, 1856–1865*. Philadelphia: University of Pennsylvania Press, 1965.

Elliott-Binns, L. E. *The Early Evangelicals: A Religious and Social History*. Greenwich, Conn.: Lutterworth Press, 1953.

Ellis, Joseph. *The New England Mind in Transition: Samuel Johnson of Connecticut, 1696–1772*. New Haven, Conn.: Yale University Press, 1973.

"Episcopal Agony over Ecclesiastical Disobedience." *Christian Century* 91 (Sept. 4, 1974): 812–14.

"Episcopal Bishop Under Attack." *Christian Century* 87 (Nov. 11, 1970): 1363.

"Episcopal Bishops Eke Out a Fragile Peace." *Christian Century* 94 (Nov. 2, 1977): 996.

Every, George. *The High Church Party 1688–1718*. London: Church Historical Society by Society for the Propagation of Christian Knowledge, 1956.

Fairbanks, Joseph. "Richard Peters (c.1704–1776), Provincial Secretary of Pennsylvania." Ph.D. diss., University of Arizona, 1972.

Feldberg, Michael. *The Philadelphia Riots of 1844: A Study of Ethnic Conflict*. Westport, Conn.: Greenwood Press, 1975.

Female Episcopal Tract Society. *Annual Report*. 1830–31. *Protestant Episcopalian* 1, 6 (1830): 234–36, 2, 7 (1831): 272–74. Philadelphia, 1830.

Foggo, Edward. *History of Recent Events in Christ Church Parish*. Philadelphia, 1880.

———. *Sermon on the Restoration of the Interior of Christ Church, Philadelphia, November 11, 1882*. Philadelphia, 1882.

———. *A Sketch of the Work in the Parish of Christ Church by the Reverend Edward Foggo*. Philadelphia, 1897.

Force, Peter, ed. *American Archives*, 4th series. Washington, D.C., by Act of Congress, 1837–53.

Fox, George. *The Journal of George Fox*. Ed. Rufus Jones. New York: Capricorn Books, 1963.

Franklin, Benjamin. *Autobiography*. Ed. Max Farrand. Berkeley and Los Angeles: University of California Press, 1949.

——. *The Papers of Benjamin Franklin*. Vols. 5 and 8. Ed. Leonard Labaree et al. New Haven, Conn.: Yale University Press, 1962, 1965.

Friary, Donald. "The Architecture of the Anglican Churches in the Northern American Colonies: A Study of Religious, Social and Cultural Expression." Ph.D. diss., University of Pennsylvania, 1974.

Gable, Martin Dewey Jr. "The Hymnody of the Church, 1789–1832." *HMPEC* 36 (1967): 249–69.

The Galilee Mission: The Church's Greatest Life Saving Station, Extracts from Annual Report, 1915. Philadelphia, 1915.

Gardner, Donald Russell. "The Society for the Advancement of Christianity in Pennsylvania." *HMPEC* 23 (1954): 321–52.

Garrett, Clark. "The Spiritual Odyssey of Jacob Duché." American Philosophical Society, *Proceedings* 119, 2 (1975): 144–55.

Geffen, Elizabeth. "Industrial Development and Social Crisis, 1841–1854." In *Philadelphia: A Three Hundred Year History*. Ed. Russell F. Weigley. New York: W.W. Norton and Company, 1982, 307–62.

Geffen, Elizabeth. "Philadelphia Protestants React to Social Reform Movements Before the Civil War." *Pennsylvania History* 30 (April 1963): 192–202

Gegenheimer, Albert Frank. *William Smith: Educator and Churchman, 1727–1803*. Philadelphia: University of Pennsylvania Press, 1943.

Gill, Bruce Cooper. "Christ Church in Philadelphia: Furnishings, The Early Years." In *The Catalog of the 1981 Antiques Show: A Benefit for the Hospital of the University of Pennsylvania*. Philadelphia: Privately printed, 1981, 129–32.

Godcharles, Frederic, ed. *Encyclopedia of Pennsylvania Biography*. New York: Lewis Historical Publishing Company, 1914.

Goodwin, Gerald. "The Anglican Middle Way in Early Eighteenth Century America." Ph.D. diss., University of Wisconsin, 1967.

Gough, Deborah. "Pluralism, Politics and Power Struggles: The Church of England in Colonial Philadelphia." Ph.D. diss., University of Pennsylvania, 1977.

Gough, Robert. "Toward a Theory of Class and Social Conflict: A Social History of Wealthy Philadelphians, 1775 and 1800." Ph.D. diss., University of Pennsylvania, 1977.

Gray, Betty. "Episcopalians Shape a New Liturgical Life." *Christian Century* 93 (Sept. 1976): 731–32.

Greenberg, Irwin F. "Charles Ingersoll: Aristocrat as Copperhead." *PMHB* 93 (1989): 190–217.

Greiff, Constance M. *Independence: The Creation of a National Park*. Philadelphia: University of Pennsylvania Press, 1987.

Gribbin, William. "American Episcopacy and the War of 1812." *HMPEC* 38 (1969): 25–36.

Griffin, Clifford. *Their Brothers' Keepers: Moral Stewardship in the United States, 1800–1865*. New Brunswick, N.J.: Rutgers University Press, 1960.

Gunderson, Joan R. "Parallel Churches: Women and the Episcopal Church, 1850–1980." *Mid-America* 69 (1987): 87–97.

Handbook of Christ Church, Philadelphia. 1892. Philadelphia, 1892.

Handbook of Christ Church, Philadelphia. 1912. Philadelphia, 1912.

Handy, Robert. T. *A Christian America: Protestant Hopes and Historical Realities*. New York: Oxford University Press, 1984.

Hardy, Edward, Jr. "Kemper's Missionary Episcopate: 1835–1859." *HMPEC* 4 (1935): 195–218.

Hatchett, Marion. *The Making of the First American Book of Common Prayer*. New York: Seabury Press, 1982.

——. "A Sunday Service in 1776 or Thereabouts." *HMPEC* 45 (1976): 369–85.

Hawke, David. *In the Midst of a Revolution: The Politics of Confrontation in Colonial America*. Philadelphia: University of Pennsylvania Press, 1961.

Hazard, Samuel et al. *Pennsylvania Archives*. 8th series. Philadelphia and Harrisburg: 1852–1935.

Helen Carpenter Washburn, 1892–1946. Philadelphia: Privately published, 1946.

Hershberg, Theodore, ed. *Philadelphia: Work, Space, Family and Group Experience in the Nineteenth Century*. New York: Oxford University Press, 1981.

Hewitt, Nancy. *Women's Activism and Social Change, Rochester, N.Y., 1822–1872*. Ithaca, N.Y.: Cornell University Press, 1984.

Hills, George. *The Wise Master Builder.* Syracuse, N.Y., 1865.

"Historic Christ Church Issues a New Declaration." *The Witness* (May 15, 1952): 1.

Hindle, Brooke. *The Pursuit of Science in Revolutionary America 1735–1789*. Chapel Hill: University of North Carolina Press, 1956.

Hodge, G. Woolsey, Admiral Fairfax, and J. Edward Carpenter. *A Reply to Certain Personal Reflections, Contained in the Speech of One of the Counsel for the Complainants in the Case of Christ Church vs. the Church of the Holy Communion*. Philadelphia, 1880.

Holmes, David. "The Episcopal Church and the American Revolution." *HMPEC* 47 (1978): 261–89.

——. "The Making of the Bishop of Pennsylvania, 1826–27." *HMPEC* 41 (1972): 225–62; 42 (1973): 171–97.

Hooker, Richard. "John Dickinson on Church and State." *American Literature* 16 (1944): 82–98.

Hopkins, J. H. *The Life of the Late Right Reverend John Henry Hopkins by one of his Sons*. New York, 1873.

Horle, Craig W. and Marianne S. Wokeck, eds. *Lawmaking and Legislators in Pennsylvania: A Biographical Dictionary*. Vol. 1. Philadelphia: University of Pennsylvania Press, 1991.

Hudson, Winthrop. *Religion in America*. 3d edition. New York: Scribner, 1981.

Humphreys, David. *An Historical Account of the Incorporated Society for the Propagation of the Gospel in Foreign Parts. . . .* London, 1730. Reprint ed. New York: J. Downing, 1969.

Hutson, James. *Pennsylvania Politics, 1746–70: The Movement for Royal Government and Its Consequences.* Princeton, N.J.: Princeton University Press, 1972.

Ingersoll, Elizabeth. "Francis Alison, American Philosophe 1705–1799." Ph.D. diss., University of Delaware, 1974.

Ireland, Owen. "The Ethnic Religious Dimension of Pennsylvania Politics, 1778–1779." *WMQ* 30 (1973): 422–48.

Isaac, Rhys. *The Transformation of Virginia, 1740–1790.* Chapel Hill: University of North Carolina Press, 1982.

Jameson, J. Parker. "The Sunday School in the National Period." *HMPEC* 51 (1982): 185–90.

Jefferys, C. P. B. *The Provincial and Revolutionary History of St. Peter's Church, Philadelphia, 1753–1783.* Philadelphia: Privately printed, n.d.

Johnson, Allen and Dumas Malone, eds. *Dictionary of American Biography.* 20 vols. New York: Scribner's, 1928–37.

Jones, Thomas Firth. *A Pair of Lawn Sleeves: A Biography of William Smith.* Philadelphia: Chilton Book Company, 1972.

Jordan, Jean Paul. "The Anglican Establishment in Colonial New York, 1693–1783." Ph.D. diss., Columbia University, 1971.

Journal of the Meetings Which Led to the Institution of a Convention of the Protestant Episcopal Church in the State of Pennsylvania Together with the Journals of the First Six Conventions of the Said Church. Philadelphia: Published by the Diocese of Pennsylvania, 1790.

Kammen, Michael. *Mystic Chords of Memory: The Transformation of Tradition in American Culture.* New York: Knopf, 1991.

Kater, John L., Jr. "Experiment in Freedom: The Episcopal Church and the Black Power Movement." *HMPEC* 48 (1979): 67–81.

Keith, Charles. *Chronicles of Pennsylvania from the English Revolution to the Peace of Aix-la-Chapelle 1688–1748.* Philadelphia: Patterson and White, 1917.

Keith, George. "A Journal of Travels from New Hampshire to Caratuck, on the Continent of North America." *HMPEC* 20 (1951): 373–479.

Kelley, Joseph. *Life and Times in Colonial Philadelphia.* Harrisburg, Pa.: Stackpole Books, 1973.

———. *Pennsylvania: The Colonial Years.* Garden City, N.Y.: Doubleday, 1980.

Kemper, Jackson. "Jackson Kemper's Journals and Letters." *HMPEC* 5 (1935): 227–44.

Ketcham, Ralph. "Benjamin Franklin and William Smith, New Light on an Old Quarrel." *PMHB* 88 (1965): 142–63.

Kincheloe, Samuel. *Research Memorandum on Religion in the Depression.* New York, 1936. Reprint, New York: Arno Press, 1972.

Kirby, Ethyn. *George Keith, 1638–1716*. New York: D. Appleton and Century Co., 1942.

Klett, Guy Souillard. *Presbyterians in Colonial Pennsylvania*. Philadelphia: University of Pennsylvania Press, 1937.

Konkle, Burton Alva. *The Life of Andrew Hamilton: Day Star of the Revolution, 1676–1741*. Philadelphia: National Publishing Company, 1941.

Ladies' Missionary Association of Christ Church, Philadelphia. *Annual Reports*. 1846–1851, 1853, 1854, 1859, 1862, 1864.

Lammers, Ann. "The Reverend Absalom Jones and the Episcopal Church: Christian Theology and Black Consciousness in a New Alliance." *HMPEC* 51 (1982): 159–84.

Lannie, Vincent P. and Bernard C. Diethorn. "For the Honor and Glory of God: The Philadelphia Bible Riots of 1844." *History of Education Quarterly* 8 (1968): 44–106.

Latham, Charles, Jr. *The Episcopal Academy, 1785–1984*. Philadelphia: William T. Cooke, Publishers, 1984.

Laurie, Bruce. *Working People of Philadelphia 1800–1850*. Philadelphia: Temple University Press, 1980.

Leeds, Daniel. *An Almanack for the Year of Christian Account 1708*. Philadelphia, 1707.

Little, David. *Religion, Order and Law: A Study in Pre-Revolutionary England*. New York: Harper and Row, 1969.

Lodge, Martin. "The Great Awakening in the Middle Colonies." Ph.D. diss., University of California, Berkeley, 1964.

Loveland, Clara. *The Critical Years: The Reconstruction of the Anglican Church in the United States of America 1780–1789*. Greenwich, Conn.: Seabury Press, 1956.

Managers of the Female Episcopal Benevolent Society. *Eighteenth Annual Report*, 1834. Philadelphia, 1834

Main, Jackson Turner. *The Social Structure of Revolutionary America*. Princeton, N.J.: Princeton University, 1965.

Manross, William. *A History of the American Episcopal Church*. New York: Morehouse Publishing, 1935.

——. "Bishop White's Theology." *HMPEC* 15 (1946): 285–97.

Marty, Martin. *The New Shape of American Religion*. New York: Harper, 1959.

——. *Righteous Empire: The Protestant Experience in America*. New York: Dial Press, 1970.

Marietta, Jack D. *The Reformation of American Quakerism, 1748–1783*. Philadelphia: University of Pennsylvania Press, 1984.

Masterman, Frederick. "Some Aspects of the Episcopate of William Heathcote DeLancey, First Bishop of the Diocese of Western New York." *HMPEC* 33 (1964): 261–77.

Maxson, Charles. *Great Awakening in the Middle Colonies*. Chicago: University of Chicago Press, 1920.

May, Henry F. *Protestant Churches and Industrial America*. New York: Harper, 1949.

Melvin, Frank Worthington. *The Miracle of Christ Church Park, Report to the Council of Colonial Society of Pennsylvania*. Colonial Society of Pennsylvania, Christ Church Park Edition. Philadelphia, 1958.

Memorial of the 200th Anniversary of the Founding of Christ Church, Philadelphia, 1695–1895. Philadelphia, 1895.

Miller, Richard G. "The Federal City, 1785–1800." In *Philadelphia: A Three Hundred Year History* ed. Russell F. Weigley. New York: W.W. Norton and Company, 1982, 155–207.

——. *Philadelphia: The Federalist City*. Port Washington, N.Y.: Kennikat Press, 1976.

Miller, Robert. "The Social Attitudes of the American Episcopal Church During Two Decades, 1919–1939." *HMPEC* 25 (1956): 162–92.

Miller, Spencer and Joseph Fletcher. *The Church and Industry*. New York: Longmans Green, 1930.

Mills, Frederick V., Sr. *Bishops by Ballot: An Eighteenth Century Ecclesiastical Revolution*. New York: Oxford University Press, 1978.

——. "The Colonial Anglican Episcopate: A Historiographical Review." *Anglican and Episcopal History* (1992): 325–45.

Minutes of the Provincial Council of Pennsylvania. 16 vols. Harrisburg, Pa.: J. Stevens and Co., 1851–53.

Minutes of the Supreme Executive Council. In *Minutes of the Provincial Council of Pennsylvania*. Harrisburg, Pa.: J. Stevens and Co., 1851–53.

Montgomery, Thomas. *A History of the University of Pennsylvania from Its Foundation to A.D. 1770*. Philadelphia: George W. Jacobs, 1900.

——. "List of Vestrymen of Christ Church, Philadelphia." *PMHB* (1895): 518–26.

Moore, Trevor Wyatt. "In Unity and Godly Love." *Christian Century* 85 (Sept. 11, 1968): 1140–41.

Morrison, Hugh. *Early American Architecture from the First Colonial Settlements to the National Period*. New York: Oxford University Press, 1952.

Muhlenberg, Henry. *The Journal of Henry Melchoir Muhlenberg*. 3 vols. Trans. Theodore Tappert and John W. Doberstein. Philadelphia: Lutheran History Society, 1947–48.

Mullin, Robert Bruce. *Episcopal Vision/American Reality: High Church Theology and Social Thought in Evangelical America*. New Haven, Conn.: Yale University Press, 1986.

Nash, Gary. *Forging Freedom: The Formation of Philadelphia's Black Community, 1720–1840*. Cambridge, Mass.: Harvard University Press, 1988.

——. *Quakers and Politics: Pennsylvania 1681–1726*. Princeton, N.J.: Princeton University Press, 1968.

——. *The Urban Crucible: Social Change, Political Consciousness, and the Origins of the American Revolution*. Cambridge, Mass.: Harvard University Press, 1979.

Nelson, John. "Anglican Missions in America, 1701–25: A Study of the Society for the Propagation of the Gospel in Foreign Parts." Ph.D. diss., Northwestern University, 1962.

Nelson, William H. *The American Tory*. Oxford: Clarendon Press, 1961.

Nicholson, Arnold. "Historic Christ Church in Philadelphia Faces Problems." *Today Magazine, Philadelphia Inquirer*, n.d. Christ Church Archives.

Oberholtzer, Ellis P. *Philadelphia: A History of the City and Its People*. 4 vols. Philadelphia: S.J. Clarke Publishing Company, [1912].

Our Common Prayer. Philadelphia: Episcopal Diocese of Pennsylvania, 1984.

"Our Good Neighbor—Old Christ Church." *The 3-3 News, Girard Trust Corn Exchange Bank*. (c. 1952): 17.

Painter, Borden W. "The Anglican Vestry in Colonial America." Ph.D. diss.: Yale University, 1965.

Parker, Peter J., "Rich and Poor in Philadelphia, 1709." *PMHB* 99 (1975): 3–19.

Pendleton, Othniel, Jr. "The Influence of the Evangelical Churches upon Humanitarian Reform: A Case Study Giving Particular Attention to Philadelphia, 1790–1840." Ph.D. diss., University of Pennsylvania, 1947.

Penn, William. *The Papers of William Penn*. Vol. 2, 1680–1694. Edited by Richard S. Dunn and Mary Maples Dunn. Philadelphia: University of Pennsylvania Press, 1982.

Pennington, Edgar. *Apostle of New Jersey: John Talbot, 1645–1725*. Philadelphia: Church Historical Society, 1935.

——. "Colonial Clergy Conventions." *HMPEC* 7 (1939): 178–218.

——. "The Reverend Robert Jenney." American Antiquarian Society *Proceedings* 61 (1941): 165–70.

Perry, William S., ed. *Historical Collections Relating to the American Colonial Church*. 5 vols. Hartford, Conn., 1871, Reprint ed. New York: AMS Press, 1969.

——. *Historical Notes and Documents*. 3 vols. Claremont, N.H.: Claremont Manufacturing Company, 1874.

——. *The History of the American Episcopal Church*. 2 vols. Boston: J. R. Osgood, 1885.

Peters, Richard. *The Last Two Sermons Preached at Christ's Church in Philadelphia, July 3, 1737*. Philadelphia: Benjamin Franklin, 1737.

Peterson, Charles E. "The Building of Christ Church, Philadelphia." In *Catalog of the 1981 Antiques Show: A Benefit for the Hospital of the University of Pennsylvania*. Philadelphia: Privately printed, 1981, 138–47.

"Philadelphia's Ills: Diagnosis by Real Estate Specialist Calls for Surgery and Rigorous Rehabilitation to Cure Bad Case of Big-City Blight." *Business Week* 649 (Feb. 7, 1942): 35–36.

Pilmore, Joseph. *The Journal of Joseph Pilmore*. Ed. Frederick E. Maser and Howard T. Maag. Philadelphia: Message Publishing Company for Historical Society of the Philadelphia Annual Conference of the United Methodist Church, 1969.

Powell, John H. *Bring Out Your Dead: The Great Plague of Yellow Fever in Phila-*

delphia in 1793. Philadelphia: University of Pennsylvania Press, 1949. Reprinted with a new Introduction by Kenneth R. Foster, Mary F. Jenkins and Anna Coxe Toogood, 1993.

Price, Charles P. for the Standing Liturgical Commission, Protestant Episcopal Church. *Introducing the Proposed Book*. New York: Church Hymnal Corporation, 1976.

A Program of Action for the Nation's Church. Philadelphia [1952].

Protestant Episcopal Sunday and Adult School Society. *Report, 1821*. Philadelphia, 1821.

The Quarterly Theological Magazine and Religious Repository. Vol. 1 (1813).

A Record. Philadelphia, 1903.

Records of the Presbyterian Church in the United States of America . . . 1706–1775. Philadelphia, 1904.

Repairs and Restoration, February 1, 1882. Philadelphia, 1882.

A Report of Christ Church in Philadelphia, 1950–1954. Philadelphia, 1954.

A Report on the United Spiritual Action Program at Christ Church in Philadelphia, March 15, 1953. Philadelphia, 1953.

Richardson, Edgar. "The Athens of America, 1800–1825." In *Philadelphia: A Three Hundred Year History*. Ed. Russell F. Weigley. New York: W.W. Norton and Company, 1982, 208–57.

Ridell, William. "Libel on the Assembly, a Pre-Revolutionary Episode." *PMHB* 52 (1928): 176–192, 249–79, 342–60.

Rightmyer, Nelson. "Swedish-English Relations in Northern Delaware." *Church History* 6 (1946): 101–15.

Roach, Hannah Benner, ed. "Philadelphia Business Directory, 1690." *Pennsylvania Genealogical Magazine* 23 (1964): 95–129.

——. "Taxables in the City of Philadelphia, 1756." Genealogical Society of Pennsylvania, *Publications* 22 (1961–62): 3–44.

Roberts, George. "History of Christ Church Hospital." *PMHB* 45 (1976): 89–102.

Robinson, James Harvey. Review of *Sources of the Constitution of the United States*, by Charles Ellis Stevens. *Annals of the American Academy of Political and Social Science* 4 (1893–94): 999.

Root, Winfred T. *The Relations of Pennsylvania with the British Government, 1695–1765*. New York: D. Appleton and Company, 1912.

Rose, Harold. *The Colonial Houses of Worship in America Built in the English Colonies Before the Republic 1607–1789 and Still Standing*. New York: Hastings House, 1963.

Rothermund, Dietmar. *The Layman's Progress: Religious and Political Experience in Colonial Pennsylvania, 1740–1770*. Philadelphia: University of Pennsylvania Press, 1961.

Rouse, Ruth and Stephen Neill, eds. *A History of the Ecumenical Movement*. Philadelphia: Westminster Press, 1954.

Rush, Benjamin. *The Autobiography of Benjamin Rush*. Ed. George W. Corner. Westport, Conn.: Greenwood Press, 1970.

Ryan, Mary. *Cradle of the Middle Class: The Family in Oneida County, New York, 1790–1865*. New York and Cambridge: Cambridge University Press, 1981.

Ryerson, Richard. *The Revolution Is Now Begun: The Radical Committees of Philadelphia, 1765–1776*. Philadelphia: University of Pennsylvania Press, 1978.

Sabine, Lorenzo. *Biographical Sketches of Loyalists of the American Revolution with an Historical Essay*. 2 vols. 1864. Reprint, Port Washington, N.Y.: Kennikat Press, 1966.

Sandel, Andreas. "Extracts from the Journal of Reverend Andreas Sandel, 1702–19." *PMHB* 30 (1906): 448–49.

Sapio, Victor. *Pennsylvania and the War of 1812*. Lexington: University Press of Kentucky, 1970.

Satcher, Herbert Boyce. "Music of the Episcopal Church in Pennsylvania in the Eighteenth Century." *HMPEC* 18 (1949): 372–413.

Scharf, J. Thomas and Thompson Westcott. *History of Philadelphia*. 3 vols. Philadelphia: L. H. Everts Co., 1883.

Schmauk, Theodore E. *A History of the Lutheran Church in Pennsylvania 1638–1800*. Lancaster, Pa.: New Era Press, 1902.

Schneider, Herbert and Carol Schneider, eds. *Samuel Johnson, President of King's College, His Career and Writings*, 4 vols. New York: Columbia University Press, 1929.

Schwartz, Bonnie Fox. "Unemployment Relief in Philadelphia, 1930–1932: A Study of the Depression's Impact on Voluntarism." *PMHB* 92 (1969): 86–108.

Seamen's Church Institute of Philadelphia, Prospectus, 1920. Philadelphia, 1920.

A Service in Honor of Louis Cope Washburn, S.T.D., And of Dedication in his Spirit to the Cause of Church Unity held Under the auspices of the Philadelphia Federation of Churches in Christ Church, Phialdelphia, Sunday, October 16, 1938. Philadelphia, 1938.

Shelling, Richard. "The Reverend William Sturgeon, Catechist to the Negroes of Philadelphia and Assistant Rector of Christ Church 1747–66." *HMPEC* 8 (1939): 388–401.

Shiels, Richard. "The Feminization of American Congregationalism, 1730–1835." *American Quarterly* 33 (1981): 46–62.

Shoemaker, Robert. "Christ Church, St. Peter's and St. Paul's in Historic Philadelphia." American Philosophical Society *Transactions* 48 (part 1, 1953): 187–98.

Simpson, Henry. *The Lives of Eminent Philadelphians Now Deceased*. Philadelphia: W. Brotherhead, 1859.

Sirkis, Nancy. *Reflections of 1776: The Colonies Revisited*. New York: Viking Press, 1974.

Sitkoff, Harvard. "The Detroit Riot of 1943." *Michigan History* 53 (1969): 183–206.

Skardon, Alvin W. *Church Leader in the Cities: William Augustus Muhlenberg*. Philadelphia: University of Pennsylvania Press, 1971.

Smith, Billy G. "Material Lives of Laboring Philadelphians." *WMQ* 38 (1981): 163–202.

Smith-Rosenberg, Carroll. *Religion and the Rise of the American City: The New York City Mission Movement, 1812–1870.* Ithaca, N.Y.: Cornell University Press, 1971.

Smith, Horace. *Life and Correspondence of the Reverend William Smith.* 2 vols. Philadelphia: S.A. George, 1879.

[Smith, William]. *Plain Truth, Addressed to the Inhabitants of America Containing Remarks on a late Pamphlet, Entitled COMMON SENSE.* London: J. Almon, 1776.

Smith, William. *The Works of William Smith. . . .* Philadelphia: H. Maxwell, 1802.

Snyder, Martin P. *City of Independence: Views of Philadelphia Before 1800 .* New York: Praeger Publishers, 1975.

Social Service Directory of Philadelphia, 1919. Compiled by Leon Stern. Philadelphia: Council of Social Agencies, 1919.

Social Service Directory of Philadelphia, 1938. Philadelphia: Council of Social Agencies, 1938.

Social Survey of the Parish. Philadelphia, 1912.

Society for the Advancement of Christianity in Pennsylvania. *Annual Reports*, 1813, 1836–1844.

Sonneck, Oscar G.T. *Francis Hopkinson . . . and James Lyon.* New York: DaCapa Press, 1967.

Spencer, David. *The Early Baptists of Philadelphia.* Philadelphia: W. Syckelmoore, 1877.

Sprague, William B. *Annals of the American Pulpit.* 5 vols. 1857–1869. Reprint edition, New York: Arno Press, 1969.

Steiner, Bruce. *Samuel Seabury, 1729–1796: A Study in the High Church Tradition.* Athens: Ohio University Press, 1972.

Stevens, C. Ellis. *The Romance of Arenfels and Other Tales of the Rhine.* New York: 1897.

——. *Sources of the Constitution of the United States Considered in Relation to Colonial and English History.* New York: Macmillan, 1894.

——. *Stevens Genealogy.* New York: Privately Printed, 1904.

——, ed. *The Genesis of the American Prayerbook.* New York, 1893.

Stevens, William Bacon. *Free and Open Churches: A Sermon Preached at the Opening of the Chapel of Christ Church.* Philadelphia, 1877.

Stone, J. S. *Memoir of the Life of James Milnor, Late Rector of St. George's Church, N.Y.* New York: American Tract Society, 1848.

Stout, Harry. *The Divine Dramatist: George Whitefield and the Rise of Modern Evangelism.* Grand Rapids, Mich.: W. B. Eerdmans, 1991.

Stowe, Walter Herbert, ed. *Life and Letters of Bishop William White.* New York: Morehouse, 1937.

———. "The Seabury Minutes of the New York Clergy Convention of 1766 and 1767." *HMPEC* 10 (1941): 125–62.

Stuckert, Howard Morris. "Jackson Kemper, Presbyter." *HMPEC* 4 (1935): 130–151.

Tatum, George. *Penn's Great Town: 250 Years of Philadelphia Architecture Illustrated in Prints and Drawings*. Philadelphia: University of Pennsylvania Press, 1961.

Taylor, Jacob. *An Almanack for the Year of Christian Account 1709*. Philadelphia, 1708.

———. "Memoir of Bishop White." Ed. John D. Kilbourne, *PMHB* 92 (1968): 48–66.

Temple, Sydney, Jr. *The Common Sense Theology of Bishop White*. New York: King's Crown Press, 1946.

Thayer, Theodore. "Town into City, 1746–1765." In *Philadelphia: A Three Hundred Year History*. Ed. Russell F. Weigley. New York: W.W. Norton and Company, 1982, 68–108.

Thomas, Gabriel. *An Historical and Geographical Account of the Province and Country of Pennsylvania*. London: A. Baldwin, 1698.

Thorpe, Francis Newton, ed. *Benjamin Franklin and the University of Pennsylvania*. Washington, D.C.: U.S. Government Printing Office, 1893.

Tinkcom, Harry. *The Republicans and Federalists in Pennsylvania 1790–1801*. Harrisburg, Pa.: Pennsylvania Historical and Museum Commission, 1950.

———. "The Revolutionary City." In *Philadelphia: A Three Hundred Year History*. Ed. Russell F. Weigley. New York: W.W. Norton and Company, 1982, 109–54.

Tinkcom, Margaret B. "Depression and War, 1929–1946." In *Philadelphia: A Three Hundred Year History*. Ed. Russell F. Weigley. New York: W.W. Norton and Company, 1982, 601–48.

Tolles, Frederick. *Meeting House and Counting House: The Quaker Merchants of Colonial Philadelphia*. New York: W.W. Norton and Company, 1948.

Trinterud, Leonard J. *The Forming of an American Tradition*. Philadelphia: Westminster Press, 1964.

Turner, William L. "The College, Academy and Charitable School of Philadelphia." Ph.D. diss., University of Pennsylvania, 1952.

Twelves, J. Wesley. *History of the Diocese of Pennsylvania of the Protestant Episcopal Church*. Philadelphia: Diocese of Pennsylvania, 1969.

Tyng, Charles. *Record of the Life and Work of the Reverend Stephen R. Tyng and History of St. George's Church*. New York: E. P. Dutton and Co., 1890.

United States Department of Commerce, Bureau of the Census. *Fifteenth Census of the United States: Metropolitan Districts*. Washington, D.C.: U.S. Government Printing Office, 1932.

Upton, Dell. *Holy Things and Profane: Anglican Parish Churches in Colonial Virginia*. Cambridge, Mass.: MIT Press, 1986.

Van Horne, John, ed. *Religious Philanthropy and Colonial Slavery: The American Correspondence of the Associates of Dr. Bray 1717–1777*. Urbana: University of Illinois Press, 1985.

Von Moschzisker, Bertha. "Ernest A. Harding: An Appreciation at the Time of His Retirement." *Preservation Post* 1, 1 (1977): 1.

4 1 4

Wainwright, Nicholas B. "The Age of Nicholas Biddle, 1825–1841." In *Philadelphia: A Three Hundred Year History*. Ed. Russell F. Weigley. New York: W.W. Norton and Company, 1982, 258–306.

Wallace, John William. *A Discourse Delivered Before the Historical Society of Pennsylvania, October 27th, 1870, Commemorative of the Reverend Benjamin Dorr, D.D.* Philadelphia, 1870.

Warburton, William. *The Alliance between Church and State: or the Necessity and Equity of an Established Religion and a Test Law, demonstrated from the essence of Nature and Nations*. 2d ed. London: F. Gyles, 1741.

Ward, Julius. *Life and Times of William White*. New York: Dodd, Mead and Company, 1892.

Warden, G.B. "The Proprietary Group in Pennsylvania 1754–1764." *WMQ* 21 (1964): 367–89.

Warne, Arthur. *Church and Society in Eighteenth Century Devon*. Newton Aboot: David and Charles, 1969.

Warner, Sam Bass. *The Private City: Philadelphia in Three Periods of Its Growth*. Philadelphia: University of Pennsylvania Press, 1968. Revised edition, 1987.

Washburn, Helen. *A Church School Looks at Christian Unity: A Seven Week Study by All the Classes in the Church School*. Philadelphia: Privately printed, 1939.

Washburn, Louis. *Christ Church, Philadelphia: A Symposium*. Philadelphia: Macrae Smith Co., 1925.

Watson, John. *Annals of Philadelphia and Pennsylvania in the Olden Times*. 3 vols. Enlarged and revised by Willis Hazard. Philadelphia: J. M. Stoddard, 1877.

Weigley, Russell F. "The Border City in Civil War, 1854–1865." In *Philadelphia: A Three Hundred Year History*. Ed. Russell F. Weigley. New York: W.W. Norton and Company, 1982, 258–306.

——, ed. *Philadelphia: A Three Hundred Year History*. New York: W. W. Norton and Company, 1982.

Weis, Frederick. *The Colonial Churches and the Colonial Clergy of the Middle and Southern Colonies, 1607–1776*. Lancaster, Mass.: Society of the Descendants of the Colonial Clergy, 1938.

Welton, Richard. *The Certain Comforts of God the Holy Ghost & Preached at the Episcopal Church in Philadelphia, Feb. 4, 1725/26* . N.p., n.d.

White, William. "The Autobiography of William White." Ed. Walter Herbert Stowe. *HMPEC* 22 (1953): 381–415.

——. *The Case of the Episcopal Churches in the United States Considered*. Philadelphia, 1782. Reprinted in *HMPEC* 22 (1953): 431–506.

——. *Memoirs of the Protestant Episcopal Church*. Ed. B. F. DeCosta. New York: S. Potter, J. Maxwell, Printer, 1820.

——. *Thoughts on the Singing of Psalms and Anthems in Churches*. Philadelphia, 1808.

Whitefield, George. *Journals 1737–1741 to Which is Prefixed His "Short Account" and "Further Account."* Gainesville, Fla.: Scholars' Facsimiles and Reprints, 1969.

Wilson, Bird. *Memoir of the Life of the Right Reverend William White, D.D., Bishop of the Protestant Episcopal Church in the State of Pennsylvania.* Philadelphia: J. Kay, 1839.

Wilson, Frank E. "Kemper's Diocesan Episcopate: 1854–1870." *HMPEC* 4 (1935): 219–24.

Wolf, Edwin. "The First Library of Christ Church." In *Catalog the 1981 Antiques Show: A Benefit for the Hospital of the University of Pennsylvania.* Philadelphia: Privately printed, 1981, 148–51.

Wolf, Edwin and Maxwell Whiteman. *The History of the Jews of Philadelphia from Colonial Times to the Age of Jackson.* Philadelphia: Jewish Publication Society of America, 1956.

Woolverton, John Frederick. *Colonial Anglicanism in North America.* Detroit: Wayne State University Press, 1984.

Wurman, Richard S. and John A. Gallery. *Man-Made Philadelphia: A Guide to Its Physical and Cultural Environment.* Cambridge, Mass.: MIT Press, 1972.

INDEX

Abercrombie, the Reverend James: background, 174–178; edits *Quarterly Theological Magazine,* 176; runs Philadelphia Academy, 176–177; political sermons, 202–203; comments on problems in Christ Church, 216; resigns, 219

Abolition Society, 197

Acevedo-Naters, the Reverend Miriam, 387–388

Act of Separation, United Churches, 219

Adams, John, 71, 98, 131

Adcock, William, 137, 188

Alison, the Reverend Francis, 116–117

Allen, the Reverend Benjamin, 212

Allen, Eric, 344

Allen, William, 57–58, 89

Allin, Bishop John M., 388

American Anti-Slavery Society, 233

American Philosophical Society, 93–94

American Protestant Association, 232

An Appeal to the Public on Behalf of the Church of England in America, 118–120

Andrews, the Reverend John, 195

Andrews, Mary, 97

Anglo-Catholic movement, 253–255, 266–267, 275

Anthony, Joseph, 197

Assheton, Ralph, 47

Atlee, William, 156

Bache, Richard, 145

Baker, William, 200

Baptismal font: William Penn baptized in, 26–27; Gostelowe font, 190, 192

Baptists, attempt to convert, 14

Barnes, the Reverend R. Hebre, 287

Baynton, John, 91

Belfield, Mrs. Helen, 307

Belfield, T. Broom, 307

Bend, the Reverend Joseph, 174

Biddle, Nicholas, 188

Bingham, James, 48

Bingham, William, 164, 197, 203

Binney, Horace, 188, 229, 233, 240

Binsfield, John, 361

Bishop of London, role in Philadelphia church, 35, 38, 51–52, 61–62, 79–80

Bishop White Club, 326

Bishop White Prayer Book Society, 240

Blacks: Jenney baptizes, 68; Catechist to the Negroes appointed, 68–69

Bok, Mary Louise Curtis (Mrs. Efrem Zimbalist): gives organ to Christ Church, 308; finances repairs, 338

Blackwell, the Reverend Robert, 144, 164, 174, 209

Bond, Phineas, 47

Bond, Phineas, Jr., 142

Bond, Thomas, 93

Book of Common Prayer: attachment to, 6;
    use in colonial services, 25–26; American,
    160–61, 189; revisions in 1890s, 277–278;
    1979 proposed, 362–363, 385
Bradford, Dr. Thomas, 305
Bray Associates: send books to Christ
    Church, 29; set up school for blacks, 69–
    70
Bray Library, catalogued, 309
Bremmer, James, 92, 98
Brooks, the Reverend Phillips, 241
Buchanan altar, 276–277

Cadwalader, George, 229, 233, 242
Cadwalader, John (b. 1742), 129, 133, 142,
    145, 188
Cadwalader, John (b. 1805), 229
Cadwalader, Thomas, 188, 229
Calvary Monumental Church, 237–238, 260
Cannon, James, 142
Carpenter, Joshua, 10
Carr, the Reverend Dabney, 359
Cary, Matthew, 198
The Case of the Episcopal Churches in the
    United States Considered (William White),
    153–155
"Cato" letters (William Smith), 136, 137
"The Centinel," 122
Chancellor, William, 197
Chandler, the Reverend Thomas Bradbury,
    118–120, 159
Chew, Benjamin, 70, 164
Childs, Allen, 305
Christ Church
    anniversary celebrations: 200th, 278;
        225th, 309; 250th, 331; 300th, 390
    buildings: first church built, 10, 19?, 309;
        second church built, 48–49; repairs and
        renovations 1760s, 98–100; 1830s and
        1850s, 234–235; 1880s, 260–261; 1920s,
        307–308; 1960s, 373–375; 1980s, 386–
        387
    confirmation: first performed in Christ
        Church, 190; number confirmed 1807–
        1810, 180; during Stevens rectorship,
        275; during Washburn rectorship, 303–

304; number of women confirmed, 190,
    229, 256, 304
financial problems: 1790s, 191–192; 1820s,
    209–210; 1830s–1840s, 235; 1850s, 244–
    245; 1880s, 271; 1890s, 276; 1930s, 305–
    306; 1949, 332; 1970s, 377
founding of, 9–12
membership: 1705, 24–25; 1730s, 47–48;
    1750s, 68; 1790–1800, 187–188; 1830s
    and 1840s, 228–229; 1870s and 1880s
    256–257; 1912–1920s, 303; 1940s, 324;
    1950s, 353–358; 1980s, 391–392
music: colonial, 25, 98; 1780s, 189–190;
    1950s and 1960s, 360–362; 1980s, 385
national shrine designation, 333
Sunday schools: founded, 199–200; 1830s
    and 1840s, 236–237; directed by Helen
    Washburn, 296–298; 1940s, 325; Sun-
    day school without walls, 364–365;
    1980s, 387
Christ Church burial ground: established,
    28–29; wall around, 306; repairs to, 358–
    359
Christ Church Chapel: founding, 264; con-
    gregation, 265–266; controversy, 266–270;
    closes, 314–315
Christ Church Declaration, 338
Christ Church Historical Association, 278
Christ Church Hospital: founding, 193;
    Joseph Dobbins bequest, 193–194; new
    building, 238–239; 1880s, 259–260; 1920s,
    314; Ladies' Committee, 314, 323; forma-
    tion of operating committee, 341; 1960s
    and 1970s, 365; 1980s, 386
Church of England, characteristics of, 8–9
Churchman, Horace, 324, 365
Civil War, Christ Church reaction to, 241–
    243
Clark, Edward L., 239, 271
Clarkson, Dr. Gerardus, 156
Clarkson, Matthew, 188
Clayton, the Reverend Thomas, 12, 14
Clymer, George, 129, 130, 142, 145, 164
Coates, Edward H., 257
Coke, the Reverend Thomas, 173
Coercive Acts, 129, 131

College of Philadelphia, 114–118; charter revoked, 145–146; charter restored, 146, 195; DeLancey becomes provost, 183

Committee of Sixty-Six, 130–131

Common Sense (Thomas Paine), 136

Commissary, powers of, 51–53

Community Investment Fund, 389

Compton, Henry, bishop of London, 11; tablet honoring, 309

Conyngham, Redmond, 91

Coombe, the Reverend Thomas: appointed assistant minister, 100–102; attitude toward other ministers, 103; position on resistance movement, 134–135; position on independence, 140–142

Coxe, Tench, 164, 196, 197, 203

Cowell, Hannah, 294, 300–301

Creth, Mrs. John, 307

Cummings, the Reverend Archibald: appointed rector, 43; appointed commissary, 51–53; theology of, 45–46; dispute with Peters, 55–59; position on Great Awakening, 54; death, 59

Curtis, Cyrus H. K., 308

DaCosta, Dr. John, 257, 279–280

DaCosta, John C., Jr., 305

Dallas, Alexander, 203

Davis, Isaac, 229

DeBordenave, the Reverend E. A.: background, 334–335; rectorship, 334–345; USA Campaign, 335–343; and college students, 342–343; denounces McCarthyism, 343; resigns, 345

DeLancey, the Reverend William Heathcote, 182–83; role in evangelical–high church dispute, 213; problems in the United Churches, 216; becomes provost of the College of Philadelphia, 183; named minister of St. Peter's, 219

Depression, Great, 299–301

DeWitt, Bishop Robert L., 367–369

Dexheimer, Mrs. Peter, 364

Dickinson, John, 120–121

Diocese of Pennsylvania, Christ Church role in, 240, 315, 366–369, 385–386

Dobbins, Joseph, 195, 238

Domestic and Foreign Missionary Society, 198

Dorcas Society, 242, 299

Dorr, the Reverend Benjamin: background, 225–227; writes *The History of a Pocket Prayerbook,* 226–227; writes *Christ Church, Philadelphia from its foundation, A.D. 1695 to 1841,* 227–228; position on slavery and Civil War, 240–241; son dies in Civil War, 243; death of, 246

Dorr, William, 243

Dorsey, John, 164, 197

Ducachet, the Reverend Henry, 238

Duché, the Reverend Jacob: appointed assistant minister, 77; appointed minister with Sturgeon, 88–89; and Peters, 90, 102; problems with Sturgeon, 90; and George Whitefield, 104; position on resistance movement, 134–135; appointed chaplain of the Continental Congress, 131; position on independence, 138–139

Duché, Jacob, Sr., 47, 93

Duffield, Edward, 70, 156

Dunlap, John, 188

Dyer, Frank, 358

East Central Social Agency, 301

Eckman, William, 346

Elder, Henry, gives estate to Christ Church, 276, 307

Emancipation Proclamation, 241–242

Epiphany Episcopal Church, 228

Episcopal Academy, 194–195, 239

Episcopal Female Tract Society of Philadelphia, 199

Episcopal Hospital, 259

Episcopate: New England clergy efforts to obtain one in the 1760s, 118–122; position of Pennsylvania clergy on, 118–120; conflict with Presbyterians over, 120–122

Evangelical–high church dispute, 166–167, 211–213

Evans, the Reverend Evan: background, 12; relations with Quakers, 14–17; cooperates with Penn, 16; dispute with Quary, 31; departure, 351

Evans, Peter: opposes Phillips, 32–33; supports Richard Welton, 37; opposes Peters, 58, 60

Ewing, John, 117

Eyre, Emmanuel, 133

Female Episcopal Benevolent Society, 199

Foggo, the Reverend Edward: background, 255; rectorship of, 255–273; builds parish house, 255–256; and neighborhood, 258–259; and restoration of sanctuary, 260–261; gives communion table, 260; Christ Church Chapel controversy, 266–271; resigns, 272–273

Francis, Tench, 47, 129, 164

Franklin, Benjamin, 44–45, 55, 71, 95, 115–116, 133, 137, 142

French and Indian War, 72

Fritzinger, Gertrude, 294

General Convention of the Protestant Episcopal Church, 156, 159

General Theological Seminary, 200–201

German Society, 112–113

Gibson, Edmund, bishop of London, 51–52, 58, 60

Gibson, John, 129–130

Girard, Stephen, 174, 188

Girls' Friendly Society, 275, 299, 325, 343

Golden Age Club, 326, 343

Gookin, Charles, 32–34

Gostelowe, Jonathan: communion table, 190, 260, 373; baptismal font, 190, 192

Governor, power in church affairs, 34, 35–36

Grace Episcopal Church, 211, 228

Gracie, the Reverend David McIver, 367

Graeme, Thomas, 47

Gray, George, 133

Great Awakening, 53–55

Greenfield, Albert, 337

Grossman, David, 326–327

Gurney, Francis, 203

Hall, William, 197

Hamilton, Andrew, 55, 57–58

Hamilton, James, 70, 93

Hand, James, 229

Hannum, Judge John, 376

Harding, the Reverend Ernest: background, 349–52; rectorship, 349–378; and purchase of rectory, 352–353; and Proposed Book of Common Prayer, 362–363; and conflicts in diocese, 366–369; and Neighborhood Businessmen's Association, 364; and improvements to Christ Church, 373–375; and Old Christ Church Preservation Trust, 375; resigns, 378

Harding, Robert, 92

Hare, Robert, 203

Harrison, Alfred Craven, 305–307

Harrison, John, 48

Hassell, Samuel, 47

Hesselius, Gusatavus, 48

Hewitt, George, restoration of Christ Church, 260–261

Hillegas, Michael, 130–188

Hillsman, Walter, 361

Hobart, Bishop John Henry, 177, 179, 183, 196

Hodge, the Reverend G. Wolsey, 264, 266–270

Holy Trinity Episcopal Church, 241

Hopkins, Bishop John Henry, 241

Hopkinson, Francis, 70, 93, 95, 98, 137, 139, 142, 152, 156, 161, 164, 188

Hopkinson, Joseph, 164, 188

Hopkinson, Thomas, 47, 70

Hubley, Adam, 130

Hughes, John, 71

Humphreys, the Reverend John, 37

Independence National Historic Park, 326, 333–334, 369–370

Ingersoll, Charles, 242

Ingersoll, Charles Jared, 229–242

Jackson, William, 197

James, the Reverend John Waller, 219, 223–224, 234

Jenney, the Reverend Robert: background, 61; and Phillips controversy, 31, 33; rectorship, 67–83; attitude toward politics,

70–75; conflict with Smith, 73–75; conflict with Macclenachan, 75–80; views on successor, 88; views on College of Philadelphia, 115; call for an episcopate, 119

Jones, the Reverend Absalom, 164, 166

Jordan, Jane, 325

Joseph Volunteers, 326

Kearsley, John: supervises building of Christ Church, 48; opposes Peters, 58, 60; and building of St. Peter's, 77; endows Christ Church Hospital, 192

Kearsley, John, Jr., 137, 142, 193

Kearsley Home. *See* Christ Church Hospital

Keith, George, 15, 16–17

Keith, William, 35–37, 38, 57

Keithian Quakers, 14

Kemper, the Reverend Jackson: background, 179–181, missionary activity, 180–181, leaves Christ Church, 210; evangelical–high church dispute, 213; problems in Christ Church, 216

King's College, 17, 114

Kloman, the Reverend Edward Felix: background, 321–323; rectorship, 323–333; and Old Christ Church Neighborhood Businessmen's Association, 326–327; and World War II, 327–331; resigns, 333

Knight, Peter, 129

Ladies' Missionary Society, 239, 260, 272, 275

Langhourne, Jeremiah, 57, 58

Laquintano, the Reverend David, 388

Lardner, Lynford, 70

Lawrence, John, 142

Lawrence, Thomas, 47, 70, 91

Lea, Sydney, 324, 366

Leaming, Jeremiah, 159

Leech, Thomas, 58, 71

Leeds, Daniel, 15–16, 17

Levy, Moses, 203

Lewis, Edwin, 334

Lewis, the Reverend W. P., 270

Lingham, Amelia, 375

Logan, James, 16, 57

Lutherans, German: number, 111–112; relations with Church of England, 112–113

Lutherans, Swedish, relations with Church of England, 112–113

McCall, Peter, 242

McCarthyism, 343

Macclenachan, the Reverend William, 78–82

McKean, the Reverend Robert, 74

McKean, the Reverend W. Roulston, 294–295, 298, 301, 325

McRae, the Reverend Cameron, 242

Maddox, Joshua, 47

Magdalene Society, 197

Masters, William, 129

Melvin, Frank Worthington, 375

Meredith, Samuel, 145, 203

Meredith, William, Jr., 229, 233, 241

Meredith, William, Sr., 178, 188, 198

Mertz, Harvey, 296, 340, 344, 360, 375

Methodists, 105–106

Midwood, the Reverend John, 387

Mikveh Israel Synagogue, 329

Milnor, the Reverend James, 181

Mohn, the Reverend Michael, 359–60, 364

Montgomery, Richard, 240

Montgomery, Thomas H., 257

Moore, John, opposes Phillips, 31–32

Moore, William, 74

Morgan, Dr. John, 93

Morris, Robert, 91, 130, 133, 137, 142, 145, 164, 188, 203

Morris Park, 309–311

Mothers' Meeting, 275, 299, 325

Muhlenberg, the Reverend Henry Melchoir, 113, 181

Muhlenberg, the Reverend William Augustus, 181–182

Murphy, Francis, 361

National Park Service, 333–334, 375; and Bicentennial, 377–378

Nativist movement, 231–233

Neighborhood House: building of, 294; activities in, 298

Neighborhood surrounding Christ Church: 1850s, 243–244; 1880, 257–259; 1912, 290–291; 1940s, 332; 1950s, 352–353, 375; 1970s, 383–384; Foggo reaches out to, 259; Washburn addresses needs of, 293–302
Neill, the Reverend Hugh, 117
NewArk Academy, 116–117
Newbold, James, 239
Newbold, John, 229
Newbold, John C. 305
Newbold, William, 239, 240
Nicholson, Francis, 11, 17, 47
Nicholson, L. Arnold, 353
New York Anglicans, 17
Nicklin, Philip, 188
Nixon, John, 130, 145, 164, 188

Oath issue, 13
Odenheimer, the Reverend William, 244
Ogilby, Bishop Lyman, 385
Old Christ Church Neighborhood Businessmen's Association, 326–327, 341, 364, 389
Old Christ Church Preservation Trust, 375
Old City Civic Association, 389
Onderdonk, Bishop Henry, 212–213
Ord, John, 128
Organ, Christ Church: purchased in 1766, 98; new organ, 1830s, 234; Curtis organ accepted, 308; major repairs to, 362
Paris, Ferdinando John, 58, 59–60
Parish house, built on to Christ Church, 256
Parish school: in colonial period, 28–29; Dorr re-establishes, 237; during Foggo's rectorship, 259
Parker, Samuel, 159
Pember, Gilbert, 313
Penn, John, 45, 56, 60–61, 93
Penn, Thomas, 56, 70, 72
Pennsylvania Hospital, 197
Pennsylvania Institution for the Deaf and Dumb, 197
Penrose, Jonathan, 197, 198
Penrose, Thomas, 130
Percival, the Reverend Henry, 266–267, 270
Perot, John, 188, 198
Peters, the Reverend Richard: background,

55, 92, 95; dispute with Archibald Cummings, 56–59; attitude toward George Whitefield, 104–105; candidate for rector in 1741, 59–61; chosen rector, 89–90; theology, 89; rectorship, 95–106; attitude toward bishopric controversy, 119; attitude toward resistance movement, 130; resignation, 138; and College of Philadelphia, 114–117
Peters, Richard, Jr., 133, 156, 197
Peterson, Charles, 334, 376
Pew: rents charged, 29–30; purchase of required, 235
Philadelphia: 1730s, 44, 1790s, 164; 1830s, 165–167; 1840–1859, 232; post-World War II, 332–333
Philadelphia Bible Society, 196
Philadelphia Dispensary, 197
Philadelphia Interfaith Action Coalition, 387
Philadelphia Federation of Churches, 315
Phillips, the Reverend Francis, 31–35
Pilmore, Joseph, 164
Plumstead, William, 47, 91
Poor relief, Christ Church provides, 68, 92, 299–300, 325
Porter, the Reverend John, 100–101
Portlock, the Reverend Edward, 12
Potter, Bishop Alonzo, 171, 238
Powel, Samuel, 93, 152, 156, 164
Poyntell, William, 164, 197
Pratt, Henry, 188, 229
Presbyterians: numbers, 111–112; and the College of Philadelphia, 114–118; oppose episcopate, 120–122; pew rents, 191
Protestant Episcopal Church, formation of, 155–161
Protestant Episcopal Sunday and Adult School Society of Philadelphia, 200
Provoost, Bishop Samuel, 152, 157
Pulpit: position of, 27, 51, 261; wine glass, 97–98, 99

Quakers: beliefs, 7–9; numbers in Philadelphia, 111–112; political conflict with Anglicans, 12–14; religious conflict with

Anglicans, 14–16; relations with Anglicans in 1740s–1760s, 112
Quary, Robert, 10, 24, 31

Read, Charles, 47
Rectory, purchase of, 353
Redman, Joseph, 47
Revolution: position of congregation of Christ Church, 141–145; position of Philadelphia clergy, before independence, 128–129, 131–136; position of Philadelphia clergy, after independence, 138–141
Riggs, the Reverend Edward, 271
Riots of 1844, 233
Roberdeau, Daniel, 71, 73–74
Ross, Betsy, 142
Robbins, George, 305
Ross, the Reverend George, 130
Royal government: Anglican attempts to obtain, 12–14; Smith opposes, 95
Rush, Benjamin, 137, 166, 196
Russian Orthodox Church, relations with, 296–297

St. Andrew's Church, 228
St. James Church, 179, 181, 199, 211, 214; founding of, 168; separation from Christ Church, 216–218
St. John's House, 301
St. Luke's Church, 244
St. Mary's Church, 388
St. Paul's Church: founding of, 80–82; reconciliation with United Churches, 104; Benjamin Allen, rector, 212
St. Peter's Church: founding of, 75–77; separates from Christ Church, 217–218; 165, 199, 211, 228, 244, 314, 342, 364
St. Thomas's African Episcopal Church, 164, 165–166, 240
St. Stephen's Church, 211
Salin-Miller, the Reverend Jean, 388
Sanctuary of Christ Church: colonial, 27, 39; 1830s, 234–236; 1880s, 260–263; 1890s, 276–277; 1920s, 307–398; 1960s, 371–373; 1980s, 386

Schnader, William, 337
Seabury, Bishop Samuel, 157–161
Seal of Christ Church, 372
Seeds, Thomas, Jr., 305
Sesquicentennial of Declaration of Independence, 310–311
Shannon, the Reverend James, 360, 364, 369; resigns, 376
Shee, John, 129
Shippen, Edward, 70
Shippen, Joseph, 47
Smith, Robert, 48, 77
Smith, Thomas, 305
Smith, the Reverend William: arrives in Philadelphia, 70–71; conflict with Robert Jenney, 73–75; conflict with Daniel Roberdeau, 73–74; and Macclenachan, 78, 80–81; and royal government movement, 95–96; and leadership of Pennsylvania church, 96; theology of, 88; and John Porter, 100; and German Society, 112–113; and College of Philadelphia, 115; attitude toward episcopate, 119–122; position on resistance movement, 120, 134, 136–137; position on independence, 141; role in formation of the Protestant Episcopal Church, 156–161
Smith, William Rudolph, 305
Social Gospel movement, 253
Society for the Advancement of Christianity in Pennsylvania, 197–199, 240
Society for the Alleviation of the Miseries of Public Prisons, 1960
Society for the Propagation of the Gospel in Foreign Parts (SPG), 33, 61, 74, 112–13, 117, 120 founding of, 15; dismisses Sturgeon, 90
Society Hill, 352–353, 384–385
Stedman, Alexander, 91
Stedman, Charles, 91
Stevens, Bishop William Bacon: consecrates Christ Church Chapel, 264; mediates Chapel controversy, 268
Stevens, the Reverend Charles Ellis, background, 273–275; rectorship, 275–281; forced resignation, 279–281

Stevenson, James H., 358
Stokes, Edward Lowber, 298, 306
Stringer, the Reverend William, 104
Sturgeon, the Reverend William: appointed
    assistant minister, 69; ministers to blacks,
    69–70; attacks Smith, 74–75; appointed
    minister, 88–90; conflict with Duché, 90;
    resigns, 90–91
Sunday School Society, 196
Swift, Joseph, 129, 156
Syng, Phillip, Jr., 48
Syng, Phillip, Sr., 48

Talbot, the Reverend John, 15
Taylor, Jacob, 16, 17
Thornton, Sandra, 376
Tilghman, James, 142
Tilghman, William, 188–189, 198, 200, 203
Till, William, 47, 70
Townsend Acts, 129
Trent, William, 31–32
Tresher, Robert, 324
Tresse, Thomas, 47, 58
Trimble, the Reverend James: background,
    385; rectorship, 385–391
Tyng, the Reverend Stephen H., 212

United Churches of Christ Church and St.
    Peter's: established, 77; obtains charter
    and adopts by-laws, 96; separation of,
    217–220
United Nations Chapel, 328–329
United Spiritual Action campaign, 335–342
Urmston, John, 37

Van Dusen, Judge Francis, 324
Van Dusen, Judge Lewis, 333
Vestry of Christ Church: role in Phillips
    controversy, 33; dispute with Vicary, 36;
    role in Peters controversy, 59, 61; and
    Revolution, 138, 143–144; disputed elec-
    tion of 1778, 143; and Christ Church
    Chapel controversy, 268–269; difficulty
    electing enough members, 304–305; elects
    woman, 358; ousts Stevens, 278–281;
    composition of, 257, 304–306, 357–358

Vestry assistants, 324
Vicary, the Reverend John, 36
Von Moschzisker, Bertha, 358

Wade, Francis, 128, 133
Wagner, Tobias, 239
Walter, Thomas U., 234
Washburn, Helen, 295–297; resigns, 325
Washburn, the Reverend Louis: back-
    ground, 288–290; rectorship, 290–316;
    outreach to neighborhood, 293–302;
    founds East Central Social Agency, 301;
    institutes Every Member Canvas, 306, in-
    terest in history, 309–313; edits, *Christ
    Church: A Symposium*, 309; and World
    War I, 315–316; resignation and death,
    316
Washburn House, 309
Washington, George, 201
Watts, Henry, 358
Watson, the Reverend Wendy, 388
Wayne, William, 240
Welton, the Reverend Richard, 37–38;
    plaque honoring, 278
West, Francis, 239, 240
West, William, 129
Whitaker, Bishop Ozi W., 278, 280
White, J. Brinton, 305
White, Robert, 133
White, Thomas, 200, 229
White, Bishop William: appointed assistant
    minister, 100–102; attitude toward fellow
    ministers, 102; position on Revolution,
    141; appointed rector, 144; role in organi-
    zation of the Protestant Episcopal
    Church, 153–160; elected bishop, 157;
    theology of, 170–174; attitude toward
    Methodists, 173; on episcopate, 153–155,
    171–173; remains put under chancel floor,
    261
White, William, Sr., 358, 366
White, William, Jr., 324
Whitefield, the Reverend George, 53, 104–
    105
Whitney, John, 324
Widing, the Reverend C. John, 358

Wilcocks, Alexander, 137
Wilcocks, John, 188
Willing, Charles, 48, 91
Willing, Richard, 133
Willing, Thomas, 91, 128, 130, 133, 137, 145, 164, 203
Wilson, James, 137, 145
Wilson Park, 375
Wiltbank, William White, 257
Window, Palladian, 49, 235, 261, 373
Windows, stained glass, 276, 307; removed, 386
Women of Christ Church: 1800–1836, 198–201; 1830s–1840s, 237–238; during Civil War, 242–243; 1910s–1930s, 299, 306; 1880s, 259; 1940s, 325–326; 1960s, 363–364
Wood, C. Francis, 279–280
Wood, John, 156
World War I, 315–316
World War II, 327–331
Worrell, James, 133
Worship services: colonial, 25–26, 1790s, 189–190; 1890s, 277; 1930s, 308; 1960s, 360–363; 1980s, 385

Yeates, Jasper, 10
Yellow fever, 164
Young People's Fellowship, 326, 343

This book was set in Perpetua and Granjon typefaces. Perpetua was designed by Eric Gill for the publication of a privately printed book entitled *The Passion of Perpetua and Felicity*. Perpetua was later cut in 1925 for the English Monotype Corporation. Granjon was designed for Merganthaler Linotype in 1928 under the supervision of George W. Jones. Granjon was named after Robert Granjon, a French type designer. Granjon is considered by many to be the best reproduction of the typeface Garamond which was issued by the Egelhoff-Berner typefoundry in 1592.

Printed on acid-free paper.